Violent Partners *boldly reveals:*

♦ **Victim and abuser collaborate in violence**
through a "dynamic of abuse" and learn these patterns
in childhood from their mothers, fathers, and siblings

♦ **Men and women abuse each other
at similar rates**, although men's injuries are often
less serious, and they are much more reticent to report them

♦ Assumptions that women are helpless victims and
men are simply brutal aggressors are **inaccurate**

♦ Given the chance to escape their abusers, most
women—more than 50 percent—**want instead
to salvage the relationship**

♦ Batterer intervention programs that emphasize
blame and shame **do not work**

♦ A judicial system that uses arrest and prosecution to
mandate separation of abuser and victim is **often
at odds with what couples want**

LINDA G. MILLS, J.D., Ph.D.,
is Founder of the Center on Violence and
Recovery at New York University, where
she is also a Professor and Senior Vice
Provost. She has appeared on "Oprah," Bill
Moyers's "Now," and "The O'Reilly Factor"
and has been featured in the *Boston Globe*,
the *New York Times Magazine*, and more.
Her op-eds have appeared in *USA Today*,
the *Los Angeles Times*, and *Newsday*.
She lives in New York City.

© Brian Dilg

A highly controversial approach to the crisis and treatment of intimate abuse, Violent Partners *offers new evidence that abuse is a* shared experience in which both victim and abuser are active participants

Linda G. Mills, J.D., Ph.D.

Violent Partners

*A Breakthrough Plan for
Ending the Cycle of Abuse*

A RADICAL NEW TAKE ON THE CRISIS of intimate abuse, *Violent Partners* argues that as a culture we misunderstand the root causes and basic effects of abuse, and until that changes there is no hope of fixing the problem. Dr. Linda Mills challenges assumptions, tears down myths, and offer solutions, all the while telling riveting stories of couples who have conquered violence in their relationships. In *Violent Partners*, she describes several programs that hold promise for addressing intimate abuse, including two nationally known and groundbreaking treatment programs— Peacemaking Circles and Healing Circles.

Controversial, provocative, and accessible, *Violent Partners* is unlike any other book on abuse and relationships, and highlights in great detail the complexities of violence through the stories of men and women who have acknowledged their abuse and sought to do something about it. This is essential reading for anyone seeking to understand violence in their own relationship, friends and family members of victims and abusers, and legal and mental health practitioners looking for a new and valuable approach to treating couples in crisis.

Psychology / Relationships

JUNE
$26.00 / $31.50 (Can.) hc
ISBN 978-0-465-04577-8
288 pages, 6-1/8 x 9-1/4
Carton quantity: 32

Selling Territory: W

First Serial, British Commonwealth, Translation & Electronic Rights: Basic Books

Audio & Performance Rights: Author

National marketing campaign

- National author publicity from New York
- 20-city radio satellite tour
- Targeted marketing to violence and recovery groups
- Tie-in with author lecture schedule

VIOLENT PARTNERS

VIOLENT PARTNERS

A Breakthrough Plan for Ending the Cycle of Abuse

LINDA G. MILLS, J.D., PH.D.

BASIC
BOOKS

A MEMBER OF THE PERSEUS BOOKS GROUP
NEW YORK

Published by Basic Books,
A Member of the Perseus Books Group

Books published by Basic Books are available at special discounts for bulk purchases in the United States by corporations, institutions, and other organizations. For more information, please contact the Special Markets Department at the Perseus Books Group, 2300 Chestnut Street, Suite 200, Philadelphia, PA 19103, or call (800) 255–1514, or e-mail special.markets@perseusbooks.com.

Designed by Timm Bryson

Library of Congress Cataloging-in-Publication Data
Mills, Linda G.
 Violent partners : a breakthrough plan for ending the cycle of abuse / Linda G. Mills.
    p. cm.
 Includes bibliographical references and index.
 ISBN 978-0-465-04577-8 (alk. paper)
 1. Family violence—United States. 2. Marital violence—United States. I. Title.
 HV6626.2.M58 2008
 362.82'920973—dc22
                              2008001189
10 9 8 7 6 5 4 3 2 1

TO PETER AND RONNIE

My profound gratitude for our *dynamic and for* your *love*

Contents

Author's Note

Many of the people I interviewed for this book have asked me to use their real names; others have wanted to remain anonymous, and so their names have been changed to protect their privacy. The notes provide supplemental information about these people and how I came to hear their stories.

The language in this book often relies on traditional terms such as "domestic violence," "battered women's movement," "battered women," "batterers," "victims," and "perpetrators," which have certain political connotations, while also using language that resonates more closely with my own political inclinations, including such terms as "abuse between intimates," "a person who has been violent," and "a person who has been victimized." While I am inclined to reject the terms that reduce people to a single quality such as "batterer" or "victim," and the gender assumptions associated with those labels, I also felt that recounting the history of the movement to address domestic violence in a language familiar to those who participated in it was respectful and important. My choices are never meant to insult or hurt those who do or do not resonate with terms from either category. In time, I hope we can move away from essentializing perspectives—a move that is consistent with my efforts to end the cycle of abuse.

Introduction

Little more than a generation ago, domestic violence was considered a private matter. Some people felt that a man's home was his castle and that it was no one's business what went on there. Others assumed that the violence in most marriages was either provoked (and therefore deserved) or rare (and therefore something to be endured, like terrible weather). Why intervene? Since so few women ever chose to prosecute, trying to arrest their violent partners was often considered a waste of the public's time and money. If these people wanted to be together and make each other miserable, well then, let them.

Now, thirty years after feminist advocates first started the fight against domestic violence, many changes have come to pass. In 2008, if a woman is hit by her husband and calls 911, the police arrive promptly and take the incident seriously. The officer doesn't suggest that his time is being wasted, and he doesn't suggest that the man step outside to cool off. Instead, he handcuffs the perpetrator and takes him to the police station, where he will be booked and jailed, while another officer offers to escort the wife and her children to a shelter. Violence against a woman in her home is now defined as a crime by our society, and the criminal justice system treats it as such.

But has this enormous revolution in both public perception and public policy made America less violent? Are there fewer batterers than before? Are batterers learning to take responsibility for their behavior? Are women safer or more in control of their own lives? Unfortunately, after years of researching this social problem, I can't answer any of these questions with a resounding yes. What's more, the ideology and rhetoric of the antidomestic violence movement have become so rigid that they have created a new set of myths—or, at the very least, a new set of highly partial truths—that can be as pernicious as those we fought so hard to dispel years ago.

This book grapples with realities that many professionals and academics in the field now take to be self-evident—even though it is still virtually forbidden to acknowledge them in public and in print:

- The popular conception of domestic violence, in which the female victim lives in terror of her controlling abuser, only represents a fraction of the American couples struggling with violence today.
- Yesterday's victims often become today's criminals. Most researchers in the fields of psychology, sociology, criminology, and social work now agree that child abuse is far more responsible for creating batterers than sexist attitudes and beliefs, and yet most batterer intervention programs fail to acknowledge this troubling legacy.
- Violence is dehumanizing not only for the victim but for the perpetrator as well. When society reinforces that shame by declaring the perpetrator a pariah, he or she is discouraged from seeking help.
- Women frequently strike out at their partners, and not simply in self-defense; in 24 percent of American marriages only the woman is physically violent.

The fact that so many crusaders against domestic violence remain either ignorant of these facts or unwilling to openly discuss them is deeply troubling. The implication is that to engage with these questions would set us back thirty years: you are either for battered women or against them. And yet if the antiñ-domestic violence movement is *really* about giving battered women more power, the 2008 scenario should evoke the following questions:

- Does the woman who calls the police necessarily want to have her husband arrested?
- Will arresting him decrease the violence in their relationship or make it worse?
- Is there any form of help we can offer, other than arresting her abuser, that might help her reduce the violence in her life?

These questions are still not being effectively addressed—just as they weren't being effectively addressed thirty years ago—even though most women do not want to sever their connection with the partner who has hurt them. They just want the violence to stop.

Furthermore, if the feminist movement is really about empowering women and ending oppression for all, it should be asking whether or not the woman who has called 911 has played any role in the altercation with her husband—whether she, too, ever participates in acts of physical or psychological aggression against her partner. At present, such questions are considered tantamount to blaming the victim. But does encouraging women in abusive relationships to think of themselves as powerless really bring them closer to transforming their lives?

Violence between intimates is almost always more complex than we are prepared to admit, and many violent relationships do not fit standard definitions. The alarming gap between our tidy conception of the problem and the far messier reality has created a new population of isolated and shame-ridden victims and perpetrators.

Brenda Aris, whom I've known for ten years, best fits the traditional description of the battered woman: she was a victim of relentless physical and sexual abuse for more than a decade. And yet Brenda never called the police— not simply because she feared her husband but also because she loved him and didn't want to put him in jail. The ramifications of his violence and her loyalty are still being felt by the Aris family today.

Jade Rubick was married while he was still in college. Before long, his wife had started hitting him, pulling his hair, and throwing things at him. Even when such incidents were occurring several times a week, he refused to admit that he was the victim of domestic violence; he had never heard of anything like this happening to another man. Finally, his employer helped him face the truth.

James and Kate's intense relationship was marked by screaming arguments. After they decided to have a baby, the tensions between them increased. During one fight, well into Kate's pregnancy, James had his wife pinned to the floor. He was told by the police he was a danger to his family; she was told by a shelter worker that her only problem was that she couldn't leave her abuser. Nevertheless, they were not ready to destroy the family they had only just begun.

When Jeff McPherson sent his wife to the emergency room with a large gash next to her eye, he was as shocked as she was. The couple had been together for eleven years, and they had three children; there had been no incidents of physical violence between them. Even so, a domestic violence advocate urged Sarah to separate from her husband. The couple felt manipulated and diminished by the very people they went to for help.

Betty Stein, an Orthodox Jewish woman, felt that her husband, Harry, physically and sexually mistreated her, but her religious beliefs made it unthinkable for her to go to the police.

These individuals refused to condone the violence in their relationships. What's more, they were all determined to take steps to end it. But they were unwilling or unable to ìfollow the scriptî—to accept all the blame or to leave their relationships—and this made their predicaments all the more desperate.

When we are lucky, crisis breeds opportunity. The unmet needs of these couples and individuals drove them to invent new solutions and explore unconventional alternatives to confront the violence in their lives. After leaving his marriage, Jade went on to help found a program called Stop Abuse for Everyone so that others ignored by the system can get the support they need. Instead of divorcing, James and Kate both took responsibility for their destructive dynamic and succeeded in salvaging their relationship. They attribute their recovery to

Violence Anonymous—a program James developed when no other treatment was working for him. Couples counseling enabled *both* Jeff and Sarah to see the ways in which they felt extremely vulnerable in the marriage and how these feelings had been the catalyst for their fateful dispute. The Steins have participated in a Healing Circle program, which brought their extended families together to explore the origins of the couple's intense unhappiness. Harry has learned to be a different kind of husband and father; Betty has come to recognize her own aggression in the marriage.

Of all the victims, Brenda paid the highest price to escape her abuse: she ended up in prison. But she was fortunate enough to take advantage of the therapeutic services that were offered her there—if only something equivalent had been available to help her separate from her husband before it was too late.

All of these people are now in much better situations because they have worked extremely hard to get there. Their stories provide a road map of the possibilities for healing intimate abuse. At the same time, it is painful to acknowledge that the criminal justice system we have put in place at great cost and effort could do little or nothing to help them.

I am a feminist who has devoted a great deal of my career to the problem of abuse in women's lives, and I am not out to demonize the battered women's movement or the criminal justice system; there is no question that dedicated professionals and volunteers who work closely with victims of domestic violence do so to make the world a better place. Clearly, hundreds of thousands of women have been helped by the system, which is much more sophisticated than it was thirty years ago. Nevertheless, I believe the needs of many more, perhaps millions, continue to go unaddressed. In this book I attempt to synthesize a broad array of studies and experiences in the fervent hope that we can expand the ways in which we think about intimate abuse and discover new paths for ending the cycle of violence.

I have come to believe that this synthesis dramatically illustrates the need for a radical change in our approach not only to intimate abuse but to aggression of all kinds. When we are forced to recognize just how much aggression there is in *all* our close relationships—between parents and children, siblings, friends, intimates—it gives us an opportunity to affirm one of the ideals implicit in the early feminist movement: everyone should have the right to lead a life free of violence and fear.

I hope that this search for answers and a new way forward will inspire all of us to rethink how we deal with intimate abuse—as a culture, as individuals, and, more often than we'd like to admit, as victims and abusers. It is time for a hard reassessment of where we've come from and where we're headed. I know we can do better.

PART ONE

A New Voice

The survey found that women who were physically assaulted by an intimate were significantly more likely than their male counterparts to report their victimization to the police (26.7 percent and 13.5 percent, respectively).

—Patricia Tjaden and Nancy Thoennes

I tried to tell the truth and cooperate in good faith. I thought the system was there to help me, but, instead, it ended up becoming my greatest enemy.

—Sarah McPherson, a victim of domestic violence

1

MY PERSONAL ENCOUNTERS
WITH INTIMATE VIOLENCE

W omen in every class of society have been discriminated against on the basis of their gender for most of human history. Yet we know that many women are extremely powerful in the lives of their families. This is one of the paradoxes at the heart of intimate violence. How do we recognize and address the victimization of women within the family without ignoring or minimizing their strength? At the same time, how do we empower women in ways that allow them to confront and transcend their victimization—rather than simply endure or deny it?

In many ways, my own life—both personally and professionally—has been an ongoing struggle with these questions. I was raised in the 1960s, when it was rarely acknowledged that girls and women are often assaulted by friends and family members. I grew up in a privileged, white, middle-class Jewish household; after college, I went on to get a law degree, a master's in social work, and a doctorate in social welfare policy. I did not come from a physically violent family. Nevertheless, before my thirtieth birthday, I had been bullied, struck, and sexually abused on several different occasions by various men whom I loved or admired.

At first, shame kept me from discussing these experiences with others. Still, I rebelled against them inwardly: I thought I was stronger than the violence that had been done to me. Years later, when I found myself in an abusive romantic relationship, denial gave way to anxiety. How had this happened to me? I became preoccupied by the apparent contradiction between my ostensible power and my moments of extreme vulnerability.

As I struggled to integrate these dissonant parts of my character and my past, I began to think about the fact that all those who experience intimate

3

violence are to some degree haunted by it. I started to wonder how those experiences affect the way we move through the world.

In a symposium at New York University's law school in 2001, I delivered an academic paper in which I argued that certain criminal convictions may be influenced by the violent histories of the jury members—even without their realizing it. I cited as an example a trial of a severely battered woman who eventually shot and killed her husband; one of the female jurors had been indefatigable in her efforts to get the defendant convicted of first-degree murder. A fellow member of the jury, in fact, accused this juror of attempting to hijack the deliberations. Years later, when I interviewed the female juror about her strong views of the defendant's guilt, she acknowledged that she herself had come from a violent household and that she held her mother largely responsible for her father's violence. ("I adored my father. My mother was a shrew.") She also explained that fourteen years before the trial, her fiancé had been shot to death in a liquor store robbery; the gunman had never been caught. In the paper I presented at NYU, I argued that this juror's own traumatic experiences may have made it impossible for her to see the facts of the criminal case clearly.

During the question-and-answer period, three academics in the audience objected to my claim, insisting that it was perfectly possible to compartmentalize one's own history of violence so that it would not affect a professional or legal judgment. I was fascinated to learn, over the next few days, that these three academics were, in fact, speaking of themselves: one by one, they approached me and explained that they had been exposed to intimate abuse during childhood but that these experiences in no way affected their thinking as adults. I suggested that their reactions to my paper illustrated my very point: if the past truly carried no emotional charge, their responses would have been far more measured.

I believe that even events we see as "minor" may have deep and lasting effects. Therefore it is in the spirit of full disclosure that I begin with a reckoning of my own encounters with violence. They are by no means extraordinary, especially when compared to some of the stories that follow, but I have come to believe that they have influenced my thinking and my actions in ways that I am still discovering to this day, and for that reason I feel compelled to set them down here.

EARLY YEARS

I was born in the suburbs of Los Angeles in 1957. I grew up thinking that I could do whatever I wanted with my life. My parents and my grandparents had all worked hard and sacrificed for the family in ways that made my own ambitions possible, and I grew up hearing stories of their struggles. Most compelling were the tales of my mother's family fleeing Europe during World War

II. My grandfather, a successful Viennese clothing manufacturer, was detained by the Nazis on Kristallnacht, in 1938, but he ultimately escaped. He was reunited with his wife and children in Los Angeles, where he rebuilt his business.

On one hand, I was keenly aware that the ease of my life was a result of the efforts of all those who'd come before me: as long as my ambitions included meaningful work and achieving some measure of financial security, I knew my parents would support me. At the same time, like many privileged children, I took my privileges for granted.

In 1971, my family moved to Trousdale Estates, a development above the Beverly Hills flatlands, so that I could attend Beverly Hills High School. Beverly, as it was called by the locals, wasn't just any high school; it was considered the best public high school in the city. More than 90 percent of the students came from wealthy and well-known families.

In this rarefied environment, I became increasingly critical of the beliefs and values that my parents seemed to represent. In Southern California in 1971, the generation gap was particularly wide. The assassination of Martin Luther King Jr. and the killings at Kent State were still fresh in everyone's memory, the Vietnam War was being protested on college campuses across the country, and the White House would be embroiled in Watergate within a matter of months. If my parents had fought hard to make their way in the world, my friends and I were questioning everything that world stood for. After all, obedience to authority was potentially lethal, as the war had so vividly demonstrated to us. Instead, the allure of drugs, sex, and music—suffused with a vague idealism—governed our teenage existence.

My father was a doctor, and my mother worked for her father. I saw them as overly materialistic and focused on the importance of getting ahead. Despite my straight A's in school, I had my own vision of success, and it didn't involve wearing suits and pleasing adults. At the same time, I assumed that my parents and their resources were at my disposal—at least until I was old enough to go out on my own. My parents had little idea of what I was up to, and no clue as to how to handle our differences. As a result, high school was an exciting and dangerous time. No one attempted to teach us how to take care of ourselves, and perhaps we wouldn't have listened if they had.

Chris

Chris was my first serious boyfriend. I met him at a party the fall of my freshman year of high school. I was desperate to meet cute guys, and I had set my sights on a boy named Jeff, but had failed to attract his attention. Chris, on the other hand, noticed me, and I found his intense stare flattering and exciting. Handsome and quiet, he had a car, which added to his appeal: I lived at the top of a hill and wouldn't be old enough to drive for another year. His family background was very different from mine. His father had left his mother, and he lived in a small one-bedroom apartment on the south side of town. I was curious to know more about a world so different from my own. I was also eager to lose my virginity, and choosing a boyfriend who was so different from me seemed very sophisticated at the time. Within a few weeks, we started going out.

A great deal of our relationship consisted of driving around, fooling around, and hiding the truth from my parents, and at first this was more than enough. Chris took care of me: he was older than I was, he had the car, and he had plenty of money from his after-school job as a stock boy at a boutique on Beverly Drive. He enjoyed buying me presents, and I enjoyed being spoiled; this ritual allowed both of us to ignore the larger disparities between us.

After six months of dating, however, I became restless and impatient with Chris's chronic petulance: he would never talk to me about his family or his feelings. Where had his father gone? Why was his mother out most nights? I was never able to penetrate his reserve, despite my ability to bring people out. I began to yearn for a boyfriend more like me. Then one day at school, an encounter with Jeff in the hallway indicated he might be interested in me. I was excited but also conflicted. Even though Chris couldn't talk to me, he cared for me, and I didn't want to hurt him.

It was during this week of uncertainty that Chris took me to Saks Fifth Avenue to buy me a birthday present. This sort of shopping excursion was one of our rituals. I eventually found a few things to try on and went into the dressing room. I emerged modeling a cute shirt, expecting Chris to like it as well.

Chris looked me over and started laughing.

"What's so funny?" I asked, angrily.

"It just looks *bad*," he said.

"Well, I like it," I said—probably thinking to myself that I didn't need to dress just to please Chris, anyway. Just then I noticed that a button had popped off the shirt onto the floor, and I bent over to retrieve it. As I stood up, Chris punched me in the chest, hitting me so hard that, for several moments, I couldn't catch my breath.

"Why did you do that?" I finally cried out. But he just stared at me. I walked back into the dressing room, quickly put on my clothes, and left. My chest was aching, and I was in complete shock. What had I done to deserve such a blow? Did Chris know about my feelings for Jeff? Had he not really wanted to buy me a gift in the first place? But why did he *hit* me? And why hadn't I seen this coming?

I had grown up in a household with a high tolerance for verbal abuse: my maternal grandfather, the patriarch of the family, was always shouting at someone. We'd arrive home to his screaming voice on the answering machine demanding his daughter's assistance, or we'd be sitting in his kitchen while he yelled at his wife that the coffee wasn't hot enough. He humiliated me in front of my friends by shouting at me for no good reason. Although I saw my grandparents often—almost every Saturday night—I found these outbursts terrifying, largely because they were so unpredictable.

The rest of the family hated them as well, but we all excused them because we thought we understood where they came from—his childhood, the Holocaust. Getting punched, however, felt totally unacceptable to me. I was sorry I hadn't been completely honest with Chris, but I also knew that I didn't deserve to be hit.

By the time Chris called a few days later to apologize, it was too late. For me, the relationship was over, and there was nothing more to talk about. I didn't really explain why I didn't want to see him anymore; indeed, I didn't think I owed him any such explanation. After this, he began calling me incessantly, but I wouldn't take his calls. No matter how much I tried to avoid him, though, he always seemed to be lurking nearby. Late at night he'd park in front of my house. I could hear his engine running, and I knew he hoped I would come outside. From my bedroom window, I could see him smoking one cigarette after another, just waiting. I found it frightening, but sad as well. I still felt that ending my relationship with him had been the right thing to do, but most of the time I chose to repress the catalyst for doing so: the punch itself.

Dudley

I met Dudley at the beginning of my sophomore year in high school, shortly before I got my driver's license. Unlike Chris, Dudley came from a rich family: his parents bought him everything he asked for. But the Jensen Healey, the stereo, and even the huge television set in his well-equipped bedroom didn't improve his romantic chances with girls. During this period, Jeff and I had an on-again off-again relationship. Dudley and I got into the habit of hanging out, and we always had a great time.

By the end of sophomore year, we had gone to most of the big high school parties together. We had a tried-and-tested approach to these evenings: Dudley would drive me there, we'd explore the party together or go our separate ways, then we'd meet up again to leave. Dudley would usually drive me back to his house, where we'd go straight to his room to listen to music and smoke pot. This routine took a lot of the social pressure off both of us, and it was a pleasure to end the evening comparing notes with Dudley because his descriptions of one classmate's ridiculous outfit or another's outlandish behavior were always hilarious. He was my first real friend of the opposite sex, and I expected to know him for the rest of my life.

Dudley and I went to a party one night, and I was crushed to see Jeff there with another girl. I wanted to leave early, and Dudley agreed to drive me home.

"Hey," he said, "why not go to my house like we usually do?" Trying to tease me into a better mood, he pressed the gas, and the car jumped forward. "C'mon, the night is young." I really wanted to go home, but I wasn't entirely surprised when we ended up at Dudley's house: this was, after all, our routine. We were both tipsy from the alcohol and drugs we'd had at the party. When he tripped going up the steps to the house, I grabbed his elbow. He wrapped his arm around my waist to steady himself. Inside the house, on the way down the hall to his room, I again felt the pressure of his arm around my waist. I tried to free myself from his embrace, but he wouldn't let go. I sensed that something was off, but I told myself that maybe he was a little more stoned than usual: after all, we'd been friends for months now, and we'd never even had an argument. Once we were in his room, though, he did something he'd never done before: he closed and locked the door and put the key on the table by the bathroom.

I was suddenly alarmed. At sixteen, Dudley was already six feet tall, and I was tiny—no more than ninety-five pounds. Dudley lumbered over to his new sound system and switched it on.

"Listen to this," he said. The Rolling Stones blared out into the room, the volume unbearably high. I knew that he wasn't worried about waking his parents, though, because his room had been soundproofed; Dudley could blast his music as loud as he wanted without disturbing anyone.

"What are you doing?" I screamed, as music bounced off the walls around us, but I was sure he couldn't hear me. Besides, he wasn't interested in anything I was saying. After standing unsteadily by the door for a few moments, he lunged toward me and pushed me onto his bed. For a few seconds, he stood over me and stared down at me. Then he jumped on top of me.

"Get off of me!" I yelled.

It was impossible to move with him lying on top of me; in fact, I could hardly breathe. I couldn't believe this was happening to me. He was one of my closest friends. When Dudley lifted himself up slightly, only to press down harder, I forced myself to look at him. His face, normally pale, was flushed, and his eyes were bloodshot. He leaned forward, pinning my flailing arms to my side. "This is the story, cunt," he hissed into my ear. "You're going to fuck me now, or I am going to beat off and come in your face. Which is it going to be?"

I knew that screaming would be hopeless. Anyway, I didn't want to wake his parents; the thought of their intervention seemed even worse than whatever Dudley was going to do to me.

"Well?" he demanded.

"I'm not going to fuck you," I said flatly.

He masturbated, came all over me, and promptly passed out.

I slowly got up and walked into the small bathroom attached to his room. Semen was smeared across my brown cotton turtleneck sweater. With tears streaming down my face, I scrubbed ineffectually at the stain—if I could get rid of it, I somehow felt, no real damage would have been done. Finally, I gave up. After opening the bedroom door, I roughly roused Dudley from his sleep.

"Take me home *now*," I demanded.

Shaken from his stupor, and noticing that the door had been opened, he zipped up his pants, turned the stereo off, and walked out behind me.

On the way back to my house, neither of us spoke. Dudley drove too fast, but I didn't care. As soon as he pulled into my driveway, I was out of the car, and I didn't look back.

Unlike Chris, Dudley never apologized. Instead, he pretended that nothing was wrong between us by trying to talk to me at school, but I always ignored him. I also vowed to myself that what happened between us would never happen to me again. Next time—if there was a next time—I would be smarter. I would get away.

Often my father would ask me why I never saw Dudley anymore. He was puzzled as to why two best friends suddenly never spoke or went out together.

"We don't have anything in common," I finally replied.

Both Chris's punch and Dudley's sexual attack felt sudden and catastrophic to me. They had come out of nowhere, and I had been utterly unprepared for them. I couldn't help feeling that I, too, was to blame. I kept these incidents a secret for many, many years. For my own part, I simply excised Chris and Dudley from my life and the memories of what they had done to me from my mind. Vowing not to see them or think about what had happened would make it all go away.

COLLEGE AND GRADUATE SCHOOL

Although the University of California, Irvine, was located just an hour from Beverly Hills, it was another world. I straightened out and started getting serious about my future. At the same time, my vague dissatisfactions with my parents' world began to take on a more definite and intellectually coherent form. Many of my professors were quite radical, especially those in the history department. I began to think about the problems of race and class in American life; I also began to consider myself a feminist. It was exciting to be a part of a larger social cause, and as an ambitious young woman in the late '70s, I quickly recognized that all the principal power structures in American life—the academy, the government, the media, the military, the judiciary—were dominated by men. Significantly, however, I never consciously connected my interest in feminism with my personal experiences. I saw the oppression of women as only one important struggle among many, and I saw myself less as a victim than as someone who was dedicated to fighting for the rights of others.

At UCI, I met many men who shared my political beliefs. Soon I began to have emotionally and sexually fulfilling relationships. These romances, which were both egalitarian and mutually supportive, emboldened me to think that my own life as a woman was destined to be exceptional: I could not only escape being victimized but help other women overcome their victimization as well. My privilege, I believed, would allow me to speak for those who couldn't, and this newfound voice could not be silenced.

My activism at college gave me a keen interest in law: I understood that for a woman to fight the system, it was useful to know how to work the system. After graduation, I went on to Hastings College of the Law in San Francisco. At Hastings, minority students were made even more uncomfortable than white women were. One event crystallized these disturbing racial dynamics for me. A white female professor would do anything to avoid calling on black students in the class, even if they had their hands raised. When the black students finally walked out one day en masse, I stood up and followed. This, I knew, was the sort of activism I wanted to practice.

After graduating from law school, I went to work at a small firm that specialized in helping people apply for Social Security disability benefits—particularly women of color. The people we served were often poorly educated and almost entirely without resources. Many of them had worked for most of their lives and then suffered some sort of injury that had forced them to stop. One of my clients, an African American woman named Versie Hawkins, had been a house cleaner and a nurse's aide who'd eventually injured her back one too many times while lifting a patient. After a five-year waiting period, she had been rejected for benefits. She asked me to help her reapply.

While working on Versie's application, I realized that my client was not only disabled but also in poor mental health—severely depressed and somewhat delusional. I used this new information to strengthen her claim for benefits, but her five-year struggle also convinced me that clients like Versie needed emotional support services as well as legal assistance: applying for benefits could be a punishing ordeal. After winning her case, I decided to pursue a master's in social work at San Francisco State so that I would be qualified to develop the sort of comprehensive program I envisioned. More than ever before, I was seeing how the personal *was* the political, and I couldn't wait to put my ideas into practice.

Keenly aware of my clients' vulnerability, I still had no sense of my own. My clients were often poor, disenfranchised, and multiply afflicted. I was a twenty-six-year-old white lawyer going back to school for a second graduate degree, financially independent and passionately engaged in my work and my life. The world was my oyster.

David

All first-year MSW students at San Francisco State were invited to attend an internship fair at the beginning of the term. This fair usually involved representatives from all the local social work agencies who were looking for free labor in exchange for professional training, and it was held in an auditorium on campus. When I walked into that auditorium, in September 1984, I saw David immediately. He wasn't conventionally handsome, but he had an intensity that attracted me. When he saw me staring at him, he gave me a welcoming grin. I practically danced over to his table. I was captivated.

David was a social worker and well-respected in his field. From the moment we met, we were inseparable. He was quick-witted and articulate. He was also argumentative in a way I admired, and he thought deeply about pressing social issues. He was a self-described feminist, a great cook, and the smartest man I'd ever encountered. Within a month of our meeting, we started dating.

David was clearly powerful and asserted that power in ways I didn't fully understand, but I welcomed the challenge; we felt evenly matched. Even so, disagreements plagued our relationship from the beginning. For one thing, he refused to be monogamous. He also demanded that I adhere to his rules: there were certain things I couldn't buy and certain things I couldn't wear. I decided that I could live with his rigid policies because I respected his views. In exchange, however, I wanted him to stop sleeping with other women. He was unwilling to do so, and this remained a major source of conflict between us. Still, I held out hope that I could win him over, and the relationship went forward.

One night, after we'd been dating for several months, we were driving home from a meeting related to our work together. I was criticizing the way he ran the meeting because I found his need to control what everyone said counterproductive. Perhaps I was expressing my own feelings of resentment at being controlled without realizing it. Nevertheless, our conversation felt to me more like an exchange of opinions than a heated argument—until David jammed his fist into my upper arm. It wasn't a tap or a slap; it was a painful punch.

"Why did you do that?" I asked. David stared straight ahead at the traffic. "Why did you hit me? That really hurt," I repeated.

He refused to answer. We ended that evening much the way Chris and I had ended our clash in the department store about a decade earlier. This time, however, I wasn't sure I wanted to walk away from the relationship. David and I had been friends before we had become lovers, and I had considered sharing a future with him—marriage, even children. I wasn't ready to give that up. At the same time, I could also feel myself withdrawing.

A few days later, David came to my house to talk about what happened. He apologized and said he didn't know what came over him. He asked for forgiveness. I found this outright apology, with no excuses, very disarming.

"I want to be open and honest with you," he continued. "You are not the first woman I've hit. I've told you about Sybil, the woman I was in love with before we met. Well, I struck her, too. And I've also had other relationships that were violent. I think the reason that I am so interested in injustice is because I wanted to understand my own abuse of power better." He looked completely stricken as he said this. "I'm working hard to understand where this violence comes from, and how I can stop it."

"What can I do?" I asked.

"Forgive me," he pleaded. "Love me. Stay with me."

This new David—anguished, confessional—was a sharp change from the usually challenging and argumentative David I was used to. I felt a rush of love for this man—I knew how much it must cost him to be so open with me about this problem. Perhaps we could work through this. We embraced, but I also felt that I had to make it clear to him that the punch had been a very serious breach of trust for me.

"I accept your apology," I said. "But if you ever hit me again, I will leave you. I mean it. I will be gone." He told me he understood, and kissed me.

"Somehow," he began, "I think my anger and violence connects to my mother. She was demanding when I was growing up, and I often had to wait on her. She was a very critical woman," he continued. "Nothing pleased her. Absolutely nothing! The tea was never hot enough. The toast was always too dry or too dark. I never moved quickly enough. No matter what I did—and I did a hell of a lot—she was just never satisfied." We talked for hours, and the revelations poured out: his father's essential absence, the toxic combination of his mother's criticism and demands, and his own anger and guilt. I could feel my sympathy growing—and I could also feel the way that these intimate events drew us closer together. I started to ask myself: Why should David suffer as an adult because he had suffered so much as a child? Surely our love could overcome his mother's rejection.

Our life together both quieted down and deepened. David's hitting me had been the worst thing that had happened to me in the relationship, but, ironically, this brief flash of violence brought us closer together. I felt that I understood him better, and he clearly felt more committed to me and available in ways I hadn't anticipated. We still argued, but our disagreements never felt particularly serious to me, and as the weeks passed, the memory of the punch gradually faded from my mind.

We started going away together. One time, we were sharing a bottle of wine in our hotel room, and I was telling him all about a piece of clothing I had seen in a store window. David was holding firm in his stance against frivolous purchases; I was excited about being on vacation and wanted to go shopping. Before I had registered the level of David's anger, he spat right in my face. I was shocked, humiliated, and furious.

"What the hell was that?" I asked. Without answering, he stormed out of the room.

When he returned, several hours later, we tried to piece together what had happened, but our attempts were less satisfying than before. He said he was deeply sorry; he had not intended to actually spit *on* me. I wasn't entirely convinced that he was being honest. I considered spitting a violent act. He disagreed. He also argued that he had been working on his violence, and he felt that he'd been doing pretty well. I agreed with him on this point. I could see, sometimes, that he was struggling with his anger and trying not to overreact, and I appreciated those efforts. Perhaps spitting *was* different from hitting; after all, it wasn't physically painful. By the end of the day, we had reconciled.

Still, I decided this was David's struggle; I refused to make it *our* struggle. I was also deeply aware of how ashamed he felt of his behavior and how much he wished he could control it. But I had meant what I said: if he ever hit me again, the relationship would be over.

For several months, no new incidents occurred. David was especially sweet. I felt that it was time for us to move in together and have a monogamous relationship, and he was now quite open to the idea. David lived in a large house, which he owned, and we agreed that my moving in there was the logical next step. The presence of another roommate made the decision to live together seem less loaded. Even so, I was going to be renting a bedroom that had been vacated by one of David's ex-girlfriends, and tensions were running high the day I moved in.

As we were unpacking my things, David declared that he would continue to see other women socially, even if we were now monogamous. In fact, he planned to have drinks with his ex-lover-housemate in the coming week. This announcement, particularly its timing, immediately made me feel anxious and upset: if I was moving in with him, I needed to be reassured that he really wanted to be with me. After a few angry exchanges, I brushed against him as I passed by carrying a box of my things. In response, David shoved me. That's it, I thought. We're finished.

"I told you that if you ever hit me again, our relationship would be over!" I said.

"I pushed you," David answered, clearly panicked. "A push isn't a *hit*," he added defensively.

"A push, a hit, it's all the same," I said. "It hurt."

What did it mean that I was choosing to live with a boyfriend who treated me like this? On the other hand, did it really make sense to turn right around and move out again? For a push? *Was* a push the same as a hit? I decided, once again, to stay, and I attempted to clarify my position with the following statement: "Let me make myself absolutely clear: if you ever hit or push me again, I will leave you."

I also thought that we needed help, and David agreed. We decided to go into therapy together, which felt like a hopeful way to embark upon this new phase of our relationship. To our surprise and disappointment, however, all three of the therapists we met with refused to treat us. They told David that he had to deal with his violence on his own before we could think about working together. This made perfect sense from my feminist perspective. Yet the side of me that was in love with David was also seeking guidance about what to do about *us*, and I very much wanted to be a part of the process. I also needed help managing my own anxiety about what might come next. I wasn't ready to leave David, but I wasn't prepared to just tolerate his rage, either. When I expressed this frustration to the therapists, they told me that my response was typical— that women always make excuses for their violent partners—but that couples counseling wouldn't solve the problem.

Sorting through these mixed messages was frustrating. On the one hand, the therapists were theoretically supportive of me. ("This is not your problem; this is not your responsibility. Cocounseling suggests that you share some fault for your relationship, and we will not permit that here. He must take responsibility for it alone.") In practical terms, however, their politically correct stance helped neither of us. David felt alone at a vulnerable time when he needed support, and I felt isolated, with nowhere to turn for help with our problems. We ended up feeling more ashamed of our predicament rather than less so.

Still, our new life together was fun and exciting. Nearly every night, David would find an excuse to bring people together to share a meal, and he was at the center of every interesting conversation. At these moments, I knew why I was living with him. But his determination to maintain platonic relationships with his ex-lovers also frequently left me alone in the evenings. Luckily, I enjoyed hanging out with his roommate, Charles, who was one of his best friends. Charles was quietly confident and comfortable with himself. His dry humor and sophistication were a welcome alternative to David's constant intensity. Charles and I particularly enjoyed talking about psychology—he wanted to return to school to become a therapist—and we shared a passion for analyzing the human psyche.

That fall, Charles and I signed up for a meditation class together. Occasionally, if David was busy, we would go out for dinner afterward, and I would use these occasions to discuss my romantic difficulties. Charles had a great deal of insight into David after their years of friendship, and I was desperate for support and advice; talking to Charles gave me the therapeutic outlet I craved. Since we both loved David, initially these discussions didn't seem disloyal to either of us; they seemed to be buttressing a fragile and demanding relationship to which I was committed.

As time went on, however, the situation became more complicated; although Charles and I didn't acknowledge it, we were attracted to each other. I was also fed up with the way David used the threat of infidelity against me, and my friendship with Charles helped level the playing field. I had thought that moving in with David would make our relationship more intimate, but we often seemed less close than before. The question of whether we were moving forward or backward was increasingly muddled for me, but I was clear about one thing: if David could have drinks with other women, I could go to meditation class with Charles. After all, we weren't doing anything wrong.

One night, Charles and I pulled up to the house after meditation class, and we stayed in the car to finish our conversation. I knew David was home, and I realized this might lead to an argument with him once I went inside. The more time I spent with Charles, the more jealous David became. On the other hand, part of me rebelled against this flicker of concern.

When I went upstairs to David, though, I felt vaguely anxious, and also irritated by my anxiety. Sure enough, when I entered his room, he was sitting on the couch waiting for me. He fired questions at me, demanding to know why I spent so long in the car talking with Charles.

Finally, I answered, "You're the one who wanted an open relationship." I knew this comment would anger him, but I didn't care.

I sat down on the water bed instead of joining him on the couch, to put some distance between us. "You know, Linda," he began, his voice hard, "you belong to me. After all," he continued, "I have been working hard to be faithful to you." David had never spoken to me in quite this way before, and I found it unnerving.

"I guess right now," I began, tentatively, "I don't know what's going on. I just don't think our relationship is working out in the way I thought it would. I . . . I don't think I belong to you. I . . . I . . . "

I could see by the look on his face that this was not the right answer. He rose from the sofa and walked over to where I was sitting. "You are mine," he yelled, towering above me. "You will always be mine."

"I am not yours," I answered. But my voice was little more than a whisper.

Sitting unsteadily on the bed beneath him, I suddenly felt sick with dread: something terrible was about to happen. He grabbed my shoulders and squeezed them until the pain coursed down my arms and up my neck. He slammed me back onto the bed, yanked my pants down, and forced himself inside me.

When I look back on my relationship with David, this incident marked the turning point in more ways than one. Although David had been violent with me before, he had never been violent with me sexually, and it felt like a terrible betrayal. Also, in the past, the violence had been over almost as soon as it had begun. This time, however, he had declared that he owned me and then, in effect, demonstrated it. And I felt absolutely powerless.

While I was involved with David, I never confided in anyone—aside from the therapists we spoke with—about his violent outbursts. Perhaps I was ashamed to be dating someone who was violent, but at the time I would have said that my silence was a matter of privacy and loyalty to him. David had built his career doing social work. Any revelations that he was violent in his personal relationships could have been damaging to his reputation. But my silence after this violent encounter was different, because I also didn't discuss it with David. Every other incident had been accompanied by a serious conversation about what had happened and why; after this, neither of us said anything. David, like Dudley, did not apologize, and—even more disturbing to me, now—I did not demand that he do so. We both just got up the next morning and pretended that the fight and the rape hadn't taken place. For me, this marks the turning point at which I became a battered woman.

Why didn't I do something? Why didn't I simply get up the next morning and move out of the house? The answers to these questions are complicated and paradoxical. When I look back on this experience now, I think I was afraid of David—truly afraid, for the first time in our relationship. I had witnessed a deeply ugly and terrifying side of him. It felt dangerous enough to have experienced this episode of violence; to draw attention to it felt unwise.

I also think that discussing what had happened between us would have meant acknowledging to myself that I was emphatically *not* in control of the relationship. Despite my frequent assertions to the contrary, I was deeply involved with a man who repeatedly permitted himself to hurt me. I felt that what it said about me was almost as horrifying as what it said about him. In short, neither of us could face the truth, which was that I had stepped out of line and been raped as punishment for doing so.

The only tangible result of this incident was that I was once more galvanized to find us a couples counselor. I located someone who would help me negotiate the boundaries of a relationship that was now scaring me—even though I wouldn't acknowledge either my fear or the particular event that precipitated it. When we first tried to go into therapy, I felt genuinely committed to working our way through our difficulties. The second time around, however—although I didn't admit it to myself at the time—too much damage had been done. Now I believe I was looking for a safe way out.

The therapist who agreed to see us together was smart and accepting. David and I talked about the violent incidents between us—except for the last—and the issues of jealousy on both sides. She was adept at getting at the underlying tensions in the relationship, and we both felt supported by her. During one session she said to me, "I don't think you'll ever leave this relationship, Linda." Looking back, I now suspect that she meant this as a challenge, but at the time I interpreted it as a straightforward prediction. This remark stayed with me. I found it frightening that she was making an assertion about my future behavior that seemed in no way contingent on David's actions. It brought out the rebel in me.

The Sunday morning after the therapist's statement, David and I went out for a walk and talked about Charles and the role he played in our relationship. We'd been in therapy for a few months, and I admitted that I was still feeling confused. David always had problems with the importance I'd given to monogamy; now I, too, was ambivalent and told him so. He became enraged. "How can you not say that you are committed to me in this way?" he asked. I hesitated, unsure of how to respond. When I remained silent, he turned beet red. Moving closer, he put his hand flat against my upper back and pushed with all his strength, sending me staggering forward. This was, in a sense, the push I'd been waiting for: angry, uncontrolled, and undeniably against our agreement. I remembered the therapist's dare, and I took it. "That's it," I said. "We're through."

I moved out. I also proudly declared the end of our relationship to the therapist in David's presence. He pleaded. But I refused to change my mind. Still, he remained on his best behavior. We spent one last night together after David promised to be "good." Although I was not ambivalent about my decision to leave him, I still cared for him and wanted things to end on as positive a note as possible. Perhaps we could really make a good clean break of it.

The next morning, David and I went down to the street to find the pavement littered with broken glass and my car missing. We found it at the impound lot: it had been set on fire. As I looked at the charred remains of my Honda, I felt that David was somehow responsible. We treated the matter as a freak act of vandalism and went our separate ways, but I was deeply shaken. Was this a warning about what would happen to me if I didn't go back to him?

As soon as my relationship with David was formally over, Charles and I became involved. In one sense, this new romance had been a long time coming, but the situation with David undeniably hurried things along. I was frightened and lonely; Charles was horrified by David's behavior and feeling protective of me. We tried to keep the fact that we were dating a secret, but David quickly found out. One night after work, Charles came home to find that his car had crashed into a lamppost at the foot of a hill. The parking brake had apparently been released. A few days later, someone slashed the tires of his motorcycle to ribbons.

David started calling my house. When I answered, he would hang up. It happened so frequently that I finally changed my phone number. He would also show up unexpectedly—at some place he knew I had to go for work or outside a restaurant where I was meeting someone for lunch. I might look up and see him, staring through the plate-glass window. When I went downstairs in the morning, he would be sitting outside my apartment, waiting. He wouldn't say anything, which somehow made it even more terrifying. I felt as though I was being hunted—but when was he actually going to make his move, and what would that move be?

Eventually, I moved across the Bay to make his unannounced appearances more difficult. But they persisted nonetheless. Charles moved out of David's house and came to live with me. He became my protector and my confidante. Ultimately, we decided to marry. Charles was the classic knight in shining armor.

VICTIM AND ACTIVIST: MY OWN
PERSONAL FEMINISM

By the time I left David, I was starting my not-for-profit organization that helped poor people get their Social Security disability benefits while also providing supportive services. I named the agency the Hawkins Center for People with Disabilities, after the woman who had inspired me to found it.

The questions I would ask my clients were far more detailed and personal than they had been in the law firm. I asked not only about their work history and education but also about their childhoods and relationships. I asked if they had ever been physically mistreated, as adults or children, or sexually abused. In many instances, I was the first person who had ever shown any interest in these questions, or suggested—simply by posing them—that they were important. And the stories came pouring out.

Initially, my practice of taking detailed histories was a legal strategy—I was casting a wide net, in an attempt to come up with information that might be useful to my clients' disability claims. What I hadn't been prepared for was the multiple levels of violence I would find—how many of the people I interviewed had histories of abuse that would qualify them for government support and a lifetime of benefits, given how traumatic the events had been and how severe an effect they had on these women's ability to function as adults.

News of the center spread quickly throughout the community. It would be years before its efficacy would be proven; the immediate basis for our popularity was simply that the women who visited us felt they were being heard—often for the first time in their lives—and our clientele quickly grew. Within the first year, I had accepted over fifty cases for legal representation.

Personally, however, I found my new job completely overwhelming. It was as if I had opened Pandora's box: I was awash in horror stories. I had also lost my earlier sense of myself as somehow "above" these questions as a privileged and powerful feminist, since I was now fleeing an abusive relationship and was still afraid of my abuser. Was my own history affecting my ability to do my work responsibly? Was my work making my own concerns about my recent past even more upsetting? I felt compelled to start seeing a therapist in an attempt to sort these questions out.

For years, I had kept all these different parts of my life apart: my childhood, my grandfather's outbursts, my scary experiences as a teenager, my feminism, my social justice advocacy, my romantic life. Only now, in therapy, did I begin to understand the ways in which the pieces fit together—that my attraction to David, for example, might have been a desire to both re-create and improve upon my relationship with my grandfather. Like David, my grandfather was an extremely bright, charismatic, and engaging man—always the life of the party. I also began to see that these "random" incidents of violence from high school were not quite as insignificant as I had allowed myself to believe.

At the very least, my experiences with Chris, Dudley, and David were evidence of my inability to recognize danger. I saw that downplaying these incidents made it more (rather than less) likely that I might experience something similar later on. If I never analyzed the circumstances that led up to them, how could I effectively avoid or mitigate such threats in the future? Many of us want to avoid thinking about a painful incident, but this desire can unwittingly lead us into situations that are similarly risky.

Once I was able to admit to myself that I had, in fact, been a victim of intimate violence, I was also able to examine what my own role in these relationships had been. This did not mean that I took responsibility for the men's violence. I believed then, as I do now, that their actions were their responsibility. But once I acknowledged how betrayed I felt by what they'd done to me, I could ask myself how they might have felt betrayed by me as well.

In the case of Chris, I think that the superficial trappings that made him seem the more powerful—his age, his gender, his car, his ability to buy me presents—couldn't disguise the larger inequities between us. What's more, I was using him, much as boys are often accused of using girls, as a short-term pleasurable distraction, and I knew he was in love with me. Did that mean that he had a right to punch me in the chest? Of course not. But should I have been allowing him to buy me a present with his hard-earned money even as I was thinking about leaving the relationship?

My friendship with Dudley was also self-serving. I assumed that my sexual indifference to Dudley absolved me of viewing him as a sexual person—an assumption that now, in hindsight, I believe enraged him. I wasn't paying attention because I didn't think that I needed to. From this vantage point, my self-involvement was not only unkind but also dangerous.

My relationship with David, on the other hand, was much more complicated than either of the prior experiences. Clearly, my attraction to him was deeply meaningful and profoundly linked to my complex relationship with my grandfather. I know that I stayed with him as long as I did because I was in some way revisiting this earlier significant relationship and trying to improve upon it at the same time: I loved both men dearly, but they also hurt me. I instinctively felt, as so many people ensnared in violent relationships do, that David was the only person with whom I could work through that painful history.

It is clear to me now that the violence in my relationship with David was significant—even life-threatening. That said, I see my strength and my tolerance for the violence—let alone my initial decision to stay, as so many women do—as an opportunity for imagining new perspectives on violence in intimate relationships.

My progress in therapy over the five years that I worked at the Hawkins Center influenced these feelings and my approach to my advocacy work in paradoxical ways. On the one hand, I felt that, for the first time in my life, I could locate my real self, with all my contradictions, at the center of my work, and I felt connected to my clients as I never had before. I was also fascinated by the lesson I was seeing repeated over and over again, which was that children exposed to abuse frequently led violent and dysfunctional adult lives. Indeed, both David's violence and my tolerance of it underscored this lesson. And yet these intergenerational connections—for example, between child abuse and wife beating—were almost never discussed; the child advocacy and domestic violence movements barely interacted. Interestingly, as much as the larger culture was recognizing the injustice of violence against women, it was not making the connections necessary to understand the origins of this abuse.

I also began to question the long-term effects of getting someone disability benefits to compensate for a history of ill treatment. Yes, most of these women were already desperate, and most had no satisfying or financially viable employment prospects, nor had they been taught the skills to truly compete in a work environment. But as the reputation of the center grew, I started seeing younger and younger women, many of them with psychological rather than physiological disabilities. Was the best solution to label these women as damaged for life? Didn't this permanently solidify their status as victim, although many of them were also tough survivors? The awarding of benefits was where our efforts for their empowerment came to an end.

In 1991, I moved to the East Coast to get my Ph.D. in social welfare policy at Brandeis University. Charles and I moved to New York for a year, but finally, after many attempts at making our relationship work, things fell apart. I moved back to California in 1995 to join the faculty at UCLA. In the meantime, the domestic violence movement had come of age in America.

I had misgivings about the way the movement had developed. To be sure, in certain respects my response to the intimate violence in my life was in keeping with feminist principles. I had objected to my treatment; I had set limits; I had walked away. In other respects, though, my responses to these men ran contrary to the stance that the feminist movement was taking on this issue. I knew that the legal system would never have been my chosen method for dealing with the episodes of violence in my life—before or after therapy. I would never have reported Chris, Dudley, or David to the authorities; indeed, I might even have protected them if someone else had. Finally, I didn't believe that punishing the men who hurt me would be any more "healing" than receiving financial compensation for abuse. A necessary response at times, certainly. But did it make sense for us to fight domestic violence almost solely on the legal front? I was dubious.

2

A BRIEF HISTORY OF THE BATTERED WOMEN'S MOVEMENT

Enormous Strides and Unexpected Consequences

THE WAY WE WERE

In the 1970s, victims of domestic violence often had no safe place to go where they couldn't be tracked down by their abusers. At the same time, with the resurgence of the feminist movement, a woman's right to protect and control her own body was becoming a powerful rallying point: every woman deserved a life free of rape, physical and sexual abuse, and unwanted children. Across the United States, former battered women and feminist advocates banded together to address the shelter needs of abused women, making this one of their highest priorities. This grassroots response was the beginning of the battered women's movement.

The first known shelter in the United States was founded in Minnesota in 1974; by 1977, there were eighty-nine shelters for battered women across the country. Initially, though, it was hard to drum up support for these shelters because the larger society didn't recognize the demand for them. By definition, shelters were invisible; their very secrecy unintentionally reinforced the shame that already surrounded the problem. Like victims of date rape and child abuse, battered women were all too often hidden casualties, treated like the property of their tormenters and expected to suffer in silence.

For those who came to their rescue, however, the realities of living with violence were often horrifyingly stark. Women would arrive at the shelter with black eyes and broken noses. Sometimes they would be in their nightgowns, having run out of the house in fear for their lives. The gulf between these nightmarish existences and the public's vast ignorance about domestic violence was

21

hard to countenance for those who were exposed to it every day. Advocates believed that for things to change, they had to take the fight against abusive men out into the open.

The tenets of the battered women's movement were roughly as follows: First and foremost, we all needed to recognize that domestic violence was caused by deeply held misogynist beliefs that allowed men to hurt women. This in turn meant that battering was a heterosexual problem caused almost exclusively by men. When women, on rare occasions, *were* violent, it was in self-defense— these actions needed to be understood as a response to the batterer's aggression rather than as aggressive acts in their own right. If women tolerated their abuse and didn't leave the relationship—and they often didn't—it was because they feared what would happen to them if they did. Indeed, these women were so intimidated by their abusers that they were incapable of reacting to the violence in their lives in ways that kept them safe: they needed the help of people and systems more powerful than their abusers. Before batterers could be held accountable for their actions, however, the criminal justice system had to be forced to take domestic violence seriously, and the first challenge was to reform the attitudes of the police.

Police officers have traditionally been unenthusiastic about responding to domestic violence calls. For one thing, these visits can be dangerous: one or even both parties can turn against the officer who arrives on the scene. Family disputes also tend to be chaotic, intensely personal, and sometimes exasperating to an outsider. It can be difficult for the officers to tell who did what; besides, haven't these people chosen to be together in the first place? For all of these reasons, many officers believed that intervening in low-level violent conflicts between lovers was not the best use of their limited resources. They did not see responding to domestic violence complaints as "real police work."

The inadequacy of this perspective was chillingly demonstrated on June 10, 1983, when Tracey Thurman, a twenty-two-year-old mother of a two-and-a-half-year-old boy, called the Torrington, Connecticut, police because her estranged husband, Charles "Buck" Thurman, had arrived at her home and was yelling outside, demanding to speak with her. Tracey had separated from her husband after he repeatedly beat her and threatened to kill her, and she secured a restraining order to keep him away; now he was outside the house, threatening to hurt their son. Tracey called the police while neighbors waited inside their homes for the situation to calm down. When fifteen minutes passed and the police still had not arrived, Tracey went outside in an attempt to appease her husband. Buck Thurman attacked Tracey, stabbing her thirteen times in the chest, neck, and throat. Finally, a single police officer showed up; he found Tracey on the ground and Buck holding a bloody knife. In the officer's presence Buck dropped the knife, kicked his wife in the head, and ran into the house, from which he soon emerged holding their son. He dropped the boy on his wounded mother and kicked her in the head again. When three more officers arrived on the scene, Thurman continued to threaten his wife. He wasn't arrested until he threatened Tracey again, this time as she lay on a stretcher waiting to be taken to the hospital.

Buck worked at a local diner frequented by police officers, and the possibility that this may have made the police especially reluctant to intervene was mentioned in newspaper accounts of the case. Tracey Thurman, who was left partially paralyzed by the attack, eventually sued the Torrington Police Department for its inadequate response, and in 1985 she was awarded $1.9 million.

The officers' astonishing passivity in the Thurman case infuriated battered women's advocates and laid the groundwork for an active campaign to overhaul the criminal justice system. Whereas in the 1960s Buck's attack probably would have been categorized as a crime of passion, it now represented for many women a political event—an indictment of American society as a whole. Men were allowed to do whatever they liked to their wives and the rest of us would simply stand by—in this instance, literally—and do nothing to stop it.

THE CRUSADE

Efforts to criminalize domestic violence began by focusing on educating police departments around the country and encouraging officers to arrest men who committed crimes like assault and battery against their wives or girlfriends. After all, police officers were the first responders: without their involvement and testimony, the courts couldn't intervene.

But significant numbers of police officers still resisted making arrests, and their reluctance couldn't be blamed on sexist attitudes alone. It was one thing to arrest the perpetrator when the victim was begging you to do so. But what were you supposed to do when the victim was begging you *not* to do so? When the woman wasn't serious about pressing charges, the entire process could be a waste of time: many officers arrested men only to be stood up in court, later on, by the victim.

In addition, officers knew from experience that determining guilt at the scene was not always as easy as some activists made it out to be. For example, a man accuses his wife of having hit him over the head with a frying pan, and he has the bump to prove it. But she claims that she hit him only after he threw a pot of boiling soup at her and missed. He denies it. Neighbors heard the yelling and called the police. Who is the guilty party? How can we really know?

Some advocates for battered women countered these concerns by arguing that the back-and-forth in any particular instance wasn't as important as which member of the couple had the upper hand. The arresting officer had to be aware of the underlying dynamics of power and control in the relationship. Perhaps the woman *did* hit her husband with a frying pan, but if he first tried to scald her and she was fighting for her life, it was an act of self-defense. Advocates also pointed out that a battered woman is often terrified of her abuser; she can't be expected to demand that he be arrested, because that act might put her at further risk once he is out on bail. Instead, state laws should institute mandatory arrest policies, so that the woman couldn't be held responsible for her partner's arrest.

To address the concerns raised by the frying-pan scenario, battered women's advocates persuaded lawmakers that the police needed first to identify the primary aggressor in the conflict. The protocol for doing so included examining the extent of any injuries, discovering whether or not any threats had been made and whether the violent act had been committed in self-defense, and determining if either participant had a history of domestic violence. This strategy was supposed to promote arrests while simultaneously discouraging the impulse to simply arrest both parties. (It should be noted, however, that this was not a protocol set up to protect the sexes equally; it was an attempt to keep women from getting ensnared in a legal process that had been designed to catch violent men.)

By 1989, just six years after the Tracey Thurman case, enormous reforms had been enacted: 84 percent of U.S. police departments had adopted aggressive arrest policies for domestic violence crimes. Yet with each new strategy developed by feminist advocates, new impediments to putting batterers behind bars emerged. A chief complaint of police officers was that men arrested for domestic violence crimes weren't being prosecuted. This was because prosecutors could still exercise some discretion over which cases they took—just as the police once could. And prosecutors were unenthusiastic about bringing to court cases that they didn't feel they could win. Too often, victims would deny what happened or change their stories to protect their husbands from being sent to jail. This unpredictability on the part of victims also made many prosecutors feel that these cases weren't worth the effort. Once more, the ostensible beneficiaries of feminist reform—battered women—were proving to be a significant stumbling block to holding batterers accountable.

In the late 1980s, prosecutors sympathetic to the cause came up with the idea of victimless prosecution—the same strategy necessarily employed in murder trials. Instead of relying on the victim's testimony, prosecutors who advocated for this approach argued that they could use ancillary evidence gathered at the scene of the crime and beyond: photos of the victim's injuries, recorded 911 calls, medical records, a ripped phone cord. The woman herself could be spared from testifying.

Soon, fighting domestic violence had become a national priority, and there was a widespread consensus throughout the country that police officers, lawyers, judges, activists, and jailers should be the principal combatants in that fight. Then, in 1994, Congress passed the Violence Against Women Act

(VAWA), which encouraged both police precincts and prosecutors' offices to develop new and innovative programs to prosecute violent crimes against women. A primary focus of this act was to serve the needs of battered women.

Other initiatives quickly followed. It became much easier for women to obtain restraining orders, which serve as official "commands" by a court prohibiting an individual from carrying out a specific action, such as touching his partner or visiting her place of employment. A restraining order that prohibits someone's boyfriend from coming within two hundred yards of her apartment cannot, of course, literally prevent him from doing exactly that. But once he knocks on her door, he has also broken a court order, which is a serious offense that can bring with it immediate arrest and jail time.

Advocates for battered women also pointed out that stalking could lead to murder. And yet stalkers engaged in very scary behavior that wasn't necessarily illegal, such as incessantly phoning an ex-wife and then hanging up, or having roses delivered with their heads cut off. As a result of such serious concerns, anti-stalking legislation became much more stringent in the early 1990s, thereby making it easier to arrest men harassing their ex-lovers—men who, before, had not technically been breaking any law.

Feminist activists also recognized that mandating health care professionals to report child abuse had become an important means of preventing such abuse. Why couldn't similar laws be applied to domestic violence? They believed that if a doctor realized that his or her female patient had not, in fact, fallen down the stairs but instead had been kicked in the jaw by her husband, the physician had an ethical obligation to intervene. And so advocates began agitating for mandatory reporting laws, which required health care professionals to call the police if they suspected that one of their patients had been a victim of intimate abuse—no hard proof was necessary. California was one of the first states to embrace this approach. By 1999, a woman's visit to an emergency room could lead law enforcement officials to her unsuspecting husband's doorstep.

NEW EXPLANATIONS FOR AGE-OLD QUESTIONS

By the 1990s, the corrective slant that feminists brought to our understanding of domestic violence—the reminder that women were frequently the victims of a crime committed by men, which often resulted in serious injury and sometimes death—had hardened into a widely supported and vigorously defended political and ideological truth: men were the batterers, and they were solely responsible for the abuse; women were the blameless victims. This was the message that needed to reach not only the police, lawyers, and judges but also society at large. Public education campaigns—posters on subways and in welfare offices—encouraged victims to seek assistance. Even neighbors were being directed to intervene if they heard fighting in the apartment next door.

Batterers also needed to be reeducated. Even with a mobilized criminal justice system, feminist advocates were concerned that minor incidents of domestic abuse might result in little or no punishment. Once aggressive arrest and prosecution policies were in place, mandatory treatment programs for batterers became an important component of the strategy to ensure some accountability while simultaneously reforming men's sexist attitudes. But there was also a fear that sexist therapeutic attitudes could be more damaging than no treatment at all. It was crucial, therefore, that the prevailing message of any treatment program be politically in tune with the principles of the movement, which asserted that men abuse women because it is part of their male prerogative in a sexist society. The batterer then habitually blames the woman—"She provoked me"—because it relieves him of taking responsibility for his unacceptable behavior. Such sexist attitudes had to be eradicated from the batterer's belief system.

Batterer intervention programs, or BIPs, were created to answer this concern. The most common BIP is called the Duluth model, which is named for the city in Minnesota where it was developed. Ellen Pence and Michael Paymar, the architects of this program, believed that if men's sexist attitudes could be altered, their behavior would change as well. As Pence and Paymar stated, the Duluth model "helps offenders to understand how their socialized beliefs about male dominance impede intimacy; [how] that violence is intentional and a choice designed to control their intimate partner; that the effects of abusive behavior damage the family; and that everyone has the ability to change."

If we as a society were supposed to be teaching men that they were solely responsible for the physical violence in their relationships, we were also supposed to relieve women of their guilt: it was never their fault, even if they stayed in the relationship. For one thing, it was much more difficult for women to leave than most people realized—for myriad financial and emotional reasons. Furthermore, many women, physically abused and psychologically diminished by their tormentors, had lost all sense of their rights and their power. Indeed, these women often showed positive feelings toward men who threatened and hurt them.

Women's loyalty to their abusers has always been difficult for outsiders to understand. To help explain it to police, prosecutors, judges, and the world at large, advocates for battered women started drawing on theories like the Stockholm Syndrome, a term that originated from a case in Sweden in the 1970s when two ex-convicts held four bank employees hostage. The victims were held under life-threatening conditions for six days, but their captors also showed them some kindness during the ordeal—playing games with them to pass the time, lending them their jackets for the cold. To everyone's surprise, after her release, one of the victims asked the police to show the gunmen mercy. When researchers sought to understand this phenomenon, they found this sympathetic reaction in all kinds of traumatized people, from concentration camp survivors to abused children. The Stockholm Syndrome came to symbolize the sentiment common among many battered women that their perpetrators weren't as bad as the outside world made them out to be.

The pioneering work of educational psychologist Lenore Walker also started to play a key role in the development of this line of argument in the courtroom. To explain the battered woman's seeming paralysis in the face of danger, Walker drew heavily on experiments by Martin Seligman, a world-renowned professor of psychology at the University of Pennsylvania.

In a series of experiments in the late 1960s and early 1970s, Seligman placed dogs in two different types of cages. In the "shock" cage, a bell would sound, and the entire cage floor would become electrified so that the dogs were shocked no matter where they stood. The second cage was similar to the first except that it contained a small area—a safe haven—where the dog could escape the charge.

Seligman observed that the dogs in the shock cage would initially search for a safe place to stand but then give up trying to escape the inevitable shocks. The dogs in the second cage would always seek out the uncharged area in their cage. More revealing, however, was that when the dogs in the shock cage were later placed in a different environment—a cage with the safe haven—they *still* did not try to seek safety. Seligman deduced that their hopeless experience in the shock cage had affected them so dramatically that they could no longer "imagine" a safe haven. From this experiment, Seligman theorized that the dogs exposed to the "no-escape" shock cage developed a "learned helplessness," which he characterized as being passive and accepting of pain—even when escape from pain later became possible.

Walker then applied Seligman's learned helplessness theory to battered women, explaining why some women were unable to leave their abusers. Once they had become accustomed to enduring the abuse, they could not recognize or imagine that escape was an option available to them. Walker tested this hypothesis by interviewing more than four hundred battered women who confirmed that while their perceptions of danger were often accurate, they had difficulty choosing an effective response to that danger, such as leaving the abusive situation when an opportunity to do so presented itself.

Walker's theory, which quickly came to be referred to as the Battered Woman Syndrome, also advanced the argument that these women were so deeply wounded by the violence they'd endured that any irrational behavior they manifested—even killing—could be explained by the abuse. As a result, Walker has become a frequent expert witness in the trials of women who eventually killed their batterers. Her theory gained significant attention in 1987, when it was used in the defense of Hedda Nussbaum, a New York book editor, who failed to protect her six-year-old adopted daughter from her abusive partner, lawyer Joel

Steinberg. He eventually beat the girl to death, and at first it seemed that Nussbaum would be charged as an accomplice in the murder. Then the photographs of Nussbaum's severely battered face and body were released to the press; eventually she was pronounced too physically and psychologically damaged to be held responsible for her inaction. Over time, Walker's theory has become the most enduring explanation for why battered women stay in abusive relationships.

HOW FAR WE'VE COME

In the past thirty years, the feminist effort to change the way we as a nation respond to a major social problem has achieved astonishing results. Most Americans no longer believe that violence against women should be tolerated, and battered women are frequently and sympathetically portrayed in the media—in newspaper accounts and on talk shows; in books like Anna Quindlen's best seller *Black and Blue* and Susan Weitzman's *Not to People Like Us*; in movies like *The Burning Bed* and *A Cry for Help: The Tracey Thurman Story.* Now almost every major American city has a shelter where a woman can seek refuge from a violent partner.

Neighbors frequently call the police when they witness domestic violence or hear someone yelling for help next door, unwilling to be complicit in the abuse through their silence. Men are arrested for their crimes; domestic violence cases are filed, and charges are brought against them. Nearly everyone convicted of a domestic violence crime is mandated to batterer intervention classes, which have been designed to help batterers unlearn their sexist attitudes and change their violent behaviors. In 2005, Congress reauthorized the 1994 Violence Against Women Act, appropriating $3.33 billion in funding for five years to improve the criminal justice, social service, and health care systems' response to violence against women.

The campaign to institute mandatory arrest laws around the country has been very successful since it was first implemented in 1984: twenty-one states and Washington, D.C., have now adopted mandatory arrest policies for domestic violence crimes, essentially forcing police officers to respond with more than just a warning when a call comes in involving intimate abuse. Visible injuries are often no longer necessary for the officer to make an arrest; a victim or child's allegation—even a neighbor's—may be enough.

At this point, Alaska is the only state that mandates prosecutors to charge all domestic violence defendants with a crime. But several states either encourage this practice or limit the prosecutors' ability to offer a plea bargain in a domestic violence case. In other words, if a defendant has been initially charged with battery, which might carry with it a period of time in jail, these prosecutors are discouraged from reducing it to a disorderly conduct charge, which may result only in counseling and a fine. Nearly every jurisdiction has also adopted victims' rights legislation, which usually includes informing the victim when and whether the defendant will be charged, consulting her before a plea bargain is accepted, and allowing her to make a statement at sentencing.

In most states, the victim's vulnerability after her abuser's arrest is also being addressed. A number of states mandate or authorize courts to issue restraining orders in domestic violence cases before the accused can be released on bail. A national registry of restraining orders now exists; thirty-six states typically require that a restraining order be submitted to the registry within twenty-four hours of being issued by the judge. This registry allows a victim to simply call the police and have her batterer arrested if he is in violation; she no longer needs to carry the protective order with her at all times.

New York has been especially creative in its effort to simplify the overwhelming legal challenges facing battered women. The state has developed Dedicated Domestic Violence Courts (which handle only intimate abuse crimes) and Integrated Domestic Violence Courts (which process both criminal and family matters, such as divorce and child custody cases). Victims of domestic violence now get support from advocates who are trained to help them, judges who know how to handle manipulative defendants, and court personnel who are familiar with the treatment options for men and women whose cases they process. In 2005, the state of New York spent over $100 million in government and private contributions to provide services for victims and their children.

Once convicted, a batterer may face jail time, judicial monitoring, and mandatory treatment. As of 2007, there were over two thousand BIPs along the lines of the Duluth model; the length of the program is often based on the severity of the violence and the frequency of arrests. Also, every convicted abuser must pay a fee to attend the BIP, on the theory that one should be financially penalized for one's crime. The Duluth model is favored to the exclusion of other treatment approaches. For example, couples counseling is discouraged, because the victim is in no way to be held responsible; in some states, couples counseling is actually legally prohibited.

Clearly, an elaborate legal and judicial infrastructure has been created in a relatively short period of time. Are people using it? Absolutely. Consider these statistics for the state of New York in 2005: 450,000 Domestic Violence Incident Reports (DIRs) were filed with local police departments, and 123,649 restraining orders were entered into the national registry. All the courts specializing in domestic violence are overwhelmed, processing hundreds of thousands of cases a year.

California has seen a similar trend. For example, in 2005, there were 181,362 domestic violence calls placed to 911 operators, and 93,000 of them involved weapons or firearms. In 2003, the State of California denied 212 permits for firearms as a result of allegations of domestic violence. That same year, 125,000 restraining orders were entered into the national registry.

The feminist effort to counteract domestic violence—both by promoting new interpretations of how the issue is viewed and by reforming the criminal justice system—has, by many measures, been extremely successful. The hostile police, dismissive prosecutors, and ignorant judges whom activists once hoped to reform are now the exception rather than the rule in criminal justice circles, and most Americans consider violence against women a serious crime. And yet the crusade has also had its fair share of unpredictable outcomes, and these are sometimes difficult for us as a nation to acknowledge and digest. The magnitude of the effort expended, coupled with our overwhelming need to believe that we are making things better for women in desperate need, encourages us to turn away from the reforms' unintended consequences. At the same time it would be both intellectually careless and morally reprehensible to ignore them.

UNINTENDED CONSEQUENCES

All of us who are committed to combating domestic abuse must continue to ask ourselves the following questions: How effective are the responses we've engineered in the last few decades at decreasing violence in people's lives? Was our original definition of domestic violence sufficiently inclusive? And if not, how can we broaden and refine it?

Are Women Safer?

Generally speaking, yes. Domestic violence homicides have dropped dramatically over the past three decades—as have homicide rates overall. Casey Gwinn, San Diego's former city attorney and one of the nation's most voluble and effective advocates of mandatory responses to domestic violence, believes that these policy changes have, in fact, reduced the murder rate. In an interview with Oprah Winfrey in 2003, Gwinn declared, "We need to be intervening earlier and earlier, holding batterers accountable and preventing escalation until we no longer have broken bones and dead bodies." Gwinn's attitude reflects the popular belief that by taking the responsibility for arrest and prosecution away from the victim and placing it in the hands of the court, the victim is insulated from a batterer's anger and retaliation and can't be coerced into dropping charges.

When one delves into the research, however, the correlation between the new policies and the drop in murder rates is far from clear. In a 2007 research report about domestic violence, Rana Sampson, a national policing consultant and a former White House Fellow, noted the general decline in nearly all forms of violent crime and then added, "It is unknown whether domestic violence is paralleling these declines for the same or different reasons." Richard L. Davis, a retired lieutenant from the Brockton, Massachusetts, police department and an independent consultant to the criminal justice system, asserts that "the majority of domestic violence abusers will discontinue their abusive behavior without an arrest being made" and points out that "to date there are no National Institute of Justice studies that provide any empirical evidence that most contemporary batterer intervention programs really work." Davis also observes that nearly every large governmental study over the last ten years has concluded that the overall effectiveness of criminal justice in domestic violence cases is very much in question.

More troubling, some studies suggest that certain women in abusive relationships may be in greater danger now than they were before these reforms were instituted. Davis cites study after study showing that while the system seems to protect some victims, these same interventions also "increase retaliation" in other cases. A Ms. Foundation study that focused on the advocacy needs of women of color expressed similar concerns, concluding that for many women "involvement with the criminal legal system has not been a positive or helpful experience." Indeed they went so far as to say that "some women are actively harmed" by the system's involvement.

The first scientifically rigorous study to look at the relationship between arrest and battering was performed in Minneapolis by Professors Richard Berk and Lawrence Sherman; it involved 314 victims of domestic violence. Published in 1984, around the same time that the Tracey Thurman case was decided, the Minneapolis study examined three alternative interventions after a violent incident: arrest, counseling the parties when the police arrived at the scene, or separating the couple for several hours after the altercation with the threat of a subsequent arrest. After a six-month follow-up, the researchers found that arresting the abuser had been the response most likely to deter a future incident of violence. This study, together with the Thurman verdict, became the impetus for encouraging arrest in domestic violence cases nationwide.

Eight years later, when Professor Sherman published a follow-up study on the same question, he drew his couples from a different city—Milwaukee, Wisconsin—with decidedly mixed results. Arrest deterred violence, he and his colleagues found, when men had something to lose as a result of the arrest, like a job or their marriage. But for those men who were unemployed, unmarried, or African American, arrest actually increased the likelihood of future violence.

Sherman underscored the significance of this discrepancy: If the Milwaukee police arrest ten thousand Caucasian men, these men subsequently commit 2,504 *fewer* acts of domestic violence than they do when they are simply warned. On the other hand, if the police in Milwaukee arrest ten thousand African American men for domestic violence crimes, these arrests subsequently produce 1,803 *more* acts of domestic violence. If these men had been warned rather than arrested, the research suggested, these acts of violence might not have occurred or would have been delayed.

Clearly, this finding is very problematic for several reasons. First, the police can't respond to an incident of domestic violence simply on the basis of the race of the defendant. In addition, many more African American men are likely to be arrested for domestic violence crimes than Caucasian men in urban centers like Milwaukee, which means that mandatory arrest policies may be *increasing* incidents of domestic violence overall. Sherman estimated that if three times as many African American men as Caucasian men are arrested in Milwaukee, a mandatory arrest policy in a city like this one would prevent 2,504 acts of violence primarily against Caucasian women at the price of 5,409 acts of violence primarily against African American women.

Sherman sadly noted that although the Minneapolis study received a great deal of attention and affirmation and was hailed by many as a "breakthrough," the Milwaukee study was widely ignored because it was delivering news that no one wanted to hear: "It is clear that our zeitgeist in the 1990s still favors 'getting tough,' and that greater severity is more politically correct than less severity among a broad coalition of both liberal and conservative groups. This carries a sobering lesson: provisional policy recommendations made on initial research results may be widely accepted in support of that broad coalition but subsequent findings that run against it may have far less influence."

A similar inconsistency came up in a 2001 report funded by the National Institute of Justice, which examined the effectiveness of restraining orders in preventing abuse and related deaths. The report concluded that bringing violations of these orders to court increased the likelihood of death for unmarried African American women and married Caucasian women.

A 2002 study also funded by the National Institute of Justice was specifically designed to address whether the criminal justice system and related strategies, such as shelter stays, were effective in reducing domestic violence homicide rates. Although there were overall declines in violence for women who visited shelters in rural areas, and shelters in urban communities contributed to declines in violence for Hispanic women, they did not have this effect on Caucasian and African American women's lives.

Furthermore, in a perplexing twist, the presence of these shelters in cities seemed to contribute to declines in domestic violence against African American *men*. In other words, sheltering African American women seemed to protect them from hurting their partners, but not the reverse. Overall, the researchers concluded that "the findings are surprising in terms of the relative weak, or null, overall net effect of criminal justice system response." It is particularly disappointing to learn that African American women, who are most at risk for homicide, are least likely to benefit from the protective strategies offered them.

These studies suggest that prevention strategies may be strongly influenced by race and class issues in ways that we are just beginning to recognize: holding abusive men accountable and encouraging their victims to seek shelter may in fact be making some women's further injury and death more likely rather than less so. Given that the largest increase in domestic violence incidents has been among African American women, and that Native American women face three times as many domestic violence attacks as white women, it is important for advocates, law enforcement officials, and the women themselves to understand just how helpful or harmful obtaining a restraining order might be. The research also suggests that we need to continue to evaluate these policies, even if—*especially if*—we may learn that they aren't as effective as we'd hoped. The battered women's movement was fueled by women's rage that society would rather turn away from domestic violence than fight to save the lives of its victims: the inconvenient truths about this social problem had to be confronted, not swept under the rug, no matter how tempting it was to do so. Now those of us who consider ourselves activists in the movement must hold ourselves to that same high standard.

Women as the New Criminals

On the evening of Monday, October 15, 2007, thirty-nine-year-old Jill Dean of Conway, South Carolina, called 911 to report that her husband had beaten her, but forty-five-year-old Charles Dean had left the house before the police arrived. He returned nine hours later and stabbed his wife to death.

Mandatory arrest policies were designed to interrupt and prevent exactly this type of life-threatening situation. For better or worse, however, this is only one type of domestic violence. As anyone who regularly watches the reality show *Cops* can tell you, the police often arrive on the scene to discover a drunk and mutually combative couple yelling at each other, shoving each other, and hotly declaring that the other person started it. Even when there is no evidence that any serious injury has been inflicted by either party, many state laws now demand that someone be arrested. And when an arrest *does* take place, it's no longer necessarily the man who gets taken in. Indeed, the largest increase in arrests of domestic violence perpetrators since mandatory or preferred arrest policies have been adopted has been among women.

In one study of California, funded by the Department of Justice, the researchers found that the increase in arrests of men between 1987 and 1995 was 37 percent, whereas the increase in arrests of women was 446 percent. Convictions for domestic violence offenses between 1987 and 1999 grew at a rate of 131 percent for men—and an astounding 1,207 percent for women.

Despite the primary aggressor laws now on the books in most states, police often feel they must arrest both parties when confronted with a he-said/she-said scenario, even though many states will force them to justify that decision in their report. In other instances, police officers conclude that it was the woman who started the violence, and arrest policies force them to incarcerate her. This was certainly not what feminist advocates originally envisioned. And when there are children at home and the police are taking away *both* parents, it can be devastating for the family as a whole.

Beyond the Reach of the Police

In 2000, Patricia Tjaden and Nancy Thoennes conducted a study funded by the National Institute of Justice and the Centers for Disease Control on the "extent, nature and consequences of intimate partner violence." Tjaden and Thoennes discovered that, even after decades of reform, only *one-fourth* of the women who experienced a physical assault called the police. A little less than two-thirds of the women who did *not* call the police said that they did not think the police would believe them; 32 percent explained that they did not want the police or courts involved. And among those women who did call the police, 99.7 percent reported that they did not think the police could do anything about their victimization. Such findings led the researchers to observe that "most victims of intimate partner violence do not consider the justice system an appropriate vehicle for resolving conflicts with intimates." Then why did they call in the first place? Moments of extreme danger often prompt us to reach out for the only help available to us, even when we are not confident that it will address the problem. If you live with a pyromaniac, you call the fire department when the house is going up in flames, even though you doubt that it will be able to stop your partner from lighting matches in the future.

Several states have instituted Fatality Review Teams—made up of police officers, court personnel, children's services workers, advocates for victims, batterer treatment personnel, and other community members—to analyze why a domestic violence death has occurred. Over a two-year period in Arizona, from 2000 to 2002, there had been prior police involvement in only 30 percent of the domestic violence fatalities. Florida's Fatality Review Team, the first in the country, discovered that 50 percent of the women killed in domestic violence homicides in 1994 never had any contact with the criminal justice system previously. When the partner also killed the children and/or himself, the rate of contact dropped to less than 35 percent. Taken together, these sober findings suggest that some of the women who most need rescuing don't actually turn to the system for help.

Who Else Has Been Left Out of the Equation?

The somewhat bewildering results of Tjaden and Thoennes's study are a telling indication of the tensions between the movement's overarching ideology and the more complicated landscape it is attempting to survey. For example, although the study ostensibly focused on violence against women, it also gathered information on all kinds of domestic violence, including the incidence and prevalence of abuse against men. Some of the results were very surprising as well as disturbing; for example, 835,000 men were victims of domestic violence, in comparison to approximately 1.5 million women—hardly the stark contrast we might have expected. Similarly, 1.5 percent of the women surveyed and 0.9 percent of the men surveyed said that they were raped and/or physically assaulted by their partner in the previous twelve months. This added up to about 4.8 million rapes and physical assaults perpetrated against women in the United States each year compared to approximately 2.9 million physical assaults and rapes perpetuated against men. Only 13.5 percent of these men reported a violent incident to the police.

These statistics, taken together, suggest that a significant number of men in this country are abused by their intimate partners, yet there has been little enthusiasm on the part of the movement about following up on this data. Indeed, this study showed that—despite the significant increase we've seen in the arrests of women in the past decade—police officers are still much more likely to take a report and make an arrest if the *victim* is a woman. This begs a new set of questions: Do we need to retrain police officers to take men's claims of abuse seriously? Do we need shelters for battered men? Do we need to tailor our treatment programs so that they also accept female abusers? Should we be encouraging men to seek help when they're being abused?

Stanley Green, a licensed engineer and graduate of Rensselaer Polytechnic Institute, is one of the few male survivors of domestic violence who has been willing to go public. On a December evening in 1990, Green was retrieving some belongings from the car he jointly owned with his estranged wife, who was also a successful professional. When she spotted him in the parking lot, she accused him of trying to steal the car and attacked him, kicking him and hitting him in the head with a heavy cell phone.

Green suffered a rib injury and a bloody head wound. When the police arrived at the scene, Green asked that a police report be made. Green's wife, who presented no physical injuries, told the police that she had tried to restrain Green from stealing her car. Even though Green was visibly hurt, the police refused to write a report.

"You're lucky that we're not hauling you off to jail," Green reports one of the officers telling him. The incident, says Green, was the final violent encounter in an eight-year marriage filled with physical and emotional abuse. Following this attack in 1990, Green made a round of calls to shelters, state agencies, legal advocacy groups, and domestic violence crisis lines. He wasn't seeking a shelter—he assumed, correctly, that no shelters for abused men existed at the time. He was trying to obtain information about services for battered men and legal advice on how to force the police to take his complaint against his wife seriously. Green reports that he was told such assistance was not available to men.

Whether we as a society are comfortable admitting it or not, many men are physically abused. Ironically, many of our assumptions, whether unspoken or otherwise, about battered men are similar to those we once held about battered women: "Why don't you fight back? Why do you stay? You're so pathetic to put up with this."

There are several important points to remember when examining these biases. As we know, fighting back can often make things worse. If you pick up a paperweight and I pick up a chair, reconciliation is unlikely to be imminent. Another obvious but frequently overlooked fact is that *not everyone is violent.* Some people may try to protect and defend themselves or flee, but attempting to hurt another person is something that they are not willing or able to do.

In his book, *Abused Men*, Philip W. Cook argues that professionals and social scientists need to confront what he characterizes as the hidden problem of male victimization. "Looking at only one side of the domestic abuse equation is not the way to create appropriate public policy," he writes, "and it does not reflect reality." Men are not the only people who have been ill-served by our narrow view of domestic violence as a crime committed by heterosexual men against heterosexual women. Indeed, when same-sex couples and couples that include at least one transgender partner are plagued by intimate abuse, they also find that there is little support available to them.

Again, this absence of support does not reflect an absence of domestic violence in the gay, lesbian, bisexual, and transgender communities. It simply illustrates the same sorts of conceptual deficiencies that our lack of services for battered women suggested thirty years ago: same-sex abuse doesn't fit in with our preconceived ideas about violent relationships, so we'd prefer not to think about it.

The significance of our unwillingness to reach out to these victims of intimate violence is twofold. First, if we as a society are committed to fighting this social problem, we must be committed to helping all those who suffer from it. Second, these "exceptional" cases raise the possibility that the central tenet of the antidomestic violence movement—that men are violent and women are their victims—is simply incorrect and needs to be reexamined. We can't be so wedded to the idea that only straight men are dangerous that we refuse to protect anyone who is being hurt by a lover who doesn't fall into that category.

SO WHO IS THE CRIMINAL JUSTICE SYSTEM WORKING FOR?

The system works best for a white heterosexual woman from the middle or upper classes who has no children and has already decided to leave her abuser before that first phone call to the police. Mandatory arrest gives this woman that brief respite—while the batterer is held overnight—to marshal her forces, get a restraining order, get out of the house, and hire a lawyer. If her violent partner pursues her, he risks jail, which he is likely to view as threatening his livelihood and his reputation.

Certainly, helping these women move on from their abusive relationships is an enormous accomplishment of the domestic violence awareness movement.

But we must also face the fact that they do not constitute the majority of people suffering from intimate violence. Tragically, although this was far from the movement's intention, we have created a situation in which the needs of the white, educated, middle- and upper-class women who *built* the system are met, while the needs of so many others are not. After all, most violent couples choose to remain together: What are we doing for them?

UNREPENTANT PERPETRATORS

Many battered women hope that if they call the police on their partners, those partners may finally be forced to get help for their violent behavior. Batterer intervention programs were supposed to answer that need. But have they?

In one of the only rigorous studies of Duluth-model batterer intervention programs, researchers followed two groups of male offenders participating in BIPs—a group in Broward County, Florida, and a group in Brooklyn, New York. The results were disappointing.

Researchers found that batterers in the Broward group who were facing the possible loss of jobs, homes, families, and good reputations were less likely to reoffend after attending the program than those who had little or nothing to lose. In other words, as the Milwaukee study on mandatory arrest also suggested, a significant number of men were "beyond the reach" of the program. Indeed, men who did not attend most or all of the sessions of the twenty-six-week BIP—approximately 34 percent of those who participated in the study—were more likely to get rearrested for violence than those *who did not attend treatment at all.* Only those men who attended all of the treatment sessions experienced a reduction in their violence. The study also found that men didn't change their attitudes about violence after attending the entire program—even when they became less violent.

The Brooklyn study revealed that men who attended treatment for a longer period of time (twenty-six weeks) were less likely to commit new acts of violence than those who only completed an eight-week program. Unfortunately, however, men were far more likely to complete the shorter program, simply because it took less time and cost less money. Here, too, there was no noted change in attitudes toward domestic violence after completing either program. In other words, the reform was based on behavior modification as a result of perceived or possible negative outcomes ("I better do this, or I'm going to be in more trouble") rather than on a new understanding that hurting one's partner is wrong ("I now see my violence and my relationship in an entirely different light and accept responsibility for my actions").

BIPs are rarely successful even to this limited extent, though, because many men find them so alienating that they drop out after the first session. Only recently have judges developed follow-up measures to ensure compliance with the treatment mandate. With judicial monitoring, the program may be more

effective than it has been alone. But as researchers at the Center for Court Innovation have pointed out in their 2007 study, it isn't enough that courts *issue* a
treatment mandate; they must also *enforce* such mandates "by sanctioning
those who are noncompliant." Many men escape detection when judges fail to
follow up on the treatment orders they issue.

Why are so many men resistant to BIPs? Consider the following scenario.
Richard is a traveling salesman; Janet, his wife, stays home with their two children. Janet's drinking is a point of tremendous tension in the marriage, but
their fights have never become physical. One evening, after Richard returns
from a road trip, Janet drunkenly announces that she has been unfaithful in his
absence. Richard flies into a rage and punches Janet in the stomach, breaking a
rib. Because Richard has never been arrested before, he is offered the option of
attending a BIP for twenty-six weeks instead of going to jail.

Richard finds the class extremely frustrating because he doesn't feel solely responsible for what happened. The teacher tells him that he needs to walk in his
wife's shoes and develop a less dominating attitude. Dominators are "losers."
Every time he raises the issue of his wife's infidelity and drinking, the teacher tells
him he is blaming her for his violence. Richard completes the program because
he is afraid of losing his job, but he is left feeling bitter and misunderstood. The
difficulties in the marriage that caused the violence remain unaddressed.

UNGRATEFUL VICTIMS

In 1999, the football star Jim Brown was prosecuted in Los Angeles for attacking his wife's car with a shovel and threatening to kill her. Mrs. Brown escaped
to a neighbor's house and called 911. When the operator asked if there was a
history of domestic violence in the relationship, she said yes.

But when the case came to trial, Monique Brown's story morphed into
something different, and she refused to testify against her husband; she told
the jury that her husband had *not* threatened to kill her. In fact, she claimed
that she'd called 911 to punish him because she believed he "was having an affair." As a result of her change of heart in the courtroom, Jim Brown was acquitted of threatening to kill his wife and convicted on a misdemeanor
vandalism charge.

Monique Brown behaved the way most victims of domestic violence behave; when faced with the likelihood of her husband going to jail, she revised
her story, choosing to protect her relationship with her husband rather than
ally herself with the criminal justice system, which sought to punish him.

Linda Fairstein, a crime novelist and former head of the Sex Crimes Unit in
the Manhattan District Attorney's office, states the problem forthrightly: "The
greatest frustration for law enforcement is the overwhelming number of times
a woman—typically, it's a woman—will call 911 to have police stop an attack.

But then they don't want the violator arrested for any number of reasons. Maybe it's, 'I love him when he's good,' or maybe it's financial."

Many of us find these stories enraging. Can't these women see their batterers for "who they are" instead of who they want them to be? Don't they realize that they are likely to become violent again? I would argue that many of these women *do* know that their partners may become violent again, and that they would welcome some other form of assistance, but throwing someone they love in jail simply isn't an acceptable alternative for them. We should ask ourselves a similar set of questions: Do we really see the criminal justice bureaucracy as it is, or as we want it to be? And do we really think that these violent men will be any less violent once they've come through the system?

It would be nice to think that the reforms of the last thirty years have made the criminal justice bureaucracy more hospitable toward battered women, but that isn't precisely the case. It has become more hospitable toward women who are sure that they are ready to leave their batterers—a small minority. For everyone else, however, it is a minefield.

When I talk with legal professionals working in the system, they often report being distressed and frustrated by what they see. One New York public defender, who spoke to me confidentially, has more than a decade of experience in handling domestic violence cases. She described Manhattan's criminal court as "miserable," place where overworked and distracted judges, prosecutors, and defense attorneys scream at one another all day, and everybody is at their "absolute worst while trying to make the most important decisions about the lives of other human beings." After all, for most people, having a relative or partner arrested is both frightening and humiliating, and other bad things frequently follow: people lose their jobs; kids get taken away from their parents; families get kicked out of public housing. In sum, she said, "Manhattan's criminal court is a dysfunctional mess," and this sentiment is not specific to New York City or defense attorneys.

One East Coast prosecutor, who also spoke on the condition of anonymity, told me that he has become totally disillusioned with the system after only a few months on the job. A particular disappointment has been the lack of domestic violence training that new prosecutors receive. He attended one three-hour session on domestic violence that included clips of bloody and bruised women. The purpose was to "scare us and show us how bad things are." But what was missing from the training—something he regarded as critically important—was insight into the psychological reasons that lead to domestic violence. This omission, he feels, contributes to a general ignorance as to why violence happens and a lack of empathy for those caught in the system. He is particularly disturbed by the way female victims are treated. "I can't count the number of times I've heard the word 'crazy' applied to victims by cops, prosecutors, victim advocates, and others," he said.

To make matters worse, the inflexibility of mandatory arrest and prosecution policies too frequently lead to the escalation of minor family incidents into serious crimes. Two years ago, Sarah McPherson, a public health expert, found her assumptions about the fundamental benevolence of the system shattered when she became unexpectedly entangled with the criminal justice bureaucracy in California. I first spoke with Sarah when she contacted me for advice on how to address her situation. "I tried to tell the truth and cooperate in good faith. I thought the system was there to help me," she said, "but, instead, it ended up becoming my greatest enemy."

One evening, Sarah and her husband, Jeff, a computer programming engineer, were just getting home, and tensions between them were running high. The family's two dogs were being especially rambunctious, and Jeff lost his temper and started hitting one of the dogs. Sarah was extremely upset by this and hurried to intervene, kicking her husband to get him away from the dog. As Jeff staggered, his glasses fell off; unable to see properly and off-balance, he pushed Sarah away, striking her in the face so that the frames of her own glasses cut her close to her eye. Both husband and wife were extremely disturbed by the incident: nothing like this had ever happened in their marriage.

The cut required stitches at the hospital, where Sarah, in the company of her husband, tried to explain frankly how she had been hurt. Sarah told the nurse that Jeff had never hit her during their fifteen years together. At the same time, she recognized that what had happened between them, while it hadn't been an intentional injury, was also a result of serious stress within the marriage. She hoped that they might receive counseling to help them negotiate this difficult period in their domestic life. What happened next, however, sent the family into an emotional and financial tailspin from which they still have not fully recovered.

Sarah says that police officers questioned her in a demeaning way, trying to "put words in my mouth." In what would become an ongoing mantra, she repeatedly told everyone at the hospital that day that the violence that occurred between her and her husband was *not* a pattern of behavior. It had been, emphatically, a onetime occurrence. She stressed that she was not battered, nor was her husband a batterer. All they wanted from the system was counseling to help them work out their problems. One of the officers responded that she "could be dead next time."

Sarah was informed that her husband was going to be arrested and that she needed to obtain a restraining order against him. She begged the officers not to put Jeff in jail. She told them that he'd just begun a new job and was required to be out of town the next morning. At that moment, all she could think about was how important this new job was; it meant financial stability for their family. At great hardship, the couple posted $11,000 in bail to keep Jeff out of jail.

A few days after the incident, a victim advocate contacted Sarah and pressed her to consider a legal separation, divorce, and/or a move to a shelter. That same day, the district attorney informed Sarah that she was charging her husband with a felony. The charge was based on the number of stitches she'd received. Had she only had severe bruising, the D.A. said, the offense would have been classified as a misdemeanor. In the end, Jeff accepted a plea bargain for a felony in exchange for lifting the restraining order; he attended fifty-two sessions of domestic violence group counseling, and the family paid some $16,000 in legal bills.

"I was shocked at how disempowered they made me feel through this whole process," says Sarah. "I was treated like a victim who was unable to think or speak for myself. It was clear that the police, the D.A., and the victim advocate viewed me as a typical battered woman and that this perception colored everything that I did or said in their eyes." The D.A. and victim advocate informed her that there were few, if any, success stories in these cases: usually, the violence continues, and the woman eventually leaves or dies. "No matter how articulate I was about what I wanted or what our family needed, no one listened to me. I wondered why I did not have a say. I wondered why everyone I came in contact with in the system assumed that our family situation would not get better and that divorce was imminent. I don't think it helped that the D.A. assigned to my case only worked with cases of domestic violence."

SILENCING THE BATTERED WOMAN

From the beginning, feminists have talked about empowering battered women. What that nearly always meant, however, was empowering battered women who were ready to leave their violent relationships. But so many of the laws that have been enacted in the name of battered women have, in fact, further stripped them of power. After a woman—often in a moment of intense fear—makes that call to the police, many of the consequences of her actions have already been decided for her. (Sarah McPherson, of course, didn't go to the police; she simply went to the hospital.) Her husband or lover may be arrested and even prosecuted and convicted without her consent. In fact, in some instances, a prosecutor will explain to the judge or jury that a woman's attempts to defend her husband—by not testifying or going so far as to testify on his behalf—are the result of the Battered Woman Syndrome.

Can these reforms really be seen as empowering strategies for women? The dismaying truth is that any woman who isn't prepared to give up her voice altogether should be wary of using the system. If the system prosecutes a man against his wife or his girlfriend's will, is this likely to weaken or strengthen the bond between them? And if the woman has herself been violent in the relationship, what are her options? To admit her guilt and get arrested herself, or to go along with the mythology of domestic violence supported by the courts, to avoid a record.

Whether we like it or not, the questions of strength and weakness, choice and coercion, are very complicated in intimate relationships. Do many battered women overestimate their power in their marriage? Yes. Do they often lose power over the course of the relationship? Yes. But at the same time, many of these women are also incredible survivors, and some even acknowledge that they participate in various destructive patterns with their partners. Is taking away even more of their power really the best way to make them stronger? Or can depriving them of their decision making ability have the opposite effect from the one we intended?

Barbara Fedders of the Criminal Justice Institute at Harvard Law School has described how the new laws can backfire:

> After an incident of domestic violence, for example, a woman might wish to call the police and have them come to her home. She might reason that a police officer could diffuse an explosive situation or frighten her batterer into ceasing his abuse. She may engage in a careful cost-benefit analysis and determine that, while police *presence* would be useful, an *arrest* would not. A woman may be dependent on the income of her batterer, for example, or she may not want their children to witness their father's arrest. Such a woman, if aware of a mandatory-arrest policy in her jurisdiction, would likely refrain from calling the police at all, and would thereby be deprived of a potentially useful tool in her struggle to end the violence in her life.

In a 2006 study entitled "What Do Battered Women Want? Victims' Opinions on Prosecution," Sara C. Hare, a sociology professor at Indiana University Southeast, noted that women are empowered when they control the prosecutorial process and can use the threat of prosecution to reduce their partners' violence. Ironically, Hare comments, "the criminal justice system is pursing a policy that takes the control away from the very group who could use it to reduce revictimization."

Creating opportunities for victims of domestic violence to tell more complete stories—whether in court or through the treatment they participate in with their partners—in ways that also ensure their safety is surely a goal we should strive to attain. A woman recanting on the witness stand, changing her testimony after an arrest has been made, or perhaps, even worse, not being given an opportunity to tell a jury what *really* happened the night her husband was arrested isn't beneficial for anyone involved. Encouraging openness and honesty among men and women, including those in same-sex couples—whether or not one's story fits the feminist mold—must be developed in ways we have not yet imagined. This is especially true for those who remain silent because they fear that their story doesn't jibe with what society thinks they should do—leave and never look back.

WHAT NEXT? CRIMINAL JUSTICE REFORM AND BEYOND

No one denies the fact that the criminal justice system is an irrefutable part of fighting domestic violence. But we still need to be vigilant about reevaluating and improving the systems we are putting in place. If BIPs are serving little purpose other than reassuring society that it is taking the "right stand," other avenues of treatment should be explored. If more African American women are being beaten by their partners than ten years ago, mandatory arrest, restraining order policies, even shelter stays need to be revisited. And if most women in abusive relationships still aren't calling the police, we shouldn't be too quick to pat ourselves on the back, thinking that we've solved the problem of domestic violence.

The larger point is that the criminal justice system cannot be the *only* method we have for confronting this social problem. The much-ignored but irrefutable fact is that most people who are involved in violent relationships do not want to end the relationships, and they certainly don't want their partners to go to prison; they simply want the violence to stop. Empowering people either to heal the relationships or to disengage from them without further violence is clearly the goal, but it is equally clear that the police and the courts are not ideally suited for this purpose.

ESCAPING TO FREEDOM VERSUS ESCAPING TO PRISON

In 1996, I was acutely aware of my good fortune: I knew that my privileged upbringing, my education, and my support network had made my escape from my abusive relationship possible. While teaching social work and law at UCLA, I became curious about women who retaliated against their abusers with violence. When I was invited to Frontera Prison to meet battered women who had killed their partners, I went with many questions: How did trapped women, women who could not readily leave their abusive relationships, fare overall? What happened when the violence was relentless, and their choices were much more limited for financial or other reasons? How did they manage this violence and their own growing anger, while continuing to live with their abusive partners? Perhaps the most important question was the one that underpinned my own ambivalence about leaving David: How many of these women still had feelings for the men who had hurt them?

When I posed this last question to the women serving life sentences for killing their abusers, to my astonishment nearly all of them raised their hands. One particularly articulate woman commented that, even ten years after shooting and killing her husband, she was still confused by her strong feelings for him. Her name was Brenda Aris.

Brenda approached me after the event and introduced herself. Governor Pete Wilson had recently granted her clemency, she told me, although her release date was still pending. I would learn later that Brenda killed Rick Aris, her husband of nine years, the same month I left David.

I soon found out that Brenda and I came from very different backgrounds, and certainly our destructive relationships had very different outcomes. But we shared one striking characteristic: both of us attempted to manage the violence in our lives without the assistance of the criminal justice system. Almost from that first meeting, I knew I wanted to tell our stories.

3

ENLARGING THE FRAME

Complicating our Perspectives on Severe Abuse

The stories we tell about intimate abuse—in both our own lives and the lives of others—are often shaped by how we choose to frame the story: what information we emphasize, what we leave out, how far back in time we go, and so on. Take the O.J. Simpson case. Many whites regarded Nicole Brown Simpson's murder and its aftermath as an all-too-familiar tale of domestic violence, whereas many blacks saw it as a typical narrative of racial injustice. Still others felt that it was a story about wealth and celebrity in America: clear proof that if you have enough money, you can get away with anything.

The Brenda and Rick Aris murder case, although far less publicized than the Simpson-Brown case, was also controversial in domestic violence and criminal justice circles—despite the fact that the murderer immediately confessed.

PERSPECTIVE #1: SNAPSHOTS AT THE CRIME SCENE

At 3:40 A.M. on August 10, 1986, the Riverside, California, police department received a call that a thirty-three-year-old male, Rick Aris, had been shot at his home. When detectives arrived at the scene, Brenda Aris, the wife of the victim, was sitting outside the house with a .22 automatic handgun, which she had stolen from her neighbor earlier that evening.

Brenda told the police that she had shot her husband both in "self-defense" and because she had "just had enough of it." She also claimed that he had beaten her up earlier that evening. She had not, however, attempted to have Rick arrested after the fight—indeed, she had never filed a complaint against her husband during all the time they had been married.

In addition, she had attacked him in his sleep, shooting him repeatedly in the back while he lay only a few feet away from two of their children. Shooting someone who is asleep does not fall within the conventional legal definition of "self-defense." The wounds that Brenda Aris had inflicted were lethal; her husband died a couple of hours later in the hospital. The following year, on November 25, 1987, a California jury convicted Brenda of second-degree murder, and she was sentenced to life in prison.

In this account of the murder—which is factually accurate—Brenda is clearly the perpetrator of the crime. And yet many people were outraged by her sentence, because they felt that the truly significant facts of her case were not being taken into account: she had, in fact, been a victim for years. If you told the *full* story, domestic violence advocates argued, you would see that it turned the question of guilt and innocence completely on its head. Rick was not a victim; he was a monster.

PERSPECTIVE #2: BRENDA ARIS AS BATTERED WOMAN

Brenda Lane and Rick Aris were married in Downy, California, on March 12, 1977, one year after they started going steady. They were both from white, working-class families who lived in Norwalk—a town located forty-five minutes outside of Los Angeles. Neither of them had finished high school: Brenda was seventeen years old and pregnant; Rick was twenty-three. The wedding day proved to be a harbinger of their life to come, with Brenda's high hopes and Rick's profound failures on glaring display.

Wedding pictures show Rick, looking tentative, his hair falling loosely to his collar, a white carnation in his lapel. Rick's parents, Emalou and Les Aris, paid for the flowers adorning the small chapel. Brenda wore a borrowed white satin wedding dress and held a small bouquet of red and white carnations. But the ceremony itself was marred by Rick's best man getting so stoned before the service that he nearly collapsed during the vows. As the newlyweds exited the chapel, they were greeted by Rick's drunken friends.

Following the wedding, the family hosted a reception at their home. In the middle of the festivities, Rick summoned Brenda into his bedroom. He was holding a box—his "special box"—and he accused Brenda of going through his stuff. Brenda told him she'd never seen the box, but he didn't believe her. He called her a "bitch," "cunt," and "slut." Then he backhanded her. Brenda's first impulse was to run away. But she had just gotten married—how could she explain herself to all the people who had gathered to toast their happiness?

When Emalou interrupted the fight and asked what was going on, Rick complained that Brenda had messed with his things.

"Oh, no, that wasn't Brenda—that was me," Emalou said. "I was looking for your cufflinks."

Emalou begged Brenda to overlook Rick's behavior: the wedding had put him under a lot of stress.

Brenda and Rick spent their wedding night in the honeymoon suite of a nearby motel. Rick immediately passed out on the bed, while Brenda, lying next to him, couldn't sleep for most of the night.

The marriage was off to a rocky start. From the beginning, Rick's drinking and his inability to hold down a job put the young couple in a precarious financial position. The birth of Lucretia in 1977 added to the strain at home, both because Rick had desperately wanted a boy—Rick angrily told Brenda that he "didn't give a shit" what she named the baby—and because Brenda's attention was now divided. Yet, at times, when he was sober, he would happily diaper Lucretia or give her a bottle.

A friend offered Rick a job in construction in Sacramento, and both Rick and Brenda jumped at the opportunity. They were away from their parents for the first time, and Brenda was thrilled; now it felt as though they were really building a life together.

The first incident of serious violence in Sacramento occurred three months after they arrived. Rick and Brenda had been invited to a party; Brenda arranged for a babysitter and was looking forward to a night out. Rick suddenly became angry, however, and told Brenda that she wasn't going anywhere. Brenda generally didn't question Rick's decisions, but life over the last few months had been so harmonious that she summoned the courage to ask Rick why she couldn't go.

"Because I said so," he snapped, and left for the party.

Brenda and the baby were still up when Rick came home drunk and pounded on the front door. Seemingly in a good mood, which was unusual when he was drunk, Rick picked up Lucretia and started playing with her—until Lucretia wet her diaper and some of the urine leaked out onto Rick's pants.

"If she's going to pee like a dog," he declared, "she can stay outside like a dog."

Rick took Lucretia and placed her outside on the porch. Brenda pleaded with Rick to let her bring the baby inside. It was cold out, and Lucretia could be killed if she fell down the porch stairs. Rick laughed at her and said he didn't give a shit what happened. Placing himself between his wife and the door, he refused to let her pass. He picked up a rope that was lying near him on the floor and started swinging it at Brenda while she begged to be allowed to retrieve their daughter from the porch. Finally, Rick relented. Lucretia was physically unharmed.

As Brenda brought the baby inside to safety, she told herself that she could no longer stay with Rick. She borrowed some money from a friend, and, a few nights later, after Rick left for the bar, she took a flight back to Los Angeles. She asked her father, Alvis, to pick her up at the airport and bring her back to Norwalk.

After a few days at home with her parents, she called her in-laws to tell them that she'd separated from Rick and that their granddaughter was safe. To Brenda's surprise, Rick answered the phone; he explained that he certainly wasn't going to stay in Sacramento by himself. Although this may have been flattering for Brenda, it also demonstrated an ominous side to Rick's character. His attachment to his wife—like his attachment to drugs and alcohol—was far stronger than his commitment to any sort of independence, financial or otherwise.

In Norwalk, Rick and Brenda lived just a few blocks from each other, which made a permanent separation very difficult to sustain. Rick felt free to visit with Brenda and the baby whenever he wanted. Moreover, he was now on extremely good behavior. Brenda recalls several lazy Sunday afternoons during this peaceful period when she and Rick, together with Lucretia, would stroll to a nearby park and spend the day together there. Rick was also coaching the Norwalk Little League; sometimes Brenda would take the baby and watch Rick coach a game. Ironically, these were the sorts of visions she'd had of family life with Rick, but now they were separated. Didn't it make sense to give him another chance?

Brenda was feeling boxed in. She didn't want to live permanently with her parents. She was approaching nineteen, she had a toddler, and she was without skills or job prospects. The only future she saw was with Rick.

Thus the pattern that would define their marriage was set. As Brenda would explain to me years later, "We had many happy times together as a family. It was a cycle. We could go for a time, and he wouldn't hit me. Then something would happen." Anything could set Rick off: the house was not clean enough. Dinner wasn't cooked right. In these cases, the violence was random and impossible to anticipate or catalogue. If the violence escalated, Brenda would leave. But then Rick would say he was sorry, and eventually she would relent: "I'd think, OK, this time he'll change. It'll be different. We can be a real family."

In June 1979, Rick and Brenda rented a small house just one block away from Les and Emalou's home. Almost as soon as they moved in, Rick's desire to appease Brenda disappeared. Once again, he was out of work, and he was frequently mean and violent. He was also developing a dependency on methamphetamine, a powerful drug that often causes anxiety, delusions, and chronic fatigue. Brenda applied for and received welfare, but soon the couple was fighting over that as well: the checks came in Brenda's name, and Rick resented being dependent on his wife for money. Rick was also extremely jealous, and at other times he would become convinced that Brenda was having an affair. Although he was repeatedly unfaithful during the marriage, Rick often threatened to kill Brenda if she fooled around with anyone else.

In 1980, Brenda's father invited his two daughters to take a trip to Las Vegas with him. Brenda, tired and depressed, begged Rick to let her go: Iona, Brenda's mother, offered to take care of Lucretia. Finally, Rick consented. Brenda had a great time with her father and sister—gambling, going to a show, and eating out three meals a day.

When Alvis and his daughters returned to Norwalk four days later, Brenda picked up Lucretia from her parents' house and went back to her own, where she fell asleep on the sofa. She woke up when Rick came home and punched her in the eye, screaming about how she'd been sleeping with some guy in Las Vegas.

"What are you talking about?" Brenda yelled back, as blood spurted from her eye. Soon blood was everywhere, and even Rick seemed shocked by what he had done. He got her a cold compress and apologized. Although Brenda went to the doctor, she did not tell the truth about how she was injured. While at the doctor's office, she also took a pregnancy test; she was two months pregnant.

In the midst of the violence and misery, there were still moments of hope. Candice, Rick and Brenda's second daughter, was born on December 17, 1980, and Brenda still remembers her arrival as a particularly joyful time.

When Brenda came home from the hospital with Candice, she discovered that Rick had cleaned the entire house and filled it with roses from his mother's garden. Brenda was deeply touched. "Those roses meant more to me than if they came from the fanciest florist in town. I felt so good knowing that *he* had done all those things just to please me."

Tragically, these interludes in part derived their power from how starkly they contrasted with Rick's usual behavior at home: the romance in the relationship had quickly deteriorated after Rick and Brenda were married. Rick was often verbally abusive to his wife, calling her a "slut" or "fucking whore" in front of friends and family, and he seemed to enjoy humiliating her. Their sex life, which had once been such a strong part of the bond between them, had become at best a burden and at worst a nightmare. In bed, too, Rick seemed to enjoy hurting and humiliating Brenda; she would later tell Lenore Walker that she had been raped hundreds of times, both vaginally and anally, throughout their marriage. Rick often demanded sex when he was drunk and then had difficulty achieving climax; the sex was so painful that Brenda eventually feared that her husband had permanently damaged her insides.

April 1982 marked another significant turning point in the marriage. Rick came home one night after making his rounds of the bars; he was drunk and completely out of control. Brenda was asleep in their bed; Steve, a friend of Rick's whom he had invited to stay with them, was sleeping on the sofa. Rick woke Brenda up and started punching her hard in the face. He was convinced that Brenda was sleeping with Steve. After trashing the bedroom, he attacked the rest of the house, yelling that Brenda was a "fucking bitch" and a "worthless cunt." He broke all the panes in the china hutch, three windows in the front of the house, and two in the kitchen. He ran into the living room and turned the coffee table over on Steve, who was now wide awake.

When Rick finally passed out, Brenda took her children and fled to her parents' house. The next morning, she couldn't move her jaw. It was broken and had to be wired shut. For six weeks, Brenda ate food through a straw and lost thirty pounds. During this period, she never told her dentist or doctor that her husband punched her—and they never asked.

When Rick sobered up and realized what he'd done, he apologized and swore he would stop drinking. He promised Brenda such violence would never happen again.

By the time Brenda's jaw had healed, she had reunited with Rick, but she was now afraid of her husband in a way that she hadn't been before. In the past when he threatened to kill her or members of her family, she hadn't believed him. Now she wondered if he wasn't capable of murder after all. It felt dangerous to be with him, but also dangerous to leave him. Within months she was pregnant with their third child.

The cycle of reunions and separations quickened. After the birth of Sheena, in August, Rick was furious: it was as if Brenda were deliberately denying him the son he craved. At thirty-one, Rick was barely employable, an alcoholic, and a drug addict; Brenda was virtually a single mother of three whose husband needed her welfare money for drugs. When Rick wasn't living with Brenda, he was broke, hungry, and often homeless, wandering from place to place in the hope that someone would take him in. Sometimes Brenda would sneak him into her parents' house, where she lived on and off, to feed him and let him take a shower. But if they got back together, the violence quickly became unbearable.

By the summer of 1985, Brenda was at the end of her rope: she couldn't imagine her life continuing this way, and yet Rick seemed unreachable. That June, she contemplated suicide and slit her right wrist. When it started bleeding heavily, she panicked and wrapped her wrist in a towel. Although she tried to hide what she had done, a part of her also hoped that Rick would realize the level of her despair. Instead, he told her that she had made the cut incorrectly, and explained how to do it "the right way." Shortly after this incident, she tried to overdose on twenty valiums, but she simply slept for a few days and woke up feeling ill. She then admitted to herself that if she succeeded in committing suicide, Rick would be her daughters' only parent; there had to be a better solution.

For the first time in her life, Brenda started looking for a way to get out of Norwalk—without Rick. She spoke to an old high school friend who lived in San Bernardino, about sixty miles away. Rent was cheap in the area, and Iona agreed to lend her money for the move. But Iona also warned her daughter that this was the last time—that if she went back to Rick, her parents would disown her. Brenda told everyone else, however, that she was moving to Washington State, so that Rick wouldn't be able to track her down. (This was prudent; later, when Rick threatened to kill her sister, Kathy, for not divulging the address, Kathy had no information to give.)

In San Bernardino, life was much calmer. Brenda was still on welfare, but she didn't have to pay for Rick's habit. She found a two-bedroom apartment, fixed it up, and began again. But the girls missed their father—especially Lucretia. After a few weeks, Brenda brought the girls back to Norwalk so that she could attend a baby shower. On her way, Brenda dropped the kids off at Kathy's house; her sister had agreed to supervise a visit with Rick. They all hung out in the backyard together, and the girls were happy to see their father. Lucretia gave Rick a school photo with the words "I love you, Daddy" written on the back.

When Brenda was ready to come back to pick up the girls, though, Rick wouldn't leave the house before she arrived. Brenda was afraid to see him, but Rick was sweet and remorseful. He begged her to reunite the family, and even cried. Brenda refused, but she was also sad to have taken the children so far away. After this encounter, she started bringing the girls back to Norwalk so that they could visit with Rick at Les and Emalou's house, but she still wouldn't tell Rick where they were living.

During one of these visits, Rick called Brenda and told her that Candice was running a high temperature, and both parents ended up in the emergency room together. At some point during the confusion of checking into the hospital, Rick saw Brenda's MediCal card and memorized her new address. Two days later, he called her in San Bernardino. The conciliatory Rick was nowhere in evidence; instead, Rick threatened her on the phone, and Brenda was terrified. He told her that he knew where she lived, and that she had two choices: she could come pick him up in Norwalk, or she could wait for him to come and get her. The first option seemed safer to Brenda than the alternative.

Brenda left Rick twenty times during the course of their nine-year marriage. Her escape to San Bernardino was the last time. Twelve months later, Rick would be dead.

As horrific as the Aris story is, it is not—in 2008—an entirely unfamiliar one. In large part thanks to the feminist movement, many Americans are now able to imagine the particulars of this sort of relationship in a way that was impossible only a few decades earlier. Many of us might say that, given the torments of Brenda Aris's marriage, she should not have had to stay in jail for the rest of her life for killing her abuser. Some of us might even feel that it was a pity she didn't kill Rick a lot sooner. This fuller history of her life is in large part why she was granted clemency for her crime by Governor Pete Wilson on May 28, 1993.

But if we are trying to *understand* domestic violence, rather than simply pass judgment on those who inflict it and experience it, does this story tell us everything we need to know? The accepted wisdom when discussing these sorts of relationships is that everything the abuser does is calculated and dishonest and that the victim is, well, entirely a victim: not present in the relationship of her own free will but instead involved because of physical, emotional, and often economic coercion. Does that mean that Brenda didn't really choose to be with Rick? Does it mean that Rick and Brenda didn't *really* love each other? And what drew them together in the first place? Where did Rick's violence come from? Was he always violent?

PERSPECTIVE #3: THE BATTERER AS VICTIM

Ricky William Aris, the first and only son of Leslie and Emalou Aris, was born in Los Angeles in 1953; four daughters would follow. The Aris family lived in Downy, California. Les worked as a machine operator. Emalou stayed home and took care of the children. Rick's father was an alcoholic who frequently beat his wife.

When Les struck Emalou, she never retaliated. She was terrified of her husband and did her best to do exactly as he ordered. When Rick was seven years old, he tried to stop Les from hitting his mother by stepping between them. Les turned on Rick and beat him up instead. That was the last time Rick ever tried to intervene between his parents.

Rick was a bright and appealing child—devoted to Emalou, playful with his sisters, and popular with other kids. He was extremely physically active; he loved to ride his bike and skateboard. But he could also spend hours taking apart clocks and radios and then putting them back together: he had a gift for figuring out how machines worked. Emalou adored her son, but Les hated him, and Rick quickly became the family scapegoat. No matter what went wrong in the Aris household, Les would hold Rick responsible. Rick complained frequently about this injustice, but there was nothing his sisters or mother could do about it. Once Emalou tried to protect her son from Les and received a black eye for her trouble. Another time, Emalou took photographs of the red welts her husband's belt had left across Rick's back, but she never had the courage to show them to people outside the immediate family.

If Rick was first introduced to physical violence at home, he also found plenty of it on the streets, where he was frequently beaten up by kids in the neighborhood. If he came home bloodied, he got no sympathy from his father. Instead, Les would send him back out, telling him not to come home again until he'd shown them who was boss. If Les wasn't satisfied with how his son had defended himself on the street, he would beat Rick himself.

When Rick was twelve, he began getting terrible headaches, possibly due to a head injury he sustained during a baseball game. Despite his complaints, his parents didn't take him to a doctor. This was not unusual: an Aris who had an injury or a toothache was simply expected to tough it out. For years afterward,

Rick would wake up in the middle of the night with severe headaches, and he took large amounts of aspirin on a regular basis to numb the pain. These headaches would persist throughout his life.

As Rick grew older, his interest in machinery developed into a real skill. But Les never encouraged his son's gifts; indeed, he made it clear to all of his children that he considered getting an education a waste of time. When Rick turned thirteen, he stole his father's car, and Les called the police. This was Rick's first brush with the law. When questioned at the station, Rick admitted that he had already used Seconal, amphetamines, marijuana, acid, and heroin. He also started getting into fistfights with Les and arguing violently with his mother.

When Rick was fourteen, he was arrested as a juvenile and charged with coercing a six-year-old boy in the neighborhood to give him oral sex. The investigation suggested that Rick was not the instigator and that the six-year-old boy had been involved in similar activities with other boys. Rick was given voluntary probation. The court also suggested counseling to improve his strained relationship with his family. No counseling ever took place. More scrapes with the law followed. Rick was involved in numerous car accidents, and at age fifteen he spent thirty-six weeks in a camp for juvenile delinquents for stealing a car.

In 1969, Les moved his family to Norwalk. This may have been the end of Les's steady employment; for the most part, the Aris family lived on Les's part-time salary in a humble three-bedroom house with concrete, uncarpeted floors and tattered furniture. Here Emalou would shuffle around during the day in her housecoat and slippers, trying to appease Les and manage the chaos of raising five children on almost no money.

By the time the Aris family arrived in Norwalk, Rick was no longer a boy. He shaved daily, had long, thick brown hair, and was six feet tall; at sixteen he passed for twenty. He soon had a string of girlfriends at his new high school, and rumors of partying, pregnancies, and abusive behavior swirled around him. Before Rick had even turned eighteen, all the destructive forces of his life were in full swing: his tendency toward violence, his lack of sexual control, his dependency on drugs, and his inability to stick with anything that might help him transform his life. While still in tenth grade, Rick dropped out of school. His father's estimation of his prospects had won out.

Soon after, Rick got into trouble again and was sent to a juvenile camp for twenty-one weeks on charges of assault and possession of drugs. After Rick returned from his stint in the camp, he occasionally did odd jobs and worked as an unskilled helper on construction sites. Mostly, however, he was dependent upon Les for spending money and room and board; not surprisingly, his unemployment, lack of prospects, and growing drug and alcohol troubles fueled his anger and his already violent relationship with his father.

In December 1973, Rick had his most serious encounter with the law. He was arrested and charged on a sodomy violation: the codefendant was learning disabled and possibly mentally retarded. Rick's defense was that he had been drinking with friends at the time of the offense. This incident, combined with his earlier sexual infraction, raises the faint but distinct possibility that Rick might have been bisexual or gay—a possibility that would have been anguishing for Rick to face even in secret, given his bigoted father, not to mention publicly. Intolerably shameful sexual feelings would also go a considerable way toward explaining Rick's rage and promiscuity.

At Rick's request, his mother wrote a letter of support to his probation officer. The heartbreaking result is at once a loyal defense of her beloved son and an apology for what she and her husband allowed him to become. Here is a portion of the letter:

> On his good points he is very practical in his wants an[d] needs, as a matter of fact one of his biggest wants is a better education and so far has not been able to fulfill this want because of his financial status and because . . . I have not been able to assist him. . . . My son is a very patient individual. . . . Also he is very reliable when needed. He is a brave individual which he had to be to come thru this mess as well as he has. . . . He has a lot of pride which has been damaged a considerable amount. He is a leader not a follower. An[d] yet he is influenced easily in some ways. . . . On his bad points, he hides his emotions well which isn't good for him because if he's pushed he explodes. I feel he should speak out more often and let his feelings be known.

Rick also wrote a statement for his probation officer explaining his behavior, a portion of which follows:

> I believe I was in the fifth stage of intoxication, which is dazed and dejected. . . . I have no doubt why it happened, from what I've heard [the other boy] has been involved in things [of] this nature before. He just hasn't been caught. I believe and have been told by one of the witnesses that [he] enticed me to take part. If I would have been sober it would never have taken place. I think about it now and it makes me sick. I believe you can understand how embarrassing it is to have people I know ask me if it is true. How do you answer something like that, with a I don't know, or that's what they say. It's pretty hard. . . . My plans for my future are to go to college or a trade school, to become [an] industrial engineer. I always have liked to build things.

All Rick's evasions are clearly in evidence here: the alacrity with which he blames the other person for his own sexual behavior, the distancing of himself from his actions, the argument that alcohol relieves him of all responsibility, the appeal to the officer's sympathy, the image of himself as a victim, the promise to reform, the fantasy that he will transform himself into something admirable and worthwhile. But as an unconscious defense of his own violent behavior in reaction to *Les*, the letter rings disconcertingly true. The child is carrying the sins of the father. Now Rick, who *could* have become an industrial engineer, has become instead something that makes him "sick"—a drunken predator. He's not quite sure how he got that way, but he knows that he wants to be someone else.

As it happened, Rick wrote this statement just a few weeks before he met Brenda.

PERSPECTIVE # 4: THE DIFFERENT FACES OF VIOLENCE

Brenda Denise Lane was born November 26, 1959, to Alvis and Iona Lane. The Lanes were frugal, working people. On three salaries they provided their children with a modest middle-class lifestyle, and they demonstrated that if you planned carefully and worked hard, you could get ahead.

Alvis started out as a ditch digger for the Southern California Gas Company and eventually was promoted to being a field planner. Iona was a full-time secretary and part-time tax preparer. They moved to Norwalk when Iona was pregnant with Brenda because they could afford a three-bedroom house there.

Brenda's closest ally growing up was her sister, Kathy, who was two years older. Her brother Jack, the eldest, was rebellious and disobedient. The youngest, Terry, was deemed "slow." Although he attended special education classes, he never learned to read or write. Brenda was close to Terry, and when he was teased by other kids, she would do her best to protect him.

In many ways, the Lane household might seem a far better environment to grow up in than the Aris household. There was much more financial stability and almost no physical violence. That said, Brenda's childhood was permeated by alcoholism and neglect. When Alvis and Iona weren't working, they could be found not at home but at the local bar. In the evenings, babysitters made dinner for the Lane children; when they got older, the kids learned how to manage for themselves. Their parents were almost never around on the weekends. The Lane kids would often have to call the bar three or four times on Saturdays, complaining that there was no food in the house and begging their parents to come home. When Alvis and Iona finally returned, any groceries they'd picked up earlier would be soggy, and food would be spoiled.

Of the two parents, Iona was the heavier drinker and refused to abstain even when she was pregnant. When Brenda and her siblings were still quite young, they were told that Iona had been repeatedly sexually abused by her father when she was a child and that Iona's mother had refused to intervene: this was the family's explanation for her heavy drinking. Iona had a deep distrust of men generally, which she did her best to communicate to her daughters. Even Alvis was never allowed to be alone with Kathy and Brenda, hug them, or give them a bath when they were little. Occasionally, Iona would go into long rants about the wickedness of men, which would customarily end when she passed out from drinking. Brenda suspected that Alvis saw drinking with his wife as the only way he could preserve their bond.

Brenda detested the effect that alcohol had on Iona; she hated her mother's slurred words and the blurriness of her existence. At the same time, she remembers how tender and protective she felt toward Iona when she was upset, and how she would embrace her and try to say comforting things to make her feel better. Brenda was never convinced that her efforts made any difference, but she still tried.

Alvis and Iona created a rigid system of rules to keep the children under control and the household running in their absence. The children were expected to do the dishes, sweep the house, vacuum, and clean the sinks and toilet. When they were disobedient, they were put in a corner; when they got older, they were grounded.

Although the Lane children were rarely hit, it was a grim and lonely existence; Terry was frequently yelled at by his father because he couldn't help wetting his bed. Unable to live on his own, Terry was doomed to remain at home, but by the time his siblings hit adolescence, they were desperate to get out.

In 1970, when Kathy was just thirteen, she met and fell in love with Mike, a fifteen year-old who was already in trouble with the law. Jack, her brother, thought that Mike was dangerous, but no one attempted to stop the romance. She married him in 1971, moved out, and soon after became pregnant. Jack had also had his fill of living at home. His parents wanted him in by nine, even though they didn't return from the bar until after midnight; they expected him to do his homework, even though they had no idea what his homework was. He ran away from home at fifteen and eventually joined the Marines.

By 1975, Brenda, too, was eager for a different sort of life. But she saw herself as a *good* girl. Although sex, drinking, and drugs were extremely popular among the working- and middle-class kids at Norwalk High School, she had little interest in partying and casual sex. She wanted to get married, and she had her future planned. She would fall in love and have a couple of kids, and she would be happy. She didn't blame Alvis and Iona for her upbringing, but she didn't want to replicate it either.

Unfortunately, Jack's estimation of his brother-in-law had been correct. Mike frequently hit and punched Kathy. Things did not improve with the birth of their daughter, and after several years Kathy divorced her husband. Mike would eventually be executed by lethal injection in Texas for participating in robbery and murder. Kathy's second husband, a heroin addict, was shooting up in the bathroom when he fell over, hit his head, and died. Kathy has also struggled with an addiction throughout her adult life.

After two court-martials and a suspended sentence for a criminal offense, Jack was dishonorably discharged from the Marines. But he has proved to be the luckiest of the Lane children, and he attributes his success—today he owns a trucking company in Redding, California—to his devoted wife, Katherine, and their two kids. His only regret is that he didn't get his "shit" together earlier. "Maybe I could have set a better example for my sisters," he says. "Maybe things would have been different."

Brenda knew that she wanted to a better life than her parents had, but she had no realistic sense of what such a life would look like. Like most of us, she found herself drawn to someone who was a complicated mixture of what she knew and what was refreshingly unfamiliar. Certain dynamics in the Aris household would have been all too recognizable to her—the way a parent can pick on one child unfairly, the way alcohol can be used as a refuge from severe abuse. This understanding greatly contributed to her sympathy for and tolerance of Rick. At the same time, the Aris family was extremely close in a way that seemed almost exotic to Brenda: the children hung around the house all the time; the parents knew all their kids' friends. Even anger and chaos can have a mesmerizing vibrancy when compared to a home with no emotional warmth at its center.

Rick, on the other hand, had been raised in a family in which the head of the household never took responsibility for his violence and the woman was a long-suffering housewife. Brenda, like Emalou, was used to living under the control of others and making the best of things. Looked at from this perspective, the deficiencies of their respective backgrounds meshed all too well: the stage was set for what was to follow. Yet—and this is the greatest tragedy, in a sense—Rick didn't marry someone like his mother. He fell in love with a stronger and more idealistic woman—a woman who repeatedly defied him, left him, and tried to stick up for herself.

PERSPECTIVE #5: RICK AND BRENDA FOREVER: THE BEGINNING

When we try to understand any domestic tragedy, it is critical to remember that the couple didn't consciously expect their life together to play out through violence—especially in the beginning. In fact, it is likely that both Brenda and Rick saw their marriage not as the fulfillment of some grim destiny foretold by their childhoods but as a hope for a different, better future. After all, they *chose* each other—and then, again and again and again, they chose to remain together. For better or for worse, this was their life, and it was something that they made as a couple. From an outsider's perspective, it seems that true transformation would have been more likely if they had separated—certainly for Brenda, and maybe even for Rick as well. But it is also possible that for them the life they wanted most—a family in which they were cherished—was simply unimaginable outside of their relationship, even as such a life was hardly tenable within it.

Brenda and Rick's mutual attraction was clear from the moment they met. Diane Aris was one of Brenda's high school classmates. The first time that Diane brought Brenda home, the girls entertained themselves by doing cartwheels on the front lawn. Rick was repairing a car in the driveway; after Brenda's last cartwheel, he walked over so that Diane could introduce them. Brenda thought Rick was beautiful. He smiled at her and said something funny, and she felt flattered by his obvious interest. Over the next few weeks, she and Rick continued to talk.

Then one January day in 1974, Rick ended up in jail. Diane told Brenda that it hadn't been her brother's fault and that alcohol was to blame. Diane asked if Brenda wanted to write to Rick in jail, but Brenda said no; despite her strong feelings, she didn't want to get involved with a criminal. Even before they started dating, then, this pattern was established: Brenda recognized her attraction to Rick and acknowledged it, but she also worried that he was too risky a romantic choice.

Four months later, Rick was released. One of the first things he did was ask Brenda for a date. At first, Brenda hesitated, but Rick was persistent, and she agreed. Soon they were an item. "He was kind and gentle," Brenda later recalled. "I knew he liked me." Rick was also funny and outgoing, and he had loads of friends. Brenda was now part of an older crowd, and—perhaps for the first time in her life—she felt wanted. She had a new boyfriend, a new social circle, and even a new family outside the confines of her own. They were in love, and for a short time they were happy together.

That summer, Rick supported himself by buying broken-down cars and then repairing and selling them. Rick would pick Brenda up in one of his fixer-uppers, and they would drive all over town. When Rick was sober, Brenda found him especially romantic. They spent hours together in Rick's bedroom, which was in the garage. Rick liked to turn the lights down, play the hit song "I Fooled Around and Fell in Love" on the stereo, and look deeply into her eyes. At such moments, Brenda believed that it would be "Rick and Brenda" forever.

⌒

We may feel that Brenda's feelings for Rick are easy to dismiss: she was extremely young, she was in love, and he was her first serious boyfriend. But what about Rick's commitment to Brenda? By all accounts, Rick was both sexually

experienced and extremely popular with girls. Brenda's sense that their relationship was special was in part due to the fact that everyone *else* thought that
it was special. Rick's sisters and parents had never seen him so serious about a
girl before. Despite the fact that she was "hard to get," she held his interest. Indeed, Brenda's hopes for the future may have been precisely what made Rick
feel that she was so valuable.

By March 1976, ten months after their first date, the two were inseparable,
and Brenda reconsidered her decision not to have sex with Rick before marriage. Soon, they were making love once a week, and Brenda began to worry
about getting pregnant. Brenda knew that she needed birth control advice, and
she decided to ask her mother what she should do. Iona was unsympathetic.
"You play," she told her daughter, "you pay."

Initially, Brenda was distressed by Iona's reaction; her other option, she
knew, was to go to the local birth control clinic, but Brenda thought that clinics
were only for "lower-class people." On the other hand, Iona's fatalistic response
also gave Brenda permission to do nothing. After all, many of her friends were
already having kids. Having a baby, being a mother—that was a brand-new
identity. Moreover, getting pregnant and having Rick's child would be the ultimate demonstration of her love.

At the same time, Brenda was disturbed by her boyfriend's heavy drinking.
She tried to think positively, telling herself over and over: "I'm the first girl this
guy has fallen in love with, and I'm going to save him. I'm going to help him
not drink." Occasionally, too, Rick would lose his temper with Brenda about a
trivial matter. She might've been five minutes late for a date or laughed too
loud at a joke. By now, Brenda had also spent enough time in the Aris household to know how Les treated Emalou, and she'd noticed how mean Rick could
be to his mother and sisters. Could Les's violence toward his wife be transmitted to his only son? At the same time, Brenda saw Rick as a victim of his upbringing. She convinced herself that their family life would never be like that.

Then one February night in 1977, while sleeping on the living room floor at
a friend's house, Brenda discovered the sort of violence Rick was capable of.
Rick was drunk and wanted to have sex; Brenda refused, afraid that they would
be interrupted, and Rick exploded. "Who cares?" he answered. Then he began
hitting her—slapping and punching her in the chest. To calm him down and
avoid a scene, Brenda relented, but the sex was brutal and left her in a state of
shock. She felt enraged but also bewildered: she couldn't believe that Rick had
been so cruel.

When Brenda confronted him the following morning, Rick claimed he was
so drunk that he had no memory of raping or punching her. Initially, Brenda
refused to reconcile with him. Being drunk was no excuse. For the first of what
would be many times, she vowed that she would never see Rick again. And for
the first of many times, Rick waged a fierce campaign to win her back. He sent

her flowers and notes, begging her to change her mind and saying that he loved and needed her.

One plea read:

> *I know I need help, I know I need you to help me.*
> *I know it is the alcohol that made me do it.*
> *Please understand.*
> *I love you.*
> *Rick*

In the end, Brenda gave in; after all, she had known Rick for more than two years, and nothing like this had happened between them in all that time. She decided to take him back. Soon, she was pregnant. Rick was thrilled. He had a steady job—making electrical signs—and he wanted to get married and take responsibility for his new family. He told everyone that Brenda was going to give him a son to carry on the Aris family name. But Brenda knew him better now, and she was concerned about his inability to stop drinking. It might be better to raise the child without him. Yet no one close to her supported this idea. Emalou thought that she was lucky to have Rick; Iona's response was, "I'm not going to tell you what to do, but how would you have liked growing up without your father?" Meanwhile, Rick promised to reform. He assured her that having a baby would change him.

⌐⌐

Three kids and nine years later, this dynamic remained essentially the same—violence, flight, pursuit, reunion—but the deep meanings that the lovers' respective stances once symbolized ("I am damaged and can't help myself"; "I deserve better"; "I love you and need you and want to change"; "I love you and forgive you") had become hopelessly corrupted, robbed of almost any positive meaning. The clichÈ "They can't live with each other; they can't live without each other" had become a vivid terrifying reality.

PERSPECTIVE # 6: RICK AND BRENDA FOREVER: THE END

Rick's arrival in San Bernardino in 1985 was disastrous on many counts. It was the end of what had been Brenda's most determined and sustained attempt at independence. But an equally painful fact about Rick's arrival in San Bernardino was that Brenda shared some responsibility for it. Her frequent trips to Norwalk had made it clear to anyone paying attention that she hadn't really moved to Washington, and they greatly increased the likelihood that Rick would eventually find out where she and the girls were living. What's more, Rick hadn't sued her for visitation rights; Brenda herself had made them possible.

Would Brenda's attachment to Rick have been so strong without their daughters? The children were the only thing that Rick and Brenda had truly made together. Rick had also proved to be better than his own father in one important respect: after that first incident on the porch with Lucretia when she was a baby, he was never intentionally violent with any of his children. Lucretia and Rick were particularly close. When we consider both Rick's childhood and his lack of emotional and physical self-control, this is a startling fact, and it meant a lot to Brenda; it also made her separations harder to justify and sustain.

Brenda was lonely in San Bernardino; although she had "started from scratch" several times by this point, it had always been either with Rick or with her parents. She had no model of any sort of life outside the orbits of these two families, and one girlfriend in an unfamiliar town was simply not enough to sustain her. Even with the visits to Norwalk, though, a more determined Brenda might have found ways to avoid contact with Rick.

Brenda's unsuccessful bid for freedom had other unintended long-term consequences. Iona had helped her daughter *only* on the condition that she never take Rick back. After Rick followed her to San Bernardino, Brenda had to keep his arrival a secret. This was a new and very dangerous development. In the past, when things had become intolerable, Brenda could always run to her parents for help. Now she had lost her sanctuary, and she had to lie to her parents to prevent them from cutting her off altogether, which bound her more irrevocably to her husband.

Shortly after Rick arrived in San Bernardino, Brenda used hard drugs for the first time. In retrospect, this change—like Brenda's suicide attempts a few months before—was a warning sign. Historically, Rick's drug use, like Brenda's ability to leave, had been one of the defining characteristics of the marriage: he was an addict; she was straight. Now it seemed that Brenda was giving up. Shooting up was a way for her to be close to Rick, just as her father had kept her mother company at the bar. After a few weeks, though, Brenda panicked and cut back on her own drug use—what if she *did* become like Rick?—but money was very tight again, and so she started dealing drugs to support Rick's habit. When Rick was stoned, she'd noticed, he mostly left her alone, and this became one of the ways in which she would try to control his violence.

Two months later, Rick lost the only unequivocal ally he'd ever had: Emalou Aris died suddenly. Brenda described Rick as "shaken to the core" by the loss.

Les had never lived alone before; Rick and Brenda, who were losing their place in San Bernardino anyway, moved back into the Aris house. Brenda told her parents that she was staying there to take care of Les, but she pretended that Rick was living elsewhere. The situation was stressful for everyone; Brenda was living a lie, Les was always drunk, and Rick and Les fought regularly.

Just after the New Year in 1986, Rick and Brenda got into an argument, and Rick punched her in the chest, breaking several ribs. Brenda told her doctor that she'd gotten into the middle of a fight between Les and Rick and was accidentally hit. She hadn't had a checkup for over a year; while she was there, she also had a routine Pap smear.

Several weeks later, John, a friend of Rick's, suggested that they move to Riverside, where he had a cheap place to stay. Brenda was relieved: her secret would be easier to keep from her parents.

Not long after the move, she learned that she had cervical cancer and had to have a hysterectomy. For Rick, this was the final betrayal: Brenda would never bear him a son. "To Rick, I was no longer a woman," Brenda said later. "I was worthless, useless, good for nothing."

Brenda found Rick's response to the cancer far more terrifying than the disease itself. On the night before the operation, Rick repeatedly hit Brenda in the face and stomach. The next day, Rick didn't call to see how the operation went. After she was discharged, he picked her up at the hospital, brought her home, and raped her.

Life in Riverside resumed. Brenda enrolled the girls in the local school and still, on occasion, made efforts to project the air of a "normal" family—planning an Easter egg hunt or trying to brighten up their new home. But Rick made any sustained sense of ordinary domestic life impossible. He refused to look for work, instead spending his days in a fog of drugs and alcohol and growing more violent and delusional with each passing day.

It wasn't simply the misery of the life Rick was leading that made everything so desperate. The dreams of respite and transformation that had kept him going for years could no longer be sustained. Brenda and the children ceased to represent the fantasy family that he could be a part of "next time"—the way they had previously, after every separation—because they could no longer escape him. Emalou, his last connection to the blameless boy he'd once been, was also gone. And, finally, his hope of more than a decade—that Brenda would have a son—had also been destroyed.

In reality, a son would probably have been a disaster for Rick; the chances that he would have been able to control his rage against a boy seem minimal. But clearly a son represented some sort of clean slate to Rick—as if he would get a second chance to grow up differently, as if Brenda, by delivering a son, could deliver Rick from the man he'd become. But now Rick was confined to a bleak and hopeless present; all he could do was make sure that Brenda's life was even narrower and more hopeless than his own.

Suspicious that Brenda was cheating on him, Rick imposed his own brand of martial law. Brenda wasn't allowed to do anything by herself other than grocery shopping. She couldn't take the girls to the park or spend any time with friends. She now did all of the laundry by hand in the kitchen sink. But even these measures didn't dampen Rick's paranoia: sometimes he would lock Brenda up in their bedroom.

Brenda stopped showering every day. She stopped wearing makeup. Her goal was to be as unappealing as possible to prove to Rick that she wasn't trying to attract the attention of other men. Just as Brenda's decision to start using and dealing drugs had been both a form of self-debasement and a last-ditch attempt at self-protection, Rick's crazed jealousy was now prompting a seemingly rational but also extremely self-destructive response. Deprived of the exit strategies she'd employed their entire married life, Brenda now lived exclusively in Rick's corrupted and confined world.

On the morning of August 9, 1986, Rick, age thirty-two, awoke from a week-long drug and alcohol binge in a foul mood. He was constipated, hung over, and out of meth. He angrily called for Brenda and demanded his coffee. Then he ordered her to get to a drugstore and buy him a laxative. Brenda told him that the van wasn't working, and she didn't have any money.

Brenda was more interested in getting Rick drugs than laxatives, because then the chances of a beating would be less. But Rick had also raided Brenda's stash, and now there was nothing left—nothing for him and nothing to sell. Not only did Brenda owe money to the dealer; she also owed money to John's father, who was coming over that night for a going-away party for his son, who was about to serve thirty days in jail for a drunk-driving offense. Brenda was hoping that he wouldn't ask her for the money; indeed, Brenda hoped she could avoid John's father altogether. It was also possible that someone would bring drugs to the party, if Rick could hold out that long.

As Rick became nastier with each passing hour, Brenda's anxiety grew. Maybe it would be safer for her to simply stay in the bedroom. Finally a friend arrived with some drugs; with her husband high, Brenda felt safer about joining the party.

In the backyard, Brenda was surprised to see so many people. It was a thrill, after the isolation of the past few months. Rick, now stoned, strolled out of the house as more cars drove up the long driveway and parked all over the lot. Brenda's closest friend, Hoodie, pulled right up to the porch, rolled down the window, and called out to her.

"Hey," Rick yelled to his wife. "Your little girlfriend is here."

Brenda ran over to give Hoodie a hug. Crouching by the car door, she chatted and giggled with her friend. Suddenly Rick interrupted their conversation.

"Come here, you fat bitch," he yelled. Reluctantly, Brenda turned back to her husband. "What do you think you're doing?" Rick hissed. Then he slapped her across the face. "Go to the fucking bedroom," he ordered.

Embarrassed, Brenda obeyed. She had been through this drill before. If she didn't listen, he'd beat her harder later. After half an hour in the bedroom, however, Brenda needed to go to the bathroom. Just as she sat down on the toilet, Rick banged on the door and yelled to be let in. When she unlocked the door, Rick pushed himself inside. When the door closed behind him, he punched Brenda in the stomach.

"I know what you and Hoodie were doing!" he screamed. "You were laughing at me!" Then he kneed her in the abdomen. When Brenda heard someone knock on the bathroom door, she was frightened rather than relieved. She didn't want anyone to get hurt trying to protect her.

"Who the fuck is it?" Rick yelled.

"Brenda, are you okay?" Hoodie asked softly.

Rick cracked the door open; "You wait until I'm through with her," he told Hoodie and slammed the door. He continued to punch Brenda while Hoodie waited outside and Brenda moaned with each new blow. Finally Rick unlocked the door and pushed his way past. Hoodie begged her friend to leave with her, but Brenda refused. Instead, Hoodie agreed that she would take Lucretia for a sleepover with her kids. Brenda didn't want Lucretia to witness another beating. Hoodie then helped Brenda back to her bedroom, where she stayed up waiting; she knew it wasn't over. A few feet away, her two younger daughters, Candice and Sheena, slept on the lower bunk of a double-decker.

Several hours later, when the party was finally winding down, Rick returned to the bedroom and woke Brenda up.

"Don't think you can laugh at me!" he screamed. Pressing her back down on the bed, he pulled her head back by the hair as far as it would go.

Brenda pleaded with Rick to stop, afraid that he was going to break her neck.

Then Rick rolled her over onto her back, sat on her knees, and kept punching. "I'm not going to let you live until morning," he said, but by this time Rick was winding down. Brenda saw his eyes flicker, and then he took a deep breath. Finally, he tipped over in exhaustion onto the bed and passed out.

As Rick lay on the bed in a stupor, Brenda sat motionless, afraid to move until she was sure he was really asleep. Miraculously, her two younger daughters had slept through the racket. Her face ached; it was bruised and swollen. She tiptoed out to the kitchen, looking for ice, but it had been used up during the party. She decided to try to get some from next door. When she knocked on her neighbor's door and asked for ice, she was invited in and told she could help herself. There, on the top of the refrigerator, was the gun.

Brenda later admitted that everyone knew her neighbor kept a loaded gun somewhere. But she insisted that she didn't know where, nor had she consciously thought of using it against Rick. In fact, Brenda had only handled a gun once in her life; years earlier, Rick and some of his friends had been firing at cans for target practice, and Rick had shown her how to release the safety catch and shoot. When she saw the gun sitting on top of the refrigerator, though, she grabbed it on impulse, placed it in a bowl with the ice, and returned to the house.

Back in the bedroom, her husband and the two girls were still asleep. Brenda pointed the gun at the middle of Rick's back and pulled the trigger. Nothing happened. Then she realized that she wasn't doing it "the right way." Remembering what her husband had taught her, Brenda released the safety catch and fired five times at Rick's back.

The two deputy sheriffs who responded to the emergency call found Rick lying face down on the blood-soaked bed. They tore off his shirt and removed his sneakers and belt. As they lifted him to the floor to start resuscitation, one of the officers noted the blue tattoo roughly inked onto Rick's upper arm. It said, "Rick and Brenda Forever."

At the hospital, Rick was pronounced dead.

ENLARGING THE FRAME: THE DEEPER DIMENSIONS OF VIOLENCE

If we expand the frame around our initial snapshot of Rick Aris's murder, we can see that Brenda certainly had reason to think that her life was in danger. Many people—including several members of Rick's own family—believe that Rick would have killed Brenda if she hadn't killed him first. And Rick certainly fits the conventional portrait of the batterer: obsessed with power and control, deeply misogynist, increasingly and perhaps lethally violent. But if we go even further back in time—to the beginning of Rick and Brenda's relationship and to their respective childhoods—a more complex picture emerges, revealing subtleties that advocates have habitually shied away from. Brenda didn't choose to leave Rick permanently and break up her family, and she never asked the police to intervene for her. Her husband had a criminal record; she didn't want him arrested. She stayed with him out of fear, certainly, but fear wasn't her only reason.

Although at times Brenda said she yearned to escape from Rick, many of her actions, whether conscious or unconscious, belied such talk. Even after she was safely settled in San Bernardino, she nevertheless returned to Norwalk and allowed Rick, once again, to force his way back into her life. Like it or not, Brenda was connected to Rick, and she was an active partner in the dynamic of their relationship.

Brenda was also tougher than the conventional notion of the battered woman who can't live without her man. She was a strong, resourceful mother who received little to no support from her husband. Forced to live a nomadic life with hardly any financial or emotional security, she always took good care of her girls and tried to provide them with a sense of home.

Although she didn't have a lot of options, she was constantly reviewing them and acting accordingly—whether we agree with her rationales or not. She also clearly recognized that in some ways she *did* have more power than Rick, even as a consistently and severely abused woman.

In fact, one of the reasons why the jury convicted Brenda to life imprisonment was that she didn't seem like a victim on the witness stand. And although Lenore Walker personally testified at the trial, Brenda simply didn't conform to the portrayal of helplessness that the psychologist painted in her testimony. And if Brenda wasn't a stunned and deranged victim, then she had to be a cold-blooded killer.

As for Rick, it is difficult to convincingly ascribe all his destructive behavior to the fact that we live in a sexist society. Long before Rick was an abuser, he was a victim—and the same can be said of Brenda. Much of the damage inflicted in both families began in the previous generation, or even before that. Drugs and alcohol were a huge part of the equation—in Rick's life and in the lives of the Lanes and Arises generally. Certainly many of Rick's actions were understood to be the result of his various addictions—none of which were ever treated.

If we truly want to fight domestic violence, we must intervene in abusive relationships long before women like Brenda Aris are facing life terms for murdering their batterers. The abuses that Brenda and Rick endured as children must be explored for their deeper meanings and for what they might teach us about the possibilities of prevention. We must also learn to identify the deeply ingrained dynamics, endemic to many violent relationships, which so often precipitate the violence in the first place.

PART TWO

A New Understanding

The beatings I took from my older brother set sparks off in me. What my father told me about not letting people run over me set off more sparks. Seeing people I cared a lot for get hurt set off still more sparks. All these things sparked me off, ignited a fire in me that wouldn't go out.

I got to the point that I wasn't going to let people run over me. I had taken, seen, and heard enough. The beatings I saw and took demonstrated to me in black and white the truth of what my father had been saying: you need to be violent sometimes.

—Teenager incarcerated for murder,
from a study by sociologist Lonnie Athens

I feel horrible about the whole thing—not only about the event, but about the implications of what it cost. $30,000—that's a lot of college education.

—Jeff McPherson, after injuring his wife

The dynamic of existing as a couple is gradually lost because any kind of dialogue is perceived as threatening, and both partners are always ready for attack or digging deeper into their defensive positions.

—Social work professors Zvi Eisikovits and
Eli Buchbinder, *Locked in a Violent Embrace*

4

THE ANATOMY OF
INTIMATE ABUSE

Violence (n): physical force used so as to injure, damage, or destroy; extreme roughness of action; . . . unjust or callous use of force or power, as in violating another's rights, sensibilities, etc.

Abuse (v): . . . to hurt by treating badly; mistreat; to use insulting, coarse, or bad language about or to; revile; (n) . . . mistreatment; injury; a bad, unjust or corrupt custom or practice.

Aggression (n): an unprovoked attack or warlike act; . . . the practice or habit of being aggressive or quarrelsome; *Psychiatry* forceful, attacking behavior, either constructively self-assertive and self-protective or destructively hostile to others or to oneself.

—*Webster's New World Dictionary*

From a drug deal gone bad on L.A.'s city streets to a school shooting in the heart of Pennsylvania's Amish country, violence in America penetrates every neighborhood—and, in turn, every family. All of us know someone who has been robbed, beaten, sexually assaulted, or killed. In 2005, there were over sixteen thousand murders in the United States, and more than two million people were incarcerated in state and federal prisons. Unfortunately, the American family is often not a haven from the dangers of the outside world but simply a different sort of menacing environment. In fact, the U.S. Centers for

Disease Control estimate that 8.5 million minor and severe incidents of violence occur each year in intimate relationships.

Spectacular forms of intimate violence often dominate the headlines for weeks, if not months, and the victims and perpetrators often become household names: Nicole Brown Simpson, Joel Steinberg, Laci Peterson, the Menendez brothers, the Bobbitts. Although we are usually quick to judge who is guilty and who is innocent, the most important questions—Why did this happen? Could it have been prevented?—often go unanswered. After all, these people once cared for each other, and some of them may care for each other still. But after the trial comes to an end and the media moves on to other stories, we usually have no better understanding than we had before of what caused this terrible violence to erupt.

Many of us have wondered, upon hearing of some shocking act of violence, How could someone do that to another human being? The more difficult question we must ask ourselves is: *Do I really want to know the answer?* After all, intimate relationships are often far messier—and therefore far more threatening—than most of us would like to admit. Looking family violence squarely in the face may mean acknowledging that those who participate in it are not quite as different from us as we would like to believe; we may also be hurting those we love in ways that we don't want to admit.

Rick and Brenda Aris, each in their own way, are poster children for intimate abuse—archetypes of the victim and the perpetrator. But once their stories are fully told, Rick is not simply a monster, nor is Brenda merely a victim. Together they experienced most of the common forms of violence we have labels for. Some of the abuse was physical and therefore easy to pin down: Brenda's broken jaw, Rick's beatings at the hands of his father. Still other forms of abuse—emotional violence and neglect, for example—are harder to capture and describe. Indeed, abuse of any kind is almost never an isolated incident, and its effects can last a lifetime. So the first step in understanding aggression between intimates is to examine its components separately: domestic violence must be acknowledged in all its many forms of abuse before it can be effectively addressed.

THE SPECTRUM OF ABUSE

Reviewing the spectrum of intimate abuse is a useful way to remind ourselves both how we are hurt by others and how our own anger and fear can affect those around us. Although there are obvious gradations of violence—it is better to be spat at, say, than shot at—"ranking" violent incidents and their significance is not as easy as it might appear: many people would rather be hit occasionally in private, for example, than routinely and systematically verbally humiliated in front of family and friends. Even if some forms of abuse are categorically worse than others, all forms of abuse are potentially significant. As the definitions at the opening of this chapter suggest, violence, abuse, and aggression, which I use interchangeably, generally mean the same thing: to mistreat someone, to attack someone, or to hurt another person.

Emotional abuse is the most elusive type of abuse in that it leaves no visible mark on the victim and therefore is the most difficult to hold others accountable for. It is also something that we have all both committed and experienced, and it can take on many, many forms.

Verbal abuse refers to using words as weapons against those around us. This includes *cursing, shouting,* and *screaming,* particularly when it is directed toward a particular person, often a close friend, relative, or partner. ("Goddamn bitch!" or "You're really a little prick, did you know that?") People who love us are especially vulnerable to this sort of attack, because they value what we think of them. Even generalized shouting in a household can have a very negative impact on others in the family, particularly children, because it suggests that the person who is yelling is unhappy, angry, and out of control.

Verbal abuse also includes *insults and sarcastic remarks.* "Take that jacket off; it looks terrible" is one such comment. Another might be: "You're a fat pig. When are you going to learn to eat less?" Rhetorical questions are particularly hurtful—"Do you always have to act like the dumbest person in the room?"—because they pretend to be an attempt to communicate when they really answer themselves.

Sometimes we feel bad after making hurtful remarks, and yet we often expect those we love to take it in stride. Indeed, "He knows how I get" and "I didn't mean anything by it" are common justifications for having been verbally abusive. But the person on the receiving end is nearly always negatively affected—unless he or she has learned to tune the speaker out entirely—and others who witness this type of exchange between couples are usually uncomfortable and embarrassed. The truth is that cruel speech can be extremely damaging; in fact, victims of both physical and emotional abuse often describe the effect of verbal insults as being worse than the scars left by physical violence.

Silence is a far more subtle form of emotional abuse, compared to verbal attacks, but it can also be devastating. Insults are not always verbal. So much in an intimate relationship is unspoken that often a partner can convey a strong emotion or opinion with a simple look. For example, some people stop talking or responding to their partners or children—sometimes for long periods of time—to punish them for some actual or perceived error or insult. For many family members, this sort of emotional withdrawal can be unbearable. The "silent treatment" can be as abusive as a verbal insult.

Another form of emotional abuse is *social isolation*—when someone discourages or prevents his or her partner from seeing friends or family. Sometimes this is accomplished in a camouflaged manner—"We have to move to California.

You know I'll have better work opportunities there," or "I'm so sorry, honey; the baby's too young for us to make the reunion this year." In other cases, social contact may simply be forbidden: "Get off the phone. Right now." Or, "If visiting your mother is more important than our marriage, I'm putting the kids in the car, and I'm leaving you."

Such strictures are especially difficult for those who rely heavily on friends and family for emotional support; social isolation undermines their happiness and sense of well-being while increasing their dependence on their partner. It can be especially devastating when other forms of abuse are also present in the relationship.

Manipulation is a common feature of emotional abuse. Often it involves *false promises.* "Please don't leave me. I don't know what came over me. I swear it will never happen again." Or, "I know I shouldn't have spent the money without asking you, baby, but next month I'll be able to pay it back. Trust me." Early in a relationship, of course, the level of cynicism in these assurances can be difficult to gauge; maybe the speaker actually believes what he or she is saying. Over time, however, it becomes clear that these statements are merely a strategy for minimizing past offenses rather than representing a real commitment to change. People also manipulate those close to them through their actions rather than their words. If your husband inevitably picks a fight with your father whenever you visit your parents' home, you may find yourself visiting your parents less frequently.

Implied or actual threats are also forms of manipulation—statements such as "Sign up for that swimming class at the Y, and I promise you'll regret it," or "Let's see how you'll look at Julie's graduation with a black eye."

Economic coercion often takes the form of forcing someone to become reliant on another's resources to create dependence on that person—denying your partner access to money or bank accounts or monitoring her spending through elaborate accounting procedures. But it can also take the form of spending large sums of money or incurring debt that your partner will be held responsible for.

Addictive behaviors—gambling, drug addiction, alcoholism, and more—are also emotionally abusive, even though this result may not necessarily be the intention of the abuser. Drug and alcohol use, for example, can induce moods and behaviors that are damaging to those who are exposed to them: rage, depression, mania. Addictions often drain a family's financial resources, taking away money needed for food, rent, or school supplies. They can cause a partner or a parent to be emotionally or physically absent for long periods of time, as alcoholism did in Brenda's family.

Neglect is another form of emotional abuse. The fact that hurting another person is not your primary goal does not minimize the possible consequences of, for example, letting strangers party in your house when your children are present, or selling the family's only car for cocaine. An act of omission—the failure to protect your child from a stoned acquaintance or to pick up your girlfriend from a dangerous street corner late at night—can be as damaging as hurting them yourself.

A number of other destructive behaviors hover between emotional and physical abuse, such as *threatening violence* with words, gestures, or the presence of weapons; *pushing someone out of the home and locking the door,* especially if they are only partially dressed or without money; *driving dangerously* with others in the car. The *destruction of property* can be extremely menacing to the people who witness it or own the destroyed object(s), especially when the object is symbolically meaningful, such as the car (a means of escape) or the phone (a connection with the outside world) or even a piece of jewelry that has sentimental value. Sometimes the destructive act involves attacking a beloved pet for the purpose of hurting its owner.

Stalking—following someone against his or her will—also falls into this grey area, especially when it involves weapons or the threat of harm. The degree of threat may vary depending on whether the stalker is known to have access to a weapon—a police officer who carries a gun or a pharmacist who has access to drugs that could be used against the victim. Stalking should always be taken seriously; many stalkers have eventually killed the former lovers or spouses they were stalking. O. J. Simpson was a stalker.

Sexual abuse, which involves coercing one's partner into engaging in sexual activity against his or her will, can be more or less "violent." It can involve direct force (overpowering the other person or putting a gun to his or her head) or emotional and verbal intimidation. ("You'll come to bed if you know what's good for you.") Both Brenda and I have acknowledged that there were occasions when we unwillingly submitted to our violent partners instead of calling for help because we were too humiliated to admit to an outsider that we were being raped. This is not an uncommon response.

Systematically and punitively withholding sex can also be very destructive, if it denies one's partner a connection he or she craves and/or undermines his or her sense of self-worth over time. Sometimes it is not acknowledged by anything more than a turning away in bed; at other times it is accompanied with a verbal insult. ("I can't even bear to look at you.") *Flaunting an extra-marital affair* in a spouse's face is also deeply hostile and humiliating.

Physical abuse can be minor or severe, but it should always be viewed as significant. On one end of the spectrum, abuse may include pushing, scratching, shoving, pinching, slapping, pulling hair, or spitting on someone. More serious offenses include twisting an arm, putting one's hand over another's mouth, pushing or shoving a person into another object (like a door or a piece of furniture) or down the stairs, punching, kicking, biting, and using a weapon to hurt another (a knife, bat, frying pan, phone, or other object).

Of course, most of the abuses listed here do not occur in isolation, and the role of violence in a relationship can also change over time. Episodes of physical or emotional violence can be sporadic or incessant. Initially, the violence in Rick and Brenda's relationship was intermittent; eventually the abuse became consistent and virtually unstoppable. Indeed, physical abuse taken to its greatest extreme can result in death.

The danger of tolerating any hurtful behavior is that it can all too quickly become the norm. If we allow ourselves to "get away" with anything we know to be destructive—such as slapping a child or partner in the face—without fully taking responsibility for the gravity of what we have done, we are that much more likely to minimize the offense: "I may have overreacted, but she's got to learn not to set me off like that." Israeli social work professors Eli Buchbinder and Zvi Eisikovits have studied this issue and have found that "because the partner is perceived as the cause of violence, the perpetrator feels justified in using it." Once the actions are justified, they are more likely to be repeated.

It is also important to remember that, in most relationships, both parties engage in some form of the abuses listed above. Angry remarks or mildly aggressive actions—insulting someone's intelligence, throwing a plate of food against the wall—can both provoke and be used to justify retaliatory actions that may be more dangerous, like pushing someone down the stairs.

On the other hand, one sort of abuse does not necessarily lead to another. Rather, whether or not violence escalates depends on the person committing it. A small percentage of abusers are very violent and will be relentless in their use of abuse. Most people who are abusive are only occasionally so, much like the pattern in my relationship with David. At the same time, it is important to remember that *all* of the behaviors described above are destructive for those who participate in them, and we must work to confront and transform them in ourselves and in our families.

WHO GETS TO DEFINE INTIMATE ABUSE?

I have offered a broad, nuanced definition of what constitutes intimate abuse. But the question remains: Who defines violence in the larger society? In a word, everyone—victims, perpetrators, family members, neighbors, witnesses, police officers, judges, lawyers, activists. As we know, however, not everyone sees violence through the same lens.

Most obviously, the law defines intimate abuse, and these definitions can be fairly crude. Except in rare cases, such as stalking or threatening another person with a deadly weapon, emotional abuse lies outside the law's jurisdiction. Acts of physical violence against another person are categorized as either a misdemeanor (less serious) or a felony (more serious), but what offense falls into which category can vary from city to city and state to state.

So do we turn to those who participate in violent relationships for "the truth" about that violence? Only in part, because we feel that they are tainted by the very situation we're examining: their opinions and judgments are suspect, in effect, because they are in this mess in the first place. We may look for "evidence," say—bruises, broken bones, smashed windows—but we are often more interested in constructing our own narratives of what happened than we are in listening to the couple's versions of their struggles.

What violence means in a relationship, to both the abuser and the abused, depends enormously on the psychological and cultural backgrounds of each person. As we've seen, how tolerant we are of physical and emotional violence often depends on how much we were exposed to it as children and how we coped with it then. If you grew up in a family in which you constantly fought with your siblings and were routinely spanked or whipped by your parents, for example, a hard shove from your partner may no longer hold much significance to you. Or it may represent everything you loathed about your childhood and prompt you to retaliate, call the police, or file for divorce. If your father routinely beat your mother senseless, you may feel outraged that your wife complains when you shout and break a few dishes—you may even fear that her willingness to stand up to you makes you less of a man.

What we think of violent behavior as adults (for example, cursing or slapping someone across the face) also depends on how such words and actions were viewed by our families and communities when we were children. If a man who grew up in a loud, emotionally expressive Italian family puts his fist through a window in a jealous rage, he may see his behavior as completely normal; if his girlfriend happened to grow up in a restrained Yankee family, however, in which voices were never raised in anger, she may find his actions terrifying and unforgivable. Conversely, her emotional withdrawal from him in times of crisis might seem to him unusually cruel and perverse.

The importance of these cultural perspectives is relevant not only to how people fight but also to the extent and nature of that fighting. For example, studies show significant differences between racial and ethnic groups as to the kinds of violence they are most likely to commit. Orthodox Jews report more incidents of psychological abuse than physical violence. A Chicago study shows that intimate partner homicide rates among whites and Latinos are considerably lower than those among African Americans. Overall, Asian/Pacific Islanders report the lowest levels of physical violence. It is important to remember that people's willingness to admit to violence also may vary from group to group, depending on psychological, financial, and regional influences.

Those of us who are not living in violent relationships must also recognize that we, too, are shaped by our own personal and cultural relationship to violence. The fact that we are "outside" a particular violent situation doesn't guarantee that our understanding of that situation is necessarily objective or complete. From the point of view of assessing whether or not a law has been broken, a complete understanding may not be necessary. But if we are trying to understand why violence occurs between people who love each other and how it can be prevented, all factors are critical.

Let's say you are a man who grew up in a household in which your mother was often hit by your stepfather. This has left you with a zero-tolerance attitude toward men abusing women. When your neighbor threatens his girlfriend with a baseball bat and you call the police, you may feel that nothing "excuses" his behavior, and you may be right. But what if you knew that, before he threatened her, she yelled at him for thirty minutes about all the ways in which he'd been inadequate as a boyfriend and sexual partner. When he tried to interrupt, she simply kept on talking. When he tried to leave, she told him that he couldn't run away, and she blocked the door—at which point he'd picked up the bat. From a legal point of view, he is still in the wrong. But from a psychological and emotional point of view, his action makes a lot more sense when placed in context: he can no longer be seen as the sole aggressor in this situation.

HOW VIOLENT IS THE AMERICAN FAMILY?

Because family and domestic violence occurs mostly behind closed doors and because, like rape and child abuse, it induces a great deal of shame in those touched by it, it is impossible for those who study abuse to come up with exact figures. Trying to quantify the number of abusive incidents per year in this country is a daunting task. Even so, the statistics gathered from national surveys, police reports, and medical records are chilling. Of the 8.5 million total incidents of violence that occur in intimate relationships in the United States each year, 2.3 million involve such significant events as rape or a severe incident of physical violence. Of those assaulted in this most violent way, 1.5 million are women, and 835,000 are men. Intimate partner violence results in nearly 2 million reported injuries in this country annually. A 2000 study funded by the Centers for Disease Control revealed that women are injured by an intimate partner at more than three times the rate of men. For the year 2005, 1,181 women and 329 men were killed by an intimate partner.

As most of these statistics are taken from criminal complaints and arrest records kept by criminal justice personnel, the incidents they refer to are more readily quantified as violent (and as crimes) than aggressive domestic incidents not reported to the police. What if we take a step back and also take into account other types of abuse in the home?

Most Americans don't see themselves as violent, nor do they view the United States as a violent nation overall. Moreover, domestic violence is rarely considered alongside other forms of abuse in the family, such as spanking, child or sibling abuse, or dating violence. When all of these statistics are taken together, however, and the patterns of abuse in the American family are fully incorporated into our view of violence, an even more disturbing picture emerges.

In a study on family violence that focused on corporal punishment by American parents, sociologist Murray Straus found that 35 percent of parents hit their infants when they believe they are misbehaving; 94 percent of parents spank their three- to four-year-olds for the same reason.

Similarly, sociologist David Finkelhor and his colleagues reported that for every thousand children with siblings, there are 355 incidents of sibling violence among them. In total, over twenty-two million American children are threatened, attacked, or hit with an object by a sibling each year. Sibling violence is most likely to occur between the ages of six and twelve, with both boys and girls experiencing near equal incidents of sibling violence against each other. Sibling violence in the family can lay the groundwork for future violence and victimization.

And what happens when we add psychological or emotional abuse to this list? In a study of over seventeen thousand Americans, approximately 13 percent of women and 8 percent of men reported experiencing emotional abuse during childhood. Emotional neglect, also in childhood, was reported by approximately 17 percent of women and 12 percent of men. The presence of substance abuse—which generally invites other sorts of abuse into a family—was even more prevalent. An estimated 30 percent of women and 24 percent of men reported living with substance abuse as a child.

ARE WOMEN AS VIOLENT AS MEN?

There is a great deal of resistance to this possibility, which is completely understandable. After thirty years of effort and tremendous struggle, the battered women's movement, together with the larger feminist movement, has successfully framed the issue of intimate abuse as a one-sided problem that involves sexist men who deliberately abuse women "because they can." This belief is an important tenet of the movement's philosophy, and one that aptly captures the perceived sexist nature of intimate abuse. But it fails to acknowledge women's contribution to intimate violence.

In 1980, sociologists Murray Straus, Richard Gelles, and Suzanne Steinmetz published a groundbreaking study on violence in the American family. They found that, for 27 percent of the married couples in the United States experiencing domestic violence, the husbands were physically abusive toward their wives and the wives did not fight back. More surprising, however, was that in another 24 percent of the cases the wives were physically abusive and their husbands did not retaliate. But, most shocking of all, in the other 49 percent of the cases *both partners actively participated in the violence.* This meant not only that both men and women were initiating the abuse, but that also, after the fight got underway, both partners were doing the hitting. The results of this research were so shocking that they sparked over a hundred follow-up studies—several by Straus himself—all of which generally confirmed the fact that men and women assault each other at roughly equal rates.

But how could this picture of domestic violence—and women's part in it—deviate so significantly from our popular conception? Perhaps because this sociological study did not comb through arrest reports but instead used a telephone survey to gather its data. The couples who engage in mutual combat were less likely to show up in police statistics because both parties were implicated in the fighting and perhaps neither one regarded his or her behavior as criminal. In addition, these men and women may not have fit into the traditional "power and control" model; they may have considered themselves evenly matched. This doesn't mean that the behavior demonstrated by mutually combative couples isn't dangerous and destructive for everyone involved, but it explains how such couples might constitute a less visible form of domestic violence.

Another reason that women's aggression has remained relatively hidden is that women are much more likely to recognize violence and admit that they are being victimized by it than men are. Emblematic of this fact is the large study on emotional abuse in the American family described at the end of the previous section: 5 percent more women than men reported experiencing psychological abuse and emotional neglect in their childhoods. One could argue that this difference is a by-product of sexism, but how can we account for the fact that 6 percent more women than men in that study reported that their parents were abusing substances? Women and men aren't sorted by gender into different families at birth. So what might explain this statistical discrepancy?

Traditionally, men are expected to tolerate hurt feelings, abuse, and even injury, since it supposedly tests their manhood, and they are often still taught that they should hide their suffering. It is ironic that although women have become far more aware of abuse by men as a result of the women's rights movement—and, simultaneously, more powerful in society overall—many men have yet to recognize women's increasing power (and women's corresponding abusive tendencies) in intimate relationships. Studies show that many men still view women's violence as "horseplay," even when the violence is serious and injurious. A holdover from sexist attitudes we're trying to move away from, this approach toward women's aggression makes it shameful for men to admit that they are getting hurt. This explains the fact that only 14 percent of men who have experienced a significant incident of intimate violence report it to the police; women report such incidents at nearly twice that rate.

Further evidence of women's violence can be found in statistics concerning abuse in the lesbian community: high rates of violence have been recorded in lesbian relationships. Members of the Task Force on Violence in Lesbian Relationships who first investigated this problem in Minnesota in 1980 later recalled that they were "surprised and saddened by the magnitude of the problem and the severity of some of the violence." They found that the prevalence of abuse in their community "deeply affected our vision of ourselves and our relationships." One study found that 90 percent of lesbians experienced verbal aggression from their female partners and 30 percent reported one or more incident(s) of physical aggression. In another study of over a thousand lesbians, approximately one-third of the women reported that they had been both physically and psychologically abused by their female partner or lover.

Although homicide statistics report that women are far more frequently killed by intimate partners than men are, another trend suggests that a different pattern may emerge in the next several years. The Department of Justice reports that between 1991 and 2000, the number of girls under eighteen convicted of aggravated assault crimes increased 44 percent, whereas for their male contemporaries, the percentage decreased by 16 percent. Similarly, crimes involving weapons increased 18 percent for girls while decreasing 29 percent for boys. These patterns have also been detected in reports of dating violence.

A study by Murray Straus published in 2008 reveals that approximately 30 percent of college students who are dating in the United States experience a physically violent episode in their relationships. Overall, Straus found that approximately 21 percent of these violent incidents were initiated by women, 10 percent by men. As these young women move into adulthood, we may very well detect an increase in intimate violence among married couples.

THE FEMINIST BACKLASH AGAINST THOSE WHO SPEAK UP

One of the most dismaying instances of women's aggression comes from within the feminist movement itself. When Straus and his colleagues published their initial study on domestic and family violence, many feminists accused them of fomenting anti-feminist sentiment and stifling efforts to protect women from men's abuse. As a result, Straus, who considers himself a feminist, was excommunicated from the movement by these activists.

Straus, now in his eighties, considers it a bitter irony that his efforts incurred the wrath of the feminist movement. Indeed, his thirty-year struggle to convince people that the patriarchal theory of dominance explains only a small part of partner violence has been marked by a series of attacks that have touched him both professionally and personally. A graduate student was warned that she'd never get a job if she did her doctoral research with him; public lectures and private addresses of his have been boycotted and disrupted. Straus says his most "painful" personal slight occurred in the early 1990s when the chairperson of the Canadian Commission on Violence Against Women accused him of beating his wife and sexually exploiting his students. Straus vehemently denied both charges.

Despite everything, Straus stands by his research. "First, I am a scientist," he says, "and my scientific commitments override my feminist commitments. Perhaps even more important, I believe that the safety and well-being of *women* requires efforts to end violence *by* women." He believes his data is valid, and he hopes that others will eventually see the perils of allowing ideology to trump research.

Gelles and Steinmetz were also the subjects of vindictive and frightening personal attacks. Steinmetz was the object of an unsuccessful letter-writing campaign urging her university to deny her tenure and government agencies to rescind her funding. She also received a bomb threat at her daughter's wedding. She no longer studies family violence.

Some women in the feminist movement have abused their power in their response to battered women as well. Imposing certain legal responses on victims of domestic violence, including the arrest and prosecution of their batterers, can reproduce the rejection, degradation, and isolation that is typical of an abusive relationship ("We don't care what you think; he's getting arrested!" or "We will prosecute him, whether or not you want to testify"). Once again, the victim has no control over her own life. To be sure, these policies sound sensible if all we are considering is the victim's safety at the moment of intervention. But what if the issue is more complicated? What if the victim has initiated the violence in some way? What if the man was the victim? If there are children in the house, do we still want the mother arrested? What if the woman loves her partner and knows that he will lose his job if he gets a criminal record?

It isn't surprising that these issues provoke such passionate responses—after all, lives are at stake. But the depth of that passion is part of what we must examine. What does it mean when a female academic receives a bomb threat for suggesting that women may be as aggressive as men—and when the perpetrator who made the threat most likely views it as a feminist act? This leads us to an even more fundamental question: How often are our responses to domestic violence as much about venting *our own* anger, fear, and frustration as they are about ameliorating the social problem we're claiming to address?

PASSING IT ON: THE NEXT GENERATION

If we expand the scope of how we think about violence in the family, we find that women are even more responsible for child abuse than we previously believed. Although patterns of child rearing have changed over the last twenty years, women still have significant influence over raising children. A large national study of child abuse and neglect confirms that mothers are more likely to be abusive toward their children than fathers; they are also more likely to kill them. A study of teen violence revealed that as many girls as boys were abusive at home: 26 percent reported that they hit or threatened to hit members of their family.

These findings have significant long-term consequences both for the children who experience the abuse and for those who may eventually be victimized by them in turn. The psychologist Miriam Ehrensaft and her colleagues found that violence in the family of origin was *the* greatest predictor of someone becoming abusive as an adult. It should therefore be no surprise that boys who were hit by a parent as children are three times more likely to become violent in their adult relationships than those who were not hit as children. Boys like Rick Aris who witness domestic violence *and* experience physical violence as children are five to nine times more likely to become abusers than boys who do not experience such abuse.

Psychologist Donald Dutton also reports that there may be a critical link between the *verbal* abuse inflicted by a mother on her male child and the likelihood of the boy becoming abusive once he grows up and becomes intimate with a female partner. Dutton's finding that verbal abuse by a mother may cause a man to have "anger and humiliation responses" toward his girlfriend or wife underscores the importance of recognizing the role women can play in both contributing to and preventing intimate abuse. This connection between psychological and physical abuse is borne out in studies of engaged and married couples. For example, psychologists Christopher Murphy and Daniel K. O'Leary found that over time, "psychologically coercive behavior" by one partner predicted the "development of physical aggression" by the other. Like male aggression, female aggression at all levels and of all kinds needs to be recognized and confronted if we are to have any hope of combating the disturbing levels of violence in our society.

THE WEB OF VIOLENCE

The web of violence encompasses all phases of a person's life, from childhood to adulthood. No matter when someone experiences abuse, and no matter what kind, each abusive experience informs the next. Like a spider's web, these episodes fuse and spread. Victims are taught to be violent, in response to someone else's violence. Rick learned from his dad, Brenda from Rick. The roles can also reverse themselves, and the victim can decide that he or she has had enough abuse, as Brenda did, and attack the aggressor. Tragically, many people don't realize when they are about to turn that corner, or even when or why they're angry in ways they cannot control. The point is not to demonize any particular group or person but to recognize how much violence we are all living with and how we continue to keep violence alive from relationship to relationship and generation to generation.

Domestic violence statistics illuminate a compelling and horrifying problem, but we must recognize that they are only one part of the story. This society experiences an unquantifiable amount of physical and emotional abuse, childhood and domestic violence, committed by boys and girls, men and women, parents and children. Expanding our definitions of the violence and acknowledging that the roles of men and women are often fluid rather than fixed clarify just how complex and far-reaching the problem is—and how critical it becomes that we all recognize our collective responsibility for it.

5

WHERE DOES INTIMATE ABUSE COME FROM?

Doctors, psychologists, and sociologists generally agree that a small number of people exhibit violent behavior for biological reasons. For example, they are born with a gene that increases their propensity for violence, or they have a dulled or dysfunctional central nervous system that prevents them from modifying their destructive behavior—even after they have been criticized or punished for it. There have also been cases of people becoming more violent after having suffered a serious head injury.

Drugs and alcohol—biological stimulants—can also greatly increase the possibility of a violent outburst. A United States Department of Justice study estimated that 75 percent of violent incidents between spouses involve alcohol. It is difficult to establish, however, when the use of stimulants in these instances is "causing" the violence and when the violent person is attracted to drugs or alcohol because they "allow" or "free" the user to exhibit an aggressive tendency usually kept under control.

Most medical and social scientists believe, however, that violence is generally learned rather than inherited. The majority of us take this assumption one step further; we think of violent behavior as a *choice*. Certainly, the criminal justice system functions on that assumption: you have voluntarily broken the law, and so you will be punished. The feminist movement has also explicitly attributed violence to culture: men are violent because they have been socialized to believe they are entitled to be.

But if violence is learned, *how* precisely is it learned? How is it actually transmitted? In order to confront this problem effectively, in our own lives and in society at large, we need to understand how both the abusers and the abused find themselves living with violence.

WHAT ROLE DOES CULTURE PLAY?

Anthropologist David Levinson's 1989 comparative study of family violence across ninety societies confirmed that domestic violence, child abuse, and sibling violence are most common in countries where men exert control over women's lives, violence in the family is considered acceptable, and mothers are primarily responsible for raising children. Levinson's Herculean investigation suggests that gender inequality contributes significantly to violence within the family—especially when men dictate where the family will live; how money is spent, inherited, or divided upon separation; what roles women are permitted to play within the family; and if and when women are allowed to divorce.

He also found that even societies that ostensibly condemn violence against family members in their religious or cultural teachings may not be living according to those stated values. For example, Cagoba, Columbia, had a very high rate of violence between spouses despite the fact that hitting one's partner is culturally prohibited there.

In the societies Levinson studied, 84 percent of the wives were beaten by their husbands, 74 percent of the children were physically punished by caretakers, and 44 percent of siblings fought with each other. In light of these findings, Levinson's conclusion that violence need not be "an inevitable consequence of family life" was somewhat surprising; to defend it, Levinson pointed to several rural communities in central and southern Thailand as examples of entire societies living virtually free of domestic and child abuse.

Bang Chan was a community of 1,700 people just an hour outside of Bangkok. With no restrictions on divorce and few cultural edicts on marriage, this mostly Buddhist community of roughly three hundred households experienced almost none of the abusive conditions that Levinson found in most other societies. In Bang Chan, the central tenet was respect for one another and for each person's desire to pursue his or her own goals. Levinson attributed the astonishing lack of family violence to a shared philosophy of equality: men and women stayed together as long as the relationship remained essentially free of serious conflict. Levinson believed that the presence of two peaceful, relatively contented parents in turn made child rearing far less stressful and burdensome, so that far fewer parents hit or otherwise abused their children. If a couple's relationship became potentially violent, each partner was more likely to have the emotional independence that would allow him or her to withdraw from the relationship—not to mention the social approval necessary to do so. As men and women were free to pursue jobs held by both genders, economic independence was also typical of both men and women in Bang Chan, enabling partners to break up without a significant financial impact.

Certainly, Levinson's study supports the belief held by many American feminists, psychologists, and sociologists that cultural norms, whether in the

United States or elsewhere, play a key role in either condoning or discouraging violence against women, and it affirms the strides we have made in educating ourselves about the realities of domestic abuse and empowering women in all sectors of society. Yet despite these strides intimate abuse remains a significant part of millions of Americans' lives. What else do we need to understand in order to reduce this threat?

PERPETRATORS OF VIOLENCE: WHO BECOMES VIOLENT AND WHY?

As I've noted, researchers have now unequivocally confirmed that the roots of family violence can nearly always be traced to the abuser's family of origin: the conditions in which we are raised will largely determine how peaceful or turbulent our intimate relationships will be when we become adults. One or both parents can be responsible for fostering violence in a child, as can grandparents, or any other significant adult in the child's life. Although what constitutes sufficient "training" for a child to grow up to "cross the line" and become violent will never be precisely quantified, we can identify four key conditions that, if present simultaneously, are very likely to turn an otherwise typical child into an angry and abusive adult.

Condition #1: Insecure Attachment

Fundamentally, all of us are born into a world of extreme danger: we arrive naked, hungry, and cold, and we are unable to take care of ourselves. If we are lucky, though, we have parents who spend a great deal of time and energy shielding us from this fact. All children need to attach themselves to a parent or caretaker, for love and survival. If they are well loved and cared for in return, they are far more likely to flourish. The study of this bond between child and parent (usually the mother) is called "attachment theory."

When the bond is a strong one, the child will initially feel secure when that parent is present and anxious when he or she is absent. This anxiety is healthy, because it represents an accurate understanding of the world ("I am far safer with those who love me than those who don't"). As the child matures, that strong connection allows him to develop a sense of self ("I know that I am valuable because I am valued"). It also allows him to perceive the world as a safe place, which over time gives him the confidence to become more independent and adventurous. When the primary caregiver is available, dependable, and willing to meet the child's practical and emotional needs, the child feels secure not only within his family but also within himself and the larger world.

Unfortunately, many parents are either unwilling or unable to meet their children's needs and provide a safe space for them. Battered women like Brenda and Emalou Aris, intensely preoccupied with the violence in their marriages and unable to stop it, fail to meet their children's needs in quite obvious ways. In other families, however, the stresses can be more subtle; the strains of overwork, financial worries, health problems, depression, drug and alcohol abuse, and a limited education all contribute to inadequate parenting. Some parents, like Brenda's mother, simply ignore their children's emotional needs. Others, like Rick's father, can be actively hostile to them and punishing in response.

When a child experiences a parent as unavailable or unpredictable, she begins to feel chronically anxious and fearful. As a result, such children—who are *not* securely attached—find it difficult to relate to people outside the family, as well. Their experiences with peers and other adults tend to be similarly distant or unstable, and they often prove to be less able to control their emotional responses—including their angry and violent impulses. The world, like the home, is a dangerous place.

John Bowlby, a British developmental psychologist, further refined how "poor attachment"can affect a child's development over time. He found that when the parental bond is unstable or insecure, it tends to breed either avoidance or resistance in the child as he matures. As the label suggests, avoidant children tend to avoid interactions with others: intimacy has already proven to be risky, and so keeping to themselves is safe and preferable. (This might be the child playing alone in the corner of the playground.) Resistant children, on the other hand, are drawn to others almost despite themselves—they can't survive without the social contact (indeed, they are often preoccupied with it), and yet they are also suspicious of it and eventually express this ambivalence in ways that can be hurtful to themselves and others. (This might be the child who invites another child to build sandcastles with him but then knocks the new playmate's castle down, thereby damaging the possibility of a stronger connection.)

An avoidant child may grow up to shun intimate relationships altogether, or she may ostensibly be part of a family but insulate herself from any real closeness with others because she fears reactivating the insecurity that was originally instilled by her caregiver. Brenda's mother, Iona, is an example of an avoidant adult. The sexual abuse she endured as a child defined her life as a parent. She was rarely at home with her children, and when she was, she used alcohol to insulate herself from those closest to her. (If Alvis Lane had repeatedly challenged the barriers behind which his wife was hiding, however, making Iona feel intolerably vulnerable, she could have become violent—as she did, in one instance when she threw a milk bottle at him during an argument.)

If two avoidant people come together in a couple, there is probably little likelihood of violence, but of course two avoidant people are by definition unlikely to find each other. More frequently, an avoidant person will end up in a relationship with a resistant person—someone who is highly ambivalent about intimacy—or two resistant people will find each other. These volatile combinations can quickly become intolerable for one or both parties. Rick's attachment to Brenda is a classic example: desperate to be with his wife when they were apart, Rick couldn't tolerate the closeness when they were together and would lash out violently against it.

In 1998, psychologists Jamila Bookwala and Bozena Zdaniuk compared two sets of college students in western Pennsylvania: those who reported aggression in their romantic relationships and those who did not. The participants who said that their relationships were aggressive also described themselves as having difficulty being intimate and being "excessively controlling of others." That same year, a study conducted by Nigel Roberts and Patricia Noller in Queensland, Australia, found that men and women who used aggression in their intimate relationships reported both high levels of anxiety about the possibility of being abandoned and having partners who were afraid of intimacy.

Canadian psychologist Antonia Henderson and colleagues published research in 2005 that similarly underscored the connection between a preoccupation with abandonment and a propensity to lash out. "Preoccupied individuals," they concluded, "are torn between a need for love and support from others and the fear of not having that need gratified. Thus, they can become increasingly demanding and potentially aggressive when attachment needs are not fulfilled." The finding proved true for both men and women. The researchers also suggested that "preoccupied individuals may be more willing than others to tolerate sustained abuse from intimate partners."

Of course, a poor attachment to one's parents as a child does not necessarily lead to a violent personal life in adulthood; in fact, it is estimated that more than half of *all* Americans exhibit an insecure attachment. When we think about domestic violence, though, the usefulness of this idea is clear, because it suggests that while outsiders may see the violent adult as operating aggressively from a position of power, his or her actions may in fact be triggered by feelings of extreme vulnerability and fear. When these feelings have been compounded by growing up in a household where physical and mental abuse were also present, the chances of such a child becoming a violent adult increase dramatically.

Condition #2: Witnessing Domestic Violence

When a spectacular case of domestic violence gains attention in the media, we've all heard a statement like the following: "At least they don't hit the kids." Everyone is grateful when children remain untouched by the physical violence between their parents. Unfortunately, living with violent parents is far more damaging for children than many of us realize—even if the children themselves are never hit. Terrible conflict between the adults within a household is extremely threatening—even if the children are sitting upstairs with their headphones on, hiding under the bed, or running down the hall to fetch the neighbors. What will become of them if their mother is killed? What will become of the family if their father leaves? How will their world hold together if its central partnership self-destructs? These are terrifying questions for any child, and they are compounded by his sense of powerlessness.

Murray Straus, Richard Gelles, and Suzanne Steinmetz's national study published in the 1980s was one of the first to test whether witnessing parental violence as a child creates the next generation's batterers. These researchers uncovered a significant correlation between witnessing abuse and subsequent partner abuse: "Men who had seen parents physically attack each other were almost three times more likely to have hit their own wives during the year of the study." Women with violent parents were also much more likely to hit their husbands.

On the strength of this study, social scientists in the 1980s started to take seriously the idea that witnessing parental violence was a significant problem. Many therapists observed that although parents in combative relationships frequently convinced themselves that their children had no idea what was happening between them, in fact these children could often provide detailed accounts of the abusive encounters they had seen and heard at home. Bonnie Carlson, a professor of social work at Arizona State University, estimated in 1984 that more than three million children in the United States between the ages of three and seventeen were at risk for being exposed to physical violence between their parents. Psychologists and social workers who observed or treated these children, often in women's shelters, reported that they were behaving aggressively with family or with teachers, asserting that hitting boyfriends or girlfriends was acceptable, and running away from home.

In 1989, psychology researchers Peter Jaffe, David Wolfe, and Susan Wilson from the University of Western Ontario conducted a small but important empirical study to explore the effects of witnessing violence on children. They matched by gender, age, family size, and income twenty-eight children who had been exposed to violence in the previous six weeks and were living in shelters with twenty-eight children not exposed to violence.

They found that children who had recently witnessed domestic violence in their families were not performing well in school, participated in fewer social activities, and expressed fewer interests overall. They also found that these children's attitudes about anger were "inappropriate"—suggesting that they might have difficulty managing their anger—and that they were considerably less knowledgeable than the children in the comparison group about basic safety skills, such as whom they might call in an emergency.

In a particularly sobering follow-up study, Jaffe and his colleagues discovered that boys who had witnessed family violence exhibited extremely similar behavior to boys who had been *directly* abused by their parents. Such behaviors included: "clinging to adults, complaining of loneliness, feeling unloved, unhappiness or sadness, easily jealous, and worrying." The researchers also found that both sets of boys exhibited: "disobedience at home or school, lying and

cheating, destroying things belonging to self or others, cruelty to others, asso-
ciating with bad friends, and fighting."All of these boys were significantly different when compared to boys from nonviolent families.

Numerous subsequent studies have confirmed how harmful witnessing domestic abuse can be for children. When violence overshadows a child's inner
world, it can literally dismantle his ability to relate to himself and others in
ways that are positive and productive, leaving him anxious, withdrawn, and depressed. Because he may feel that his life, literally, depends on it, he becomes
intensely preoccupied with urgent and upsetting questions: "Why are my parents hurting each other?" "Does it have to do with me?" "Where will we live
now?" The psychological and emotional energy spent in fearing and anticipat-
ing the next incident of violence leaves the child ill-equipped to focus on the
other demands of ordinary life, such as school, play, and making friends.

Violence between parents, no matter how fervently we may wish to believe
otherwise, doesn't stay between parents. The children of violent couples inherit
not only an increased likelihood that they will have trouble negotiating their
own lives but also a significant chance that violence will resurface later on in
their own intimate relationships.

Condition #3: Child Abuse and Punishment

Many Americans physically punish their children, and many of us were physically punished as children. When does corporal punishment, which involves
inflicting physical pain for the purpose of punishing a child or correcting his
behavior, constitute physical abuse? I would argue that all corporal punishment is potentially damaging for a child. The degree of damage, however, depends on many factors: the severity of the punishment; the rationale (or lack
thereof) behind the punishment; the degree to which the child is being unfairly treated; the level of anger in the parent; the resiliency of the child. Spanking a child very rarely for a serious infraction—stealing, for example; or
running into traffic—is obviously very different from scalding an infant in the
tub because "she just wouldn't shut up."

No child feels good about physical punishment at the time (although many
children will justify their parents' actions much later on), but the significance
of that punishment is also determined by the culture of the family and the culture surrounding the family. In the Aris family, for example, even Rick's mother
and sisters recognized that Rick was a scapegoat for Les's anger.

When a child is directly abused by a parent (whether ostensibly as a means
of punishment or simply abused), there is a significantly increased likelihood
that she will become a violent adult. Indeed, Straus, Gelles, and Steinmetz unequivocally concluded that as the amount of physical punishment experienced
as a child goes up, the rates of wife beating and husband beating also go up. In
2003, psychology researcher Miriam Ehrensaft and her colleagues confirmed

these findings in a study on how violence is transmitted from one generation to the next, concluding that punishment that is excessively physical, overbearing, and unpredictable increases the likelihood that the child on the receiving end will become an adult abuser.

The age of the child may also be significant. While we may instinctively understand that beating a one-year-old could be both physically and psychologically damaging, beating teenagers can also have catastrophic repercussions. Straus and his colleagues discovered a high correlation between abused teenagers and people who used severe violence against their intimate partners (kicking, biting, punching, hitting with an object, beating up, threatening with a gun or knife, or actually using a knife or gun). Overall, they concluded that about one quarter of the people who experienced corporal punishment as teenagers hit their partners during the year of the study. Not surprisingly, domestic violence and child abuse are often present in the same family, although studies have yet to be precise in their estimates. Researchers have found that in approximately 40 percent of the families in which violence exists between parents, the children are also physically abused.

It is instructive, though, to remember that nearly all forms of child abuse are explained by the abuser as a form of deserved punishment. Very few parents admit to taking their rage out on their children simply because they have the power to do so. And even those of us who hit children for the "right" reasons will concede that the severity of our response is usually not determined *solely* on the basis of the infraction but on a host of other reasons as well—trouble at work, a quarrel with our neighbor, the fact that we were too busy to eat lunch— that have little or nothing to do with the situation at hand. If we can't honestly guarantee that the child is *only* being punished for his or her particular crime, how can we justify our use of physical force? It's a slippery slope.

Corporal punishment's "cloak of righteousness"—the notion that venting one's anger at a much smaller and more vulnerable person is not only acceptable but "for the kid's own good"—can be an extremely dangerous form of self-deception, and perhaps that is reason enough to refrain from raising a hand or belt to strike a child. Even if there were only a slight chance that it would make our son or daughter violent later on, would it really be worth the risk?

Condition #4: Teaching Violence

Lonnie Athens, a criminologist who studies violence, has always been interested in the relationship between child abuse and adult behavior. Athens was severely abused both physically and mentally by his father. His mother and his brother were also abused. Why do some people—like himself—still manage to avoid a life of crime while others do not? To answer this question, he conducted qualitative sociological research, in which he extensively interviewed people serving time in prison for significant crimes (theft, armed robbery, rape, murder). He interviewed over one hundred people, including men and women of all races, classes, and religions, ranging in age from fifteen to forty years old.

Athens's startling discovery was that many of these adults had not only been witnesses and victims of physical abuse as children but had also been encouraged, or taught, to be violent by some important adult in their life. He also found that this "coaching" of the child—the "novice," as Athens describes the child in training—was not casual, not simply a matter of modeling the violent behavior but instead deliberate, explicit, and systematic: "Novices are always taught that taking violent action against a protagonist is a *personal responsibility* which they cannot evade, but must discharge regardless of whether they are a man or woman, young or old, large or small, or what their prior beliefs about hurting others may have been."

One of Athens's interviewees, a female teenager incarcerated for criminal homicide, explained:

> My mother and grandmother didn't believe in letting people run over them, but believed in standing up for yourself and fighting even if you were a woman. They didn't believe in letting anyone insult, bully, or threaten them. My mother and grandmother just wouldn't stand for people messing with them. They were bold women and would fight a man or a woman.
>
> If they both told me once, they told me a hundred times that I better learn to stand up for myself. They said, "You can't depend upon a man, a man is not always going to take up for you and may try to hurt you, so you better learn to take up for yourself. A woman has to act, not just react, when people mess with her."

The extremity of Rick Aris's behavior as an adult is less bewildering when we recognize that *all four* of the conditions that encourage children to become violent in their intimate relationships were present in his childhood. His mother loved him, but she was unable to provide him with a safe home; he watched his father hit his mother; he was beaten regularly by his father; and he was encouraged and taught by his father to be violent with others. The fact that Rick couldn't protect his mother, couldn't protect himself, and apparently wasn't worth protecting would have been a source of deep shame.

THE MECHANICS OF SHAME: HOW CAN SHAME LEAD TO VIOLENCE?

Shame is one of the most understudied and misunderstood human emotions, yet it is also one of the most complex and potentially dangerous. Sadness, anger, and even guilt can sometimes feel useful or satisfying or even cathartic;

no one feels ambivalent about the experience of shame. Many people remember the sting of shameful incidents for decades afterwards, notwithstanding the fact that the source of the shame may have long since been discounted. ("Why did I even care what that drunken moron thought of my appearance?") Even when we know that we were completely innocent, or unfairly treated, we often feel somehow tainted by the contempt or cruelty of those who shamed us. The mere fact of our vulnerability can make us hate ourselves.

Shame has been defined as a "negative and disturbing emotional experience involving feelings of self-condemnation and the desire to hide the damaged self from others." The word "shame" is derived from the Indo-European root *skam*, which means to cover—our first response is to somehow escape our terrible sense of exposure. Shame can encompass many feelings and has been closely associated with humiliation, disgrace, embarrassment, even mortification. ("If anyone knows this happened to me, I'd die.") Shame is buried, hidden, and covered up at all costs. It is therefore easy to overlook the importance of shame—both because it is invisible and because we all have such a deep, visceral aversion to even the threat of experiencing it. Yet it plays a profoundly destructive role in any physically or psychologically abusive household.

All children experience shame at some point, from knowingly or unknowingly breaking a rule deemed important by their elders or their peers. When a child is on the receiving end of someone's anger, violence, or ridicule, he often feels condemned and diminished. Ideally, the child can share this terrible feeling with a parent who can alleviate his unhappiness and reassure him that the terrible moment—and its accompanying judgment—will pass. If a grandmother yells at her granddaughter for breaking a vase, say, the parent can minimize the importance of the crime ("Don't worry—it was only a vase"), affirm the child's feelings of self-worth ("You didn't do it on purpose"), and empower the child by suggesting that she can avoid such mistakes in the future ("You'll be more careful next time"). The parent might even diminish the power of the punishing adult ("Your grandmother's arthritis is really bothering her. That's why she's so cranky today.") Obviously, positive communication is essential for this restorative process to occur. If the child cannot express her feelings, or if the parent is unwilling or unable to come to the child's aid, the shame is simply buried.

Unfortunately, the sorts of experiences that are likely to produce the most overwhelming amounts of shame—rape, torture, beatings—are often the ones that are the most difficult to talk about or share, and the damage is compounded when the violence has been inflicted by someone who is supposed to love you and take care of you. In these instances, the child cannot carry his or her shame to the parent, because the parent is often partly or wholly responsible for what has happened. Even when parents feel terrible about what has happened to the child—as Emalou Aris did—they, too, may be so ashamed that they cannot openly admit or discuss what has taken place.

Because the child is left to deal with these feelings on his own, he has no real opportunity to come to terms with the hurtful incident. Whether children blame themselves or the person who caused the violence becomes secondary to the fact that the event is now *theirs* in some way, because it happened to *them*. They will therefore usually try to deny it or forget it as soon as possible—a typical self-protective mechanism. The entire family can become complicit in whatever wrong has been done, bound together in a conspiracy of silence.

For children, this burying of their terrible feelings—not only their fear, anxiety, and sadness, but also the sense that it is somehow their fault, or that they deserve no better—is especially devastating. Their inner reality, which should provide a place of safety and solace from life's difficulties, is no longer a place to be trusted: it has become the place where the bad feelings are locked away.

This unresolved shame is unlikely to dissipate; at some point, often when the child enters adolescence, it erupts in meaningful and hurtful behaviors, including cutting oneself, eating too much or too little, drinking or taking drugs, experiencing suicidal urges. For those who come to believe that the blame for the violence should be placed on someone else, this is when the anger often turns to aggression and, at the extreme end of the spectrum, manifests in violence against other people.

THE TRIGGERING EVENT

Again and again, in accounts of violent incidents in the home or elsewhere, the victim is caught completely off-guard by the attack. ("He just snapped." "It came out of nowhere." "I still don't understand exactly what happened.") This was certainly true for me in my first violent encounters with the men who abused me. What triggers these seemingly disproportionate responses?

James Gilligan, a psychiatrist who has worked extensively with people in prison, wrote a book entitled *Violence: Reflections on a National Epidemic*, which drew heavily on his clinical experiences with inmates. Gilligan discovered that many people who experienced terrible humiliation as children also learned that violence is the way to distance themselves from reexperiencing those feelings. If a child feels implicated by being a witness to or victim of violence, a common solution is to shift places with the abuser—to expel rather than absorb those feelings of powerlessness by asserting power over other people.

Of course, while the abused person is still young and physically small, that shift may not be possible. The shame has to be continually repressed, even as the need to expel it may be increasing over time. Later, in adolescence or adulthood, the tables can be turned: if that sense of humiliation is somehow triggered and brought to the surface—if that person is somehow "disrespected" by a lukewarm cup of coffee, say, or a sarcastic remark—he or she may now be in a position to retaliate. These people are like ticking bombs; it's only a matter of time before an event sparks their combustible feelings.

Lonnie Athens, who discovered the importance of an adult's influence on a child's violent development, describes humiliation, a form of shame, as central to the process of becoming violent. The "brutalization" process, as Athens calls it, occurs when a child is literally taught to be violent by an adult. This teaching—or "coaching," to use Athens's word—involves numerous shame-producing techniques, including explicit instructions on how to respond violently toward others when such violence is called for (which is almost always) and inflicting violence directly on the child in order to set an example of how to use violence to get one's way. Eventually, the person who has been subjected to these lessons will ask himself, "How can I stop feeling ashamed and start doing the shaming?" Athens refers to this as the process of becoming belligerent, which literally means "the state of being at war." At this point, the person begins to take violent action against anyone who provokes him, having been taught that most situations call for a violent response. One of the inmates Athens interviewed, a male teenager incarcerated for homicide, described how he was coached toward violence:

> The beatings I took from my older brother set sparks off in me. What my father told me about not letting people run over me set off more sparks. Seeing people I cared a lot for get hurt set off still more sparks. All these things sparked me off, ignited a fire in me that wouldn't go out.
>
> I got to the point that I wasn't going to let people run over me. I had taken, seen, and heard enough. The beatings I saw and took demonstrated to me in black and white the truth of what my father had been saying: you need to be violent sometimes. There was no more room in my life for people talking crazy and hurting me any more. I was going to stand up and stop people one way or another from doing that to me. Whatever it took, I was going to do it. I wasn't going to be down on myself any more for not having guts enough to show people they can't mess with me like that and get away with it. No one has a right to talk crazy or hurt me, no one.

This helps to explain why so many violent actions seem irrational from an outsider's perspective. It is more useful to think of a shamed person's violent response as *an internal recalibration of an intolerable emotion* than as *a meaningful declaration of injustice against a particular enemy*. A teenager from a violent household convinces himself that another kid in his class is giving him dirty looks so that he can beat him up in response. The infraction may be invented—as so many of Brenda's infractions were invented by Rick—but objective reality is almost meaningless here; violence, this teenager has been taught, is an effective way of replacing his bad feelings with a sense of power over his world.

A murder that took place in New York City in 2005 illustrates very clearly how shame can turn to violence. A twenty-eight-year-old actress named Nicole duFresne was with some friends in the Lower East Side late at night when they were mugged by a group of young people. Rudy Fleming, who was armed, pistol whipped duFresne's boyfriend, Jeffrey Sparks, and grabbed another woman's purse. Sparks's face was bleeding profusely; when the attacker still lingered, duFresne shouted, "What are you going to do, shoot us?" In response, the attacker shot her in the chest; she died within minutes.

We can never know what, precisely, duFresne was thinking when she yelled at Fleming, but in all likelihood she was speaking from a position of enraged fear and powerlessness. At the same time, the fact that her anger got the upper hand of her fear also suggests her personal strength. We might surmise that Fleming, even with a gun in his hands, felt so threatened by her question that he couldn't just walk away. Even with the money and the weapon, he was still afraid of being the loser. In that instant, pulling the trigger was the preferable alternative.

In the immediate aftermath of duFresne's murder, the National Crime Prevention Council cautioned that the victim's behavior "may have antagonized the criminal," encouraging him to shoot. Sparks contested this interpretation of his girlfriend's murder, adding, "I would disagree with anyone that blamed her for it." Certainly duFresne was not responsible for her murder—Fleming was. But that does not negate the value of the Council's warning: any sarcastic remark or antagonistic behavior that might trigger shame in another person—and then a violent response to negate that sense of shame—can have lethal consequences, no matter how irrational or extreme the response may seem to others.

Gilligan explains that many violent criminals lack the emotional capacity or language to cope with the feelings that are stimulated by shame in the first place. Violence *is* the language, the communication—just as Fleming's gunshot was his answer to duFresne's verbal challenge.

Some people react impulsively as Brenda did; others plan their violence ahead of time. Fleming could belong in either category—after all, he was wandering the streets with a gun in his hand. Perhaps he was simply looking for trouble, waiting for the catalyst that would allow him to release his explosive feelings into the world. But it is possible that even those who carry out quite intricate plots against their partners are in the grip of some prior slight or humiliation.

The morning when David and I "discovered" my burned out car together was unnerving in this sense. Nothing that had happened between us in the previous twenty-four hours had in any way suggested that level of hostility on his part, and yet I was sure that he was responsible, that his rage must have been bubbling just beneath the surface. The invisibility of those intense emotions during everyday life explains why such experiences can be so terrifying for the person on the receiving end of a sudden outburst of violence—on the one hand, the violence feels intensely personal; on the other, its source seems to lie beyond the victim's frame of reference.

Although we often tend to think of the abuser as the more powerful partner in these moments, it is important to remember that this person nearly always has something to lose as a result of resorting to violence (exposure, further shame, loss of self-respect, perhaps even jail). The abuser must therefore feel very threatened if he or she acts out in any event, despite the likely consequences. Whether the violence is planned or not is irrelevant—either way, it feels justified or necessary, given this person's mind-set and tortured personal history.

The terrible and often conflicting feelings produced by this sort of history is vividly captured in the statements made by some of the criminals Athens interviewed. Their belligerence is often fused with their anguished and ongoing sense of victimization at the hands of others. This is where shame intersects with the four conditions that lead to violence in an individual. Consider the explanation given by a male teen whose offense was aggravated assault:

> I still get upset when I think about all the things that happened. I can never forget the beatings that my father gave me, the beatings that I saw my mother and older sister take from him and all his loud bragging about what he had done to people. The things my father did to us made me feel ashamed and mad. It built my anger up and up until I got mean and crazy. . . . I was ready to kill people who fooled and fooled around with me and wouldn't stop.

Another example Athens highlighted involved a young man in his mid-teens, whose offense was armed robbery:

> The beatings my stepfather laid on me, the terrible beatings he laid on my mother, and all the violent rhetoric took their toll on my mind. It inflamed me and made me want to go for bad. I was tired of always being messed with by people. . . . I was going to stop them from messing bad with me. If I had to, I would use a gun, knife, or anything. . . . My days of being a chump who was too frightened and scared to hurt people for messing with him were over.

The final example comes from a man in his late twenties who was incarcerated for criminal homicide:

> After I got my ass whipped bad a few times, I realized that being a loser was not where it was at. I didn't want to be a loser any more and get my ass

whipped. I wasn't running from people. I didn't go for that. I learned that I had to hurt somebody bad before they hurt me. If I couldn't hurt them bad with my hands, then I would use a brick, rock, board, knife, or gun to hurt them. Since I was small, I usually needed more than my hands to hurt someone bad. I needed leverage. I don't care how big a guy is, a knife or gun will cut him down to my size.

Central to each of these stories is the history of violence witnessed and experienced by a child, and the anger, shame, and accompanying aggression it subsequently produced.

These young men have been subjected to and committed acts of extreme violence. They have also been locked up for their crimes and extensively questioned about them by a criminologist. These factors may contribute to their level of awareness: they have had to explain, both to others and to themselves, what has happened to them. Tragically, however, this awareness has come too late: both their own lives and the lives of others have already been destroyed. That's why it's important to teach children to develop ways of talking about their pain and shame, and to help those who already communicate primarily through violence to learn new ways of expressing themselves.

Athens's cases are extreme. But many of us have tried to suppress our unhappy childhoods, and the price of that buried past may be making itself felt in the present—in bullying junior colleagues at work or unnecessary disputes with strangers in restaurants. Before we have even realized what is happening, our hostility has become an ingrained response, a way of being in the world.

THE VICTIM: WHO IS ATTRACTED TO VIOLENCE AND WHY?

Victims and perpetrators of domestic violence often come from very similar family backgrounds. In their longitudinal study mentioned earlier, which traced violence across the generations, Miriam Ehrensaft and her colleagues also found that early exposure to abuse in the home helps to determine who will end up battered: "Exposure to violence between parents, which probably begins when a child is young, seems to pose the greatest independent risk for being the victim of any act of partner violence."

These children's expectations of intimate relationships are skewed because their primary attachments with their caretakers are unstable. The resulting anxiety increases the risk that these vulnerable children will play out their insecurities in similarly dysfunctional relationships with peers and, ultimately, with intimate partners.

Rejection by one's peers—which is common when a person's expectations of others are based on a destructive family dynamic—leads adolescents to other rejected peers. As an adolescent, Brenda was a bit of an outsider. So was Rick. Superficially, of course, the two were very different: Brenda was a "good" girl from an emotionally violent family; Rick was a "bad" boy from a physically violent household. It was these conditions in their childhoods that made their need for each other so great but also left them incapable of meeting that need. Such "outsiders" further initiate each other into antisocial and violent behavior, including substance abuse and partner violence.

It is important to underscore just how unconscious the process of victimization can be: the Lanes' alcoholism never even came up at their daughter Brenda's trial; indeed, I spent over three years talking to Brenda about her life before she revealed her parents' drinking patterns and related neglect. When I asked her why she had never told me about her feelings of abandonment, she was perplexed by my question: "I didn't think it was a big deal," she said.

I, too, had a difficult time seeing any connection between my childhood experiences and my vulnerability to domestic violence. It took me many years to understand how my grandfather's emotional badgering affected me later, in my own romantic relationships.

My grandfather was a very powerful person in my early life, just as Brenda's mother was in hers. But like Brenda, I recognized that this authority figure was also a victim: my mother had often told me of my grandfather's difficult childhood. My great-grandparents, who lived in Poland in the late 1800s, were very poor, and my great-grandmother supported the family as a peddler. Her husband, who was very religious and had no interest in taking care of the household, was left at home to raise the four children, and he proved to be a brutal parent. He was so frightening, in fact, that my grandfather ran away from home when he was only twelve years old.

How had he managed on his own after he'd run away? How had he escaped the Holocaust? I was obsessed with these questions as a child, and I would often interrogate my grandfather about his past, which he proudly shared with me. He explained that he'd sold buttons on the street for cash and that he'd outsmarted the Nazi soldiers in the camp by running under the fence when they weren't looking. I was impressed. Like Brenda's mother, my grandfather survived such terrible ordeals that any complaints I might have had about my own life felt insignificant by comparison. But I found it very difficult to reconcile my grandfather's funny, brilliant, gregarious side with his hostile outbursts, and I hated the fact that I could never predict what his mood would be at any given moment. Hoping to draw out his best side, I would always be surprised when I was greeted with hostility; I felt helpless and inadequate when I could not turn his anger into affection. This sense of humiliation at my inability to transform my emotional world became a deep part of me—although I was completely unaware of it.

David represented my old dilemma in the guise of something completely different. His volatile mix of humor, intelligence, love, and hostility was deeply familiar to me: I was returning to what I knew. But David was also a chance to change the pattern. I was stronger now and had more to give, and David, too, was a victim: Couldn't my love and my tolerance for all he'd been through help to fix him, as I could never fix my grandfather, and heal our relationship?

A contradictory but equally seductive urge was to express my anger at the injustice of my treatment in a way that I never could with my grandfather. After all, what right did either of these men have to treat me this way and to make me feel bad for things that weren't my fault? This time around, I was stronger and had ways of defending myself: I could hurt David, to get him back for the hurt he inflicted on me, and I did—by falling in love with Charles. This betrayal of David was in part fuelled by my earlier experience of violence and shame with someone I loved but could never fully bond with, because the aggression was always in the way. Paradoxically, then, my romance with David was not simply an attempt to remedy my earlier relationship with my grandfather but also to avenge it.

THE VICTIM'S SHAME: DAMAGE SEEKING DAMAGE

What is the mechanism of shame that triggers someone to put himself in an unsafe situation or expose herself to violence? If we think of shame as an unresolved emotion, it's easy to see how a history of abuse can trigger either a vulnerability or attraction to someone who is violent. Often, once the violence has expressed itself, the connection can have a terrible yet compelling foreordained quality—abuse once again speaking to shame. A victim might say things like, "I guess I deserve no better," or "I somehow bring this on myself." If the victim has struggled to repress his or her violent past and the shame surrounding it, the romance may also have a seductive intimacy: "For years, I have hidden my true self. But this person *sees* me." In the case of those who were neglected or abandoned as children, the intensity of the relationship can feel like true attachment and true affection: "She may sometimes lash out, but at least she needs me. Her violence shows me that she cares."

Bernice Andrews, a professor at Royal Holloway and Bedford New College in London, England, and a colleague, Chris Brewin, conducted a study of battered women from North London and found that women who had been repeatedly physically and sexually abused in childhood experienced feelings of inadequacy when they found themselves in violent relationships as adults—so much so that they blamed themselves for their partners' abuse.

The *hope* is that the love—or attraction or attention or interest—will eradicate the earlier sense of shame and abandonment; the *likelihood* is that the adult relationship will simply reinforce the earlier destructive pattern for both parties, if in different ways. Brenda saw Rick as the answer to her future, just as

I thought that David was destined to be my husband, and yet we both had in fact chosen men who were singularly incapable of the roles we had assigned to them.

In an enlightening study of the feelings elicited by violent relationships, Eli Buchbinder and Zvi Eisikovits found that shame from childhood was a major factor in how female victims conceptualized their violent partnerships later in life. In an attempt to overcome their shame, they would seek out shameful experiences similar to their childhoods, in an effort to correct their dysfunctional histories. When they were, in turn, shamed by their violent partners, they had no choice but to relive their childhood experiences of feeling ashamed—which they then tried to overcome once again, by reengaging with the violent partner, and the cycle would continue. Just as perpetrators will ultimately pay for the terrible shame they feel when they express violence, victims find no comfort in the people they seek to remedy their shame.

HOW HARD IS IT TO ESCAPE A VIOLENT PAST?

Certainly, many people who have been exposed to violence in some of the ways described here manage to escape participating in abusive relationships later in life. Usually it is because they received strength or protection from an adult who acted as a substitute for the parent who was abusive or neglectful. This nurturing caregiver can be a grandparent, an aunt or uncle, a teacher, a coach, a minister, or any other influential person in the child's life. Such adults represent several crucial things: a nonviolent role model, an interaction that isn't defined by violence, and a sense of self that isn't tainted by violence.

A child who is unusually intelligent or creative can sometimes build an internal world and sense of self that makes him more resilient in the face of domestic hostilities, but this is a rare occurrence. Samuel Aymer, a social work professor in New York City, is interested in how teens cope with domestic violence and what contributes to their resiliency. He did an in-depth study of ten male adolescents of color who came from poor families and who were receiving counseling for emotional and behavioral problems. Many of the young men had criminal histories; they had all been exposed to domestic abuse. His subjects cited community centers and activities as being extremely important in counteracting their turbulent home lives. A basketball program or a quiet library to retreat to provided opportunities to seek more positive experiences while simultaneously minimizing the negative ones. It is important to remember that many children living with domestic violence will not talk about what is happening at home for fear of getting their parents in trouble. A teacher or sports coach can therefore be far more important than he or she realizes to a child in crisis. One of Aymer's subjects recalled, "I like my coach 'cause he was nice. He made us work, too, 'cause we had to get to practice early and he would yell at you if you come late. He was alright. Know what I am saying? Better than my father. The other boys like him, too. Our team was the best. We won a lot of games all the time. I never told him about my parent's situation, though."

Unfortunately, all too often, frightened and angry parents are threatened by their children's desire to escape the violence: as a result, they systematically denigrate and undermine the very opportunities that their children so desperately need to survive and to transcend their family's misery. Andrea Ashworth's book *Once in a House on Fire* explores the author's violent childhood and the ways in which her stepfather was hostile to any sign—a love of books, skill at drawing, close friends—that his children had an inner life or a life outside the family's shame-bound existence. If he heard about or suspected some type of social activity, there were always more chores to be done around the house: "It was easier not to go out at all, to avoid the anger it would stir up, ready to burst in your face when you stepped back through the door."

Ashworth's mother was secretly proud of her children but too greedy for her moments of intimacy with her husband to stick up for them. As one of Ashworth's sisters bitterly observed, "Why does it have to be Them against Us . . . whenever it's not Him against Her?" Inevitably, the house's atmosphere of doom and entrapment filled Ashworth with a sense of hopelessness. In high school, when she read Thomas Hardy's *Tess of the d'Urbervilles* and discovered that Tess is ruined by her tainted past, she immediately felt a flash of recognition: "For years, I had lived with a sticky sense of being spoiled. I could almost feel it clogging my veins, making me feel mucky inside." Ashworth eventually escaped to Oxford, but her sisters were not as fortunate: one was denied a chance to attend a dance school in London; the other was given lengthy boxing lessons by their stepfather so that she could go up against her enemies in the schoolyard.

THE LEGACY OF INTIMATE VIOLENCE: LUCRETIA ARIS

If Rick grew up in an abusive family, and Brenda grew up in an emotionally withdrawn household, their children had the misfortune of growing up in both: before Lucretia turned twenty-one, the violence and neglect that had respectively marked her parents' lives had been repeated in her own, and their devastating effects were in ample evidence.

Lucretia's memories of life in Riverside are not completely unhappy ones—in part, perhaps, because it was the last place she would live with her parents before her dad died. She remembers the swing Rick built on the porch of the house, and the afternoons she spent hanging out there with her father and sisters. In retrospect, of course, there were many signs that things were terribly wrong: her maternal grandparents weren't supposed to know that Rick and

Brenda were back together; Rick was always around because he was virtually unemployable; the one time Lucretia invited a friend from school to come over, the little girl was attacked by their pit bull.

Lucretia also remembers living in constant dread of setting her father off. The days were easier than the evenings, because he was less likely to be high and out of control, but she remembers always "walking on eggshells" in her father's company. By this point, Brenda was also rarely allowed to leave the house: she often had to ask her nine-year-old daughter to bike to the drugstore for her, to pick up supplies, or make a call from the payphone nearby. At the time, however, Lucretia didn't understand that this was unusual.

On the night of Rick's death, Lucretia was relieved when she found out she was sleeping over at Hoodie's. She still remembers the backyard filling up with drunk and stoned guests and her father banging on the door while her mother hid inside the bathroom. She knew from experience that things were unlikely to get better as the evening wore on. That said, she also had no inkling of what was to come. The following morning, her Aunt Kathy gathered Lucretia, Candice, and Sheena together and told them the news: their father was dead, their mother was in jail, and they were going to live with their Grandma Iona.

Although Brenda had never managed to extricate herself from her marriage, she had been a steady and loving presence for her girls, even under the most difficult circumstances. But life in Grandma Lane's house was now, if anything, even grimmer than it had been when Brenda was so anxious to leave it a decade earlier. Although Lucretia was thankful that her grandparents never badmouthed her father, they also never discussed the fact that the children were practically orphaned. "In Iona's house," Lucretia said later, "I couldn't talk about what had happened. I couldn't grieve."

Soon after Brenda went to prison, Grandpa Alvis died, leaving Iona even more depressed than usual. As the eldest child, Lucretia was expected to be the babysitter, the housekeeper, and the cook. Iona, drink in hand, would bark orders at Lucretia from her chair in the living room about the right ways to prepare each meal. On Saturdays the entire house had to be scrubbed down, including the two bathrooms, before her granddaughter would be allowed to go out with friends. "Meanwhile," Lucretia said, "Iona drank until she couldn't get out of bed to drink any more."

While Lucretia was living with Iona, the reality of her childhood and its consequences finally dawned on her. "I felt ashamed and guilty," she later recalled. "I came from a screwed-up home. This realization set in soon after my dad's death. The pain of what happened was too awful. As a child, I was closed to discussing what had happened. But it was something I always carried with me."

The children were allowed to see Brenda for two nights in prison every three months; in other words, the family could be together for twelve days a year. According to Lucretia, these visits were packed with loving and intense discussions about what had happened to them as a family. Brenda also called her children from prison as frequently as she could. Still, those brief visits couldn't compensate for the bleakness of their present lives or the horror of their family's past.

At fourteen, after spending almost five years with Iona, Lucretia ran away from home. Although she would periodically return to her grandmother's to check on her two younger sisters, she mostly bounced between her Aunt Anita's house (Rick's sister) and her Aunt Kathy's. Both women were struggling with drug addictions, but at least they didn't spend all of their time telling her what to do. She dropped out of school, joined a gang, and began experimenting with drugs. She frequently got into fights, priding herself on her tough style and the fact that she didn't take "shit" from anybody.

The following year, Lucretia met Bobby, a sixteen-year-old car thief. The pair immediately became best friends. Their chief preoccupations were stealing cars, drinking beer, smoking weed, and snorting and smoking methamphetamine. From Lucretia's viewpoint, life was vastly improved. Bobby was charming, funny, loyal, and a good companion. He was also her first serious boyfriend, and the bond was extremely powerful. Soon she was pregnant.

After their daughter was born, Lucretia's relationship with Bobby proved to be as volatile as her parents' had been. The striking difference was that Brenda and Rick's respective roles—good/bad, law-abiding/criminal, victim/perpetrator—were blurred in the dynamic between the younger couple from the beginning. Like Rick, Bobby expected the mother of his child to settle down and be a housewife, but Lucretia wasn't interested. Lucretia recalls the day Bobby spat in her face—she responded by hitting him over the head with a case of baby formula.

Before long, Bobby's parents had relieved the young couple of the baby, but the pattern between them was set: they couldn't get along, but they also couldn't make a complete break. Eventually, Bobby was arrested for stealing cars. Over the next few years, both of them were in and out of jail, Lucretia for check fraud and drug possession. When she and Bobby reunited, as they often did, it always ended in violence.

Bobby not only refused to be faithful to Lucretia but also flaunted his cheating—just as her father had. On one occasion, Lucretia came after him at the home of one of his girlfriends. Bobby, livid, hit Lucretia hard on the head with a gun. On another occasion, Bobby and Lucretia were visiting Iona when another girlfriend showed up for a date. Lucretia, humiliated and seething at yet another betrayal, tried to knock Bobby to the ground and started beating his chest with her fists. It took several people to pull her off of him. During a later incident, Bobby picked up a girlfriend in his car, and a fight ensued when Lucretia, spotting them together, tried to attack the girl with a screwdriver.

Bobby and Lucretia were a perfect example of a couple engaged in mutual combat, both ready and willing to physically strike out against the other. The tenor of their relationship feels very different from the relationship between Rick and Brenda. Lucretia was, in a sense, following in the footsteps of both of her parents simultaneously: obsessively attached to Bobby, she was perversely loyal to him, as her mother was to her father, and yet she rejected the role of the passive wife and mother, which Brenda embraced right up until the end, and instead went at the world with all of her father's rage.

Lucretia's relationship with Bobby could easily have proved as lethal as her parents' marriage did. The prevalence of drugs and weapons in their lives, combined with their deep need for one another and their equally deep fury at one another, produced some unnervingly close calls. After Lucretia spent one evening helping her Aunt Anita move, she returned to find Bobby convinced that she'd been flirting with the moving men. Bobby called her a bitch and a whore, but the fight unexpectedly became more serious when he suddenly pointed a loaded gun at her head and said he was going to kill her. "Luckily," Lucretia recalled, "after a while he quieted down."

Lucretia remembers another evening when Bobby really wanted them to go to the movies together. After the show, he insisted they go to a motel room. Lucretia, who was supposed to go to work that night, felt compelled to call in sick. This wasn't the first time she'd made excuses for her absences, and a few days later, she was fired. She came home after hearing the news, in a funk and "totally stoned," vowing to kill Bobby. Luckily, she passed out, but not before announcing to her lover: "One of us is leaving in a hearse, the other in a cop car"—a scenario that would have eerily echoed her own family history.

Lucretia and Bobby never managed to separate voluntarily. In 2000, they were separated by the State of California: Lucretia was convicted of car theft, and Bobby was convicted of attempted murder, after shooting a man in the chest who was involved in an argument with one of his friends. He was sentenced to a twenty-three-year term.

THE DYNAMICS OF INTIMATE ABUSE

WHO STARTED IT VERSUS BLAMING THE VICTIM

When parents are trying to sort out a fight between children, one of the first questions they ask is often, "Who started it?" Let's say Jimmy punches his sister Suzanna in the leg while they are watching TV. Maybe Jimmy's actions had nothing to do with his sister; he is angry because he has just been told he won't be getting a new computer game for Christmas. But perhaps Suzanna said or did something mean to her brother. Or she said something that unintentionally provoked her brother's anger. Ideally, the adults involved are not only trying to figure out which child deserves to be punished but also trying to understand the dynamic between the siblings so that they can improve it.

We all recognize the importance of dynamics in our intimate relationships. Negative patterns established in childhood often pursue us into adult life. For example, it may be predictable that when you arrive home for Christmas, your mother greets you by criticizing your outfit, and then she complains that your foul moods always ruin your holidays together. Similarly, couples have their own lists of long-standing grievances: A husband habitually leaves the bathroom looking like a pigsty and then seems surprised when his wife is upset. He doesn't understand why she's giving him the silent treatment; she wonders why he always insists on making a mess when he knows it upsets her.

When it comes to such grievances in *violent* relationships, however, exploring the dynamic—who started what, when and how it happened, and what happened next—is taboo. The battered women's movement taught us that any exploration of this dynamic would be blaming the victim: For example, if Stacey refused to wash her husband's work clothes, that didn't mean he had a right to slap her across the face. And often, of course, as we saw in the last chapter, and in Rick and Brenda's story, the "trigger" for the violence can be very obscure; the recipient of the abuse is merely standing in for the original object of the abuser's rage.

Our fear of blaming the victim is admirable, but it too has had unintended consequences. For one thing, it presumes that the violence is always one-sided, when it often goes both ways. It also overlooks the fact that victims frequently do feel in some way responsible; simply telling them not to feel guilty doesn't make those feelings go away. Those guilty feelings can also fester into anger. Understanding the dynamic in abusive relationships is key to preventing the recurrence of violence in the future.

WHAT INFLUENCES A VIOLENT DYNAMIC?

"Dynamics" is a word of Greek origin describing the way in which "forces shift or change in relation to each other." The dynamic is the force created between two people—the exchange that exists as a result of two people's contributions to a joint enterprise. Each person's contribution to the dynamic is independent, but those independent contributions, when mixed together, become the dynamic

As we have already explored, many different factors influence the dynamic of a violent relationship—just as they do any relationship. At the most particular level, there are the personal characteristics of each partner. ("I hate being nagged." "He can't stand being ignored." "She refuses to tell me what she's thinking.") Then there is his or her personal history—how the person was raised and how he or she responded to that upbringing. ("Everyone in my family is like that—screaming constantly." "Her mother was an alcoholic, so my wife had to raise her siblings.").

Then there are the larger cultural contexts in which the couple lives, the expectations associated with gender, religion, race, and class. ("It's his job to support the family." "She'll have as many children as I say." "No real man would cry in front of his children." "To disobey the head of the family is a sin against God.").

We also need to ask, Who has the power in the relationship? Who asserts it, how, when, and with what degree of force? ("I am always walking on eggshells. I never know what will set him off." "Day and night, she's after me, running me down for God knows what." "If he hits me, he knows I'll give it right back to him—that's who I am.")

What is the nature of the connection in the couple? Do they share a mythology about their intimacy? ("We have tough times, but we're soul mates.

We couldn't live without each other.") Or do they tell very different stories? ("She's the most selfish person alive." "He makes my life a living hell.") Do they seem loosely or tightly bound together, and by what—love, fear, habit, animosity, need? Finally, what is the evolution of the violent dynamic—how does it grow and change over time? Even when the pattern *doesn't* change, the meaning of the pattern can shift for the couple involved, and that can be equally significant.

When we review, after the fact, the specifics of a violent domestic incident, the facts can seem fairly straightforward—and from a legal point of view, perhaps they are. If, however, one wants to understand the dynamic that produced the violence and the nature of the back-and-forth, all the influences I have listed may significantly alter one's initial assessment of the violent incident.

A particularly striking example of these forces at work can be seen in a case study by Melvin Lansky, a psychiatrist who oversaw the Los Angeles Family Treatment Program. Lansky describes the therapy sessions of a couple named Mario and Anna. Initially, Mario appears to be the aggressor, and Anna appears to be the victim. But Lansky's portrait of their relationship—which relies heavily on the transcripts of their joint counseling sessions—presents a more nuanced picture. As Lansky outlines the nature of their dynamic, all the influences listed above are starkly illustrated.

MINING THE LAYERS OF AGGRESSION

Mario, thirty-two, and Anna, forty-six, have been together for a year and a half and married for six months when Mario doesn't return home one night. Then the next day, on her way to church, Anna sees Mario with another woman— driving in the car that Anna had bought for him. In the ensuing confrontations between the couple over this incident, Mario hits Anna for the first time and then hits her again in two subsequent fights that same week. Mario agrees with Anna that he is out of control: both husband and wife appear eager for couples counseling.

In Lansky's account of the therapy, however, it seems that neither of them is particularly concerned about Mario's infidelity—or for that matter, his physical aggression. Instead, Anna is anxious to explain that Mario is a terrible provider. Although he is good at getting jobs, he seems incapable of keeping them—"either he is not experienced enough," she guesses, "or his emotional problems have affected his ability to work." How, she asks the therapist, can she be expected to take care of them both financially?

Mario feels that Anna is consistently unsupportive of his ambitions and goals. He argues that he wants to work, but that he has trouble getting along with other people—that's why he is keen to open up his own mechanic shop. If you tell a brake lining to go to hell, he points out, nobody cares. And Anna has the savings, so why does she refuse to help him? Isn't that what a loving wife should do—support her husband's attempts to fulfill his dreams for their life together? Their respective complaints demonstrate that both Anna and Mario want to be taken care of by the other while maintaining a sense of independence and control. Moreover, both of them rely on conventional expectations about how husbands and wives should behave in order to buttress their arguments.

As the sessions proceed, the therapist tries to explore the ways in which the couple's past histories may be affecting their marriage. Anna was one of seven children; her father was a drinker, and her mother yelled a lot. Growing up, she almost always sided with her mother. It also gradually becomes clear that she has been married not twice, as she originally implies, but four times before, and that all of her husbands have disappointed her in some way: one couldn't satisfy her sexually; the last one before Mario was an alcoholic. "Mario doesn't drink," Anna says. "He doesn't work either. At least Paul worked." But although Anna constantly uses her past husbands against Mario, she of course can't deny that she is the common denominator in all of these failed marriages.

Mario, on the other hand, is still haunted by his father, a Marine drill sergeant who deliberately humiliated his son throughout his childhood. "He made me feel like an idiot," says Mario. "He didn't know how to handle a kid. . . . He was used to handling eighteen-year-olds on the drill field. . . . They understood it, why couldn't I? But I wasn't old enough to understand it." Now he has married a woman who is equally uncomprehending. "She has no idea what my experience levels are," Mario complains bitterly, "and she'll sit there and say I'd better crawl before I can walk, and I've heard my father say that all my goddamn life." In this violent relationship, Lansky points out, *both* partners trigger a feeling of shame in the other. Much of their aggressive and shaming behavior is a response to being shamed themselves.

Ironically, although it quickly becomes clear how all of these influences have contributed to the destructive dynamic between Anna and Mario, they show no signs of increased empathy or understanding of their predicament. The transcripts reveal not a dialogue but two competing monologues: both husband and wife are invested in being heard by the therapist, but they don't appear remotely interested in the opinions or feelings of the other. What, precisely, binds them together? There are no signs of affection in their exchanges, and yet they are deeply enmeshed: Mario struggles to understand why he makes himself vulnerable to Anna. ("Anna seems to have a talent for pushing buttons that make me go. . . . Nobody's been able to get to those buttons before because I always protected them very well. . . . I'm much more emotional with her than I ever would get with anybody else.") Anna struggles to understand why she stays with a man who doesn't meet her expectations. Perhaps the failure implicit in parting is unbearable, but the prognosis for change in the relationship seems equally poor. One is not surprised to learn that the couple abandons the therapy abruptly, disappointed and angry at the therapist's failure to meet their needs.

Perhaps the most illuminating aspect of Lansky's case study, however, is that its generous use of dialogue conveys a vivid sense of the back-and-forth between the couple, and it is *Anna* rather than Mario who comes across as the more aggressive party. Although Mario proudly describes himself at one point as a man powerful enough to take a pipe and bend it "into a pretzel," he is unremittingly under attack during their counseling sessions: almost the entire discussion consists of Anna running him down while he attempts to defend himself. Even his criticisms of her revolve around her treatment of him, whereas her unsolicited comments are all about his character. Most striking is the fact that Mario can barely get a sentence out before Anna has interrupted to disagree with him—despite assurances from the therapist that she will have her time to speak. Clearly Anna is correct in her assessment that Mario has psychological difficulties in working with others, but her unconscious desire seems to be to keep him in that damaged place.

"He wants to start at the top," Anna says at one point. "Everybody would like to, but unfortunately everybody doesn't get to. . . . Last week he was talking about his ideas. Every time he has an idea he brings it up, and I squash it. . . . He's got a lot to learn." And although Mario often recognizes the truth of Anna's criticism, her relentlessly aggressive and belittling approach both enrages and disorients him: "I can sit there for three hours and listen. But I can't speak for about 1 minute before she steps on me, stomps, and I have to start all over." Mario and Anna only participated in four therapy sessions, but these recorded exchanges between them provide a revealing glimpse of how complicated and layered the dynamic of intimate abuse can be. The psychic violence inherent in their language predicts the likelihood that physical violence will follow. By the time Mario says, "It's almost like I have to hit her to get her attention," the ways in which Anna's aggression elicited his own are all too clear.

WHAT DOES VIOLENCE SAY?

All forms of violence, whether physical, sexual, or emotional, are also messages—powerful, destructive gestures that communicate how someone is feeling. Speaking *through* violence is almost always an attempt to get the other person's attention through verbal or physical contact. ("I can't get her off the phone unless I threaten to hit her." "He doesn't listen until I scream at him." "He only notices when I refuse to say a word.")

Communication styles involving violence obviously vary. Some people fight with words; others fight with fists or with silence. These styles of communication, violent or otherwise, are nearly always learned in childhood. It is predictable that someone who grew up in an extremely verbally aggressive family would experience a partner's yelling differently from someone who grew up in a family where insults were rarely exchanged. But violence that is learned *always* comes with a story—why someone believes that she must be violent, or that she can't help being violent, or that her violence is justified.

Most often that story is a simple one—someone hurt me, and so I have to strike back. Sometimes the victim is the same person who inflicted the earlier hurt; sometimes it is another person who caused the initial pain. In general, society dismisses the reasons offered by perpetrators for their behavior as being merely self-serving. Dismissing these reasons without examining them, however, forgoes an opportunity to understand intimate violence, let alone do something about it.

Viewing violence as communication—or, more accurately, as failed communication—also helps explain why victims and perpetrators often play both roles. In my relationship with David, the aggressive communication was like a volley. Sometimes David's communication was intentionally hurtful; sometimes mine was. In Mario and Anna's relationship, Mario's violence was physical; Anna's was verbal. Finding a nonviolent language to express feelings, especially anger, is one objective for those struggling to break the cycle of abuse.

Two overlapping needs often prompt violent communication: the need for release and the need for control. Understanding the differences between these two needs takes us closer to clarifying what the violent speaker hopes to communicate.

Many of us experience physical and emotional abuse as a release of the other person's inner feelings—a release we often find ourselves unable to fend off or soften. We've all been exposed to anger that seems to come out of nowhere, as though a switch has been flipped. We may also have experienced that lack of command over our own feelings. A person in this situation appears to be in the grip of a strong emotion that must be released, causing him to lash out. Often he appears to be possessed by something larger than himself, perhaps prompting the comment, "What's gotten into you?" These moments of transformation don't have to be physically violent to be troubling: the fact that a loved one may suddenly look or sound like a completely different person is upsetting enough.

At the same time, most of us have learned by now that intimate violence can also be used to control one's partner and diminish his or her power in the process. Controlling access to friends and family, exerting financial control, and manipulating someone into behaving in a particular way are all forms of coercion. Domestic violence advocates have pointed out that most abusers have no difficulty controlling their anger at work or in public. By implication, if they are violent only toward their partners but not elsewhere, it is because they give themselves permission to behave that way. Even Rick, who was an extremely violent person, usually refrained from hitting his children.

This issue of control, however, is more complicated than it at first appears: We must consider where that desire for control comes from. The person who is the victim of this kind of controlling behavior will frequently argue, for example, that the lover's controlling impulse paradoxically comes from feeling *out of control*. ("He just lost his job. I know he's just trying to get his life back by controlling me.") This understanding may lead to a tolerance of the abuse that outsiders find mystifying. Yet the person being controlled understands all too well. ("This always happens whenever my wife gets really anxious about something.") Over time, though, the person who is being controlled may—and probably should—stop tolerating this behavior.

I often experienced David's violence as *releasing* the tension that built up within him when he was angry. Perhaps it was because I thought I understood where the tension came from (anger at his mother) that I tolerated his outbursts as long as I did. David's verbal attempts to *control* my life—telling me what I could wear and whom I could see—felt different from these moments of release and seemed to come from his need to exert power over me. Interestingly, the moments in which David communicated his need for domination were more difficult for me to sympathize with than the moments in which he released his anger toward me.

I also used to manipulate David, of course: continuing to see Charles, despite David's objections, gave me more leverage in the relationship. I felt that I needed this leverage to maintain some balance of power in the relationship. And ultimately, I rejected David's control over me by rejecting him altogether. It is important to keep in mind that, even though one partner may be more abusive than the other, often both parties are engaging in hostile communications and power plays.

The larger problem is that both these strategies—violence as a form of release and violence as a means of control—are abusive and dysfunctional: if such gestures *do* constitute a communication, it is a declaration rather than a real invitation to discuss. Nevertheless, learning to recognize their underlying purpose is the first step to dismantling the highly destructive habits that plague so many of our intimate relationships.

NOT ALL VIOLENT DYNAMICS ARE THE SAME

During the last thirty years, while activists and reformers have fought to define domestic violence as men exerting power and control over women, researchers have discovered that violence between intimate partners is often far more complex than the original feminist vision anticipated. Who would have thought then, as we see now, that women could be violent, too, or that wives would be getting arrested for domestic violence crimes? Mario and Anna's interactions support the idea that issues of power and control are key to understanding how and why violence erupts in personal relationships, but they also prove that these elements don't always play out in predictable ways.

Michael Johnson, associate emeritus professor of sociology, women's studies, and African American studies at Pennsylvania State University, believes that the issue of who controls what in a violent relationship is key, but he does *not* believe that every violent relationship is merely an exercise in control. He has therefore developed a broader set of definitions in an attempt to accommodate all forms of domestic abuse.

Most dangerous, according to Johnson, are those who exert a great deal of power and control over their partners. High controllers like O. J. Simpson and Rick Aris exhibit behavior that Johnson characterizes as "intimate terrorism"; their violence is likely to escalate over time, and it can prove to be lethal. These are the cases we are most likely to read about in the paper or see on the six o'-clock news. In 97 percent of these relationships, the man is the one in control; his victim is nearly always female.

But all dynamics are, by their very nature, *dynamic*: Occasionally, the victim of this sort of violence will fight back, exploding the power structure of the relationship and seriously injuring or killing the aggressor: Johnson refers to this behavior as violent resistance. After years of either enduring or trying to escape Rick's battering, Brenda turned the tables and shot her husband; in Johnson's terms she would be a violent resistor. She went from having little or no control over the relationship to taking total control by ending Rick's life. In 96 percent of these cases, the resistor is a woman.

Rick and Brenda's relationship is the sort that battered women's advocates educated us about—in fact, one could argue that men like Rick became synonymous with the label "batterer." But there are lots of other men and women living with violence who don't fall squarely into the intimate terrorism or violent resistance model. In fact, batterers like Rick and victims like Brenda are quite rare.

Sometimes, for example, *both* members of the couple are high controllers. According to Johnson's categories, Lucretia's relationship to Bobby is an example of "mutual violent control." This sort of relationship, which is also uncommon, may be less disturbing than Rick and Brenda's because the power seems more evenly distributed in the relationship and neither party seems to fear the other. After all, who exactly is the victim? But it can still be extremely dangerous, especially when there are drugs or weapons involved.

Most violent couples are engaged in what Johnson calls "situational couple violence"—these men and women physically or psychologically go after one another when specific tensions in the relationship erupt, rather than as part of an overall attempt to control the other partner. Often both men and women initiate and participate in this sort of low-level violence. Sometimes this involves some back-and-forth, but it rarely becomes life-threatening. Once again, the partners tend to be more evenly matched, and—as they are not attempting a "total win," the way a high controller might—the situations tend to be far less volatile. This sort of low-level abuse certainly isn't healthy, but it is generally more common, less dangerous, and less unjust.

In a recent article he wrote with Janel Leone, Johnson reminds us that these questions of categorization are not merely academic. Recognizing the particularities of violent dynamics and what they mean determines how we respond to them—as individuals and as a society: "Just as intimate terrorism and situational couple violence have different outcomes, they probably have different causes and remedies. Only research that attends to these differences can effectively inform social policy, educational efforts, and intervention strategies."

7

SITUATIONAL COUPLE VIOLENCE

When psychologist Antonia Henderson began her study of why women remain in relationships with intimate terrorists, she realized that this type of relationship was only one possible dynamic; most of the women she spoke with, in fact, had simply not experienced the type of violence she'd anticipated uncovering. Henderson writes, "It was also evident that the aggression was going both ways—that women were just as likely to be psychologically aggressive or to occasionally push, shove, or slap a partner as vice versa. And it was also clear that this kind of aggression, or relationship dysfunction, was damaging to men as well as to women. My original question of why women stay with abusive partners was meaningless in this context."

The sort of dynamic that Henderson describes here is a perfect example of Michael Johnson's situational couple violence. The violence that erupted in Jeff and Sarah McPherson's marriage falls squarely into this category.

Jeff and Sarah are low controllers—partners whose problems often spring from familiar conflicts about children and money and household arrangements. They consider themselves equals, and neither one expresses any interest in dominating the other. That does not mean, however, that control is not important, or that each of them does not try to exercise it within the dynamic of their relationship. In fact, a sense of being overwhelmed and out of control has contributed significantly to their marital difficulties.

Sarah and Jeff agree that a strong friendship existed between them from the earliest days of their relationship, about fifteen years ago. They fell in love quickly and lived together for four years before getting married.

Both Jeff and Sarah experienced tumultuous childhoods. For most of his formative years, Jeff's family lived a nomadic life, moving from town to town as his father tried to eke out a living as a mechanic. Jeff was one of seven children, and he always felt that he was the "black sheep" in his family. He was regularly hit and humiliated by his father. Typically, he would be forced to bend over and grab his ankles so that his parents could spank him—sometimes with a hand, sometimes with a belt or a paddle. He was also beaten up by his older brother on a regular basis. On one occasion, while he was sleeping, his sister told his father that Jeff had been rude to her. "My father stormed into the room, grabbed me by my hair, pulled me out of bed, dragged me across the floor, down the hallway, and into the living room," Jeff recalls bitterly. "There he ordered me to beg my sister for forgiveness for whatever it was I supposedly had done."

Jeff's unhappiness at home came out in other ways. Throughout his teenage years, he was involved in frequent fights in school, and he was arrested for smoking pot. When he was sixteen, he moved out. Sometimes he lived on the street; sometimes he stayed with other relatives. He supported himself by doing odd jobs.

Life was difficult on his own, but it was also less hostile and more secure; Jeff was able to build a good life for himself. He put himself through college, paid back all his debts to his parents, established himself professionally, and even bought a house. As he looked back on his childhood, he understood that his parents had been "overwhelmed" by the responsibilities—financially and emotionally—of parenting seven children. He hoped that if he one day decided to marry, his future wife would share his determination not to repeat their mistakes. "I had my own home," he tells me, "and things were comfortable for me."

Sarah also had a difficult childhood. Her stepfather was "horrible," a large, scary man who constantly yelled and did things like pull phone cords out of walls. "He had a daughter, and he was always comparing us," Sarah recalls. "One time, he was angry at me because I joined a church group. Can you imagine?" Her mother never stuck up for her, and she felt abandoned. She had a number of animals as a kid, and she saw these relationships as key in getting her through her lonely and chaotic existence. Rather than share Jeff's wariness of dependents, she has embraced a life of children and pets.

Temperamentally, Jeff and Sarah complement each other. Jeff is cautious by nature; security is paramount to him, so he is averse to taking risks and trying new things. Sarah is impulsive and in constant motion, energetic and eager to say yes. As Jeff describes her, "She throws herself to the wind." She also has a history of responding to anxiety by spending money she doesn't have—a compulsion Jeff has helped her curtail. When things are going well, the couple's dynamic is therefore quite healthy: Sarah has drawn Jeff out into a wider, richer life, while he has given her stability. Both Sarah and Jeff felt that they had found a haven in their marriage. Together they created the family that neither of them ever had, and they have made a huge effort not to pass along to their kids the legacy of physical and emotional abuse that they themselves endured as children.

In times of tension, however, we all know that the same qualities that once seemed so alluring or consoling in a partner can quickly become threatening and unbearable. Ever since things first became serious between Jeff and Sarah, there has been a push-me/pull-you dynamic between the two lovers—as there often is in adults who had insecure attachments to their parents in childhood. Clinically, Jeff would be described as avoidant. Before they married, the couple even separated for a time; although Jeff loved Sarah, he wasn't sure that he wanted to "go on Sarah's roller coaster." Marriage was an opportunity, yes, but marriage to an impulsive woman like Sarah was also a threat.

Sarah, on the other hand, could be described as anxious or preoccupied in her attachments—strongly drawn to others, even if the connection is problematic. Certainly it was problematic with Jeff. He was quite grumpy—just like her grandfather, Sarah later realized, who had been one of the only positive male presences in her childhood. But she could see that Jeff was also a good and loyal person underneath his pessimism and gloom, and she felt that they had a profound connection. During their separation Sarah suffered crippling anxiety attacks, as if her entire world was coming apart: "I just felt this void without him, and it was awful." Eventually, they decided to reconcile and commit to having children together. Jeff made it clear, however, that there was a limit to what he felt willing to take on. "We had a well-established agreement," he says. "I would get married. I also consented to one child, but *absolutely* no more than two."

Over the next six years, only one significant act of violence scarred the relationship, and it was directed not at Sarah but at a complete stranger. Jeff was often moved to punish the aggressive behavior of others on the road, and he rarely kept these feelings in check; Sarah frequently complained about her husband's driving. One day, when Sarah was pregnant with their second child and they were driving to a wedding, Jeff cut off a motorcyclist towing a trailer who had cut him off seconds before. When the driver gave him the finger, Jeff slammed on the brakes. The motorcyclist couldn't stop in time, swerved, wiped out, and was horribly injured. Jeff was arrested, and forced to go into therapy and take anger management classes. The McPhersons were also sued and came close to losing their house. In the end, the accident cost them $50,000 and almost ruined their marriage. Jeff felt terrible about the consequences of his impulses; Sarah was beside herself with anger.

Clearly Jeff's road rage was deeply connected to his childhood. It also became a part of the dynamic of his marriage: Sarah and the children had to pay the price for Jeff's actions, even if they were not responsible for inflicting the original hurt that made Jeff so angry in the first place. But it is also important to ask whether there was any stress *within* the marriage at this point that might have pushed Jeff to the breaking point.

Given both the timing and the consequences of his actions here, one can't help but wonder if they were in any way unconsciously related to the impending pressures of having a second child—he was, after all, literally slamming on the brakes. Jeff also knew that Sarah hated this sort of behavior in the car, so the act was also indirectly hostile to his wife. Ironically, of course, the accident diminished rather than strengthened Jeff's power in the relationship, realizing his worst fears: his increased responsibilities for his wife and his children now coincided with diminished resources to provide for them.

Whatever the source of Jeff's anger, the accident was a perfect example of an act of humiliation precipitating an act of violence. It also encapsulates Jeff's implicitly defensive posture, which characterizes so much about his approach to both his marriage and the world in general. Jeff doesn't cut people off on the road as a matter of course; he cuts people off who cut *him* off. The world, like his family of origin, is not a safe place to be; he needs to take action as soon as he is threatened, or everyone will walk all over him. While Jeff's road rage is an expression of control, the framework of the gesture is entirely reactive. Jeff is not fighting for new territory, so to speak, but simply trying to hold on to his own.

At home, as the years passed, this proved to be a losing battle. Examining their respective accounts of what happened between them, we can trace a shift in the McPherson household over time. The family no longer sounds like an entity belonging to and created by both of them—a compromise between Sarah's rushing forward and Jeff's holding back. Instead, Sarah's assertive style seems to have gained momentum and become the dominant force within the family.

After the birth of their second child, Jeff's home was too small for their growing family. Sarah persuaded Jeff to buy a larger, older house that he would remodel. "Suddenly, we had taken on a significant amount of debt," Jeff explains. "This made me very uncomfortable. Sarah is also much more likely to spend money than I am. As a result, we've had constant money problems. On top of everything, both of us have very stressful and demanding jobs." When he wasn't working or taking care of the kids, there was always work to be done on the house. Life seemed to have become one long list of chores, leaving Jeff sullen and withdrawn.

Sarah loved having pets, but Jeff felt that they added to the general sense of stress and chaos at home. For Jeff, one cat and one dog was enough. Then Sarah found a stray cat. "I said, 'No more animals right now,'" Jeff recalls. "OK, we end up keeping that cat. Kind of like, 'Kids, you can keep the cat unless Dad says no.'" Then three months later, Sarah told her husband that they needed to get another dog. Their dog was her running companion, but now he was too old to keep up with her. Jeff said no to the dog, but Sarah got one anyway—a rambunctious pure-bred Labrador who loved to chew the moldings off the walls. "This was a house that I had spent years remodeling," Jeff observes, "so I wasn't too happy about that."

The last straw for Jeff, however, was when Sarah told him that she was expecting another baby. This explicitly violated the agreement they had made when they'd gotten married. "'Oops, oh, by the way, I'm pregnant again,'" Jeff says, mimicking his wife. "Now we were up to three cats, two dogs, and three kids. Let's just say that I wasn't on board for all of the above."

Sarah agrees that she broke her agreement with Jeff, but adds that the pregnancy was an accident. She explains that "it simply wasn't in my DNA to have an abortion," but she also adds that it wasn't "in Jeff's DNA to have a third child." Again, the language here is revealing. Having a third child is no longer a matter of shared responsibility and shared decision making but instead a question of DNA—something that, like an accident, lies outside of the couple's control.

Certainly the additions of a puppy and a newborn increased the stress on the marriage. Both Jeff and Sarah were always exhausted, and money was even tighter. "Jeff's always had a short temper," Sarah says. "Now with the third baby, he was constantly irritated. Also, we had no sex life. I felt a low-grade frustration in which nobody was getting their needs met." Sarah feared that Jeff wasn't bonding with the new baby, which she found very upsetting.

Another flashpoint in the marriage became the cooking, which Sarah experienced as a tremendous burden and which Jeff wasn't willing to help with. But Jeff insisted that his wife had made the kitchen "an impossible and dangerous place to work." He could never find anything in the drawers. When he opened the cabinets, things would fall out. Worst of all, the pots hanging overhead were often precarious. "Two or three times, heavy enameled pots hanging on hooks have crashed to the floor, narrowly missing me," Jeff complained. "It's just madness and chaos. I can't stand it. And I won't cook there." He offered to help her reorganize it, but Sarah refused. She saw Jeff's worrying as the cause of his problems, not as the result of some other problem. "When he gets stressed or anxious, he blows up," she explains. "It's small things, like—I'm just making this up—'The toaster just dropped crumbs on the counter,' and it's a crisis." The kitchen remained as it was.

From one angle, the McPhersons were a fairly ordinary American family, struggling with the responsibilities of work and home. Yet at the same time, they were re-creating the landscape of their respective childhoods, in which they had each felt abandoned and unsafe in different ways. Their ongoing dispute about the kitchen functioned as a perfect metaphor for their estrangement. As any couple knows, these "small" issues often represent deep fears and power struggles within the relationship and can be of critical importance to the couple's future happiness. This was the state of the marriage when it turned suddenly violent in 2005.

It was a typical evening. Jeff had just picked up the three kids from day care; Sarah was not yet home. The dogs, who'd been cooped up in the basement all day, were barking loudly, anxious to be let upstairs. After strapping the baby into the high chair, Jeff went down to let them out.

"On the staircase," he says, "I had a problem with the Lab."

The younger dog jumped up onto Jeff and pushed him into a framed poster hanging on the wall, which then fell and broke, so that the stairs around them were suddenly covered with glass, but the Lab was still jumping. Sarah arrived home and heard Jeff cursing and struggling with the dog below. She came to the top of the basement stairs. Realizing she was about to enter the fray, Jeff ordered her to "stay back." But Sarah, believing Jeff needed help and feeling the dog was being mistreated, headed down the staircase. Upon seeing Sarah, the Lab became even more excited. Jeff, trying vainly to contain the situation, punched the dog hard and yanked his collar. Sarah approached Jeff and grabbed for the dog's collar.

"We then began fighting over control of the dog," Sarah remembers.

Their stories explaining what happened next differ.

During the struggle, Sarah believes that she kicked Jeff in the leg to get him to move away from the Lab, so that she could take control. Jeff says that Sarah kicked him in the face and that the blow knocked off his glasses. Without his glasses Jeff is legally blind. Jeff remembers trying to retrieve them as the dog continued to jump and bark. Jeff says he then lost his balance and fell two or three steps, his arm striking Sarah in the face. He remembers intending to push her—in what he describes as a "'what are we doing here, fighting over the dog?' kind of way"—before he fell. Sarah, however, remembers the blow as a deliberate punch.

"I knew that he was mad. I think he lost it for a moment—just the flicker of a moment—and then realized what he did," Sarah recalls. "Later, he just kept saying, 'Oh, my God, if you just hadn't come down the stairs.'" Sarah was wearing metal-framed glasses, and Jeff's blow smashed them into her face, causing a deep gash dangerously close to her right eye. Blood spurted over Sarah's face and neck. Later, there would be severe bruising.

The fact that Jeff and Sarah don't remember what happened in exactly the same way is not unusual, and it doesn't necessarily mean that one of them is deliberately lying. Different versions of violent events, *especially* when both parties are actively engaged in the moment of conflict, are common. What is perhaps more significant—and more hopeful for the McPhersons' marriage— is that they were willing to admit that there *were* two plausible versions of what had happened. Not surprisingly, each of them favors his or her own version, but both acknowledge that it might not be correct. Equally important, both of them immediately recognized the gravity of the situation.

"At that moment," remembers Jeff, "everything stopped, and everything changed." Sarah agrees. "I was like, 'Am I in somebody else's nightmare? This can't be happening to me.'" She remembers sitting with her husband in the ER, waiting: "I just kept looking at him, saying, 'What were you thinking? I can't believe that you did this!' And he was looking back at me, going, 'I don't know; I feel awful; I'm so sorry.'"

Ideally, a couple seeks help before their relationship turns violent. Unfortunately, however, even after this sort of explosion, many couples choose to deny the seriousness of their situation, and the McPhersons' example makes it easy to understand the temptation. After all, from one perspective, Sarah and Jeff were simply unlucky. What if the struggle hadn't taken place on the stairs, or around broken glass, which greatly exacerbated both the danger and Jeff's anxiety about it? What if Sarah had arrived home one minute later? The entire situation might have been avoided. The "special" nature of such moments encourages couples to simply bury them in horror. The "violence presents them with a distorted and ugly image of themselves and their partners," Eisikovits and Buchbinder observe, "which they feel a need to reject." In other words, it was an accident, and it won't ever happen again. The fact that our society still reinforces that "ugly" image by demonizing abusers only further discourages such couples from seeking help.

If we examine this particular incident closely, however, it seems obvious that through counseling, both members of the couple could come to better understand the dynamic and its predictability given each of their family histories. Jeff is overwhelmed—literally, in this case—by his wife's dog: "I am trying to get him up the stairs and keep him out of the glass and keep him somewhat under control." He is trying to protect the dog, but he is also angry at the dog: it's an emotionally loaded moment. Sarah intervenes, as she habitually does when Jeff seems overwhelmed, hoping to help. But she is also disregarding Jeff's warning not to come down the stairs, and she further excites the dog. Jeff then starts punching the dog, ostensibly to bring him under control but also because he's so angry. Sarah kicks Jeff in defense of the dog. Although she is the first person to initiate violence between them, she is so emotionally close to her animal that it almost feels like self-defense to her, or as if she is defending a child. From Jeff's perspective, however, she is joining forces with the dog against him—which, symbolically, she already has, by bringing the dog into his life in the first place. Within seconds he is attacked, blinded, and dangerously off-balance. In this enraged and vulnerable state, he strikes back. And just as in his road rage incident, the consequences of his actions are so grave that the potentially legitimate frustrations that provoked them are forgotten. Once more, he is in the wrong, the "black sheep of the family."

Even though Sarah blamed Jeff for hitting her, she still recognized that the violence between them was a shared problem—a result of the larger pressures on the marriage—and she was determined to get them into therapy. This was one of the reasons that Sarah told the truth at the hospital about what happened in the first place: she thought that they could be referred to community resources and counseling through their health plan. Jeff was ambivalent about the consequences of this honesty—since it eventually earned him a felony conviction and threatened his job status—but for him, too, the "we-ness" of the couple was still intact. He had the choice of doing community service instead of paying a large fine, but chose to pay because the service option would have meant six months away from the family on weekends. "I feel horrible about the whole thing—not only about the event, but about the implications of what it cost," he says. "$30,000—that's a lot of college education."

Months after Jeff's arrest, when things finally calmed down, he and Sarah searched for a private therapist who would work with them, and they began couples counseling. Now, nearly three years later, there is still some bitterness and distrust on both sides, but they agree that it has been extremely helpful. Unlike their encounter with the legal system, which seemed determined to break them apart, they are now working within a framework that supports them as a family and encourages them to change the destructive aspects of their dynamic.

Because Sarah is the preoccupied type, she has always felt that she has to manage the family and manage Jeff's own anger and anxiety—to put herself, in a sense, "between" Jeff and the world. For the preoccupied person, engagement is nearly always the immediate response, even when it repeatedly doesn't prove useful. For example, Sarah always wants to discuss everything until she feels it is resolved, whereas Jeff sometimes feels that he just needs to take a break to restore his sense of self. Sarah's engagement can be seen as cooperative or caretaking, but it can also be interfering and aggressive—just as it was when she tried to "help" Jeff with the dog.

On the other hand, even before their third child, Jeff was pulling away from his wife, and his habitually avoidant tendency was painful for her. It is easy to see how Sarah's need for connection and engagement may have unconsciously encouraged her to increase the size of her household—a need that has, in turn, further distanced her husband. Therapy, even in such a difficult period of their marriage, has restored Sarah's sense of intimacy and connection: "I think we could get through anything now." Their joint sessions have also helped Sarah to see that sometimes it is better to simply leave Jeff to find his own way through his emotions, even when she may think that she understands better or could manage things more effectively.

For Jeff, the therapy sessions have provided, in his words, a "safe" place in which his longstanding complaints about the marital dynamic can be validated. Their therapist has suggested that the circumstances of Jeff's childhood have left him in a state of hypervigilance, and that it is important for both him and Sarah to be alert to that. He has also given Jeff a sense that his marriage is finally, in small but concrete ways, moving in a positive direction.

One weekend, the McPhersons even hired a babysitter and began to reorganize the kitchen together. Sarah admitted that it worked better afterward. For Jeff, this was tremendously significant. It proved his willingness to actively participate in the marriage, but also that he wasn't willing to sacrifice his own needs entirely to hers: "Unless I have some say in making things work, I won't be engaged." Slowly but surely, both Sarah and Jeff are trying to learn when to separate and when to come together in more loving and productive ways, thereby greatly diminishing the chance that violence will recur between them. Only if the couple actively and consciously addresses the dynamic can the relationship change. Otherwise, the script begins to write itself.

What would have happened if the McPhersons hadn't confronted their issues in therapy? Eisikovits and Buchbinder, who have studied violent couples who stay together, stress that there are many different variant dynamics within that group; nevertheless, they trace several possible stages that these couples can go through, if the dynamic isn't altered. Even though they are studying physical violence, the stages they highlight in their research are also applicable to couples who are only verbally aggressive or psychologically violent with one another.

In the first stage, an isolated violent act is in response to a specific "infraction" committed by the other party and seen as having an objective. In the case of the McPhersons, Sarah kicked her husband to get him to stop hitting the dog; he struck her in response to being kicked. Each act was specifically rooted in time and place, a means to an end. Often such acts of violence are seen by those who commit them as being "for the good of the family"—necessary to address some threat. A husband who slapped his wife might say, "She went out and bought a couch that she knew we couldn't afford. She knew what was coming." A wife who threw a plate of food at her husband might say, "He thinks he can just flirt like crazy with our neighbor and then come in and eat the dinner I slaved over? I showed him what he could do with his dinner."

These incidents are often sparked by conflicts relating to domestic and family life but are also rooted in the inequality between the genders, as these topics suggest: child care, education, spending, employment, household chores. Although both partners in the examples above are being undeniably aggressive, there is still a sense of commonality—what Eisikovits and Buchbinder call "we-ness"—that each half of the couple thinks he or she is fighting to preserve: a solvent family or a romantically intact partnership.

If these sorts of incidents solidify into a pattern, however, they become more generalized, harder to change. The violence doesn't need an obvious catalyst. It can be triggered by a reminder of a past infraction or a suspicion of a future one: a husband is paying the bills, finds they are short on money, and assumes that his wife has spent it unwisely because she has done so in the past. A wife is waiting for her husband to come home, he is late for dinner, and she assumes that he is with another woman because he's cheated on her before. Each instance is seen as justification for some sort of attack, even before any real threat or wrongdoing has been established. Trust quickly erodes, and real communication becomes impossible. The couple's conversations become like Mario and Anna's therapy sessions: nothing is actually being heard, in any productive sense, by either party.

At this point, each member of the couple is on the defensive, and turns to protecting his or her own interests and sense of self. As each partner becomes more deeply entrenched in his or her position, the other partner is correspondingly more demonized. ("Yes, maybe I take money from him from time to time without telling him. But that's because I can't even buy myself a new blouse without getting hit for it. I do everything for him and the kids as it is. Does he ask me before he buys himself a new pair of shoes? He's impossible.") Communication becomes pointless, so deception becomes easily justified, even called for. ("How could I tell her there'd be other women at the conference? My wife is a lunatic. If I hadn't lied to her, she'd be calling me on the cell every half hour, making me look like an idiot in front of my employees. The less she knows about my business, the better.")

Eisikovits and Buchbinder describe how compromise has become tactically dangerous, because it might expose a weakness that could later be exploited. ("If I agree to review all my expenditures with him now, he's bound to use it against me later." "If I'm honest about this conference, she'll find a way to forbid me from going next time.") Both parties come to see compromise as morally suspect—a form of self-betrayal. ("He just wants me to play along with his games, but I won't. I refuse to live a lie." Or, "A man who lets his wife tell him what to do is a nothing, a zero. This is a matter of my self respect.") The other person has become the enemy, and yet the enemy is essential to each partner's sense of self because each one is now defined against the other. It is the tension of that resistance, in a sense, that keeps them standing: without the other, they lose their identity.

By now, both partners are leading parallel lives with parallel narratives, unable to come together in a happy or productive way. Fighting becomes the connection they share; violence becomes their shared life. By this stage, the dynamic continually reinforces itself:

> The vicious circle is further exacerbated by the fact that each partner interprets the other's behavior as provocative: The woman screams, the man refuses to hear, the woman screams louder, the man hits her, the

woman reciprocates. The woman wants to continue screaming but also wants her partner to stop beating her. The man similarly wants to keep slapping the woman and wants her to stop screaming. Each is focused on controlling the other rather than himself or herself. Once the script takes effect, violent incidents are transformed into a violent way of life. The conversion is complete, and the ritual of violence is their new religion. They are committed to it, and no specific reason is needed to trigger it.

Like a wheel rolling downhill, these abusive dynamics only gain momentum if they go unchecked.

8
THINKING BEYOND LABELS

The Odiernos and the Woodses

Although Michael Johnson's categories (described in chapter 6) are useful for reminding us that violent relationships can differ widely from one another, it is critical to remember that couples don't necessarily fit into any particular category and that no dynamic is necessarily fixed. A mutually violent couple might find themselves becoming increasingly controlling and volatile, for example. Or a relationship that initially looks fairly safe—like my relationship with David—can become a struggle marked by sexual intimidation and slashed tires. A relationship is organic rather than static: everything between two people is constantly evolving.

The marriages portrayed in this chapter don't subscribe to the standard definitions of domestic violence. Neither couple accurately represents the model of situational couple violence described in the previous chapter. At the same time, neither relationship supports our notion of what intimate terrorism looks like. Finally, both of these stories underscore once again the importance of recognizing that intimate violence is potentially deadly; even if you do not fear your partner, your belief that you can "manage" your abusive relationship may very well be an illusion.

THE LETHAL CONSEQUENCES OF PSYCHOLOGICAL ABUSE

In April 2005, Ben Odierno, a seventy-one-year-old real-estate millionaire on Manhattan's Upper East Side, fatally attacked his fifty-six-year-old wife during an argument over their separation agreement, stabbing her more than twenty times with a kitchen knife. The pastor next door to their townhouse called 911 when he heard a woman screaming. The police responding to the call encountered the

Odiernos' sons, Marcus, twenty-three, and Stephan, twenty-eight, chatting on a front stoop across the street; Stephan volunteered to unlock the door for the police. Stephan led them in and according to his report, found his parents lying together on the kitchen floor, covered in blood. When the police entered, Christine Odierno told them, "My husband did this. My husband stabbed me in the heart." Shortly afterward, she died. The final pathologist's report would state that Christine had almost forty cuts, bruises, abrasions, and stab wounds on her body.

Anyone who has been reading the newspapers for the last twenty years would say that this scenario resembles a classic example of domestic violence taken to its fatal extreme—and in fact that was what the prosecutor, Kerry O'-Connell, would eventually argue in court: that Christine was increasingly unhappy and fearful in her marriage to an extremely rich and controlling husband. When she finally had the courage to leave him, he killed her in a rage. Within days, neighbors had also come forward and told reporters that the Odiernos had been arguing for months. One woman said that Christine had predicted that her husband might harm her, and had confessed that she said she was afraid for her life.

The great surprise, however, was that the defense also argued that this was a case of domestic violence—and that Ben Odierno was the victim. And this, as it turned out, was the narrative of the marriage that was supported by the Odiernos' two sons: a history of psychological deterioration and mental cruelty that only came to an end when their father suddenly snapped. Preposterous as this might have seemed initially, news accounts of the trial and interviews with individual jurors afterward make it clear that the jury eventually found the defense's claims too compelling to be dismissed.

Friends and strangers alike testified that the Odiernos had a very good marriage for almost twenty years. Ben adored his pretty wife, who looked young enough to be his daughter, and Christine was a good mother. Still, Ben seemed to have been the primary nurturer of the two children. He loved to cook, and Christine loved to entertain; for years, the Odiernos regularly invited friends to their estate in the Catskills. Ben later recalled it as "a marriage made in heaven." But in 1996, around her fiftieth birthday, Christine started becoming increasingly hostile and withdrawn; she stopped giving parties, and guests were no longer so welcome in her home. Marcus testified at his father's trial that a friend of his was once asked to leave because his cologne was too strong.

As the years passed, her suspicion and hostility—especially where Ben was concerned—became increasingly pronounced. According to Ben's testimony at the trial, Christine refused to have sex with her husband, and after Stephan moved out to go to college, she forced Ben to share a room with Marcus. The younger son said that while he and his father slept, his mother would come into their room and wake them by rummaging through the closet or turning off the air-conditioning. In the mornings, she would sometimes lock herself in the bathroom for hours, refusing to get out when Marcus needed to get ready for school. Although Ben did most of the family's shopping and cooking, Christine would pointedly clear every plate at the table except for his, saying, "I'm not your maid." She took the boys on vacations, refusing to let Ben come along.

Christine began taunting and humiliating her husband, sometimes in front of other people, calling him "fat," "a slob," "a lazy bum," and a "piggy, piggy, oink, oink." Witnesses testified that Ben never responded angrily to her insults. Both he and his sons said that they loved her very much and believed that she was suffering from some sort of mental illness. By 2005, Christine had lost a great deal of weight, was eating only salad for dinner, and was hoarding large quantities of various items in garbage bags in the basement—bars of soap, cologne, empty water bottles, and picture frames.

When the prosecutor asked Ben why he didn't try to get his unstable wife committed, he said that he simply couldn't bear to do that to her. The sons reiterated that their father had often begged Christine to get psychiatric help, but that she had refused. "I'm not crazy," she'd yell. "You're the crazy one." In fact, she eventually convinced Ben to see a psychiatrist, who prescribed medication for depression, and although she refused to prepare food for him, Christine dispensed his medications to him daily.

Prosecutor O'Connell argued that Ben and his sons were colluding against Christine, and that the father used his money to manipulate the boys into supporting him—certainly a plausible scenario. But some of the most damning testimony came from outside the family. A neighbor reported that she'd met Ben while he was picking up his prescriptions at a local pharmacy. As they chatted, Ben showed her the long list of drugs he was taking. The neighbor, who favored homeopathic remedies, was horrified and told him so. As they walked back to their homes together, Christine pulled up in her Mercedes convertible, jumped out of the car, and asked the neighbor what she was doing with Ben. The neighbor explained that she'd told Ben that he shouldn't be taking so many drugs. At that point, the neighbor testified, Christine went "crazy" in the street, saying that she had no business helping Ben.

"Don't you understand?" Christine screamed. "I want him dead." Ben did not respond angrily to his wife's attack, the neighbor said, but simply retreated into his house.

In court, Stephan recalled a particularly unsettling incident that occurred in Hawaii, where he and his mother were looking at real estate. When the broker asked Christine if she was married, she said no, that she was a widow—an answer that echoes her remark to the neighbor that she wanted her husband dead. At the same time, in the months before her death, Christine often played the part of the victim. She went to a lawyer to discuss getting a divorce, telling him that she was physically and psychologically abused by her husband, who, she claimed, had moved money out of their joint accounts and hidden large amounts of cash in the basement ceiling. The lawyer who testified at the trial described her as "a frightened woman," but other people accused her of *literally* acting. Stephan's former girlfriend, who'd spent a lot of time at the Odiernos' house, testified that if you accidentally bumped into Christine in the kitchen, she would scream, "Get your hands off me—you're hurting me," and her sons claimed that she shouted similar things into the backyard, as if for the neighbors' benefit.

But it is also possible that Christine genuinely believed the essential truth of her position, even if she sometimes lied about the particulars. By the last year of her life, she also seemed to be harboring specific fantasies that her husband and sons wanted her dead. Marcus testified that his mother would hold a knife to her own neck and taunt her husband and sons to slit her throat. In either scenario—Christine as the widow or Christine as the murder victim—it was as if she envisioned a future big enough for only one of them, herself or her husband.

By January 2005, the problems in the Odierno family were becoming more public. At this time, Marcus had an apartment in the basement of his parents' townhouse; Stephan lived in another building that the Odiernos owned, several blocks away. One day, Marcus got mad at his mother because the garbage bags filled with her hoarded items were spreading into his room. An argument ensued, and Marcus threw an empty water bottle, which hit Christine's arm. She screamed, "You're trying to hurt me!" and called 911.

A police officer arrived and assessed the situation. According to Michael Stoller, one of the jurors at the trial, the officer, after observing that Christine was unhurt, spoke to all of them individually and recommended that the family seek psychological help for Christine.

After the incident in January, Christine continued to deteriorate and began to tell neighbors that Ben was trying to hurt her. In one instance, Christine went to a neighbor and asked her to write a letter to Christine's eighty-six-year-old mother, Jennie Kramer, who lived in Pennsylvania, to tell her that Christine was afraid of Ben. In another, Christine broke her wrist and told neighbors that Ben did it, although her family said that she had broken it at their home in the Catskills, when she fell off a stone wall. The medical report, based on Christine's own statements, eventually confirmed the latter story.

In early April, Christine went to a lawyer and filed for a separation—the first step to getting a divorce in New York. One peculiarity in their separation agreement, later to be emphasized by defense lawyer Jack Litman, was that Christine agreed to have Ben remain in the townhouse until the divorce was settled. Litman contended that if Christine truly feared Ben, she wouldn't have allowed him to continue living with her. In the meantime, a friend told Ben that if Christine threatened him, he should call the police—even if he wasn't afraid—just to have her threats on the record.

Ben claimed that he had been ready to sign the separation papers when his wife delivered them, the week before she was killed, but his sons insisted that he get his own lawyer. He met with an attorney, who told him not to sign the agreement, and they made another appointment for the following week. The lawyer later testified that Ben—who had lost more than fifty pounds in the previous six months due to the psychological strain of his home life—"looked like a whipped dog."

The following day, when Ben told Christine that he wouldn't sign, she became enraged and threatened to cut off his penis. Following his friend's advice, Ben called the police to report the threat. When the police arrived at the house, they told Ben that if he filed an incident report against his wife, Christine would be arrested. Ben refused. When he was asked in court whether he believed that his wife would have really cut off his penis, he said that he didn't know.

Marcus and Stephan, knowing their father's history of making concessions to his wife, were concerned that he would give in and sign the agreement before returning to his lawyer the following week. Without either parent's knowledge, they removed the separation agreement's signing page, making it impossible for Ben to legally capitulate over the weekend.

On the night of the killing, Christine and Ben were in the kitchen when they began to argue over the separation agreement. Christine was using a knife to prepare her evening salad. The couple was alone in the house; Marcus and Stephan were out having dinner together. This time, the couple started arguing over who would get final ownership of the Catskill estate. Ben wanted to be certain the boys received the estate after Christine's death. Christine didn't want to put this stipulation into the agreement. Exactly what happened next, no one will ever know.

The prosecution and the defense agreed that Ben stabbed Christine with a six-inch kitchen knife. The prosecutor contended that Ben attacked Christine first and stabbed himself afterward with Christine's knife so that he could claim self-defense. Ben testified that he remembered his wife coming at him with a knife and stabbing him. He then grabbed a knife. Otherwise he had no recollection of the specifics of the fight. When the prosecutor said to him incredulously, "You stood there for three stabs?" Ben answered, "I stood there for thirty years." Some of the jurors felt that this answer summed up Ben's defense.

At the start of deliberations, two members of the jury voted for a guilty verdict, five were undecided, and five voted not guilty. The defense had certainly been successful in building a claim that Ben Odierno had been the victim of psychological abuse and that his wife had been mentally unstable: more than forty witnesses testified for the defense. The prosecution's portrait of Christine Odierno as a battered woman, on the other hand, was full of inconsistencies. There was no medical or legal evidence that Odierno had ever been physically violent with his wife before the evening of her death. And although Jennie

Kramer, Christine's mother, movingly and convincingly spoke of her daughter's fear that she was going to be murdered, she then either couldn't or wouldn't point out the defendant—even when Ben obligingly raised his hand to identify himself. This behavior baffled the jurors and seriously damaged her credibility. In addition, Christine's brother and two sisters never testified, although they were often in the courtroom. To at least one member of the jury, this was telling: they would not lend support to their deceased sister if it meant besmirching her accused husband.

As the jurors' discussions progressed, they wrestled with the case's complexities. They allowed that a woman could be as abusive as a man. They saw how emotional abuse could be just as damaging as physical abuse. At the same time, Ben Odierno had committed a terrible crime: Could he plausibly have initially responded in self-defense and then lost control? "We hoped we wouldn't have done what Ben did," says Joanne McGrath, one of the jurors. "But, in the end, we knew we didn't know how we would react in such a situation."

"This was a case in which we didn't find Ben Odierno innocent," says juror Michael Stoller, "but we couldn't find him guilty either. Reasonable doubt was the centerpiece." Another juror, Mark Flowers, told a reporter, "We'll never know what happened inside that kitchen." After deliberating for five hours, the jury acquitted Ben Odierno.

Doubtless there are people who think that Ben got away with murder—as Christine's parents do. Even when people have undeniably suffered, as Ben Odierno and Brenda Aris did, it is difficult to excuse such violence. But if we look beyond the questions of guilt and innocence, crime and punishment, what can this particular dynamic teach us about domestic violence—before it ends up in the courtroom?

In this relationship, as in many relationships, the psychological abuse increased gradually over time, and Christine's husband and children drastically underestimated the need to confront the growing crisis in their family. Unsure of what had happened to Christine in the first place, they may have irrationally hoped that she would simply "snap out of it," although in retrospect it is clear that that was highly unlikely. Instead, the entire family was sucked into playing a role in her deadly fantasies until it became the family's shared truth: her husband was charged with murder, and her sons were standing by him. The power of words—and the violence those words can provoke in others—cannot be underestimated in any abusive relationship.

THE PRICE OF STAYING TOGETHER

The violent pattern between Christine and Ben was less obvious to everyone involved not because the abuser's behavior was unfamiliar—after all, Christine displayed many of the psychological characteristics of an abuser—but because she was a woman. Our difficulty imagining women in these roles affects their victims as well: Ben was tragically slow to recognize the gravity of his situation. We all need to realize that women, just like men, *can be* extremely violent both physically and psychologically, and that this can have enormous repercussions for themselves, their partners, and their children. It is also important to remember that the legacy of these injuries lives on long after the injuries themselves may have healed, as the Woodses' experience shows us.

For years, no one took Ruth Woods's violence against her husband seriously—especially Ruth herself, who would experience blackouts during her rages. She still claims to have little or no reliable memories of many of the terrible fights she had with David over their twenty-six years of marriage. This meant that David had to endure not only his wife's physical attacks but also the assumptions of others—police officers, friends of Ruth's—that he, in fact, was the guilty party.

Then, in 2003, they both ended up in the emergency room and attracted the attention of the criminal justice system; the events that followed prompted a radical change in their relationship. In fact, when they were subsequently invited to appear on NBC's *John Walsh Show* about women and violence the following year, the host presented them as a success story. After all, Ruth was acknowledging—to herself, to David, and to the world at large—that she had been physically abusive in her marriage. David was exonerated, they were still together, and the violence, after two decades, had finally come to an end.

Last year, however, when I interviewed both Ruth and David, a far more painful reality emerged. Yes, it was true that Ruth no longer hit her husband. But the dynamic that had given birth to the violence in the first place—not to mention the legacy of having lived with it for so long—still marred both their lives.

David and Ruth met in 1980, when they were working in the same hospital in Oklahoma City: David was a twenty-five-year-old orderly; Ruth was a thirty-one-year-old licensed practical nurse. One day, David, whose foot was in a cast at the time, delivered a patient with heart palpitations to Ruth's care. In her haste to respond to the crisis, she ran the patient's bed over David's foot without realizing it, and he had to get the cast fixed. When she saw him a few weeks later, she asked what had happened to him; he teased her, reminding her that she had broken his cast. Ruth says that when she offered to make amends by taking him out for pizza, David replied, "Since you make more money than I do, sure!"

In some ways, this exchange contained many of the elements that would become emblematic of their relationship: Ruth's aggression, her single-minded dedication to her work, her obliviousness; David's need for attention, his acute awareness of her superior earning power, his quick sense of humor. Within months they were good friends; soon afterward they became lovers. By the following spring, Ruth was pregnant with their eldest daughter; they decided to get married.

Although both Ruth and David found their marriage difficult from the start, their horizons had already been narrowed by other disappointments. In the late sixties, Ruth had intended to become a registered nurse but then flunked out of college, which forced her to become an LPN instead. She then married and had a son with a man who turned out to be an alcoholic. It ended when, after eleven years, she discovered that he was chronically unfaithful as well. "So I moved him out," Ruth recalled. "Took all of his stuff over to her place and dumped it." Her son was seven; at first, he lived with Ruth, but within two years he would be living full-time with his father.

In 1975, David had received a hardship discharge from the Marines so that he could come home and help support his sick parents. At first, this arrangement had worked well for him: he found that he could attend college part-time while making good money working as a bodyguard and in construction. Then, a few years before he met Ruth, he severely injured his knee: David refers to it as an accidental fall in a dark parking lot, but Ruth says that he was held down by a group of guys who shattered his knee with a baseball bat. Even after many operations, his leg was never the same, and he found his earning power suddenly and drastically reduced. (Now David has such severe degenerative arthritis in that leg that he receives disability payments from the government; he is in almost constant pain, and his medications make it impossible for him to drive.)

Because Ruth could make much more money than David, they decided that he would stay at home—first with their older child, who was born in 1982, and then with their younger child, who was born two years later. In many ways, they both concede, it was a wise decision: Ruth admits that David was a far more patient parent that she could have been, and David has tremendous respect for Ruth's professional abilities. Still, the reversal in traditional gender roles clearly left both of them feeling insecure and resentful. Ruth hated missing her daughters' early childhoods. David hated giving up his dreams of finishing college and becoming a professor.

When asked about the problems in his marriage, David described his wife as a "power-obsessed control freak" who was always so afraid that he would leave her after they were married that she was constantly telling him to get out if he didn't agree with what she wanted. "She learned fairly early on that that would work—that she could start that crap, and I would start accommodating and compromising," he said. "Like a spoiled child, the first time she throws a temper tantrum she screams and gets away with it, the next time she screams and stomps her feet, and the next time she screams and stomps her feet and throws a toy." One can't help but notice, though, that some resistance is implied

by the very example he gives: it isn't that David doesn't resist Ruth, one suspects, but that she is always willing to up the ante.

The principal flashpoint in the marriage was money. Ruth made it and
therefore felt that she could do with it what she pleased; David believed in
budgeting and planning for the future: "If you give a checkbook to Ruth, it's
like giving a checkbook to an eight-year-old. She has no sense of responsibility." But when he would talk about going back to school or trying to get part-
time work, he said that Ruth would accuse him of plotting to leave the
marriage and tell him to get out—"Go live under a bridge"—making their life
hell until he gave up his plan.

At other times, David said, Ruth would simply rage at him until he finally
lost his temper and gave her the fight she wanted. Then she would turn the tables and claim that the fight began with his response: "The reason she had been
a shrieking, screaming harpy for four days was because on the fifth day I lost
my temper."

At first, the couple's fights were verbal; then, after their second child was
born and they moved to California, away from Ruth's former job and friends,
the violence escalated. By this time, David said, he felt trapped—not only by his
inability to financially support himself or his family but also by his fear for his
daughters if he and Ruth separated. In the mid–80s, he recalled, when their
older daughter was four, she appeared one day in front of her parents wearing
some costume jewelry and a feather boa. Ruth lost it.

As David explained, "She was talking about, 'I'm not going to have you
dressing like a whore.' To a four-year-old kid! And with one hand she grabbed
her by the hair and began jerking her around, and with the other hand began
slapping her."

When David tried to break them apart, Ruth attacked him in turn; finally,
when Ruth wouldn't turn the child loose, David slapped her. "And Ruth
stepped back and acted as if she had been peeling potatoes, or knitting a
sweater—'How dare you?'—and that was the first time that Ruth ever called
the police on me."

The police didn't arrest David, but they told him next time that he wasn't to
touch his wife; he was simply to call 911—despite the fact that the child could
have been seriously injured if he hadn't intervened. On the other hand, David
pointed out, many men who are married to abusive women get arrested in just
these sorts of situations, leaving their children even more vulnerable: "What's
going to happen to your kids when you're away in jail?"

Ironically, the other reason for David remaining with Ruth was the same
thing that often drove them apart: financial need. After the children were older,
David left Ruth several times to escape the toxicity of their relationship, but
never for good. He couldn't afford to live on his disability payments alone, and

Ruth couldn't afford to keep up with her rent and pay David alimony. And so, repeatedly, they reunited to make ends meet.

When I spoke with Ruth, she was accommodating and friendly. Although her version of various disputes often didn't match up with her husband's, she expressed no need to be believed; she freely conceded that there was a lot she didn't remember about the violent episodes in the relationship; several times she even qualified some detail as if in deference to the fact that David's account of the same event might be starkly different. She was never defensive in our conversation, despite the fact that the couple's narrative of their marriage cast her unequivocally as the aggressor. At the same time, however, she seemed emotionally disconnected from the highly charged subject at hand—as if, when she is not in the midst of a triggering event, her experience is very difficult for her to analyze or recapture.

Certainly it was not surprising to learn that Ruth herself had grown up with a great deal of physical abuse masquerading as deserved corporal punishment. Both her parents "corrected" her (her father with his army belt, her mother with whatever came to hand—an open palm, a switch, a flyswatter) almost every other day, starting when she was about five or six. She was punished severely for "dangerous" behavior but also hit, she believes, because her mother was a very frustrated person. Ruth speaks of this without rancor (in fact it was David, not Ruth, who would later paint for me a vivid verbal portrait of her parents' hateful behavior). In her account of adult life, however, she freely admits that she can't stand being corrected and interprets almost any opposing view as a direct challenge.

She recalled one serious incident of violence in her marriage that erupted because David was trying to hurry her out of the house. This was during a period when she was always late for work: "Instead of doing the things that I thought David could do to help things go along a good way, he would just start kind of badgering, or—you know how you think of yip-yip dogs? You know, they just irritate the daylights out of you until you finally put them outside? That's what he reminded me of that morning. And it didn't matter what I said or what I did, he was right there, 'Come on, you gotta hurry, come on,' etc." Despite her dismissive analogy here, she clearly experienced David as deeply threatening, because she went for the shotgun. In another incident, when he persisted in talking to her when she was trying to cook dinner, she threatened him with a knife.

Although Ruth now sees her fights with David far more clearly, she refers to them both as "controllers" and would probably categorize them as a mutually combative couple. In one of her first memories of conflict in the marriage, when she was pregnant with their first child, she recalled angrily banging drawers and cabinet doors in the kitchen and then hearing David, who was in the next room, tip over the dining room table in response. In her stories she is both the grown-up who, like Ruth's own mother, cannot tolerate being challenged and the child who feels that any opposing viewpoint or suggestion is an attempt to annihilate her spirit—as perhaps, in her childhood, it was. Although this rage was entirely absent from our conversation, it has clearly dominated Ruth's life with her family.

David's descriptions of his marriage, on the other hand, more closely resemble an intimate-terrorism model, in which one partner uses money, verbal aggression, and physical violence to control the other. As it happened, David had also been terrorized in his home as a child—not by his parents, but by an angry half-brother who himself was the object of severe bullying in their tough neighborhood. When left alone in the house with David, the older boy would torture and humiliate him until David was finally old enough to fight him off. In his marriage David portrays himself as equally blameless and trapped. He fiercely rejects any suggestion that he has been in any way complicit in the violence, and he was "annoyed" after he and Ruth appeared on television, because a guest therapist on the show had suggested that violent couples stay together because the violence "works" for them. He also repeatedly reminded me of his physical injuries, referring to himself, only half-jokingly, as old and crippled.

At the same time, he abhors the notion that he in any way has been *passive* in the face of Ruth's attacks; his need to fight off the bully in the house is key to David's sense of himself, and he returned to it again and again during our conversations. He has pulled Ruth off the kids, twisted weapons out of her hands, restrained her forcefully enough to bruise her arms—but never initiated the violence. In a sentence that captures both his vulnerability and his own contained violence, he explained, "I'm a sick, weak, feeble, broken-down old man, compared to what I used to be, and yet I can still go to the mall and people get out of my way. If I hit her, I could kill her. I know that. I don't hit her."

The turning point in the Woodses' marriage came after a huge fight in 2003. Not surprisingly, David and Ruth's accounts of what happened bear little resemblance to each other. Ruth told me that she has no memory of what they were fighting about—"It was about everything; it was about nothing. One of those." She did acknowledge that she couldn't bear to be told "what I think, what I want, what I need to do." Everything David would say, she would try to match with equal hostility. "He would say something like, 'You don't even know how to write a letter, or make a sentence that expresses something.' And I'd say, "At least I can hold a job, and have for thirty-five years." She concedes that the fight was very insulting on both sides: "There was a lot of shaming, and I think I did my fair share of it, too." The fight went on for days until finally David, desperate for some rest, took medication in order to sleep.

Ruth says that she was too angry to sleep in the same bed with David. Before leaving the room, however, she pulled up David's blanket, because he had been experiencing some arthritis in his shoulder. David, thinking that she was attacking him in his sleep, sprang up instantly. "The next thing I knew, I was up against the wall," Ruth said. "I had a velour-type lounge shirt on, and he had gathered it up and was choking me. And it just went from bad to worse, you know, 'Please let me go'; 'I'm going to kill you.'" When Ruth couldn't pull him off her throat, she used some self-defense moves that David had taught her, and they ended up in a forty-minute knock-down drag-out fight in the bedroom.

Toward the end, they were standing face-to-face when David pushed her back onto the bed while her foot was still twisted and wedged against his, and she could feel the ligament in her knee tearing as she went down. "So all of a sudden I'm screaming, "Oh my god, oh my god, it's broken, it's broken, it's broken," and he goes, "The hell it is. Would you like for me to break it?" Ruth begged to be allowed to go to the bathroom to examine her injury; by the time she emerged, David had passed out on the bed, and she called her older daughter to take her to the emergency room. When, at the hospital, she was encouraged to file charges against her husband, she said yes.

David, on the other hand, remembers the subject of their fight vividly; as was often the case, they were arguing about money. In his version, Ruth had been struggling to pay off more than $8,000 in fines to the state nursing board, and he had been giving her a substantial chunk of his meager $800 disability check for many months. Then he discovered that she'd paid only a fraction of what was owed. "She started trying to impress upon me how she had to have the money or she was going to lose her license. And I said, "I already gave it to you. I gave you $8,750, something like that. Go fish.'" Eventually, David said, Ruth started hitting him, and they ended up wrestling on the floor.

David had neglected to put his shotgun away earlier in the week, and Ruth made a grab for it; soon they were struggling over the gun. "I was trying to remember, 'Oh my god, did I unload this bastard? Did I unload this?'" Finally, he wrested the shotgun away from Ruth, and as he checked to see if it was loaded, Ruth hit him over the head with something—"I believe it was one of those cute little Jane Fonda workout dumbbells"—and he passed out.

When he came to, he was alone, with several lumps on his head, blood matted in his hair, and a sore jaw. His younger daughter took him to the emergency room; when he explained that he had been attacked by his wife, the sheriff was notified, and David was taken into custody; there was already a warrant out for his arrest.

For David, the arrest was only the first in a series of outrages and humiliations. He soon discovered that Ruth—perhaps to mitigate her allegations—had told the police that David had only attacked her because he was suicidal; this meant that he was taken, against his will, to the psychiatry unit. When he eventually managed to get a hearing, the judge insisted that he be released.

Since the struggle had involved a firearm, David had been charged with three felony counts, each of which carried a minimum sentence of ten years. The only rational option, the public defender told him, was to plead guilty; then he might get only a few months in jail and several years' probation. But this, for David, was the last straw.

"I said, 'Not guilty.' He said, 'You can't plead not guilty.' 'Yeah? I didn't do it!' And my public defender, the public defender's office was outraged, they were literally *outraged* that I was going to plead not guilty. They said, 'Well, we just don't know if we can help you.' I said, 'Well, try—you're my attorneys.'"

David learned that if he could establish that there had been a pattern of threats and violent actions committed against him by Ruth during the marriage, and if he could get a significant number of witnesses to corroborate his testimony, he could submit it to the judge in his defense, and that the judge might be persuaded to dismiss the charges. And so he and his younger daughter, over the next few months, did exactly that; finally, that August, the judge agreed to dismiss the charges against him.

Ruth told me that she had no idea what was going on with David during this time, other than that he'd been arrested: "There was an automatic court order, a restraining order, and for once I stuck to it." In terrific pain from her knee injury, Ruth finally went to a hospital in Wyoming for a special procedure to have her ligament replaced. It was a particularly angry time: she was furious about her leg, furious about missing so much work, furious about the financial jeopardy her injury was placing her in. Finally, a friend of hers who was a Vietnam vet told her that it was time for her to get help.

"He says, 'Ruth, I think that you need to talk to the guy that I talk to.' And I said, 'Why?' And he said, "Well, you've got anger issues, kid.' And I said, 'Okay, I'll talk to this guy.'" When Ruth came home, she sought out an anger management group for women whose violence had gotten them in trouble with the law. Ruth only attended occasionally, since her participation was voluntary and her work schedule demanding, but she still found it helpful. Upon her return home, she was surprised to learn that the charges against David had been dropped—and even more surprised when she learned that so many of their friends and acquaintances had been willing to testify against her. Along with her friend's comments and the anger management class, these witnesses reinforced the possibility of a larger reality outside her own.

But the real turning point came one day when she was driving David to the doctor in the car. In what David claims was a common pattern in their relationship, Ruth was not taking the most efficient route to the doctor's office, and David was afraid that they would be late for his appointment; when he tried to correct her, Ruth started hitting him with her free hand. "And finally, after the second or third time she hit me, she just all of a sudden stopped and she started crying, and she started, 'I do hit; I do do it; I really do do it.' We had to pull over to the side of the road, and she sobbed for about ten minutes." Ruth had, in a manner of speaking, caught herself in the act. "That was a cathartic moment for her," David recalled, "a very self-revelatory moment."

From this point on, Ruth accepted that her own sense of her marital history was not reliable. She also actively began to change her behavior. Her anger management classes helped her understand that she had never learned how to discuss anything with a partner—she only knew how to fight. David, she told me, was very supportive and wanted to hear about everything she was learning, but eventually she became resentful. "I wanted him to get his own knowledge," Ruth explained. "He accepted that, and started reading and investigating things on the Internet."

As Ruth began to take responsibility for her own violence, she also began to feel less guilty about other things. She tried to forgive herself for not having been there for her children. She vowed to stop feeling so responsible for her husband's unhappiness. She even pointed out to David that although her memory was unreliable, his wasn't always completely accurate, either. Certainly, progress has been made in the marriage, but Ruth admitted to me that she and David still sometimes have terrible arguments. "I wish we could say we're 100 percent different, but we're not."

David was far more negative about the relationship. Although the violence has stopped, he still felt like "the nothing" in the marriage: "I am marginalized; I am trivialized; I am treated with complete and utter disregard." He also acknowledged that he is holding on to an enormous amount of resentment. "Ruth did things to me that nobody's ever done to me," David said. "I don't know whether it's that I can't forgive or that I can't forget." The consequences of this residual anger are obviously severe for both of them.

For the outsider, in fact, David's anger is one of the defining characteristics of his personality—along with his formidable intelligence and his keen sense of injury. The dynamic in the Woodses' marriage is more familiar when the genders are reversed: although only one is the physical aggressor, both partners seem equally (if differently) matched. The anger, bitterness, and sense of moral superiority that fuel David's perspective are so forceful that, for better or for worse, it is impossible to see him as powerless in the dynamic.

The real "trap" for David is perhaps that he cannot reconcile his grievances with his sense of himself as a strong person—that any acknowledgment that he wields power carries with it the damning whiff of responsibility. In truth, however, only by fully owning his power will he be able to change his place in his world, and that includes acknowledging his dynamic with Ruth in all its complexity.

My interview with Ruth occurred shortly after David had a heart attack. He was clearly going to recover, but I had the sense that the crisis had softened her a little toward him. She spoke repeatedly of his intelligence and was brutally honest in her assessment that he was the more loving and competent parent. Her respect and affection were evident, and I felt hopeful when we ended our conversation. Then, the following day—as if to discourage me from having any expectations that she could improve her marriage—she sent me the following email:

> I am not a person who can communicate well. I will not make a commit-ment to David even though we have been married for 26 years. I have not set any goals for our relationship. Matter of fact I do not set goals at all. I just do what I need to do to survive, get by, or float along. When David talks about what to do I believe he is trying to control *me*. But at the same time I do not know what to do. So I wait until David makes a decision and then I do the opposite. The relationship we have is very dysfunctional.

Several months later, I received an email from David that sounded equally despairing: "In some ways, I have to admit that I have given up. I don't see a way out for me. . . . I don't see any alternative to living here, living this life, for the rest of my life. Somewhere . . . at some point . . . I stopped hoping."

The Woodses' predicament sounds dismayingly close to Eisikovits and Buchbinder's description of what situational couples' violence often becomes over time—even though Ruth is no longer abusive: "Their joint reality is sub-stituted by a polarity in which they continue living side by side. The dynamic of existing as a couple is gradually lost because any kind of dialogue is per-ceived as threatening, and both partners are always ready for attack or digging deeper into their defensive positions."

Nevertheless, their identities are so enmeshed that it is difficult to imagine them apart. Ruth is the doer, the earner, living in the present moment; psycho-logical analysis is implicitly understood to be David's territory, and therefore it makes sense that she is wary of venturing into it—even though she avoids it at great cost to herself. David is the thinker, the scorekeeper, the couple's institu-tional memory; he is so weighed down by the injustices of the past and his own physical disabilities that establishing any meaningful connection with the "world"—Ruth's territory—has become impossible.

And so if the tragedy of the Odiernos illustrates the importance of getting help before physical violence erupts, the misery of the Woodses points to its value even after the physical violence has ended. Seeking ongoing help—ei-ther individually or as a couple—seems the only positive way for them to move forward.

THE LARGER DYNAMIC: THEM AND US

Can violent relationships change? Some can, and some can't. But individuals caught within a violent dynamic are often incapable of correctly evaluating their situation without assistance: Brenda Aris held out hope for her marriage for years after most of us would have stopped supporting her decision to stay. What sort of intervention do violent couples see as available to them?

As a society, our primary collective response to domestic violence has been a legal one, but for the people introduced in these chapters, the criminal justice system was of limited use. For the McPhersons, Jeff's arrest certainly underscored the gravity of what had happened, but it is highly probable that they would have taken it seriously even if the law hadn't intervened. For the Woodses, the intervention by the court set in motion a series of events that resulted in Ruth's epiphany, but without long-term help their marriage remains barely tenable. As for the Odiernos, the police were incapable of responding to what was happening—until it was too late.

Violent couples desperately need some sort of intervention, and the criminal justice system—which necessarily functions in terms of guilt and innocence, crime and punishment—is simply not properly equipped to deal with the underlying questions that they need answered. ("Can he kill me?" "Can she change?" "Am I somehow complicit in the violence?" "Does my boyfriend even *want* to stop hitting me?") Other venues for exploring abusive relationships have to be encouraged—not because all abusive relationships can or should be healed, but because only when help is genuinely available can we accurately determine who, finally, isn't willing or able to accept it.

PART THREE

New Approaches

People are now realizing that "pure" positions, like treating men and women separately, have largely failed.

—Virginia Goldner, psychologist and former codirector of the Gender and Violence Project, Ackerman Institute for the Family

At that moment, I felt like a warrior who'd waged and won a great and lonely battle.

—James M., Founder, Violence Anonymous)

9
COUPLES COUNSELING

ouples counseling has long been banned from the list of acceptable treatments for domestic violence. As far back as 1987, the battered women's movement took the position that couples counseling was to be discouraged—even when a woman wanted to participate in counseling with her violent partner.

One of the earliest declarations of opposition to couples counseling comes from social worker Susan Schechter, who described couples counseling as "an inappropriate intervention that further endangers the woman." Schechter explained:

> It encourages the abuser to blame the victim by examining her "role" in his problem. By seeing the couple together, the therapist erroneously suggests that the partner, too, is responsible for the abuser's behavior. Many women have been beaten brutally following couples counseling sessions in which they disclosed violence or coercion. The abuser alone must take responsibility for the assaults and understand that family reunification is not his treatment goal; the goal is to stop the violence.

Today's advocates have incorporated these same negative judgments of couples counseling into both practice and policy perspectives. Take, for example, the policy developed by the Coalition to End Domestic Violence and Sexual Assault, which calls on all courts in Rockland County, New York, to end the use of couples counseling in domestic violence cases.

> People who are being either hit, intimidated or controlled through threats or other coercive means by their partners are not free to engage in an open dia-

logue. If placed in couples counseling, a person would be encouraged to speak openly about their partner's behavior and address problems in the relationship in the presence of an abusive partner. People who do so are often at risk of retaliatory tactics from the abuser, thereby jeopardizing their safety.

Some states, including New York and California, legally prohibit the use of couples counseling when one member of the couple is charged with a domestic violence crime. In other words, these states prohibit a court from referring a defendant to couples counseling as part of the treatment mandate. In the brochure highlighting the frequently asked questions posed by people experiencing domestic abuse, the New York State Office for the Prevention of Domestic Violence explains why couples treatment is not an acceptable approach to healing abuse:

> According to battered women who have gone for marriage or couples counseling, it not only doesn't work, it often makes things worse. One explanation for this is that going to counseling together suggests that a woman shares some of the responsibility for her partner's violence, a belief that many abusive men already have. So, couples counseling can help batterers to justify blaming their partners, and give them even more excuses for being violent. A batterer's violence is his responsibility, no one else's. It is unlikely that he will change unless he accepts full responsibility for his actions.

Just because a court is prohibited from referring a defendant to couples counseling doesn't mean the couple can't, on their own, seek such treatment; doing so can be important to a couple's recovery, as mine was. Given my own difficulty in finding a counselor, and the number of people who have asked me for referrals to couples counselors following a violent incident, I have felt compelled over the course of my research to ask practicing therapists who work with couples struggling with violence how their work addressed this critique.

I spoke with five prominent therapists who have had extensive experience treating couples with a history of intimate violence. Nearly all of them work in private practice and see clients who choose to seek couples counseling treatment on their own. Some of the counselors I spoke with did couples work as part of the services offered at a clinic—although this option has become less and less available as domestic violence advocates become more vocal about their concerns. Many of the counselors I spoke to have published research on the issue of couples counseling and domestic violence, and a couple of them are considered among the nation's experts on the topic. I discovered that all of them are committed to using couples counseling to address the issue of violence in at least some intimate relationships, and that all of them believed that treatment could help manage the violence, rather than make it worse.

THE COUNSELORS

Nearly all the therapists interviewed here identified themselves as feminists, and in fact, many of them started their work in traditional domestic violence treatment settings. Samuel Aymer and Mat Williams, for example, started their clinical careers doing batterer treatment: Aymer at Safe Horizons, a victims services agency in New York City, and Williams at a batterer program in upstate New York. Both became disillusioned with the highly regimented "one-size-fits-all" approach, which seemed psychologically crude and often ineffectual. Williams eventually went to work for the Stonybrook Marital Therapy Clinic in New York, which was founded by K. Daniel O'Leary, one of the leading practitioners and researchers in the field of counseling for violent couples. Dr. Williams has been doing couples counseling since 2003. Dr. Aymer also branched out on his own; he has been working with violent couples in his private practice for more than twenty years. Aymer is a professor of social work at the Hunter College School of Social Work. His research, presented in chapter 5, focuses on the effects of domestic violence on teenage boys and how they cope with the chaos in their families; he is also interested in the complex dynamics between couples.

Williams admits that he was initially skeptical about the efficacy of couples counseling as a response to domestic violence. Over time, however, he came to see how bringing both parties together could "make a huge difference" in addressing the problem: "Couples counseling reduces aggression, often heals and halts the violence, and offers the promise of restoring families." Aymer agrees: "The work is really rewarding—you can see that treating the couple together can really change their dynamic."

Janet Geller has been doing couples counseling for more than two decades. Her book, Breaking Destructive Patterns: Multiple Strategies for Treating Partner Abuse, was published in 1992, and she has made numerous television appearances in connection with her work. She has been employed for the past thirteen years as a consultant for domestic violence programs at New York City's Jewish Board of Family and Children's Services. She also works with violent couples in her private practice. Geller, who has a doctorate in education and a master's degree in social work, started her domestic violence work in 1974, when she landed her first job as a social worker in a women's center: almost immediately, she recalled, her feminist beliefs came into conflict with her professional responsibilities.

The center's services included a twenty-four-hour hotline for women who had been raped. No one who worked there was prepared, however, for the outpouring of married women who called for help. A woman would call and say she was being abused by her husband. The center responded by offering the options that were available for battered women: shelter, orders of protection, even divorce. "The problem was that's not what they wanted. When the women started dropping out of our victim support program, we asked them why." Finally, Geller says, one woman explained, "You were all so nice, and although I thought about leaving my husband, I changed my mind. I didn't have the heart to come back and say I don't really want to end the relationship."

When Geller realized that her clients were, in effect, protecting the feelings of the social workers hired to help them, she knew that she needed to rethink her entire approach to domestic violence.

Bill Burmester is a licensed marriage and family therapist in Berkeley, California; he treats couples in crisis and is also affiliated with the Men's Center for Counseling and Psychotherapy in Berkeley. If Geller's work complicated her notion of what victims of intimate abuse needed, Burmester came to couples counseling with a more nuanced understanding of the perpetrator, having previously treated men with histories of sexual abuse.

He describes how the vulnerabilities of men who have been abused are compounded by their socialization as children, which often discourages or prevents them from having "effective, empowering relationships" in which they are permitted to share their emotions. As adults, these men are sitting on a powder keg that often frightens them as well as their family members; the smallest incident or slight can suddenly make them feel emotionally overwhelmed.

"Every man," Burmester offers, "learns early on that powerlessness is intolerable, that it is shameful." To respond to the shameful feelings, Burmester suggests, "there's a surge of self-assertion to deny it's happening." Burmester describes how domestic violence is "compensation for an internal collapse." This does not, he is quick to add, excuse the violence, but it does make it more comprehensible. In treatment Burmester focuses on recognizing the legacy of violent and traumatic childhoods, observing the influence of socialization on marital and romantic expectations, and teaching the couple how to break their dysfunctional patterns of communication.

Dr. Virginia Goldner is a psychologist who served as codirector of the Gender and Violence Project at the Ackerman Institute for the Family from around 1985 to 1999. Both Goldner and Julianne Walker, the other codirector at the Project, considered themselves feminists as well as family therapists. They were committed to bringing a perspective that incorporated an awareness of gender and inequality into their counseling work. At the same time, Goldner recalls, "family therapy needed a system's perspective for why women kept going back to violent men, and a simple feminist outlook wouldn't suffice." It was time, Goldner says, to do the "hardest work"—to come up with a therapeutic approach that recognized the importance of "holding violent men's feet to the fire" without at the same time "having too simplistic a view of what people do to each other in relationships." Although Goldner has left the Ackerman Institute, she continues to see emotionally violent couples in private practice.

THE DANGER

All of the therapists with whom I spoke took the responsibility of assessing the severity of violence in the couples they were seeing very seriously.

Samuel Aymer sees each member of the couple alone for at least three sessions before seeing them together. In these initial sessions, Aymer tries to determine how and when violence erupts in the relationship and how dangerous it is. If the woman is afraid of her partner, or if there are weapons involved in the violence, Aymer won't bring the couple together. Either way, he believes that bringing both parties to counseling—separately or together—can help pave the way to recovery.

Janet Geller also sees each member of the couple alone before seeing them together. Dividing the first session in half, she interviews each person separately—both to learn about the level and frequency of the abuse and to prepare the couple for the challenges of working together. "I ask the woman questions like: 'If something happens during session that makes him angry, are you in danger after that?' If she says yes, they aren't ready to be seen together. If she says it's fine, then the couples work can begin." Initially, Geller admits, it is very tense. If she has reservations about bringing the couple together, she holds off: "I postpone that part of the work until the behavior is under control."

Geller also demands that the couple agree to sign a contract about the violence, promising that it will stop. Several of the therapists described using this technique during their sessions. The contract's effectiveness lies in the discussion that surrounds the agreement, including possible consequences for violations. Those consequences may include a forced separation of the couple for some period, termination of the couples counseling, or even a notation in the therapist's record, which could be subpoenaed later. I asked Geller whether she felt confident that the violence stopped once there was a contract in place. She said that, in her experience, it nearly always had: "I have found that men learn other ways of dealing with their feelings of anger—and, eventually, it turns into a typical marital counseling case."

Mat Williams manages the couple's history of abuse by only agreeing to take on cases involving low-level violence. Of course, initially, a couple may not be entirely honest about their history; in the instance of Nora and Bailey, whose story I will tell in more detail later in this chapter, Williams did not learn about their most violent episode until they were two months into the therapy. He decided to keep seeing them. "By then," Williams says, "I felt assured that their violence was controlled."

Virginia Goldner, like most of the therapists I talked with, considers the initial session not simply as an opportunity to assess the threat of violence but also as a meaningful part of the therapy. She and her codirector would begin a couple's treatment with a two-hour session. Initially they would meet both members of the couple together, to observe how they interacted. Then they would separate and interview each partner alone. The next step was to consult with each other to compare notes and decide what course of action seemed most appropriate for this particular couple. Once that was done, they would call the couple back together to provide them with their assessment of the situation. Goldner and Walker would take into consideration such issues as intimidation, self-defense, and any childhood history of violence, together with the cultural context of the violence. These factors helped them determine an appropriate treatment plan while preparing the couple for the work ahead. They found that this intensive initial session was not only revealing for the therapist but also deeply meaningful for the patients. "At the end of the two hours," Goldner observes, "the couple felt very held and cared for by us."

The therapists I interviewed described the anxiety they sometimes felt about the danger of working with violent couples. Despite their concerns, none of them felt they would have stopped doing the work as a result. Mat Williams sums up the feelings of all the therapists I spoke with: "It's no different than treating suicidal patients," he explains. "There's always risk, but that doesn't mean you don't treat them. It just means you have to stay attuned to the risk."

THE ALLIANCE

All of the therapists that I focus on in this chapter describe the importance of aligning themselves with both members of the couple, in order to make the treatment successful. Burmester notes, "The basis of a good therapeutic relationship is having an empathic connection to each person, without that, nothing happens. Unless a client feels they're getting a fair shake, it won't go far." He continues, "Shame has everything to do with a sense of collapse of the self. The only way to repair that collapse in therapy is through the client's belief that the process can help you up." That happens, Burmester adds, "through a therapist's strong and respectful relationship with the client."

Samuel Aymer finds it helpful to remember what he has learned from his years of experience—that today's abuser is often yesterday's ill-treated child: "Over and over, with men and women from all racial groups, you learn that there is a history of violence in their childhoods—either they were exposed to it, or they were a direct recipient of it. This is always coupled with shame. If I don't listen with empathy, that's participating in the shame." This doesn't mean that the violence is condoned or accepted, but it does mean that the essential humanity of the abuser is recognized. Otherwise, there is little incentive for the abuser to trust the process.

Geller says that as a female therapist, she must stay particularly attuned to her relationship with the man in the couple: "I need him to feel I am on his side—when a man sees me, he automatically assumes I'm on her side. He needs some convincing that I'm not just on her side. So I try and build a relationship in the initial individual session, but it is a constant effort to make him feel safe enough so that he can say what's really going on, and that I'm there for him too."

Goldner describes walking this line in a particularly moving way:

> To succeed in this work, the therapist must create a context in which the woman can speak the truth about her life under siege and her partner, and the therapist can suffer that truth in the act of listening. At the same time, the man must also be recognized in his full subjectivity, not only in terms of his shameful identity as an offender. In many cases, abusive men carry inside them a child-victim who also has a story that must be told.

Once again, feminist fears that supporting the batterer encourages more battering are not borne out by the experiences of those who do the therapeutic work; in fact, the opposite seems to be the case. Pamela Brown and her colleague K. Daniel O'Leary found that the formation of a positive connection between the aggressor and the therapist decreased the likelihood of both physical and psychological aggression in the relationship after treatment. This fits with Janet Geller's observation about the significance of building this alliance:

> I'm a therapist first, a mental health practitioner, and I believe that every person deserves the opportunity to get help if they want it: he has a heart that beats within too, he has blood that goes through his veins too. I see more to him than just his violence. So I'm able to suspend my own personal feelings about someone who is abusive because deep in my heart, if he's coming in, I want to give him a chance to see if he can change his behavior.

THE CHILDHOOD

Usually, as the danger is assessed by the therapist and the story of violence unfolds, a history of childhood victimization also reveals itself. All of the therapists commented on this phenomenon, and each of them had come to accept that couples work is paradoxical in that the abuser has often also been a victim. They observed how sad it was that couples in violent relationships were frequently repeating and reenacting their childhood experiences.

Samuel Aymer has seen this over and over again with the men of color in his practice. He describes how "stoic these men are, despite the fact that their parents often called them names, hit them, and yelled at them as children." Aymer talks about how he has to become the client's "observing ego" by helping him stand back from a childhood experience and revisit, from a distance, what happened to him. This can be especially complicated, Aymer says, when the abusive adult was the mother. In situations like these, Aymer might say something like: "If I were in your position, I might have a lot of feelings, given that my mother was never there for me." His clients are often surprised by this observation. "In a lot of these communities," Aymer continues, "you're not supposed to say anything against the mother, the sacrificial lamb, the martyr—she's raised you and had fifteen jobs. . . . But without giving these men a forum to talk about their relationship with their mother, they can't recover."

Bill Burmester agrees: "Therapy has to facilitate the reenactment of the childhood trauma, so that it's not just a repetition and retraumatizing but instead has the chance of leading to a different outcome. But if you never get into that history with somebody, the things that need to be healed never get engaged." Burmester is suggesting that as childhood memories surface, therapy should give people the opportunity to address and heal those wounds while also recognizing that difficult childhood experiences, once acknowledged, can be viewed in a more positive way. Jeff McPherson's defensiveness was a perfect example of this: when it manifests as road rage, it is potentially lethal; when it is harnessed into reorganizing his kitchen and joining his wife to cook in it, it is a force for increased intimacy. Janet Geller couldn't agree more: "My experience with men—with the exception of their abusive behavior, which is terrible and horrible and I hate it—is that they can be tender and loving, they can cry and have feelings about what happened to them as children, and there's much more to them than their abuse. And when you see that, and you support it, they can stop the abuse, too."

THE DYNAMIC

All of the therapists here agree that doing couples counseling allows the dynamic to be more easily revealed and addressed. Most admit that at first they found it difficult to accept that the victim might in some way be contributing to the violence, but all came to see that the dynamic and the violence often went hand in hand.

When I asked Virginia Goldner about the role of dynamics in couples treatment, she confessed that initially, when her patients didn't conform to type, it surprised her. Gradually, her views evolved: "We were forced to see men as child victims of abusive families, men not fitting into a masculine stereotype. Women were not shrinking violets, but dark, confrontational, heavy-duty to manage." She sighed, concluding, "It's just an enormously complex prism."

Bill Burmester expresses a more spiritual perspective on this issue. He believes that two people find each other in order to "reenact their unfinished business." He goes on to say that "clients in distress with each other 'deserve each other'—in the good sense." As to the gender dimensions of the dynamic, Burmester wonders whether some men "let themselves get into relationships where their tenderness and dependency get stirred up," only to then find themselves terrified and overwhelmed. "Because really, who is showing up is the kids—the kids who never got developmentally finished with those needs, and are somehow not yet ready to let go of them and live in the adult world. It's almost as though men want all that emotion in their relationships, but then once they have it, they don't have the capacity to manage it."

He continues, "I wonder if the worst violence doesn't come out of a sort of gender polarization—where women play a stereotypical needy role and can't let go, and men are attracted to them because it represents something unfinished in them—the desire to be needy—but they are also under pressure to be strong." In the end, Bill believes that "women's power comes from their availability to attach; women can exert power by withdrawing—that's only one of the ways to do it. This can stir things up in men; they can become enraged."

Both Aymer and Geller believe that a couple's ability to recognize their dynamic in therapy often comes after a period of self-reflection and an acknowledgment of responsibility for the violence that has occurred. This allows everyone some distance and an opportunity to evaluate what is actually triggering the violence.

Aymer and Geller also explain that looking at the partnership as a system allows them to stand back from the violence and work without judging who is right and who is wrong. This part of the therapy is crucial for encouraging people to control their violent urges while giving them a platform to better understand them. This effort combines reflecting on the clients' childhoods while simultaneously recognizing that the present relationship appeared to be triggering a painful history. Both therapists believe that this combustible combination of past and present is often what unleashes their clients' aggression.

Although the physical abuse may be what brings people into counseling, exploring the triggers for that abuse frequently uncovers the fact that both partners are often psychologically abusive, which can also trigger physical violence—as we've seen in many of the cases we've examined thus far. Looking at the dynamic of the relationship for both psychological and physical abuse, and discovering what sets it off, becomes an opportunity for reducing the violence overall.

Several studies now confirm that marital problems contribute dramatically to the risk of men's physical aggression in a marriage. In a study of more than eleven thousand military men, psychologists Helen Pan, Peter Neidig, and K. Daniel O'Leary concluded, "When developing strategies to treat or prevent marital aggression, researchers should give significant priority to the improvement of marital relations if the couple chooses to stay together."

THE DIALOGUE

All these therapists understood that modes of communication between couples in violent relationships are at the heart of improving marital relations, and without a concentrated focus on communication, a change in the dynamic is unlikely. Each therapist viewed violence as a form of failed communication and realized the importance of providing both members of the couple with techniques that could improve communication.

Bill Burmester's work is worth noting here. He relies on a method developed in the early 1980s by the now legendary Harville Hendrix, a clinical pastoral counselor who holds a Ph.D. in psychology and theology, and his wife, Helen LaKelly Hunt, who holds a master's degree in counseling and a doctoral degree in theology. Together, Hendrix and Hunt developed Imago Relationship Therapy, which has become a classic approach to couples counseling, used by therapists around the world.

The specific method of communication that Burmester uses, which grows out of Imago Relationship Therapy, is called the "Couple's Dialogue." Burmester describes this practice as involving three levels, or sequences, of communication.

The first level of the Couple's Dialogue is mirroring: the partners take turns trying to communicate something about themselves to the other—something important that they want to make sure the other person understands. A wife might say something like, "I feel terrible that you forgot our anniversary," rather than "Only a creep would forget our anniversary." "The reason the statement should be self-focused," Burmester offers, "is that it is less likely to trigger defensiveness by the listening partner." He continues, "The listening partner has the really difficult job of putting his or her own point of view on hold while listening actively to what the other is saying." Burmester then asks the listening partner to repeat the statement he or she has just heard as precisely as possible.

Initially, he acknowledges, the work is artificial, slow, and awkward. But that is part of the point: to dismantle the well-established back-and-forth of the dysfunctional relationship, in which neither person is really being heard. Burmester describes how this exercise sensitizes both halves of the couple by showing them how they are understood by each other—and what a difference a few words can make. The receiving partner, once he or she has repeated back what the speaking partner has said, is encouraged to ask something like, "Did I get it?" Or, "Did I miss something?" The speaker then responds by saying, "Yes, you got it exactly right," or "No, I didn't say that I 'was furious.' I said I 'felt terrible.'" And so on.

When the speaking partner finishes, the listening partner asks: "Is there more?" There almost always is more, and often this is when the more painful content is revealed. Of course, some partners don't really want to hear any more, and will therefore ask the question in a sarcastic or aggressive way. "When that happens," Burmester says, "I just ask the speaking partner, 'Does that really make you want to say more? What was it about the invitation that doesn't work?' And they'll say, 'Well, he said it in a really hostile way.' Then I'll turn to the listening partner and say, 'Is there a way you can emphasize really wanting to know more? If not, let us know.' This forces each speaker to take responsibility for not only what he is saying but the way he is saying it." The couple is laying the groundwork for listening and speaking in a more nuanced and sensitive way.

The next step involves validating the sentiment behind the communication rather than simply parroting the speaker's words. Burmester says to the receiving partner, "If you put yourself in your partner's shoes, how would you explain why the things she said are important to her?" The purpose of this is to gauge whether the person receiving the information is getting the other person "from the inside." Burmester might pose the following question to determine just how far the listener is understanding the speaker: "Think of it as, 'Remembering our anniversary is important to you because you're the kind of person who . . .'" Burmester then stops there and has the listening partner complete the sentence. This validation technique is essential to building a strong bond between the partners as they move on to the next phase of the work.

The third step involves identifying what is unspoken in the spoken words. Here the listening partner might be asked to provide a simple list of emotions that they believe they have interpreted from the words expressed thus far, such as: "I think you feel disappointed, hurt, angry, forgotten, not important." Then the listening partner will stop and say: "I think that's it. Does that capture what's going on emotionally for you?" And the speaking partner might say, "Yes, all those are there, but there's something more—I feel sad." The listening partner will acknowledge this by saying, "In addition, you feel sad."

"If they get the spirit of it right," Burmester says, "it's profound—the whole interaction is profound. If they don't get it, which is often the case the first time around, we will keep working at it." Often he spends his sessions focusing as much on a speaker's nonverbal cues—the speed with which they repeat something back, the intonation, the facial expressions—as on the words themselves. How do we rile each other up, with only a glance or a gesture? How do we shut each other down? "It's great work," Burmester offers, "because it's a kind of scaffolding that one can develop with all sorts of subtlety."

Especially for violent couples, the experience of being listened to can be key: "Without that, there's no communication because the other person is just waiting to make their next point." A male patient who has benefited from this technique agrees: "One of the things that we learned from Bill is that you really have to make sure the other person is on board. Otherwise, no matter how much you want to push some issue, it's not working. In fact, it becomes counterproductive at the point that you see them tuning out. Realizing that some of the more subtle body language matters has been good."

Indeed, improving communication between partners who are experiencing situational couple violence has been shown to be effective in reducing abuse.

According to University of Houston psychology professor Julia Babcock and her colleagues, "improved communication skills was found to be one of the four variables contributing to change among men who successfully became nonabusive." (The other three variables are accepting increased responsibility for their past abusive behavior, developing empathy for their partners' victimization, and reducing their own levels of dependency on their partners.) Babcock recommends that when violence is "tied to poor communication skills, problem-solving techniques, and entrenched patterns of conflict," couples treatment may be warranted.

To understand more fully how all these influences are at play in couples counseling sessions, I spoke with Mat Williams about a couple he'd previously treated. Nora and Bailey Richmond, whose names have been changed, illustrate how couples counseling can be effective in addressing not only the violence and aggression in a relationship, but in improving the couple's experience of themselves and each other overall.

NORA AND BAILEY RICHMOND

For almost two years, Mat Williams treated the Richmonds—Bailey, forty-eight, and Nora, forty-four—a white, upper-middle-class couple who lived in New York State. Married nearly twenty years, the Richmonds had two children in middle school at the time Mat treated them.

The first incident of violence between Bailey and Nora occurred approximately one year after they were married. They couldn't exactly recall how the conflict began, but the details of the violence remained vivid. In the midst of an argument, Bailey pushed Nora through a door that broke on impact. When Nora went to the emergency room and was questioned by a doctor about what had happened, she lied, saying that she'd accidentally fallen through the door after tripping over a table.

Nora didn't lie about her injuries to her family, however. She told them point-blank that Bailey had attacked her. She even told Bailey's family. Nora explained in no uncertain terms that if her husband ever physically attacked her again, she would leave him for good. The couple didn't seek professional treatment after the fight; several years passed before they went to see Mat Williams.

Mat described Bailey as a stubborn, articulate, charismatic, self-made man who successfully ran his own company. Nora, according to Mat, was athletic and outgoing. She had had a successful career before marrying Bailey; then she became a stay-at-home wife and mom. The Richmonds lived in a large house with their children and their pets.

It was Nora who finally insisted that they go to couples counseling. Not because of a recurrence of physical violence between them—nothing of the magnitude of that first event had ever happened again. But the emotional abuse—and neglect—continued, and it worsened over the years. Nora said that Bailey's hot temper and his distance from her could be unbearable; she did not feel that her emotional needs were being met. According to Nora, Bailey was always dismissive and sometimes "horribly nasty." Ugly fights would erupt, often in front of the children. Nora felt that she and Bailey never talked and that he never listened. "He acts as though I'm an irritation rather than a valued partner," Mat recalled her saying. Now middle-aged, Nora was clear—she wanted more for herself, her husband, and her marriage. Divorce remained an option for Nora, but it was not her preferred choice.

Bailey, who had a traditional view of marriage, felt that his ability to provide for his family financially made him a "great" husband: from his point of view, he had given his family everything they needed. He also felt that Nora's emotional demands were "unnecessary" and "impossible" to meet. "She's always at me," he would complain to Mat. Although Bailey agreed that he and Nora had their share of problems, he started the therapy feeling that it was a waste of time. "I'd rather be on my boat," he announced to Mat at their first session. Not knowing what else his wife wanted, he would declare he'd given her everything she needed.

Still, Bailey had good reasons for coming to the couple's sessions. A divorce could mean separation from his children, whom he loved. A divorce would be embarrassing. Bailey was worried what his parents would think if his wife of two decades divorced him. Divorce was also expensive; Bailey felt he'd worked too hard to now reduce his holdings by half.

The Richmonds agreed on a couple of important points. Both loved their children very much, and both said that their sex life was the most consistent and pleasurable aspect of the time they spent together.

At the outset, the Richmonds' sessions focused primarily on Nora's desire to be emotionally closer to Bailey; there was no mention of any physical violence between them, and it wasn't until two months into the treatment that Nora revealed that Bailey had seriously hurt her early in their marriage. Bailey admitted that he'd been violent and said he still felt ashamed and remorseful about Nora's injuries. But Bailey stressed that the incident was "ancient history." Nora agreed that despite the early incident and the ongoing undercurrent of aggression and neglect in her marriage, she was not in any way afraid of Bailey. But then she quickly added that she wasn't happy either.

The mention of the early violence and Nora's visit to the emergency room opened the door to further revelations about the combative nature of their marriage; soon, it was revealed that Nora was often the provocateur. She described how many of their fights began when she would try to talk to Bailey. When he was preoccupied or otherwise unwilling to engage, she said, she would sometimes try to get his attention by angrily tossing symbolic items such as gifts, flowers, or her wedding ring out the window.

Nora tearfully described a painful fight that they'd once had on Mother's Day. It started when Nora tried to have a "decent conversation" with Bailey; as usual, he wasn't interested. When she pressed him further, he left the room. Nora continued her pursuit until he screamed at her that she should go kill herself.

As Nora related incidents like this to Mat, she began to see the dynamic of abuse in her marriage more clearly. The scenario between the couple, almost always the same, began with her pleading for conversation and attention from him. The more insistent she became, the more Bailey resisted. Then the abuse would begin, with him insulting and cursing at her. She'd become frantic and grab at him, and he'd push her away. The more he pushed, the more she grabbed. Sometimes Bailey, fed up with the dynamic, would slap her or knock her down. In a rage, he'd flee the house, leaving Nora miserable and longing for connection.

Later, he would return. Usually, their pattern would be to withdraw to the bedroom, make up, and have sex. In therapy, Nora saw how the trigger point for the abuse and violence in her marriage was invariably her desperate need for intimacy.

As Nora opened up in therapy, Mat noticed a corresponding increase in Bailey's annoyance. Bailey would interrupt Nora, calling her crazy and claiming that nothing pleased her. She responded by saying how she wanted to share her fears with him. He didn't really care, he would say.

Angry and fed up, Bailey began to tell his side of the story. He talked about how hard he'd worked to build his business, how proud he felt of his accomplishments, and how unappreciated he felt. But it was deeper than that. He believed that Nora was just like his parents. He complained that, his whole life, he'd never gotten the praise and understanding he deserved.

Bailey had been alienated from his parents for years. He said that his parents fawned over his siblings but largely ignored him, which made him furious. In fact, his parents had recently turned over the family business to his brothers but had given him nothing. He believed that what they'd done was unforgivable.

Clearly his grievance from childhood was carrying over into his marriage: his wife refused to be satisfied with all of his accomplishments as a husband and father, just as his parents had never seen his good qualities as a child. Nora insisted on standards Bailey couldn't meet and then used them against him to make him feel bad about himself. But Bailey, unlike his wife, refused to reflect on his own actions or concede, in any way, that his behavior might have alienated his parents and damaged his marriage.

In counseling the Richmonds, Williams took a two-pronged approach to therapy. Early on, he emphasized to Nora and Bailey that they must start by being "accountable" for their behavior. Typically, Williams says, each partner blames the other for starting an argument: "What Nora and Bailey needed to understand was that just because one of them says something provocative, it doesn't mean the other has to respond by being verbally abusive. Each of them has a choice as to how they respond."

Despite this reminder, the couple sometimes experienced heated arguments in their sessions with Williams. He followed up with frequent phone calls and individual meetings, closely monitoring every back-and-forth between them to de-escalate the aggression. Williams concedes that he sometimes fears violence will erupt in couples counseling, but he adds, "It's my job to manage it—and to help my patients develop tools so that they can manage it, too."

Williams was especially attuned to educating the Richmonds about how toxic psychological and emotional abuse can be to families and how each party has a role to play in reducing its presence. He drew on the strength of their love for their children and on their desire to provide an environment in which their kids could thrive. But he also admits that the connection Nora hoped to achieve with Bailey never happened. "Some people in counseling are determined not to change," says Williams, "but that doesn't mean they didn't feel better as a result of the treatment."

Overall, Nora and Bailey both felt there were fewer blow-ups between them as a result of the counseling and that they were happier as a couple. This was in large part, Williams believes, because Nora understood that she had some control over what happened in her relationship, and she found other outlets to help balance out her need for Bailey's attention. She also started to understand, Williams observed, that *her* actions could trigger Bailey's abusiveness. Controlling her need to rely on him meant that she had some control over the aggression he expressed toward her. This surprised but also empowered her: it gave her some sense of how she could improve her relationship with her husband.

Nora had long been aware of the limitations of her marriage; that was what had brought her into therapy in the first place. But couples counseling changed her relationship to those limitations in a profound way. Perhaps Bailey was unwilling to change, but she could make a decision for herself about how *she* wanted to proceed. She realized that she could ask herself several key questions and that she controlled the answers: Did she want a divorce? Did she want to stay in the marriage and make the best of it? If so, could she accept that he was never going to change? And what could she do to fill her unmet emotional needs and reduce the aggression that made her feel so bad?

In the end, Nora decided she loved Bailey and didn't want to leave him. She recognized his good qualities—he was a loving father, a great lover, and a superb provider. At the same time, she also saw that her happiness could not hinge on Bailey's responses to her and that she needed to ensure that her emotional needs were met elsewhere. Nora has since gone back to work and is also developing a community of friends with whom she has forged close relationships. Once Nora expanded her life and nurtured some of her emotional needs, her demands on Bailey lessened; not coincidentally, so did the abuse in the marriage. It may not have been a perfect solution, but both Nora and Bailey had a better marriage as a result.

From a traditional feminist perspective, everything about this story is wrong. Bailey never admitted that he had a problem. Nora not only stayed in her marriage but also took on the primary responsibility for "fixing" it. In another sense, though, Nora's story is an inspiring one: she stopped feeling like a victim and ceased to encourage her own further victimization. She also stopped looking to her husband for things she knew he could never give her. She broadened her life both personally and professionally. And she was stronger and happier as a result—within her family but also within herself. Although Bailey never explicitly admitted that his aggression was inappropriate or uncalled for, he reduced his violence overall. Isn't this a kind of empowerment for women that we can live with?

STAYING OR LEAVING

Traditionally, domestic violence advocates feel that couples counseling might force the couple to stay together (or more accurately, pressure the wife to stay). In addition, an abusive husband might somehow use the therapy to justify or explain his abusive behavior. From one feminist perspective, the Richmonds' work with Mat Williams was typically harmful: Nora really should have left Bailey, but the couples counseling discouraged her from doing so.

I asked Aymer, Williams, Burmester, Geller, and Goldner whether they felt that the men and women who came to them for couples counseling secretly harbored conflicting agendas: were the women looking for an escape, whereas the men were hoping to undermine their partners' independence? I was also interested in how the therapists managed their own judgments about who should remain together and who should ultimately separate. The answers they gave me were surprising.

Aymer believes that most violent couples who seek treatment are unusually close and allied: generally, those who do not truly want to stay together are unwilling to share the shameful truths of their relationship with a professional. By the time they get to Aymer, he says, "they really want to make the relationship work."

Aymer takes this point one step further. He believes that couples experiencing violence are particularly poised to do productive therapeutic work together: "When couples come in with violence as a presenting problem, it is external, something that's happening, they can see it, feel it. It is something they can have control over. On the other hand, couples who come in without a violent history have vague complaints such as, 'He isn't listening.'" Aymer says that "it is much harder to pinpoint what the deeper problem is when the complaint is "not listening." "Violence," Aymer reports, "focuses the couple's attention."

He also suggests that a good therapist does not allow himself to be manipulated by the clients but instead can reframe even a negative experience into a therapeutic opportunity. "In one couple I was working with," Aymer says, "the woman decided she wanted a break from the relationship, and she announced this in one of our sessions." Initially, the man was unhappy with his wife's decision, but Aymer pointed out that it would give him a chance to explore his own issues: "We took the time during the separation for him to work on himself. When the wife returned three months later, things were much better. And the whole time during the separation, I could help monitor how he was doing. He wasn't obsessing about her because he had this safe place to focus on himself."

Virginia Goldner agrees and says that her experience at the Ackerman Institute revealed that when separation was likely, it became obvious to her very early on in the assessment process. In these cases the couple is "much more alienated, much more volatile," Goldner says. "It is like any couple that comes to treatment too late—there is not much of a bond, if any, left in these cases." Goldner and her codirector handled couples who seemed likely to separate differently from those who sought treatment to stay together: "We usually did not offer to do couples work, because it is a modality that intensifies affect. We would be more likely to try to arrange a number of referrals—individual therapists, a men's group, a women's support group, etc."

Janet Geller, who has worked with hundreds of abusive couples, admits she sometimes believes that the best solution for certain relationships is for the woman to leave. "But that's her decision, not mine. I think we should be respectful of what people want for themselves. I can point out options such as, 'Maybe this isn't the best relationship for you,' and I can help her explore what keeps her attached to him, but it's not my decision, and I would never make that decision for anyone, no matter how I feel about it."

I asked Geller why she did not feel that she could be more forceful in these cases. Geller, who learned early on that a therapist's pronouncements can serve to alienate a client, had no qualms about defending her position: "My job is to help those who want to be helped and to be open to what's possible, but never to tell them that this is what they should do. That would be disrespectful and would be just like an abuser who goes around telling a woman what to do."

In addition, her judgments have not always borne out. "In one of my recent cases," Geller says, "I saw this couple and I thought, 'What is she doing with this guy? She should get out.' As it turns out, he's stopped his violent behavior, and in many ways he's a lovely guy. I was very wrong about that couple. I have lots of years of experience doing this work, and I was dead wrong."

Like Geller, the couples counselor I saw with my partner, David, did not tell me what to do—but she did make her views clear in another way. Rather than suggesting that I leave David—which might very well have served to rupture the alliance she had built with me—she offered a simple offhand statement: "I don't think you'll ever leave David." Her comment stuck with me, and later that week I made the decision to separate. I ended the relationship altogether at the next couples session. Even though my decision to leave that week was precipitated by David pushing me, I still wonder today if I would have been so clear had she not offered such a provocative comment.

Can couples counseling also be helpful to couples when one or both partners may want to separate? Bill Burmester says absolutely. In one couple he's treating, the woman is determined to remain apart, whereas the husband would like them to stay together. They have two children. Burmester has found that their joint sessions have allowed them to "communicate about what wasn't spoken about earlier." This enhanced communication facilitates a kind of spirit of cooperation on other issues they must discuss together and make decisions about, such as their children's lives.

Burmester also doesn't reject the possibility of treating couples who have experienced violence or aggression for the purpose of helping them to separate peacefully: "Drawing on their mutual love for the children can be a powerful motivator for people." Indeed, Burmester believes that therapy can provide parents who are separating the chance to "team up and create an experience with one another with their children in mind. It can provide an experience that counteracts the acrimony of the violence."

WHERE DO WE GO FROM HERE?

When I asked the therapists I interviewed whether they thought that people were more open to treatments such as couples counseling than they were years ago, they all resoundingly said yes. When I asked them what the possibilities were for a future that included couples counseling, each of them commented on the importance of this work for improving treatment options for people in violent relationships. Virginia Goldner believes that domestic violence policymakers and practitioners "are now looking for treatments that work and looking for ways to complicate the approach to treatment. People are now realizing that 'pure' positions, like treating men and women separately, have largely failed." Goldner continues, "What seems clear is that the feminist movement's fear of complexity and ambiguity in violent relationships has been a real inhibitor in the development of complicated kinds of treatment that might actually have a chance of addressing the problem of domestic violence." She sums up: "Even politically oriented people are starting to realize that abuse can happen to anyone and that women and communities need empowerment that doesn't support the violence but does support men and women raising families."

Janet Geller sees the progress this way: "The main issue for me is that one treatment method does not fit all. Things are changing in a way that allows us to think more creatively about the possibilities. Couples counseling is definitely a part of that landscape, and should be."

Bill Burmester describes the work as "very energizing because you can see the progress a couple is making." Of one violent couple he's counseling, he says: "They're coming in with the real thing, and we're addressing it. They're getting what they need to correct the past and carry on in a new way in the future."

Of course, couples counseling has long been available to people who seek out such treatment and can afford to pay for it. Still, such approaches are not socially sanctioned and are now often unavailable to people who must attend (and pay for) treatment as a result of a domestic violence conviction. Those who are relegated to the options provided by the legal system are often left without the possibility of working *with* their partners to make the relationship better.

10
THE NEW GRASSROOTS MOVEMENT

SAFE and Violence Anonymous

Over the past thirty years, the battered women's movement has inspired many former victims of domestic violence to invest their efforts in addressing the absence of effective programs and policies, in order to help those who are still embroiled in abusive relationships. These grassroots efforts have consistently filled important voids in services. Many of the reforms inspired by the women's movement have succeeded in transforming not only how we treat the problem of intimate violence but also how we think about it.

The birth of the shelter system for battered women is a perfect example. For many Americans, the fact that battered women needed to escape their homes was, literally, inconceivable. But then willing community members who were more familiar with the disturbing truth about domestic abuse in this country started offering battered women a place to stay, free of charge. This informal assistance eventually grew into a network of more than two thousand shelters across the country. Similarly, many of the first domestic abuse hotlines were started by formerly battered women—they knew just how important it was to give women who were being abused a safe space to talk about their experiences and work through their options. The battered women's movement has had a long history of innovation by the very people who have experienced violence—and by friends and family members who have become inspired to help them. Now there are some new voices.

STOP ABUSE FOR EVERYONE

Jade Rubick is the founder of Stop Abuse for Everyone (SAFE). SAFE describes itself as a human rights organization that provides services, publications, and training in order to serve "those who typically fall between the cracks of domestic violence services: straight men, gays and lesbians, teens, and the elderly." Jade started SAFE in 1996, after his marriage fell apart and he came to terms with the fact that he was a battered man.

Jade Rubick was raised in Oregon by his mother in the Baha'i religious tradition. In 1993, as a nineteen-year-old student at the University of Oregon, studying Japanese, Asian studies, and computer sciences, Jade met and quickly married an international student who was seven years older than he was. Soon after marrying, his wife started abusing him verbally and physically: slapping him, striking him in the groin, pulling his hair, and throwing things at him. The incidents occurred as often as several times a week.

At the time, Jade was a foot taller and thirty pounds heavier than his wife, but he points out that height and weight differentials are only part of the equation when it comes to intimate violence:

> What matters really is *not* how strong you are, but the limits you put on your own behavior. And a person who truly has no limits, no matter how big or small they are, will use all sorts of nasty tricks to overpower you— they'll wear you down by arguing with you all night, they'll take it as far as they can. So it's really not about strength. It's about limits.

Jade remained in the relationship despite these attacks in part to honor his commitment and in part because his wife was mentally fragile and he worried that she might kill herself if he left her. He now believes that there was something else going on, as well: without realizing it, he had gradually fallen under her control. He remembers one night when they were quarrelling and his wife asked him to lie down on the bed; she then pulled his hair with both hands as hard as she could. When Jade asked her why, she said that she "needed to do it" because it "made her feel better."

At work, his employer noticed heavy bruising on his legs and confronted him, but Jade denied that anything was wrong at home: by not talking about it and enduring the abuse, he thought he was being "strong." He elaborated: "I kind of had a martyr complex. I was doing everything possible to make the relationship work by staying in it, and sticking by her was a sign of toughness. I was doing everything to make it work—even if it meant submitting myself to her rages."

Eventually his boss accused him of lying about his injuries, and he came clean. Together they developed an exit strategy, and his boss told him that when the time came, he would help Jade find a place to stay until he got himself back on his feet. Several months later, after yet another fight, Jade decided that he was ready; when his wife left for work, he gathered together a few of his things and moved out for good.

Then a junior in college, Jade looked to the university to help him under-stand what he'd been through. Was he the only man experiencing abuse? He decided to go to the library to research the issue, where he found the studies that Straus, Gelles, and Steinmetz conducted in the 1970s and 80s:

> I was shocked. I'd never heard of it at all, but the research was saying being battered as a man was pretty common. My first instinct was, This is crazy. I've never heard of this; this must be by crazy reactionaries, crazy anti-feminist researchers. I was raised very pro-feminist, so that was my in-stinct—to really question it. So I attempted to delve deeply into this issue, to make sure the researchers had used sound methodology. The more I looked into it, the more I was convinced.

Soon he realized that there must be thousands of men who felt as lonely and bewildered as he had. He also realized that his ignorance about his situation had made everything so much worse: "When I reflected on my own experi-ence, isolation was a very large part of it. You get that same thing in other abu-sive relationships, but add to that a feeling of shame that this is happening to you because you've never heard of it happening to other men—it feels emascu-lating. But that's kind of an intellectual response. Emotionally, it was very painful."

As part of a course on leadership that he was taking that year, Jade devel-oped the idea for a hotline and support group in his community in Eugene, Oregon. The first thing he did was create a website called Stop Abuse for Everyone (SAFE). The idea was to see how much interest there was in the issue of male abuse and to start a dialogue about it. When he received an unexpected amount of email from people living all over the world—"people working on this issue in isolation, counselors who'd discovered this problem among their clients, people ranging from wackos to the sincere"—he knew how important it was to move his idea forward.

What surprised him most about these responses was the severity of the physical abuse men were describing—"I thought I'd had it really bad, but then I heard about men in abusive relationships for twenty years, beat up every day, people whose partners were pretty close to killing them at times, stabbing their beds when they were asleep—clearly very, very abusive situations." In fact, the majority of men who contacted him were in relationships so physically violent that they felt they were in real danger.

Jade's research on available programs for men didn't turn up much: all of the programs he discovered served only battered women. Galvanized, he started to make contacts with people who might help him start a hotline for abused men. Every week, he would dedicate himself to making some progress toward this dream. After three years at the University of Toronto as a graduate student, he moved back to Portland and, working with Phil Cook, became determined to get SAFE up and running as a formal organization.

Phil and Jade then asked Stanley Green to join their steering committee. Jade had met Stanley online through the SAFE website, and Phil knew him from interviews he'd done for his book. Together, they got SAFE incorporated, designing it to be a chapter organization, so that people from different states who wanted to join the effort could do so; eventually, they hoped to create a truly national organization.

They made public education their top priority. Through the SAFE Speakers Bureau, men and women spoke honestly about all kinds of intimate abuse to audiences who were willing to listen. Focusing on populations generally ignored by the battered women's movement, they developed pamphlets for heterosexual men and gay, lesbian, bisexual, and transgender victims of intimate partner violence. They compiled research on men who were abused by women and started to make mainstream media appearances.

"Dear Abby was one of the first to promote us," Jade reports, "and she's been a contributor ever since. I wrote to her a few times in response to letters from men who were abused, and she was very responsive. I encouraged her to read the research, and she contacted us for more information. She clearly did her homework," he says proudly.

A few years ago, when Dr. Jack Turteltaub, a psychologist and member of the SAFE Board of Directors, was selected by the National Organization for Women to participate in the Gay and Lesbian Task Force charged with recommending changes to the Violence Against Women Act, Jade knew they were on the right track: "Building coalitions between heterosexual men and other underserved groups, such as gay men, lesbians, and transgendered people is the way to help repair divisions in this field."

For the past five years, SAFE has also participated in the International Conference on Violence, Abuse and Trauma, held in San Diego. Over 1,500 people and agencies attend this conference every year, giving SAFE the opportunity to talk to hundreds of advocates about the importance of responding to the needs of untraditional victims.

It has become the custom at domestic violence conferences to display cutouts of women who were killed by their male partners, each printed with her name and the date of her death. SAFE convinced the conference organizers to also display images of men who have died at the hands of their female partners. This is a clear sign of the progress they've made in penetrating more traditional venues.

SAFE also persuaded several people who were organizing the National Advisory Committee (NAC) on Violence Against Women to invite them to testify about the experiences of male victims. The NAC on VAW was established in January 2006 to "provide policy advice to the Attorney General and Secretary of Health and Human Services concerning the implementation of the Violence

Against Women Act, raising public awareness regarding violence against women, and facilitating cooperation among members of the criminal justice system and our communities." Although SAFE's presence was resisted by some committee members, it was clear that their message was heard by others. In fact, the following appears in NAC's Committee Recommendations: "While victims of domestic violence, sexual assault and stalking are predominantly female and female teens experience the highest rates of domestic violence and sexual violence, it must be noted that males are also victims." Although some of these concessions may still feel begrudging, these changes show that SAFE's more inclusive point of view is beginning to take hold.

SAFE-New Hampshire

Victims of intimate abuse like Jade Rubick turn to doing domestic violence work to help others who are facing the same difficulties that they have overcome. Some victims of domestic violence, however, are drawn to the work for reasons that they themselves don't fully understand: Lee Newman was one of those people.

In 1987, Lee became involved with a highly abusive woman in New Hampshire. He finally fled both the relationship and the state in 1994. Six years later, Lee returned to New Hampshire to go back to school. To help pay for it, he became an AmeriCorps volunteer advocating for victims of domestic violence—one of the first and only men to serve in this position at that time. He chose to volunteer at an organization called A Safe Place in New Hampshire because he wanted to be able to help women in need; he drew no parallels, however, between their situation and his own history.

Then one day, while he was taking calls on the hotline, a woman asked him if he had ever been a victim of domestic violence. When he heard himself saying, "I don't know if you'd call it that," he suddenly realized that that's exactly what he *should* have called it. And yet he'd never quite made the connection before. Shocked by this realization, he confided in two friends at the agency about his physically abusive relationship.

As the story spilled out, Lee and his coworkers realized that A Safe Place, which served only women at the time, would not have welcomed him had he gone there for help. Lee and his colleagues were also offended that the agency trained its employees to discourage lesbian victims from coming into the shelter. According to Newman, the agency felt that these cases challenged its basic assumption that women were always victims and men were always perpetrators. "Rather than figure out a way to handle the complexity," Newman reports, the agency "just cut these people loose, and didn't help them to the fullest extent." No matter how hard Lee and his friends tried to change the agency from the inside, A Safe Place didn't adapt. Eventually, Lee and his colleagues decided to form their own organization.

In 2002, their organization was absorbed by SAFE as an official chapter. Lee is now the executive director of SAFE New Hampshire. The following year, the SAFE hotline went national—twenty-four hours a day, seven days a week.

SAFE's program in New Hampshire is still quite small: Lee and a few dedicated volunteers manage the hotline. All federal funding for this sort of work must come through the New Hampshire Coalition Against Domestic and Sexual Violence, which has thus far refused to admit that battered men's needs are not being adequately met. Without federal support, SAFE has to rely on foundation and private donations, and so far they have not secured any large grants for their work. The little they do receive goes to a travel fund for engagements like the NAC meeting in Washington, DC, or the San Diego Violence, Abuse and Trauma conference, and to the costs of running a hotline.

SAFE's involvement in cases has increased significantly since they decided to offer the hotline nationally. In 2003, they had fewer than 400 calls; in 2004 and 2005, they had approximately 1,200 calls. Volunteers in 2006 put in 4,317 hours to support SAFE's work in New Hampshire.

As for the individuals SAFE serves, the latest numbers come from Newman's office in New Hampshire for 2005: nearly 1,200 heterosexual male victims of domestic violence and over 160 heterosexual female victims contacted SAFE New Hampshire by phone or email that year. In addition, SAFE New Hampshire assisted twenty-three gay male victims and thirty-four lesbian victims in 2005. They assisted a total of nineteen transgender victims, both male and female. Victims of school bullying and sibling violence were also served by SAFE that year. The alleged perpetrators in these cases were described by victims as a diverse group of men and women, boys and girls, heterosexuals and homosexuals.

Several other developments suggest just how influential SAFE has become, particularly in New Hampshire. For example, all members of the New Hampshire Coalition Against Domestic and Sexual Violence are supposed to serve men as well as women. In addition, the coalition members know that Lee is likely to find out about what's going on around town: if the member agencies aren't doing what the Coalition's director, Grace Mattern, has claimed they are doing—serving all victims—Lee is unlikely to stay silent about it. At a recent police training, for example, the domestic violence advocate giving the presentation referred to victims of domestic violence exclusively as women—until she noticed Lee in the room. She quickly incorporated more neutral and inclusive language into her lecture. "Sometimes I feel like a watchdog," Lee says, "but I've learned that if I stay quiet, nothing will change."

Placing his work in a larger context, Lee explains that he doesn't just receive calls from New Hampshire: "We get people from all over the country." In one case that Lee had been intimately involved with, a battered woman contacted the Illinois chapter of SAFE after her call to a domestic violence national hotline proved useless; Lee learned of her situation when his SAFE chapter partner, Cindy Wallace, called him from Illinois.

The woman had learned that her violent husband was planning to relocate the family to a right-wing separatist commune in a distant state. He was on a business trip, and expected his wife to be ready for the move when he returned. The house was filled with weapons, the woman reported, and he had threatened to use them if she didn't comply. She needed to find shelter immediately.

When she called the National Domestic Violence Hotline, however, she was devastated to learn that there was nothing they could do for her. Three of her children were teenage boys, and the hotline knew of no battered women's shelters in the country that would accept teen males. It was by chance that the victim had heard about SAFE and called the Illinois office. In two days, Lee, working closely with Cindy, found the entire family the shelter they needed and had arranged for their numerous legal issues—restraining orders, name changes—to be addressed.

"A man stepped forward from a local church and put up some money to help the family get out," Lee says. "It was amazing." Pleased with the work SAFE did to help this family, he adds, "By the time her husband returned, they were long gone, safely where they needed to be."

The case also solidified Lee's relationship with the Illinois chapter of SAFE in a way that he couldn't possibly have anticipated. At present there are only three chapters nationwide, but Lee would like to see a chapter in every state: "We could change a lot. The thought sends chills up my spine."

VIOLENCE ANONYMOUS

I first met James when he contacted me unexpectedly in early 2006 about a program he'd started called Violence Anonymous. James had been trolling the internet for people who might help him offer VA as an option for domestic violence treatment to individuals in need, and he came across my work on violence and recovery.

He explained that his new program was based on the principles of Alcoholics Anonymous. Meetings were held by phone every Sunday at eight P.M. Central Time. Those wishing to join the meetings simply called a number and punched in an access code. Anonymity was always guaranteed. James facilitated the meetings, and about six to eight people participated in each session.

"Many of the people calling in have attended treatment for different addictions, including anger, drug addiction, and sexual abuse," James wrote me. "We are just people recovering from violent behavior."

Several months later, I met James and his wife, Kate, in person. We agreed that, in the tradition of AA, I would not reveal their last names or the particulars of where they currently live. But both James and Kate were very eager to talk about their troubled history and how they were struggling to come to terms with it. They believed that intimate abuse needs to "come out of the closet" and that honesty is a vital part of real change.

When James first met Kate in 1998, he was a struggling musician in New York City. His childhood had been an abusive and unhappy one, and he'd gone on to have serious problems with drugs and alcohol in his teens and twenties. But now, at the age of thirty, he had been clean for over four years. He attended some sort of 12-step meeting—Alcoholics Anonymous, Debtors Anonymous—every day; it didn't matter what the topic of the meeting was as long as it was a 12-step program; he found the format extremely sustaining. He was working hard on his music and feeling committed to his recovery. He was full of hope for a different kind of future.

Kate, who was thirty-three, was visiting New York from England. Like James, she was a musician. She'd also grappled with the difficult circumstances of her childhood, which had been followed by a long and destructive bout with drug addiction. In addition to 12-step programs, Kate says that she had participated in nearly every form of therapy "known to man." By 1998, she was feeling grounded in her life and passionate about her music. She felt ready to put destructive relationships behind her and settle down.

They met at a Debtors Anonymous meeting, and the attraction was immediate. Both of them felt that their love for each other was different from anything they had experienced before. They courted for several months before becoming engaged, and only then did they have sex with each other. They also shared their darkest secrets, met each other's friends, and played music together. It was amazingly intense and special, and they were determined not to mess up what they had created between them. Then they got married in May 2000—and everything began to fall apart.

After the wedding, they settled in a Southern city, where James had a steady job in the music business. Kate felt fine about being away from her native country; the only problem was that she didn't have a green card yet, so she couldn't work. For the time being, however, they could easily get by on James's salary. Almost immediately, however, James came home after work one day and announced that he'd lost his job; he had gotten into a fight with his boss. Kate was angry and upset. She knew that James often had trouble getting along with people—especially authority figures—but she didn't think he would risk their security over a meaningless spat with his employer. In addition, for the first time in their relationship, he was yelling a lot about issues that seemed quite insignificant to Kate. One afternoon when Kate was cooking, she accidentally splattered oil onto their new kettle; James got very agitated, even though the fat was easily washed off. Kate didn't yet understand just how far all of this could go.

For his part, James knew at some very deep level that he was terrified of intimacy; he had been sexually abused by a trusted family member at a very young age, which made him suspicious of those closest to him—and Kate was now closer to him than anyone else. He thought he'd dealt with all of his fears long before his marriage, so he felt ambushed by the unexpected ambivalence he was feeling. On one hand, he knew he could count on Kate for her support; he felt comfortable, perhaps for the first time in his life, opening up to a woman. On the other hand, there were moments when he felt terrified, and all he wanted to do was run away. He was the perfect embodiment of the fearfully attached partner.

Kate, in the meantime, found herself at the mercy of a range of contradictory emotions. She could sense that James was struggling with something very important, and she was deeply sympathetic; at the same time, she was anxious about having her own needs met. After all, she had given up a lot to be with James—she'd moved halfway around the world for him. Didn't she deserve some attention? She felt abandoned by the man who should have taken care of her. She vacillated back and forth between inelegantly asserting her own needs ("You are being selfish; I need you to be there for me") and trying to be more supportive of him ("What you're going through is so difficult—what can I do for you?")

Money became very tight after James lost his job; James, feeling the pressure, turned his anger on Kate. She couldn't get a job without working papers, but she wasn't going to sit back and take his rage either: "I am married now, and I need to make sure I get taken care of," she found herself saying to him. Before long, they'd been evicted from their townhouse for their noisy quarrels. "Too much fighting," the landlord said. "We don't need your screaming so close to our peaceful household."

Kate's AA sponsor came to the rescue by providing them with a temporary place to live, but the tension between them only continued to build. James found himself increasingly besieged by excruciating memories from his childhood. In one, he remembered waiting to see whether it would be him or his brother who would be summoned to his relative's bed. He also recalled the time he ran away from home and lived on the street when he was in elementary school. After witnessing someone get killed over a bit of money, he tried to find his house again. He managed to make his way back to his school, which he recognized. The school then notified his mother, who came to bring him home. But were all of these memories real, and if so, how could he have forgotten them in the first place, and what did they mean about his past? Why were they all flooding to the surface now?

He was also becoming both more fearful and more aggressive. He developed an intense response to knives, even though he couldn't remember why or how they might have been significant to him as a child. Kate liked to cook, and she felt this was one way that she could take care of him. But every time she had a knife in her hand, he would become anxious. "Get that thing away from me," he'd say.

One night, half asleep, James kicked his slumbering wife so hard that she fell off the bed and hit the wardrobe. The next morning she had bruises on her legs. Kate didn't ask for an explanation—she was too shocked and too scared—and James wouldn't have been able to explain himself if she had. "I had no idea what I was doing back then," James recalls. "I was completely lost in my memories and couldn't find a way through it."

Later that night, a quarrel escalated into a major fight. It became so heated that James, not knowing how to put an end to it, called the police. Two officers answered the call, a male and a female, and they talked to James and Kate separately. Initially, Kate mentioned the incident in bed, but then she amended her original statement when she realized that it could land James in jail. At the end of the interview, the cops told James that he needed to leave the house—that he was putting his wife at risk. But Kate knew that James was in no shape to function in the outside world. "Fuck it," she thought. "I'll just go." She gathered a few things, and the officers drove her to the local women's shelter.

Kate was shocked by what she saw at the shelter—women whose teeth had been knocked out by their boyfriends or who'd suffered other acts of extreme violence at the hands of their lovers. She didn't believe that her situation with James would ever reach that point, but she agreed that a temporary separation was the best thing for both of them.

"In the shelter, I spoke to a social worker. I explained my predicament. I was literally begging for help. Where could I go? Whom could I talk to? What agency or organization assisted violent couples? What were people who loved each other but were in abusive relationships supposed to do? That was my quandary! The answer I got from the social worker was: 'He's never going to change. The violence is all *his* fault. You're the *victim* in this relationship. The only true problem you have is that *you* are refusing to leave.'"

Kate argued that she didn't, in fact, want to leave her partner—that she loved him. What she wanted was to find some way to work out her problems *with* her partner. But apparently that was considered beyond the realm of possibility. "Something good did come out of my talk with that deaf social worker," Kate says now. "The conversation made me think. It made me realize that as a person in an abusive relationship, I was on my own. I had to figure out my problems for myself."

Although the shelter rules prohibited her from seeing James, she was still allowed to attend her 12-step meetings every day. She worked out that she had about ten minutes at the end of each meeting before she was expected to be back at the shelter. During this short period of time she would visit with James—even though she risked being kicked out of the shelter—and they would talk and cry together.

Part of the problem, Kate realized, was that she could sense James pulling away from her as he became increasingly consumed by his childhood memories. This made her feel abandoned, even though she understood that his preoccupations with his past had nothing to do with her. This sense of loneliness triggered bad feelings that Kate carried around from her own past. "I grew up needy," she told me, "always wanting more from my parents. I wanted their attention and love, but I never really got it—or at least enough of it." But she also came to see that her preoccupation with getting James's attention when he was at his most vulnerable and incapable of giving her what she needed constituted a form of emotional violence. Perhaps it was time she took responsibility for what *she* could change.

Kate stayed at the shelter for almost two months. By the time she was ready to come home, both she and James knew that they needed to be in therapy. Luckily, unlike so many other couples struggling with violence, they were used to confronting their demons. James took a week in a mental health recovery center, and Kate went to the same recovery center the following week. At the center, James was diagnosed with Post Traumatic Stress Disorder, which helped to explain his mood swings and his unpredictable reactions. They entered couples counseling, and they did individual therapy as well. They also went to 12-step meetings every day.

Once James and Kate started living together again, they believed that they had a shared understanding of the problem. But when the reality of daily life kicked in, things quickly took a turn for the worse. Kate started earning some money so that James could take time off and address his childhood trauma in therapy. But this only fueled his sense of self-loathing, and he became increasingly remote. Kate could see that she needed to minimize the demands she placed on James, and so she started building a network of supports outside the marriage—attending AA meetings on her own, arranging lunches and evenings with friends, thinking about her own music. This shared understanding of what they each needed wasn't blame—again, their 12-step work had taught them that blame wasn't particularly useful—but rather a belief that it was up to both of them to take care of themselves as well as each other.

Time moved on, and things calmed. Still, every six months or so they would have some screaming match about how one or both of them felt let down by the other. Usually, they could draw on the well of strength they had developed over the many months of their recovery together. At other times, though, they seemed powerless to stop the back-and-forth. During one of these arguments, James was in the car, and Kate was standing beside it. James turned the engine on, and Kate sat on the front of the car to prevent him from driving away. James took off with Kate holding on to the windshield. They were playing out the dynamic that was all too familiar to them: James wanted to leave, and Kate didn't want him to go. But they stayed together and continued to work through their difficulties.

Kate was pregnant by the end of 2004. On one hand, they were both thrilled; they had been together for six years, which felt like a tribute to the work they'd done on their own and the progress they had made together. Still, their intermittent fights did not entirely reassure them that this new stage—and further commitment—would be without conflict. And they were right.

Five months into her pregnancy, Kate and James started fighting over what often came between them—his distant behavior. "You're not going to treat me this way when I am pregnant," she warned. Her belligerent tone completely set James off.

James's and Kate's versions of the argument differ at this point. Kate remembers confronting James and being "very much in his face." James remembers Kate's confrontational tone but also her flailing arms, which felt threatening to him. Either way, the situation quickly escalated, and within minutes James had wrestled Kate to the floor and pinned her arms.

It was a shocking moment for both of them, similar to the climactic fight between Jeff and Sarah McPherson, except in this case—perhaps because of all the work they'd already done as a couple—they managed to break apart without either of them doing serious harm. James was horrified by how close he'd come to actually hitting Kate: "How could I live with myself if I injured my wife and unborn child? I rose from the floor, and I left the house. I just left. I really fled. I was so grateful that I hadn't hurt her. But I was also so scared that that moment of violence could come again. Now it wasn't just Kate and me. Now it was Kate, me, and our baby. I had to do something."

Kate had promised herself a long time ago that if James was ever violent again she would call the police. When they arrived a few minutes after she'd called, they took pictures of Kate's bruises for the police report. A few days later, a prosecutor called Kate and told her that it was up to his office—not her—whether they would file charges and that he had two years to take action. They would hold the case open. However, James was never formally arrested— probably because there were no additional incidents reported.

Every couple of weeks, a detective would call Kate and inquire about whether there were any new incidents of violence. "No," Kate would report honestly.

Kate and James lived apart over the next eight months. They started writing letters to each other about how much they loved each other and wanted to make it work. For James, the question was how. By this point, James felt that there wasn't a program he hadn't tried over the years to help him recover from his troubled past. "Despite all this," he says, "I found that I was unable to control my violent outbursts no matter how hard I tried—and I tried really, really hard." This wasn't to say that he felt the work he'd done was useless. "Understand," he says, "everything that I've done to help myself has helped me. I've educated myself. I've kept myself out of jail. And thank God, I've never seriously injured anyone." But it also wasn't enough. "I knew in my heart that I was getting progressively worse. I was getting angrier and angrier. I could feel it. And I couldn't find anything in all these programs that I've been to that could stop my violent behavior."

James's experience isn't uncommon. Often people plagued by addictions assume that if only they could break their dependencies, all of their problems would be over. But of course many of us turn to drugs and alcohol in the first place as an escape or means of obliterating some terrible unhappiness that has come before. When the narcotics that have kept the original pain at bay are finally removed and new pressures are introduced—in this case, the threat of intimacy in marriage—the original damage can suddenly and starkly reveal itself in other ways.

Initially, James tried to deal with his violence by "going directly at it," but that wasn't getting him anywhere. "I needed a step-by-step process—something that broke it all down into pieces—so that I could see how my anger gets stimulated in the moment as clearly as I could see, overall, how abusive I'd become."

James's epiphany was similar to Kate's earlier realization in the shelter: he was going to have to discover whatever help he needed within himself. He also needed something that would specifically address his violence. He found himself turning toward models he knew so well. "I have for a long time been a true believer in AA's 12-step approach. I know from experience that it can work."

Each of the 12-step programs has developed a slightly different version of the steps people follow on their path toward recovery; nevertheless, there are several essential components that are always a part of the process: For example, a person in 12-step must admit powerlessness over his addiction and the importance of turning himself over to a higher power; he must take a "moral inventory" of himself—in other words, review how he's doing from a moral point of view. He must admit to at least one other person the nature of these wrongs and ask "God" or a higher power to remove his shortcomings. (Twelve-step guides usually specify that the term "God" signifies "God as we understand him"—a universal spiritual power that signifies a force larger than ourselves.) He must make a list of the people harmed by his addiction and develop a willingness to make amends to those people whenever possible. In addition, he must stay vigilant in monitoring his behavior, practicing spirituality so that the connection with a higher power is always available, and, finally, stay open to recovery in all aspects of life.

The person who seeks recovery through a 12-step program works through the steps one at a time. It is thought that by the time you reach the end of the twelve steps, you are well on the way to recovery. Many people then start at the beginning again, to learn more about what they might have missed the first time around.

Members of AA and companion programs for family members, like Al-Anon, gather together daily in group meetings around the world to tell their stories to each other. At the heart of AA is the notion of fellowship—the belief that people can help each other through the process of spiritual conversion and recovery.

In January 2005 James decided to start a 12-step program for people living with violence. In other words, he invented the solution he so desperately needed, because he didn't know where else to turn.

"At that point, all I had was an idea. I soon found out that it's the *implementation* of a great idea that's the real accomplishment. The first thing I did was go to a local church and tell them about my idea. The folks at the church were extremely generous, and they immediately gave me a free room to hold weekly meetings."

"My second task—a much, much harder one—was to find violent men who would agree to attend my meetings. I began by going to AA meetings, and other local meetings, around town. I talked about Violence Anonymous, and I invited the men in these meetings to join me, if they felt they had a problem. Many times I spoke directly to men whom I knew had serious problems with violence. They would say, 'Oh, that's a great idea, a Violence Anonymous! I need to come. I *really* need to come.' Anyway, whether people came or didn't, the meetings continued," James recalls. "I know this sounds crazy, but I would sit alone in that room in the church, and I'd conduct a meeting by myself. What was happening in my essentially one-person Violence Anonymous meetings was that I'd just talk and talk about what I was feeling, what was going on, and also about the particular step I was working on. And the walls listened."

As the weeks passed, James began to see that his violent behavior exhibited itself in many ways: "Sometimes it was through manipulation and control. Or sometimes I would make *myself* a victim in a situation and then use my being a victim as a reason to exert control. When this happened, I could see how I was just looking to start a fight. Slowly, I began to understand myself much better. I became much more aware of what I was doing, and as the months went by, I began to feel as though, for the first time, I had the power to control my abusiveness."

Kate was less clear about what she needed to do, but she did realize that taking care of James at the expense of her own needs was never going to work out over time. "Really, for me, I needed to take responsibility for valuing myself, instead of getting angry that James wasn't valuing me, and getting into a violent exchange. What I realized was that when I am angry at James for not respecting me, usually it means that I'm not respecting myself. It's 95 percent me, 5 percent James. Usually what's behind it is my childhood and a great deal of sadness, and I notice that to avoid the sadness, I prefer to pin my feelings on someone else. Then we would have three days of drama—that was the passion for me."

But Kate could see that James was changing in new and profound ways: "James was literally transforming before my eyes." He was much less willing to engage in his wife's dramas—her need for negative attention—and he was finding new ways to manage his anger. Her confidence in their future together was growing.

James's desire for a real support group deepened. But where could he find other members? Ideally, his fellowship would be made up of both victims and abusers—he wanted anyone struggling with violence to feel welcome, and his own experience had taught him that sometimes both members of the couple could be, in different moments, the aggressor or the victim. Then one week, James spoke at a teleconference meeting of Debtors Anonymous. Over the past few years, using the telephone had become a new avenue for holding 12-step meetings. After James spoke, several women asked James if he'd have an open VA meeting over the phone. When Kate heard from James that he was going to start a telephone fellowship, she knew that she wanted to join.

"On that phone call, I had this epiphany," James recalls. "I realized that people simply cannot come to an open 12-step meeting that is only about violence. The reason was suddenly so obvious to me; it was just too awful for people to publicly admit that they are abusers or victims of violence." James finds the intensity of the shame especially notable in light of the fact that we live in an era of self-exposure. Admitting you're violent or a victim of violence is still very taboo.

"At this point in our cultural evolution, it's simply too humiliating for a woman to come and talk *openly* about her husband raping or beating her, controlling her every action, treating her like a servant, threatening to take her kids from her, or constantly putting her down. It's likewise too humiliating for a guy to come and talk *openly* about his wife beating him up, pointing a gun at him, wrecking his car, torturing his dog, making light of the abuse, or saying he's a liar."

James now has the ability to see some humor in his earlier naïveté: "My brilliant idea of having weekly meetings for people embroiled in violence in a room in a church in a small town in the American South was just never going to happen." But he couldn't bear to give up, and he knew the call-in system was the solution. "'That could actually work,' I thought. Because on the telephone, you're invisible—you're just a voice with a first name. A person can say whatever they want and not have to worry about exposure. I'd finally found *the* way to overcome the humiliation of in-person meetings." James was ecstatic. "At that moment," he adds, "I felt like a warrior who'd waged and won a great and lonely battle."

The Telephone Fellowship

The format of the VA program is simple. James starts every meeting with the Violence Anonymous Preamble, which he wrote:

> Violence Anonymous is a program for women and men who, through shared experience, strength, hope and honesty are recovering from violent behavior. Whether the violence happened as adults or as children, Vio-

lence Anonymous welcomes everyone who wants to stop the emotional, physical or mental violence in their lives. Are you ready to stop the cycle of abuse in your relationships? So are we.

Physical and sexual assaults, or threats to commit them, are the most apparent forms of violence and are usually the actions that allow others to become aware of the problem. However, regular use of other abusive behaviors, when reinforced by one or more acts of physical violence, makes up a larger system of abuse. Although physical assaults may occur only once or occasionally, they instill threat of future violent attacks and allow the abuser to take control of the partner's life and circumstances.

These are some of the ways violence is carried out:

- Intimidation
- Emotional abuse
- Isolation
- Minimizing, denying, and blaming
- Using children
- Economic abuse
- Male privilege
- Coercion and threats
- Spiritual violence

There are those among us who found that the behaviors of violence, whether emotional, psychological or physical, stem from a desire to exhibit power and control over people and circumstance. We have found that without a spiritual awakening, this condition is progressive and untreated can result in imprisonment and death. For those of you who are sincerely willing to change, there is hope. May you find it now.

James then reads the twelve steps of recovery for Violence Anonymous, which he adapted from Alcoholics Anonymous:

1. We admitted we were powerless over violence—that our lives had become unmanageable.
2. We came to believe that a power greater than ourselves could restore us to sanity.
3. We made a decision to turn our will and our lives over to the care of God as we understood God.
4. We made a searching and fearless moral inventory of ourselves.
5. We admitted to God, to ourselves and to another human being the exact nature of our wrongs.
6. We were entirely ready to have God remove all these defects of character.

7. We humbly asked him to remove our shortcomings.
8. We made a list of all persons we had harmed, and became willing to make amends to them all.
9. We made direct amends to such people wherever possible, except when to do so would injure them or others.
10. We continued to take personal inventory, and when we were wrong promptly admitted it.
11. We sought through prayer and meditation to improve our conscious contact with God as we understood God, praying only for knowledge of God's will for us and the power to carry that out.
12. Having had a spiritual awakening as the result of these steps, we tried to carry this message to perpetrators of violence and to practice these principles in all our affairs.

Once the meeting is opened, participants simply tell their stories. A participant might talk about a specific violent or abusive experience and how that fit in with her recovery, or the step she was focusing on at the time. She might share how she came to Violence Anonymous. Or she might let other members know how her life has changed since joining the fellowship.

Four basic principles dominate each meeting: anonymity, group support, learning by listening, and learning by telling. "The everyday face of intimate abuse," James says, "needs to be exposed in order for people to feel comfortable talking about it. Violence Anonymous helps accomplish that simple goal." Violence Anonymous also has a website announcing the number people can call and when.

One anonymous caller agreed to share her VA experience with me by email.

I grew up in a middle-class Jewish family. My mother never worked, and my father was never home. He owned restaurants and kept very late hours.

For as early as I can remember my father would come in my bedroom late at night after I was crying or asking for attention of some sort, I was only 7 years old. He told me if I didn't shut up I was going to get it. I always just asked a question like please talk to me I'm scared of the dark and I want to know what to dream about. I would persist and he would start beating me with a leather strap until I was crying myself to sleep. This happened on more occasions than not.

I have had a long and painful love life because of my father—by the way, my mother was in the room next door and never even got out of bed on any of those occasions.

I've been in therapy for over 20 years and found VA on the phone meeting lines. When I found VA it put many of the missing pieces together for me. I found other people like me who would attract violent men into their lives and go as far as to provoke the violent person until they would get enraged, it was almost an addiction.

The enormous gains that so many people in AA have made in their struggles with alcoholism give us an appreciation of the potential for this new program. If Violence Anonymous had only a fraction of AA's success, thousands of people experiencing intimate abuse would at last have—for the cost of a phone call—virtually instant access to help and support.

Inevitably, there will always be people who are highly resistant to the idea that a support group could successfully combat domestic violence. But it is important to remember that, at AA's inception in the 1930s, those same doubts existed about its efficacy. After all, alcohol, like violence, is a formidable and destructive force that has torn apart hundreds of thousands of families. And yet, for those who are truly ready to change their lives, AA has proved to be transformative—again and again and again.

The model of AA also offers some useful parallels when it comes to questions of taking responsibility for one's violence. Many people who don't know much about AA find the idea of "admitting one's powerlessness" and "turning oneself over to a higher power" slippery and dishonest: Isn't this sort of thinking simply a crutch, an excuse for one's bad behavior? In fact, AA's policy of accepting the humanity of the person but never the inhumanity and destructiveness of the *behavior* is an important feature of its success. The principal thrust of the program for its participants is not evading responsibility but assuming it—often for the first time in their lives. At the same time, these troubled individuals are being drawn back into the community in a healthy and forgiving way. The parallels that this model holds for families living with violence—angry and afraid of one another, but also often deeply ostracized and alienated from the larger culture—is impossible to ignore.

Kate and James Today

Since January 2005, James has worked through the Violence Anonymous twelve steps twice—as someone who is addicted to violence and as someone who is enabling someone else's violence. Kate has done one full cycle and is working on the second, but in the opposite order. Both of them feel transformed by it—as individuals and as a couple.

In my conversations with Kate about her experience of VA, she explains that it has been enormously helpful to her, and she acknowledges her debt to her husband for having founded it. Finally, the pieces of her past are coming together for her, as well.

"As a young woman," Kate says, "I was a drug addict. I've been clean and sober since 1989. I spent the first ten years of my recovery attending 12-step meetings and helping other addicts, as well as myself." But for Kate, as for

James, her addictions had been masking deeper problems. "I still sometimes found myself in relationships with men who were disrespectful. These men would verbally and emotionally abuse me. I felt very ashamed when this was happening. I kept much of it a secret from my friends and family. But I had an even deeper secret than my abusive relationships. My deepest secret was that in my heart, I thought I deserved the abuse that was being heaped upon me. When it was happening, I believed all the terrible things that I was told—the put-downs, the name calling, and the mind games designed to make me think I was crazy and stupid."

As Kate worked on step 4—conducting a searching moral inventory—she began to see that her problems with these abusive lovers were really problems with herself: "I have been struggling with who I am. I know, of course, that many of my problems go back to my childhood. I don't want to put the blame on my parents. They tried hard, and I know they love me. And I love them dearly. But my childhood was difficult. My parents were divorced. My father was sick. My mother seemed unhappy and angry much of the time. I now think my childhood paved the way for my troubling relationships with men."

It was only in VA that Kate developed the ability to examine the particulars of her violent relationship with James, and this enabled her to see her part in their ongoing dynamic. Suddenly her past and her present, her anger and her fears, all began to fit together and make sense in a new way: "I began to see how I was incredibly needy with my partners. I wanted love, love, love, and more love. I simply couldn't get enough of love. But then when my partner tried to come close, I'd become this cold-hearted bitch. I wanted the love, but I couldn't accept the love. I couldn't accept the intimacy."

"That moment of switching to being a bitch was the moment of combustion. That's when my partner would become abusive. And when the explosion of abuse happened, I'd switch back to being that needy little girl again. 'Why are you yelling at me?' I'd scream. 'Why are you so angry with me? Why are you treating me this way? I haven't done anything wrong.' I was back to my childhood, feeling incredibly needy and very much the victim, again."

Kate believes that James must take responsibility for his abusive behavior, but that she must also take responsibility for the ways in which she triggers that behavior: "To be free of abuse, I also have to change."

In some ways this has been a very painful period for her: "I've wasted so much time being a victim. I'm grieving for my lost past." On the other hand, for the first time in her life, she is no longer so terrified of intimacy, and although there is always a temptation to play the victim and push James away, she no longer indulges it: "Some terrible fear inside me has been lifted. God has granted me a moment in which I am able to step out of the abuse that was so much a part of my life. James and I now have a beautiful little boy, and we want him to grow up with two happy, healthy, and peaceful parents."

James and Kate confirm that there has been no act of physical violence in their lives together since the founding of VA. But it isn't simply the absence of physical abuse that is significant here; it's that the dynamic between them as a couple has radically changed. The screaming matches, once the trademark of their relationship, have disappeared. There are still tensions during periods of transition—"I don't know; maybe we're hardwired to be violent during these stages when everything's changing," Kate says—but they have learned not to engage with each other at these moments. James has set up "bottom lines" for himself about raising his voice, for example, and that has also helped. "It's a lot easier to just be there, and tolerate it, and not feel threatened by it, not take it personally," James explains. "To just watch it, be as supportive as you can, and then get out of the way when and if necessary." They are learning how to solve their differences "in a far more adult way, not like a couple of teenagers having a temper tantrum—and then a power struggle."

James and Kate find it both amusing and gratifying that people now comment on how wonderfully they communicate with each other and how pleasurable it is to spend time with them as a couple; in the past, their fighting cost them many relationships with both friends and fellow musicians. "It's a real turnaround," Kate says wryly, "from people literally running away when they saw us to people running towards us."

Perhaps most surprising is that James's work in VA has also changed his relationships outside of his marriage. Now that he is less anxious, for example, he doesn't try to control his professional relationships so aggressively, which often damaged them in the past. He has also stopped looking for validation for his talents from people or situations in which it's unlikely to be forthcoming: "Instead, I put my energy into other opportunities that are more attractive, and where I feel like I'm getting what I need."

So at present, after almost ten years of hard work, Kate and James are happier than they have ever been in their personal lives and more successful professionally than ever before. Theirs is a story of tremendous struggle but also one of great hope. "Just as stories are at the heart of AA, stories are also at the heart of Violence Anonymous," James says. "There are many lessons to be learned from our experience."

THE POWER OF THE GROUP

Not only have victims and perpetrators developed innovations in programming for victims of intimate abuse and their families; professionals have also recognized and responded to gaps in services. I found several programs—Family Wellness in New York City, the Marriage and Family Therapy Program in Virginia, and Northwest Network in Washington—that challenged the conventional thinking about intimate abuse. I was struck by the fact that all three of these organizations draw on the strength of a tried-and-tested approach to recovery: bringing a group of people together to support one another as they go through the difficult process of trying to improve their lives.

FAMILY WELLNESS PROGRAM, NEW YORK CITY

In 1996, Dr. Peggy Grauwiler, a social worker by training, was hired to work with the New York criminal court system to provide services to victims who were cycling through the dedicated domestic violence court in Brooklyn. This job exposed Grauwiler to scores of victims assistance programs; her task was to identify the programs she felt best met the needs of their clients. She observed that almost no program at the time provided services for women who were still undecided about leaving their abusive partners.

Several years later, however, while she was working on her doctorate in social work, Grauwiler came across the Children's Aid Society's Family Wellness Program, which was founded in 2000. Unlike most programs specifically dealing with violence prevention and intervention, Family Wellness serves the whole family: men can receive group treatment for their physical, emotional, or sexual violence before the criminal justice system intervenes; women can join a support group for victims; and teens and children can participate in groups that recognize the devastating effects of witnessing abuse in the family. In other words, Children's Aid sees that the wellness of the child cannot be easily separated from the wellness of the parents—a common notion in child welfare circles, perhaps, but more rare among advocates for victims of domestic violence. Although Children's Aid doesn't offer family therapy for violent couples, their belief that all members of the family—including men—can benefit from treatment is a very unusual one.

Kerry Moles, a social worker and the director of Family Wellness, observes that the agency's long history of helping families experiencing violence taught them about the inadequacy of relying solely on the criminal justice system. "When there's abuse in the family, every single member of the family is affected," Moles told me. "The only way that people can heal is if everybody in the family can heal." It was also clear to Children's Aid administrators that the families they were seeing "didn't fit the services being provided."

Grauwiler was particularly interested in the Women's Group at Family Wellness because it made all battered women feel welcome. Grauwiler interviewed ten women who had participated in the group in order to find out whether it had been helpful to them. Emily was one of them.

SUPPORT WITHOUT JUDGMENT

Emily met Frank at church. She joined a new congregation when she started college, and Frank's father was its pastor. From the very early stages of their relationship, Emily supported them both with her job as a paralegal.

For the first two years, Emily said her relationship with Frank was "good" and "a lot of fun." Then, at age twenty-two, she became pregnant with their first child, and they decided to move in together. The relationship quickly deteriorated. It started with insults and Frank's attempts to control their finances, even though Emily was the primary breadwinner. As time went on, Frank also tried to control Emily's movements outside the house. Then, when she was eight months pregnant, Frank choked her during an argument because "he didn't like the tone of her voice." She was terrified. For the first time, Emily realized that Frank could kill her.

The next morning, Emily called her mother for advice. Her mother told her that she should pack up and get out; Emily moved to her mother's, where she lived until she gave birth. Afterward, Emily moved back in with Frank, believing she should try and make the relationship work "for the baby's sake." She also felt that the apartment Frank was now living in was her home, and she wasn't ready to give it up. But Frank continued to be violent. When the abuse persisted during her second pregnancy, Emily wanted to learn what her options were. She called the New York City domestic violence hotline.

"I wanted, number one, somebody who would listen to me," Emily explained. "There were a lot of things on my mind I had to get straight. Everything was confused; everything was in a blur. I didn't know right from left, up from down. I really needed guidance. I also needed assistance because my bills were a little behind, and I just needed somebody to show me, tell me how I could get out of this situation, give me a game plan, show me how I can do this without having to leave everything I've worked hard for."

To her disappointment, however, the hotline counselor had only one thing to say: "'Pick up your stuff and go'" Emily felt that this response wasn't helpful to her. "There are some people who are not ready to leave the home," she pointed out. "It's not going to be a situation where you always find a person who's like, 'I need to get out of the house now.'" The hotline recommended a shelter for battered women. But Emily didn't feel that a shelter was the right move for her.

Eventually, Emily settled on kicking Frank out of the apartment, and he complied; she also applied for a restraining order. This course of action had its own set of challenges. Even as a paralegal, she found the legal process frustrating: "To get an order of protection it takes a whole day. You have to spend the whole day in family court. They make it so hard. You stand in line. You fill out forms. You hand in the forms. You have to wait for them to call you. Everything could be done in two seconds, but it takes the whole day to do it. . . . The court officers have a lousy attitude." All this made her want to give up. "So by the time you sit down, read the paper, and are trying to fill out everything, you're like, 'Oh, I just feel like leaving.'"

Everywhere Emily turned, she was encouraged to leave the abusive relationship, but whenever she asked for help in doing so, she felt that she was blocked from getting the kind of assistance she needed. Instead of someone helping her to sort out her next steps, she was told what to do; instead of the court granting the order of protection in a few hours, she had to miss work and spend the whole day sitting around. And on top of everything else, when she visited the welfare office to seek financial assistance, she was told that they couldn't help her because she was working. When Emily encountered these difficulties, she felt she was running into "brick walls." Sometimes she'd see it as a sign that she was doing the wrong thing. At other times, she'd bounce back and look for more help: "There was a part of me that just kept saying, 'Don't give up. Don't give up.'"

From the perspective of many outsiders, Emily had already solved her domestic violence problem; she had left Frank and gotten a restraining order. But she didn't feel that way about it: she still felt "in" it, even if Frank was no longer in the apartment. For one thing, he was still in her life because of the children; Emily believed strongly that kids shouldn't be penalized for "the problems between their parents," and didn't want to do anything to harm the connection they had with their father. Still, this made it more difficult for her to move on with her life;

she wasn't always sure that she was doing the right thing. Finally, Emily came across the Family Wellness Program and joined the Women's Support Group.

Emily was both taken aback and pleased by the group's supportiveness; what mattered was where she was, not where the counselors wanted her to be: "No matter who's your counselor [at Family Wellness], they all listen to you. They don't take the approach, 'Oh, I know what you need, here take it, you're wrong.' They listen to you. They understand." In this atmosphere of nonjudgmental support, Emily felt safe enough to begin exploring the meaning of her relationship with Frank—both in the past and in the present.

The Women's Support Group, which lasted eighteen weeks, was made up of women from all races, educational backgrounds, and incomes. All of them had children; most of them had come to the Children's Aid Society as mothers. Several of the women were in Emily's situation—they had *some* contact with their abusive partners. Others were still living with the men who abused them; still others had left their relationships altogether and had never looked back. The one thing all the women had in common in the group was that they had children. The group provided a safe place for women facing similar struggles to consider the destructive dynamics in their personal lives.

Each week the group focused on specific exercises outlined in *The Relationship Workbook*, depending on the particular needs of the group participants. The *Workbook* contains over fifty activities and worksheets to help women analyze what has gone wrong in the past and what they might do to improve things in the future. For example, the women were asked to read about "Lucy and Will" and then answer questions about their relationship.

Lucy and Will have been living together for a year when Lucy comes to counseling because she feels "depressed and anxious." She describes how Will has felt unsatisfied sexually and says that he blames her for the problem. Lucy attends school during the day and works at night. When she tells Will she's too tired to have sex, Will tells her how selfish she's being. He encourages Lucy to drop out of college and start taking care of him and their home. He also tells her "there are a lot of women who would be happy to take care of" his needs. Lucy is worried that Will might leave her for another woman.

For this exercise, the women in the group were encouraged to "describe examples of the 'power and control' tactics found in this case study." By the time they got to this exercise—about a quarter of the way through the workbook—they had heard a lot about power and control in abusive relationships. Once they were done writing down their answers, they discussed the case study with the group. This discussion gave the women an opportunity to explore not only what's unhealthy about Will and Lucy's relationship but also how it might relate to their own lives.

Another important exercise in the workbook is called "For Adults from Abusive Homes." This exercise encouraged participants to think about their childhoods and to connect what is happening in the present with what happened to them in the past. Helen, another participant at Family Wellness, was grappling with how her mother had spoken to her when she was little and how that might be affecting her current relationship. Helen remembered sitting on her mother's bed just after getting her first period, at the age of eight, and being told that no man would ever marry her: "They're just going to use you," her mother said. "You're too dark. Your hair is too short. You're ugly. You're worthless." Helen came to realize that she had gradually started to believe her mother's words.

Emily recalled that Frank's father had been physically and verbally abusive to his mother—teaching Frank, in effect, that an easy way to build yourself up was to put your partner down. In Emily's words: "He needed to feel that he was higher or more important, and I have a very strong character."

With the guidance of the *Workbook*, the Women's Support Group took into account not only Emily's present struggles but also the legacies of the past and her hopes for the future. By illuminating the web of violence in which she and Frank were enmeshed, the work of the group helped her to extricate herself from it.

After participating in the group, Emily regained some of her former confidence. Her boss told her he'd originally hired her because she was "a real firecracker," but then he noticed that she'd lost her spark during the time she was with Frank. Now, she felt that she was more like "the old me."

Frank was still a complicated part of Emily's life. He occasionally harassed her or refused to drop the kids off at an agreed-upon location. But she learned how to manage the ways Frank disobeyed the visitation agreement they had established—as well as the aggression Frank expressed toward her. In the past, Emily would have confronted Frank. But this, she found, only made him more hostile. It was common for Frank to challenge Emily with statements like "Do you have a problem with that?" After participating in the support group, Emily realized that she could overlook the ways Frank didn't meet her expectations while still maintaining control over her own life. "Before, I used to question him, saying, 'Why did you do this?' I'm never going to get an answer, a real answer."

Leaving an abusive relationship is far more complex than walking out or getting a restraining order. By accepting Emily's ambivalence and helping her work through it, the support group made her stronger rather than weaker—and safer as a result.

Safety on the Victim's Terms

The Family Wellness Program is distinct from many other domestic violence service agencies because its philosophy is not to convince women to adopt a predetermined course of action but instead to support them and help them develop the tools to manage their own lives. Kerry Moles says that "harm reduction" lies at the heart of the program's philosophy.

A harm-reduction model encourages people to reflect on the danger they are being exposed to and then learn to reduce the risks, so that they are less likely to put themselves in harm's way. "If you're going to be in a relationship that has the potential to be violent," Moles says, "it is important to figure out how to help you be there in a safe way, or in as safe a way as possible—to keep yourself safe and to keep your children safe. So helping a woman to better understand warning signs, cues, or what happens before there's an incident is key to our work—also advocating and helping to empower them."

Many feminist advocates resist the idea of supporting a woman who is living with her abuser because they see it as somehow the equivalent of endorsing the abuse. But by refusing to extend support to those women who are not ready or able to leave their violent partners, these advocates isolate and alienate the victims even more. Family Wellness, on the other hand, recognizes that no one understands the particulars of a victim's life more than the victim herself; the organization's job is to strengthen her position. "Bottom line," says Moles, "it's the women who are recognizing that their situations are escalating or dangerous—all we can do is give them the tools to make change."

I asked Moles if she ever felt that a woman in her program was in life-threatening danger. "There are certainly situations where we think a woman is minimizing the situation, and we worry about her, and sometimes we struggle with it," Moles answered. "But unless we're in a position where we feel certain that something's going to happen tonight, and somebody's going to get killed, then it's not our decision to make. We're here to give the women the tools—not to use the tools for them." Moles believes that there are a lot of good reasons why women stay in these relationships. "Our job is to empower these women, not tell them what to do."

In 2000, Professor Einat Peled and colleagues at the University of Haifa published an article in *Social Work* in which they asserted the importance of this perspective when providing services for battered women. They argued that staying in the abusive relationship must be presented as one of the legitimate choices that battered women make. They also emphasized that making the decision to stay "does not preclude fighting intimate violence within the relationship." Such an approach, Peled asserted, helps women feel accepted for the choices they are making, and more informed about what the risks are in staying in the relationship. By being better informed, women feel better about themselves and, in turn, are more likely to keep themselves safe.

Emily's experience with Family Wellness exemplifies the advantages of such an approach. The support group provided her with a forum to explore whatever issues she felt were important, without forcing any judgments on her for what she was and wasn't ready to do.

THE MARRIAGE AND FAMILY
THERAPY PROGRAM, VIRGINIA

The Marriage and Family Therapy Program at Virginia Tech Center for Family Services provides two treatment options to couples who are experiencing violence: traditional couples counseling or a couples group. If the couple chooses to attend traditional couples counseling, they meet with two therapists on a weekly basis. The weekly meetings are open-ended; the therapists direct the work depending on the issues being presented to them.

The couples group, however, combines couples counseling with group therapy by bringing five to seven couples together over an eighteen-week period to help one another address the violence in their relationships. Although group treatment does not follow a rigid schedule, it typically starts with six sessions in which men and women meet in separate groups—primarily to be educated about issues related to abuse and victimization. Classes on power and control and equality in relationships are also offered to the participating couples. These classes are followed by twelve sessions in which all of the couples meet together with two counselors. The couples group is highly unusual in that it acknowledges that bringing violent men together with victims in a group setting can be a positive force for change—that perhaps these men can help themselves, other abusers, and even victims to recover from violence.

Dr. Sandra Stith

Sandra Stith, who was the director of the Marriage and Family Therapy Program until the summer of 2007, has a Ph.D. in marriage and family therapy and first started working in the field of domestic violence as a shelter worker in the early 1980s. "Back then," she says, "I felt strongly that you didn't do couples counseling if violence was occurring. I did not believe that you'd ever work with couples together."

Everything changed for Stith in the mid 1980s, when she started conducting research on what the risk factors were for someone experiencing domestic violence. "I realized that violence between partners was more complicated than I had first understood," Stith says. She began to see how the couple's verbal interactions—the back-and-forth—could contribute to the violence. Around the same time, Stith started looking at the kinds of issues that marital clinics generally addressed. When she studied the clients at a marital clinic in Kansas, she was stunned to realize that as many as 40 percent of them shared a history of intimate violence. Stith wondered if having the couple meet together with a counselor was safe for the victims. "In my heart," she told me, "I kept asking myself, 'Is this right?'

"Finally, I decided that if we are going to do this kind of work with couples, then we needed to develop a treatment program that was safe and that we could prove was effective. I wasn't thinking at the time that couples counseling would be better, but rather that if we were doing it anyway, we may as well do it safely." Stith was also encouraged by the studies published by psychologists like Daniel O'Leary, which suggested that couples counseling was as effective as treating men alone: "All this gave me confidence that we could do couples counseling with careful screening."

In 1997, Stith, together with two colleagues, Eric McCollum, who is currently the program director, and Karen Rosen, decided to develop a systematic treatment approach for couples experiencing violence. Then something surprising happened. During conversations with a project manager at the National Institute of Mental Health, Stith and her partners were encouraged to compare a traditional couples counseling approach to a group format that brought several couples together for treatment; they would also study which approach was more effective.

Responsibility and Hope

Whether therapists at the Marriage and Family Therapy Program are doing traditional couples counseling or couples group work, their treatment is guided by several agreed-upon principles. First, they believe that behaving violently is a choice and that "each person is responsible for his or her own behavior." Second, safety is of paramount importance. Therapists must stay attuned "to the potential risk when violent couples discuss difficult topics" and "take a clear position that violence is always unacceptable." Third, they believe that couples who choose to remain together can do so nonviolently with treatment. Fourth, they assume that even couples who are in violent relationships can make sound decisions for themselves and for the relationship. Finally, they commit to making the work solution-focused, always guiding clients toward a set of mutually established goals that encompass taking responsibility for one's behavior, decreasing anger levels between the partners, recognizing success in developing solutions, and ending violence in the relationship—the overall goal.

To ensure that the couple can adhere to these principles, all couples are screened before they become eligible for treatment. Screenings are done alone, with each member of the couple. The screening focuses on the partner's level of violence, substance abuse, depression, relationship satisfaction, and risk for homicide and suicide. The center does not shy away from physical violence: indeed, couples are *accepted* into treatment (assuming all other conditions are met) if either partner reports one incident of physical violence in the past year or ongoing psychological aggression over the past year. Court-ordered participants are excluded from the program for complicated reasons including the fact that if the couple separates, the defendant can no longer continue with the treatment when he may need it most. They also refuse to work with couples in which one party has not consented to treatment or otherwise feels coerced. Finally, they will not work with potential participants who are unwilling to remove guns from their home. A "no-violence" contract is a precondition for participating, as is a willingness by both parties to dedicate themselves to the specific purpose of ending violence in their relationship.

Stith expressed an immense confidence in couples work and now believes "that failing to provide services to both parties in an ongoing relationship may inadvertently disadvantage the female partner who chooses to stay." One female participant who had previously attended a women-only support group, articulates the problem as follows:

> You go into an isolated group of women. . . . We all talked a lot. But we're just in there supporting each other and saying how wrong [things are]. . . . This doesn't feel right; this doesn't feel good. Pointing out the things that aren't right. That escalates. . . . It's like they're building each other up. But separately. [The men] are getting support in the [anger management] program to feel better about themselves, maybe to help control the anger. In the women's support group they're getting support to build them up. But what are you doing for the couple? . . . Doing this . . . in a vacuum, for us was not working. I don't know how it can with anyone. Someone just attending the [anger management] program and . . . not having any interaction with the women. It was like one-sided. My going to [victim's support group], I got support there, but when I tried to communicate what I was learning from [it] there was resistance [by my partner]. It was like we weren't in the same show.

Stith and McCollum helped clients understand the importance of assessing the dynamics in a relationship. They divided the dynamic work into two distinct components: first, they encouraged the two members of the couple to recognize that they were responsible for their own actions. McCollum explains, "Each person comes to understand that, first and foremost, they are responsible for their abuse—if they are abusive." Second, the therapists emphasized with the couple that their actions occurred in a context and that both members of the couple are also responsible for improving the environment in which the abuse habitually took place.

Commenting on this duality, one male participant underscored how important couples work can be when addressing violence:

> [Men's groups] can't really address relationships because they're only seeing one half of the issue. . . . The primary function was to persuade the people to stop [violence] and give them tools to help them do that. However—I mean, that was good; that was right; that's what they should be do-

ing. The other side of that is these people are involved in relationships, and there may have been something wrong with the relationship. Yes, it was a bad attribute of the guy's behavior, but there was something else there too, and that needs at some point to be addressed.

Like Violence Anonymous, the Marriage and Family Therapy Program is emphatic about the importance of taking responsibility for one's behavior and making safety paramount while also empowering those who participate in the treatment to believe they have control over their lives and their relationships.

Results

In 2004, seven years after starting their research on the two treatment approaches (they also compared these couples to couples who did not receive any sort of treatment), Stith and her colleagues were surprised to find that the innovative group approach suggested by the NIMH project manager in 1996 turned out to be even more effective than traditional couples treatment. Stith says that, compared to couples counseling and no treatment at all, the group approach was "the *most* effective modality for decreasing psychological and physical violence."

Stith and her colleagues measured the percentage of repeat offenses between the three groups; any physical aggression constituted a reoffense. Their results were startling: six months after the treatment started, 67 percent of those who did not receive treatment experienced another violent offense; 43 percent of those in the traditional couples treatment reoffended, and 25 percent of the couples receiving the group couples treatment reoffended.

Even more surprising was the fact that couples reported significantly more satisfaction with their marriage after participating in the couples group. Moreover, those participating in the couples group were most likely to change their views about wife beating (to reject it as acceptable behavior). These views did not change for those who participated in the traditional couples treatment or for those who received no treatment at all. It is interesting to note that the couples group is more successful than either batterer intervention programs (which are single-sex) or couples counseling (which involves only one's partner) at fundamentally changing the abuser's thinking about his violence.

It also appears to strengthen the participants' sense of community and collective responsibility. Stith believes that the group format is incredibly effective because "learning from each other and being committed to the group" makes a significant difference to the participants. To her amazement, Stith has observed that people in the couples group "don't quit even if they feel they've got what they've needed, because they care about the group." "We developed what we call an 'alumni group,'" she explains, "in order to respond to the requests of clients who want to come back and see how Bob and Mary are doing." This underscores the importance of not only receiving something of value in a therapeutic setting but also feeling that one has something of value to give to others—which group work emphasizes.

THE NORTHWEST NETWORK, WASHINGTON

The innovations of the Family Wellness Program and the Marriage and Family Therapy Program notwithstanding, both of these groups still fall back on a relatively traditional paradigm: that men are the batterers and women are their victims. The Northwest Network of Bi, Trans, Lesbian and Gay Survivors of Abuse, located in Seattle, Washington, scrupulously avoids such stereotypical thinking.

The Northwest Network opened its doors in 1987 to help those in the bisexual, transgender, lesbian, and gay community who were struggling with intimate abuse. They provide free and confidential community education and advocacy services, such as support groups and classes, referrals, safety planning, and community organizing. "Whether we're at a drag king show or a city council meeting," their website states, "we weave education about domestic violence, support services, anti-oppression, and safety planning through all our interactions."

Certainly the Network cannot assume that a woman who comes in complaining that her partner is "abusive" is necessarily the only one feeling victimized. When men date men, women date women, and some people in their program are transitioning from one gender to another, labels that rely on pronouns are clearly inadequate. "The Network never assumes that the surface interactions are all that's going on," Connie Burk, the Network's executive director explains. So when the Network's founders started to conceptualize their mission, they knew they needed a different starting point.

The Relationship Skills class is one of the Network's signature initiatives. The class is offered to about twenty people every few months and involves a two-hour weekly seminar that runs for six weeks. Anyone can sign up—in other words, the Network doesn't take responsibility for sorting people into "victim" and "perpetrator" groups but, rather, offers a forum in which each participant can learn how to define his or her own behavior. The centerpiece of the class is the Network's "Assessment Tool Worksheet." Like the *Relationship Workbook* at Family Wellness, the worksheet is the jumping-off point for discussing and addressing issues raised by members of the class. The facilitators then try to help people understand the dynamics that underpin their nontraditional relationships. The emphasis is less on accepting or rejecting various labels than on refining the participants' understanding of their relationships in a useful way—whether or wherever they happen to fall in the spectrum of abuse.

Their objective for the class is to "get the skills you need for the relationships you want."

Context, Intent, Effect

The Network uses the terms "context," "intent," and "effect" to describe the dynamics in an abusive relationship; the distinctions between these words are important to the program. *Context* refers to both the specific behaviors surrounding an event and the contours of the relationship over time. "To understand context," Burk elaborates, "it is important to ask questions that consider both partners' perspectives: 'What are you like when you are angry? How does your partner respond? What is the outcome? What is your partner like when she is angry? How do you respond? What is the outcome?' Or, 'Have you ever prevented your partner from leaving during a fight? How? What happened? Has your partner ever prevented you from leaving during a fight? How? What happened?'"

By *intent* the Network means finding ways to understand how the partners use power and control: "the real, imagined, perceived, expressed or intuited reasons for the behavior." To delve deeper into intent, one needs to ask such questions as the following: "What is the goal of each partner's behavior? Was the behavior used to establish control over someone else, or was it used to regain control over oneself? For example, did a person lie because they feared for their own safety, or because they want to maintain an isolating condition for their partner?"

The *effect* describes whether the violence was successful in victimizing the other person. To understand effect, Burk said we should consider the following: "Whose life is smaller as a result of the behavior? Who is being controlled, manipulated, coerced, exploited, or hurt as a consequence of the behavior?" This analysis of the end result is important because, Burk believes, aggressive behavior often masquerades as victimization. By examining the effect of a particular action, one can see whether the person is, in fact, losing or gaining ground in the partnership.

For Burk, these issues are key to understanding how abuse operates. Burk told me how, in her own family, her mother would direct aggressive comments toward her father to get his attention. Even her mother's escalating psychological abuse did not engage him, however. Instead, her father would instantly dismiss her with such comments as "You've had too much pie," implying that if she ate less sugar, she would be less angry. Burk feels that the effect of her mother's comments on her father were relatively nil, while her father's dismissive remarks really stuck. "He didn't internalize my mother's messages, as my mother did his," she says. "My mother didn't have the sexist privilege or the expectation that she could control his life, and he didn't have the expectation that he might be controlled by a woman."

But Burk also concedes that—with changing gender roles, greater acceptance of lesbian relationships, and women's enhanced power in society—the traditional notions of male privilege that existed in her parents' relationship are much more ambiguous in the twenty-first century: "This notion today that people use their own vulnerabilities to further their power and control is very different from the notion in the past, of a big, strong man beating up a tiny lady." As a result, our analysis of abusive relationships must become far more nuanced.

Defining the Parameters of Being Supportive

Erin K. told me that she first visited the Northwest Network in October 2005, after trying, on her own, to understand better what was happening in her relationship. She was especially interested in learning techniques that would help de-escalate the verbally abusive arguments she was having with her partner of eight months—a woman who was making the transition to being a man. When an advocate at the Network suggested that she take the Relationship Skills class, Erin jumped at the chance. "It seemed like a really safe place which was open to all genders and sexual identities. It was also kink friendly," Erin says.

Erin explains that when she was first introduced to the person who would become her new lover, she was confident she could handle whatever challenges this relationship would bring. "I was raised by a lesbian," she says. "I grew up with an ability to discuss complicated topics." Her childhood household created "a space which is accepting of everyone's situation, and boundaries were clearly laid to keep it open and safe for everyone."

Still, Erin wasn't quite sure what to expect from her partner's experience of transitioning. Previously, Erin had "pretty much identified as heterosexual." When Erin's partner wouldn't allow her to talk to anyone about what they were going through, Erin became confused and uncertain. She knew from her childhood how stressful these periods of change could be: her father had found it very difficult when her mother left him for a woman, and Erin had been exposed to his judgments and anger as a result. When her partner became increasingly difficult to communicate with, Erin wasn't sure what it meant: Was it temporary? Was it to be expected?

"Because I couldn't talk to anyone about it, I had no way to validate if his behavior was normal," she says. Erin wanted to support her partner in becoming a man, but she also knew how important it was to get the support *she* needed: "I didn't know what was okay and what wasn't, and I was blindsided by it." When her lover started to pressure Erin to minimize contact with her family and friends, Erin got scared. She started to ask herself if she was in an abusive relationship.

Connie Burk points out that sometimes the person who appears to be the victim is actually the perpetrator of violence: "Sometimes a person will be fired from their job for being gay. Then that person will tell their partner that they have to be the provider for the whole family, to make up for the gap in money, all because the person who was fired experienced homophobia." This is how victims are made to feel responsible for a partner's vulnerability. One also sometimes sees this, Burk says, when an individual is recovering from an addiction: "Women in recovery might say, 'If *you* can't keep alcohol away from me, then *I* might drink and who knows what will happen.'

"Another thing that occurs pretty frequently," Burk continues, "is that women who are survivors of childhood sexual assault will have all these rules around sleeping. We noticed that women we were working with weren't allowed to get up in the night, or move when they were sleeping, because their partner had been assaulted as a child. So these women who had sexual abuse histories would attack their partners, or punish them for moving, because they had failed to meet their needs as a childhood sexual assault survivor." Burk quickly realized when she started to do this work that "we need to honor the fact that people who batter *do* experience racism, *have* been hurt, have feelings, may feel hopeless. That is real. People need to feel that and be sensitive to it, but that doesn't give anyone a license to hurt other people with it. That's the essence of our Relationships Skills class—it doesn't make distinctions between abusers and victims but helps people assess their own behavior."

For Erin, the Relationship Skills class was extremely helpful. She realized that her partner was using the gender transition in an abusive way: "It definitely reframed things for me." When I asked Erin whether it troubled her that the Network didn't screen out abusers from the Relationship Skills class, she said that it did not: "It makes sense that the Network makes an effort to include everyone. Regardless of what type of relationship someone is in, abuse can occur, and there needs to be support for victims and abusers, regardless of gender or identity."

After she completed the Network's program, Erin decided to end all contact with her abusive partner. She also decided to join the Network's board of directors. "I do performance art to learn from my mistakes. I put it out there that people go through these experiences, and it's okay to get help. Everyone deserves a nonabusive relationship, whether they've been raised by trans, gays, or not—whatever!"

The courage of the Network's decision to avoid terms like "batterer" and "victim" is commendable—first, because the organization honors the intent of the participant to grow by taking a stand against certain *behaviors* rather than against particular people or categories of people; second, because it honors the process by giving it more importance than the labels we are so eager to attach to people struggling with these issues.

PART FOUR
A New Vision

The healing power of connecting with others in community, the wisdom of those who have traveled hard roads, the transforming experience of listening and speaking with respect, and the little touches of care and love that make a big difference: these potentials are present in us and in our communities. . . . Circles connect us in ways that help us find them in each other."

—Kay Pranis, Barry Stuart, and
Mark Wedge, *Peacemaking Circles:
From Crime to Community)*

As I continued with the circle I started to see changes in my life. I learned that it takes hard work to change a bad habit and form a good one.

—Participant, Constructing Circles of
Peace Program, Nogales, Arizona)

MY POLITICAL ENCOUNTERS WITH INTIMATE ABUSE

THE BIG STICK: HOW FAR CAN THE CRIMINAL JUSTICE SYSTEM TAKE US?

In September 1996, two years after my arrival at UCLA as a professor of social welfare, I was asked by the university's law school to participate in a legislative forum on mandatory prosecution. California lawyers, legislators, and scholars had been invited to discuss the merits of forcing prosecutors to bring charges against men accused of domestic violence crimes. The event included a debate between me, arguing against mandatory prosecution, and Donna Wills, head deputy of the Family Violence Division of the Los Angeles County District Attorney's Office, who was in favor of adopting a mandatory prosecution policy. Sheila James Kuehl—then the temporary Speaker of the House in the California State Assembly and now a state senator—served as the facilitator.

By the mid '90s, mandating the arrest of abusers had taken hold in most police departments in the United States. Prosecutors, however, were still reluctant to bring charges against defendants arrested for domestic violence crimes, even though states like California encouraged them to do so. They argued that most victims were unwilling to testify against their partners; legally mandating prosecution wouldn't change that. Without the victims' testimony, the cases were often very difficult to win. California lawmakers like Sheila Kuehl, a longstanding advocate for battered women, were grappling with whether these policies actually helped victims of domestic violence. Could they legally mandate prosecution in these cases?

Generally, prosecuting attorneys who worked for the city, county, or state were given the *discretion* to bring cases to court that they believed were supported by the evidence. In other words, they were never forced to take a case they didn't think they could win. But Cheryl Hanna, a former prosecutor and law professor at Vermont Law School, had just published a powerful and persuasive account of the importance of mandating prosecution in domestic violence cases in the *Harvard Law Review*, one of the most prestigious and widely read scholarly law journals in the United States. This article, along with the ongoing pressure exerted by battered women's advocates, placed the issue of mandatory prosecution front and center.

Donna Wills argued that a mandatory prosecution policy was an "enlightened approach to domestic violence" because it took the difficult decision of whether or not to prosecute "off the victim's shoulders" and put it where it belonged: with those whose job it was "to enforce society's criminal laws and hold offenders accountable for their crimes." She drew on a homicide case she had brought to trial nine years earlier, in which the victim, Donna Houston, a mother of two young children, had been given at least two opportunities to bring charges against her violent husband and declined. After the first violent episode, Houston reconciled with her partner. After the second, she left him, but she also made herself unavailable to testify, and the charges were dropped. Eventually, he murdered her. Wills argued that prosecutors "need to be able to say that despite a battered woman's ambivalence, we did everything within our discretion to rein in the batterer, to protect the victim and her children, and to stop the abuser before it was too late." Advocates like Wills believe that other forms of evidence besides testimony—photos, 911 calls, and statements made by suspects when the police arrived at their homes—can be the evidence used to prove that the crime occurred, and that this type of evidence is enough to counteract the victim's refusal to testify at trial.

My arguments focused on how mandatory prosecution may in fact escalate harm to victims, both physically and emotionally, and should be used with caution. Prosecutors, I asserted, are in an excellent position to use their expertise and intuition to work together with victims to reduce their risk of harm. I argued that a conversation between a prosecutor and a victim was the best approach to ensure both her safety and her trust, rather than mandating what should happen in all cases. It was my position that mandating prosecution in cases like Donna Houston's might not have saved her—and might even have hastened her death.

My perspective was in part informed by a study on mandatory prosecution that had been published in 1986 by sociologists David Ford and Jean Regoli. The study showed that the least safe option was for a woman to refrain from prosecuting her partner when she was given the option. But the study also showed that women experienced less violence following a prosecution when they were given the option to prosecute and took that option, compared to when the prosecution was imposed on them by a mandatory policy. On the strength of these results, it stood to reason that *encouraging* women to assert their power to prosecute outweighed state intervention into women's lives against their wishes.

My personal and professional experiences further fueled my point of view. After all, I had never used the criminal justice system to deal with the violence in my life—and I'd never regretted that decision. As a feminist lawyer, I also saw how aggressive the criminal justice system could be when given a mandate, and I'd come to believe that, without significant reform, the courts were usually not the proper forum to address this complex issue. As a social worker, I was convinced that the criminal justice system could not provide the emotional support battered women needed for themselves and their families and that, without meaningful treatment, the violence was likely to continue. In fact, I had come to believe that using the criminal justice system as the primary instrument for addressing domestic violence was the antithesis of empowering battered women.

When I stood up and made these arguments to the hundred or so people who attended the forum at the law school, my comments were dismissed. When I suggested that battered women might be *capable* of making positive decisions for themselves—especially with the help of informed advocates such as prosecutors—the audience became palpably angry. When I said that I had been a battered woman who'd never used the criminal justice system and had no regrets about my choices, I was chastised for deserting the cause.

It appeared that nearly everyone in the mostly female audience believed strongly that women who are abused by their partners *could not* decide whether to prosecute their lovers—only a skilled prosecutor could or should do that. Taking the decision out of battered women's hands was justified on one of two bases: we were either "saving them from themselves" or taking the aggressive measures that they apparently approved of but were too afraid to pursue on their own.

Just as I finished speaking, a female prosecutor jumped up and started shouting at me, telling me that she had worked on domestic abuse cases for years and that she knew what was best for battered women. My crazy ideas, she claimed, would endanger vulnerable victims and set us back when the solution was a simple one: prosecutors needed a big stick to counteract the abuser's violence, and the criminal justice system was the biggest stick out there. I realized I'd hit a nerve, and the emotional violence of her response to batterers was crystal clear: "You want to be violent? I'll show you violence. You won't even know what hit you."

This vituperative response helped me to refine my objections to using the criminal justice system in domestic violence cases. After all, as feminist advocates, didn't we also need to think seriously about the institutional violence of the system *we* were employing—and why it appealed to us? How had we, as feminists, strayed so far from our belief that women should be free not only from the abuse of men but also from *all* forces trying to control them against their will—even feminists?

In 1999, I published an article in the *Harvard Law* Review entitled "Killing Her Softly: Intimate Abuse and the Violence of State Intervention." In it I argued that the criminal justice system's imposition of power over battered women's decision making looked and felt like what batterers do to battered women. Forcing women to testify against their batterers by subpoenaing them—a practice that was becoming common across the United States—could be as coercive and terrorizing as the batterer's behavior. This practice further isolated and degraded women who were already isolated and degraded by their abusers, alienating them from the larger society that was attempting to protect them. It could also have the unintended effect of sending these alienated women back to the men who abused them.

Many people believed that my arguments in this article crossed the line. How could I allege that well-intentioned police officers, prosecutors, and battered women's advocates were acting like batterers? I had clearly abandoned my feminism; perhaps I was really more sympathetic to men who battered than I was to their victims. Slowly, however, other advocates began approaching me, both publicly and privately, to voice their concerns about the direction the struggle against domestic violence was taking. A small but growing movement of dissent was taking hold.

An important influence on my own thinking was Professor KimberlÈ Crenshaw, a law professor at UCLA and Columbia. In an article published in 1991 in the *Stanford Law Review,* Crenshaw argued that domestic violence policies that served the interests of white middle-class women failed to recognize the complexities of identity that women of color encountered when *they* experienced violence.

Crenshaw encouraged her audience to consider the predicament of many immigrant women: what *we* might do if faced with the decision to prosecute an abuser—or to tolerate his violence—when we were dependent on him for citizenship. Or what if the abused woman was the citizen and her lover was the immigrant—how might she feel if reporting a black eye might lead to his deportation? Crenshaw also argued that an African American woman, acutely aware of the racism in the criminal justice system, might fear that the police would brutalize her partner in some way. In addition, she might believe that testifying against her husband in open court would only serve to contribute to long-standing stereotypes that African American men are more violent than other men.

Crenshaw recognized that these "other considerations" did not always take into account the women's safety. But that didn't make them any less significant.

Whatever a battered woman ultimately decided to do, we needed to understand that issues of class, race, religion, and ethnicity strongly influenced whether a woman would call the police and whether she might prosecute. Crenshaw believed that policies like mandating arrest or prosecution in domestic violence cases, which served to override the importance of these concerns, were "a deadly serious matter of who will survive—and who will not."

Crenshaw went on to explain, "Women of color are differently situated in the economic, social and political worlds. When reform efforts undertaken on behalf of women neglect this fact, women of color are less likely to have their needs met than women who are racially privileged."

THE LESSONS OF 9/11

By the time I moved to New York in 2000 to become a professor at NYU, my perspective had started to gain attention on a national level. Shortly after my arrival, I was invited to give a keynote address on the question of mandatory arrest and prosecution at the New York City Human Resources Administration (HRA), Department of Social Services conference. This conference, which is generally attended by more than a thousand social workers, lawyers, and child welfare workers, was scheduled for late September 2001.

On September 11, my husband, Peter, and I walked our son to the public elementary school located closest to the World Trade Center. It was his third day of kindergarten. Peter and I were still in the school playground with other parents when the first plane hit the North Tower; pandemonium at the school was instantaneous. We found our son ten minutes later and decided to take him home. Just as we emerged from the building, the second plane hit the South Tower and we ran for cover. A few days later, I received a phone call notifying me that the social services conference, which was to be held a few blocks from the World Trade Center, had been postponed; the entire neighborhood was shut down.

For the next several months, along with the rest of the country, I tried to sort out my feelings about 9/11. On the one hand, my neighborhood had been the target of the largest terrorist attack in US history, and my family had observed this terrible event at close range. I felt frightened, grief-stricken, and angry. But I also felt that the United States had some responsibility for what had happened to our country. Of course, I didn't think that anyone who was hurt or killed was specifically to blame for the violence of that day, but I did think that what America represented in the world—and the power that we cavalierly wielded over other nations—was at least in part responsible for why people attacked us.

This idea and the aftermath of September 11 in turn penetrated my thinking about family violence. I started to reconsider what I already knew about the problem: that batterers as adults were usually victims as children; that we teach men to become abusive—they aren't born that way; and that all of us, men and women, are responsible for making people violent. I also started to recognize that many of us were far more complicit than we realized in contributing somehow to a violent dynamic—that mothers and wives, as often as fathers and husbands, could do an enormous amount to reduce violence if we were willing to take the time to understand how we all played a role in it. This, I decided, was what I wanted to talk about at the HRA conference.

Six months later, I presented this new topic to the planning group responsible for the conference. I explained to them that although the opinions expressed in my *Harvard Law Review* article were still important to me, my thinking on the subject of domestic violence had expanded to incorporate larger notions of responsibility—including the role that women played in the violent dynamic. The planning committee was horrified. Even those present who conceded that my ideas had some merit didn't think it was a good idea to present them to a group of a thousand people.

A small contingent of the conference planning group moved quickly to try and prevent me from speaking. But freedom-of-speech concerns prevailed, and instead the organizers invited fourteen panelists to counteract my position. After my hour-long keynote presentation, I was essentially ordered to sit on the stage and listen—for three hours—to what were largely opposing points of view. Deborah Sontag, a reporter who was covering the event for a *New York Times Magazine* story entitled "Fierce Entanglements," noted the chilly reception my speech received: "Many in the audience shuddered." But she also observed, "Mills . . . was asking publicly questions that some in the field have been asking privately."

A great deal of media attention followed, which created valuable catalysts for discussion in domestic violence advocacy circles. But I also realized that I was seen by many as nothing more than a naysayer—someone who seemed to revel in tearing down the reforms that others had spent so many years trying to put into place. If I wanted to truly change the way people thought about this issue that I also cared so deeply about, I had to offer concrete solutions as well as criticisms.

RETRIBUTIVE VERSUS RESTORATIVE JUSTICE

Over the next few years, I wrote *Insult to Injury: Rethinking Our Response to Intimate Abuse* (2003). For this book, I investigated not only the possibilities available for victims of abuse in the United States but also approaches to violence that had been tried in other countries. Many programs weren't willing to take on all the issues that I was eager to address: the value for women of recognizing their contribution to the violence in their lives; the fluidity often found between the roles of victim and victimizer; the significance of seeing violent men as potentially capable of change. Most important, I was searching for an approach that could intervene on behalf of the whole family in order to interrupt the vicious cycle of abuse over generations.

It was abundantly clear that the counseling options being provided to literally thousands of men across the nation weren't working. Batterer's Intervention Programs were, for the most part, a failure. Many men didn't continue with the treatment after the first or second visit; those who *did* continue in treatment became "slightly less likely to be arrested than similarly situated men who attended no sessions." Furthermore, even those who stopped their violence did not change their attitudes toward women or toward battering as a crime.

These programs were failing for many reasons, but principally because they wanted to reduce the problem to the following premise: If men simply unlearned their misogynist attitudes toward women, their violence would diminish. Whereas the men kept asserting that the problem *wasn't* so simple—that they needed to process their childhood histories and work through the issues they had with their partners. Sadly, most domestic violence advocates didn't want to hear it. Nor were advocates fully confronting the fact that at least half of the women who had gone to a domestic violence shelter went back to their abusers—no matter how many posters had been put up in the subways. I was convinced that if we didn't find a way to provide holistic, meaningful treatment options that gave couples the option of confronting their violence together, we couldn't make a significant dent in the problem. Then I came upon the concept of restorative justice.

Restorative justice imagines bringing everyone in a room together to discuss the effects of a particular crime on their lives. It has given rise to many different sorts of specific programs around the world designed to promote healing among the affected parties after acts of violence. Its goal is to help the group develop insights together on what happened among them and why, so that everyone can come to terms with the past as well as alter the course of the future. For me, restorative justice was exciting because it provided both an alternative to the criminal justice system and possibly an enhancement to it.

Retributive justice, the theory that best describes the criminal justice system, is almost entirely geared toward punishing those who break the law. The ultimate purpose of that punishment is not usually to rehabilitate the offender but simply to repair the unfair advantage the offender gained over society by not obeying its rules. (Perhaps the reasons that advocates who promote a criminal justice response to domestic violence aren't looking for a more effective treatment option than batterer intervention programs is because their main objective is to punish, not to rehabilitate.) According to Immanuel Kant, who advanced the idea of retributive justice in the late 1700s and who still stands as its most persuasive advocate, society has a moral duty to punish the person who breaks the law in order to avoid the appearance that society has been complicit with the crime.

On an abstract level, this makes a great deal of sense. As children, we learn that if someone doesn't follow the rules, there should be consequences for disobeying them. Without such consequences there could be chaos—those who follow the rules would be discouraged from bothering to do so in the future. But when the theory is deconstructed, and the experience of punishment is felt at the human level, often very little is gained. Victims who are actively involved with their cases as they move through the criminal justice system—helping to decide whether to prosecute, testify in court, preparing victim impact statements—find that involvement therapeutic. At the same time, many victims are quite lenient when it comes to sentencing, and they do not believe that punishment alone will help the offender reform his criminal behavior.

Still other victims believe that apologies or even forgiveness is the best approach. The Amish community's reaction to the murders of five of their children in 2006 led their leaders to the house of the dead killer, where they formally forgave him for his heinous crime in front of his wife and father. Such public acts of forgiveness are now much more common. Some victims, of course, aren't interested in mercy, but that doesn't necessarily mean they feel a sense of healing once the sentence is carried out. Indeed, many family members of homicide victims express absolutely no relief after the murderer has been executed.

Retributive justice also often fails to prevent future crime, because criminals are so rarely rehabilitated in prison. Indeed, there is some evidence to suggest that criminal behavior in one generation is replicated in the next unless the cycle is interrupted. I knew that this was particularly true of domestic violence crimes, in which the victim and perpetrator are likely to have a family together and one or both may be physically violent with the children, as well. Brenda Aris finally put an end to Rick's violence, but she was far less successful at protecting her own children from the same destructive influences that had been so damaging to her and her husband, as we saw in Lucretia's case.

When apartheid was abolished in South Africa, Archbishop Desmond Tutu knew that retributive justice could not address the sins of the country's past; a different approach was necessary. And so he set up the world's largest Truth and Reconciliation Commission, which was founded on the principle that "reconciliation depends on forgiveness and that forgiveness can only take place if gross violations of human rights are fully disclosed." Although some victims' families objected to the exchange of truth for amnesty, the vast majority of black South Africans supported this process.

In exchange for sparing their perpetrators jail time, victims got the opportunity to find out what really happened to their loved ones. They also received financial support for their families by garnering the wages of the perpetrators, and they received apologies. The fact that victims had the opportunity to dictate what they might get from the perpetrators helped them feel at least partially restored and empowered.

If South Africans considered reconciliation a viable response to its century of racial violence and oppression, it seemed reasonable to think that such an approach might be helpful to those struggling with all sorts of traumas and crimes.

Once I became interested in restorative approaches, I began finding them in many different contexts and settings—whether at the heart of the South African Truth and Reconciliation Commission or embedded in small programs being adopted by child welfare agencies across the United States, Canada, and the United Kingdom. Sometimes these programs are referred to as "Circles" programs because of their collaborative and nonhierarchical design. Hawaii is using Circles to help people who've been in prison reconnect to the community after serving their sentences. Minnesota is using Circles to bring victim and offender together with other affected community members to determine the appropriate sentence following a domestic violence conviction. England has incorporated the use of Circle-type programs in their response to delinquency crimes.

Let's consider what such a Circle program might look like for a juvenile arrested for breaking into his elderly neighbor's house. It would involve the perpetrator and the victim but also, perhaps, the victim's neighbor or best friend, a priest, or a local activist who works closely with the elderly. It might also include support for the teenager—his parents, a cousin, a teacher. No one participates in the circle program who doesn't feel comfortable doing so, however—including the victim. Such an approach to healing must be voluntary for it to work. The Circle would be facilitated by a Circle keeper—someone who understands the overall purpose of the program and ensures that everyone has a chance to speak and be heard.

The Circle keeper is responsible for ensuring that the process continues until a natural conclusion is reached to repair the harm done—and, just as important, to prevent it from recurring in the future. This usually involves some sort of agreement signed by all of the participants, which is sometimes called a Social Compact. Ideally, both the perpetrator and the victim are supported by other members of the circle in new and inventive ways; the priest might help the teenager repair the woman's broken window; the elderly woman's neighbor might check in on her more often; the activist might find the boy some part-time work to help encourage a feeling that he was contributing to the community in a positive way.

CIRCLES AND DOMESTIC VIOLENCE

Circles are actually ancient in origin. In their book, *Peacemaking Circles,* Kay Pranis—one of the nation's leaders in promoting restorative approaches to crime—and her colleagues, Barry Stuart and Mark Wedge, describe how aboriginal communities used the sacred circle to pass on "ancient wisdom about how to call forth the best in us when we need it most." According to William Isaacs, a professor at MIT who wrote *Dialogue and the Art of Thinking Together*, "no indigenous culture has yet been found that does not have the practice of sitting in a circle and talking." These circles are also akin to what many families do: sit around the table and talk. That is why the circle formula has such rich potential for a family struggling with violence.

Social workers Joan Pennell and Gale Burford, who are also experts in restorative justice, have experimented with circles for child welfare cases in which domestic violence was also present. They found that domestic violence was reduced when the whole family was brought together in an intensive yet supportive way to address the problem. Circles are being used by Kay Pranis and others in sentencing domestic violence offenders; victim, offender, and other affected family and friends come together to advise the judge on an appropriate sentence for the crime committed. Pranis reports that these Circles—which gives the offender a voice in his sentencing—increases the likelihood that the defendant will fulfill the requirements of his sentence, which generally tends to involve making amends in the community in some way for the harm he has done. Just as the victim is healed by actively participating in the criminal justice process, so is the offender.

My vision for Circles, however, was more ambitious. I wanted them to be used for long-term treatment rather than as a one-time intervention. What would such a circle program for domestic violence look like? Ideally, it would include both members of the couple, but it could also include the couple's parents, who might have taught them to become violent in the first place, and any children who are being exposed to violence. Even extended family members and neighbors could participate—both to better understand how the violence got started and what each of them could do to help stop it. Restorative justice in this context could draw on the partners' own cultural and racial identities, sexual orientation, and religious heritage to tailor the process to their needs. A shared prayer might be key in one family; shared food might be significant in another. Most important, though, this process could help the group develop insights into the history of violence in a family and to find specific responses to it.

Again, the victim's participation would be voluntary; no battered person would be coerced into participating in a Circle. Rather, Circles would be available for couples that wanted to be treated together. At the same time, it shouldn't be seen as a treatment *only* for couples who wanted to stay together; it could also provide a mechanism for ending relationships more peacefully and humanely, so that there is some forum for processing the intense anger and sadness that often accompanies such transitions. (What would the end of my relationship with David have looked like, for example, if both of us had had that sort of support network?) This might be especially useful for couples who've had children together. The flexibility of the Circle format allows the couple to include anyone they want to participate—anyone they think might help them recover. And this work, in turn, reconnects them to their immediate communities in beneficial ways.

Circles could also be extremely useful at placing violent events in their larger contexts (childhood history; drug or alcohol addictions; cultural, religious, and gender considerations); this would, in turn, assist everyone involved in coming to some sort of shared understanding, even when they didn't entirely agree with one another on every point. Without such a process, though, the couple could not move on from the violence, and the family would be overshadowed by it. Without incorporating everyone (victim, perpetrator, parents, children) into the process, there was a greater likelihood that the violence would be passed on. Inviting all those touched by the crime to participate in a Circle—together— would give the family the greatest chance for a full recovery.

According to Pranis, "the healing power of connecting with others in community, the wisdom of those who have traveled hard roads, the transforming experience of listening and speaking with respect, and the little touches of care and love that make a big difference: these potentials are present in us and in our communities. . . . Circles connect us in ways that help us find them in each other."

My idea was all still theoretical, however. I hadn't yet implemented such a program, and many of my critics argued that the idea wasn't viable.

PUTTING THEORY INTO PRACTICE

In 2004, I hosted a roundtable discussion for experts in restorative justice and domestic violence who wanted to develop an alternative treatment program for couples struggling with abuse. Two Circle programs were developed at that roundtable: Peacemaking Circles and Healing Circles. Peacemaking Circles would be available to people arrested for domestic violence crimes. Healing Circles would be available to people who were seeking help before they had come to the attention of the criminal justice system.

Kay Pranis, Gale Burford, and John Braithwaite, a law professor in Australia who is considered one of the founders of the modern restorative justice movement, were among the people who evaluated the feasibility of developing this radical new treatment that would bring the whole family together in a Circle over several months to address the violence. We agreed that certain key features would be indispensable.

To ensure that no one person dominates the Circle, but rather that all voices are heard, the Circle keeper uses a talking piece. Only the person holding the talking piece can talk; others must wait until they receive the talking piece to speak. If a participant is unwilling to talk, he or she can simply pass the talking piece to someone else. Sometimes the talking piece might be passed around the circle, but at other times the Circle keeper might direct its movements—to prevent a particular participant from dominating the conversation, say, or to make the exchange a more productive one.

The Circle keeper and the talking piece help those harmed by the crime feel that they are being heard by the offending party, but they also help the offender to understand and confront the consequences of his or her actions, and encourage taking steps to correct those actions in the future. What we know is that without giving the offending person an opportunity to be integrated back into the community—and a chance to air his or her concerns publicly—he or she will probably continue to harbor those hostile feelings and harm someone again. The very process of talking to one another helps family members reconnect and develop a new pattern of communicating when things go wrong. The method used to understand the problem—talking openly and honestly—also helps people imagine the solution. All participants are held accountable in the Circle, but they are also *held*.

My consultations with other experts such as Joan Pennell suggested that in addition to the Circle keeper, a safety monitor would be necessary to keep a close eye on the family dynamics when the Circle wasn't meeting. A neighbor, cousin, sister, or brother would be appointed to this role; these monitors became an important cornerstone for ensuring that someone was watching the family for increasing tension or anger. This approach complemented the current practice, which relies entirely on probation or parole officers who tend to check in with defendants by phone or in their offices, and not more than once a month.

It was against this backdrop that Healing and Peacemaking Circles came into being in 2004.

13
HEALING CIRCLES

A lyssa Nice is a clinical social worker and an Orthodox Jewish woman who has been working with Orthodox families affected by domestic violence for more than twenty years. I first met Alyssa in 2000, when I attended a meeting to address domestic violence in the Orthodox Jewish community. When I introduced the idea of Circles to Alyssa in 2003, she was immediately intrigued, and she became one of the people who helped me develop the Healing Circle model. I was especially excited to have Alyssa participate because I thought that Circles were particularly suitable for Orthodox Jewish couples and others who were likely to stay married despite the violence.

Two-thirds of Orthodox women are married at the age of twenty-five—and usually after only a few dates, which are almost always arranged by their parents. Because of their ages, the newlyweds are frequently still enmeshed in their families of origin. This is further complicated by the community's emphasis on the importance of procreation—on average, an Orthodox Jewish family has five children. These large families can also be haunted by memories of those lost in the Holocaust, making it even more difficult for children to separate from the parents they have been encouraged to depend on. At the same time, it is exceedingly important to maintain an appearance of physical and mental health: since marriages are often arranged, a young person's chances of making a good match can be damaged by any history of mental illness, alcoholism, or abuse within the family. Orthodox families often live in close proximity to their place of worship because Jewish law dictates that everyone must walk to synagogue on the Sabbath; they also often work together and go to school together as well as pray together. In such a tight-knit community, secrets are hard to keep. Certainly, the last thing a married couple is likely to do if they are fighting—let alone being violent—is call the police.

With this in mind, Alyssa Nice decided that Healing Circles could be very beneficial to the Orthodox Jewish community, and Betty and Harry Stein became her first case.

Betty was twenty-seven when she first met Alyssa; Harry was thirty-two. They had three children. They lived in a small town in the Northeast, where Harry was working as a real-estate salesman, but only sporadically. His primary responsibility was doing volunteer work within his community. Betty, the family's main breadwinner, was an accountant for a large company.

The Steins came to the attention of their rabbi, who suspected that something "weird and possibly violent" was going on in the Stein family. Alyssa was then called in because she is seen as an expert in family violence in her community; rabbis and social services often consult her in cases of suspected abuse.

When Alyssa contacted the Steins, Betty told her that there were "problems in the marriage." Alyssa told her about the Healing Circles, and Betty accepted Alyssa's offer of help. Alyssa's first meeting was with Betty only; Harry refused to attend.

In the initial visit, Betty said that she and Harry had been in marriage counseling with both a therapist and a rabbi, but it had not been successful. Harry was frequently violent and aggressive. Their sex life, Betty reported tearfully, was horrible: "He would suddenly grab me against my will, pick up my skirt, and have sex with me," cried Betty. "There was never anything emotional or romantic about it . . . never, never, never. . . . I've told him, no more sex." Recently, after becoming very suspicious, she'd discovered that her husband had a girlfriend—she knew this because she'd figured out Harry's password to his computer and found a series of incriminating emails. When she printed them and confronted him with the evidence, he flew into a rage and slashed her leg with a knife.

Alyssa's first impression was that Betty was a victimized, depressed, and unloved woman, terrified of her husband and miserable in her marriage. During their second meeting, however, a different Betty emerged. Now she presented herself as an overworked career woman who seemed to enjoy that she was both the breadwinner and the matriarch of her family. This time, Betty explained that she was furious that Harry wasn't pulling his financial weight; she also mentioned that her parents helped support the family. She again raised Harry's affair—she'd learned from Harry that his girlfriend was younger and unmarried—and focused on the content of his emails, which were laced with compliments and sexual innuendo and addressed to "Sweetie" and "Honey." Why, Betty wondered aloud, wasn't she getting this kind of "romantic treatment"?

Harry attended the third meeting with Alyssa, together with Betty and their rabbi. Harry said he was coming to "set the record straight." Alyssa had asked the rabbi to be present because she didn't really know what to expect from

Harry; she was prepared, she told me later, for "a monster to show up." Instead, Harry turned out to be a small, unimposing, "regular guy," who began by talking about his volunteer work. He emphasized that his reputation was important to him and that he was worried about losing the role that gave him stature in his community.

Harry also talked about his extramarital relationship. Even though he readily admitted pursuing another woman, he maintained that nothing actually happened between them. Indeed, he told Alyssa, they'd never even met in person—it was an online relationship only. The only reason he was involved with another woman, he said, was because he needed someone to talk to. This other woman listened to him; Betty screamed at him from the moment he walked in the door in the evening until the moment he left the next morning.

"She pummels me," he said, "you know, just constantly pummeling about how little money I make, what a terrible father I am, what a bad husband I am, how she won't have sex anymore. . . . It's constant, constant pummeling, never a kind word. I'm so tense; I smoke two packs a day. I'm a mess. . . . I need relief."

The conversation turned to money. Betty started complaining that she worked all the time. She wanted to be a full-time mother, but Harry didn't make enough money for her to stay at home. She reiterated that her parents were helping to pay their mortgage and other bills. As Betty spoke about her parents, Harry's face reddened with anger. Believing that there was more to the story, Alyssa probed further. In the ensuing conversation about Betty's close relationship with her mother, Betty revealed that her mother called the house every morning at six-thirty A.M., "like clockwork." Nothing important was said on these early morning calls, said Betty—"it was just chitchat."

Harry's temper suddenly flared. "Those calls every morning wake us up," he said. "They also interrupt our lives. I want the calls to stop. I want Betty to tell her mother that my feelings—her husband's feelings—come first. This is my house, my wife, my family—I have rights, too."

They ended this session with an agreement from Harry that he would no longer threaten or otherwise touch Betty in a violent way. He would also stop all contact with the other woman. Betty was already feeling much better. When asked outside of Harry's presence whether she felt threatened, she said "No, not at all," reassuring Alyssa, "I feel completely safe with Harry under your watchful eye." The rabbi reported to Alyssa that he was impressed at how much important ground had been covered in the session.

Over the next several months, further glimpses of the dynamic between the couple emerged. "For me," Alyssa says, "Betty was getting bigger and bigger, and Harry was getting smaller and smaller, meeker and meeker. What was clear was that Betty, while having been abused, wasn't subservient, and that Harry, while at times abusive, wasn't an ogre. Somewhere in between—in the history and complexities of their case—lay the truth."

After eight months of using what Alyssa calls "the preparation process" for Healing Circles, she started to understand that the Steins' difficulties somehow involved Betty's mother and Harry's father (and possibly other family members). When Alyssa proposed bringing all of the relevant parties together in one large circle, however, both Betty and Harry were immediately worried. Alyssa assured them that this circle could provide an opportunity for people in their extended family to speak candidly about their needs, pain, and anger. She told them that Circles are a lot more than a bunch of people sitting in a circle talking. She described how the talking piece guaranteed the right to speak without being cut short and how storytelling in circles delivered information in a way that allowed for easy and accessible listening. After some thought, Harry and Betty agreed to participate, but they felt that it was important to separate the in-laws, who didn't get along that well. Bringing everyone together at once might make things worse. It was decided that Betty's parents, Moshe and Hadassah, would attend first.

On the day that Moshe and Hadassah came for their first circle session, Betty seemed excited and optimistic. In her eyes, her parents were the most wonderful people in the world: they babysat, they helped support the family, and, most important, they knew the *true* story of Harry's failures as a father, husband, and provider. All of her complaints, at last, would be supported by her parents' voices.

Alyssa, aware of Betty's expectations, wanted to be especially careful not to let the Circle disintegrate into a laundry list of Harry's faults. Circles, Alyssa reemphasized, were not about casting blame, but rather about gaining insights and moving participants to a place in which they can live together as a family.

As the Circle began, Moshe, a serious and highly educated teacher sat silent. It was clear that he was going to let his wife do the talking. Each participant understood that they must be holding the talking piece in order to have the floor. The Book of Psalms was chosen as their talking piece. It symbolized asking G-d to help them with the work they needed to do to make progress.

In the first twenty minutes of the Circle with Betty's parents, the conversation centered on the close and loving relationship Hadassah had with Betty. Feeling that the circle was not yet addressing the problems at hand, Alyssa took the talking piece and asked Hadassah how often she spoke to her daughter on the phone; Alyssa was aware that this was a significant point of conflict in Betty and Harry's marriage.

"I probably talk to her twenty times a day," Hadassah said proudly. "We talk about everything."

"At what time of day do these phone calls start?" Alyssa asked.

"Six-thirty A.M.," Hadassah answered.

Without hesitating, Alyssa again asked for the talking piece from Hadassah. "Do you think calling at six-thirty in the morning might affect your daughter's relationship with her husband?" Alyssa, as Circle facilitator, handed the talking piece back to Hadassah. Hadassah avoided the question. Instead, she described how lucky she was to have such a close relationship with her daughter. At that point, Moshe, springing to life, asked for the talking piece.

"This is the first I've heard of Hadassah calling Betty at six-thirty in the morning," Moshe said. "You must call right after I go to shul, right?"

Hadassah nodded. Typically men in the Orthodox community attend services early in the morning.

"Now, I know it's not uncommon in our community for mothers to talk to their daughters on a regular basis," he continued. "But perhaps six-thirty in the morning is too early to be calling."

Hadassah squirmed in her seat.

"Perhaps you shouldn't call every day at that time," he suggested.

Hadassah reached for the talking piece.

"You're not serious!" she asked.

"I am serious," said Moshe, taking the talking piece back.

Again, Hadassah reached for the talking piece.

"What's the big deal about calling my daughter?" Hadassah responded, an edge in her voice.

"I just think six-thirty A.M. is perhaps too early," said Moshe.

"Why is that such a bad thing to do?" Hadassah snapped. "No, it's not a bad thing to do. We're very connected. After all, I do everything for her. I pay her rent. I babysit. I am at her beck and call. Always! There's nothing wrong with me calling at six-thirty every morning."

Moshe asked for the talking piece and stood his ground.

"I think—perhaps—calling every morning at six-thirty A.M. is not good," he reiterated. "Perhaps you shouldn't call every morning."

Betty and Harry remained silent, although Alyssa later reported that Betty was stunned by her parents' exchange. In her experience, her father rarely, if ever, crossed her mother.

Alyssa asked for the talking piece. "How would you feel if you were at home with your husband and his mother called *him* at six-thirty every morning?" she asked Hadassah gently. Alyssa's point was made, and everybody in the Circle knew it. Hadassah again asked for the talking piece and held it in her hands several moments before speaking. All of the attention in the Circle was focused on her, as the others waited and wondered what she would say.

"Perhaps I could call only a few mornings a week. . . ," Hadassah offered.

Moshe smiled at his wife. Harry then asked for the talking piece and spoke directly to his mother-in-law.

"I am thankful for your help," said Harry. "But it would be good for our family if you didn't call every morning."

One of the hallmarks of Circles is that it provides those who are often struggling to find their voice with a forum in which to speak. Having found their voices, Moshe and Harry were heard in ways that they'd rarely experienced in their families.

The Circle was also an important moment for Betty. For most of her life, she'd seen her parents' relationship as static. But now the circle process revealed a different kind of interaction between her parents. Betty could see that the Circle process could shake things up in a good way. She could see that it was extremely positive for her dad to be able to speak up about his feelings. Even though it meant that she would not talk to her mom quite as often, she "knew this was probably for the better." This gave Betty hope.

Harry saw the Healing Circle with Moshe and Hadassah as the beginning of a new kind of communication with his wife. "The session with Betty's parents opened my eyes because when we communicated," he said, "we began to understand and respect each other. That is so much better than getting upset, not talking, not listening, and having all hell break loose."

A few weeks later, Harry's father, Seymour, a rabbinical scholar, attended a Circle with Harry and Betty. Harry's mother, Sophie, declined to attend. This was not a surprise to Harry, who said his mother rarely spoke or, for that matter, even left her home. He doubted that his mother would feel comfortable talking about private matters in a Circle. He also added that she was always ruled by his father's wishes.

After Harry called his parents to invite them to the Circle, Alyssa called Seymour Stein to tell him what to expect. After speaking with him, Alyssa encouraged Betty to call him as well so that all the key Circle participants would have touched base before they came together. Betty called Seymour to discuss how unhappy she was with Harry. She wondered aloud whether Seymour could help their marriage get better. Perhaps that is why, on the day of the Circle, Seymour simply walked in, sat down, took off his hat, and started talking: "Do you want me to tell you why Harry is the way that he is?"

Betty, Harry, and Alyssa nodded; the circle had obviously started without any prompting.

Alyssa handed Seymour the talking piece, the Book of Psalms, and he held it in his hands as he spoke: "Until Harry was eleven and in the fifth grade, he was a good boy. He was well behaved. He was smart. His teachers loved him. In fact, everybody loved him. Then, I don't know what happened, but one day I got a phone call from school saying Harry was playing hooky and running around. When he came home that day, I never asked him why or what happened. All I did was beat him. I beat him that first day; when his bad behavior continued, I beat him the next day. He just wouldn't stop being bad. So I beat him every single day after that. I never spoke to him. Not once. And that is why he can get so angry and violent. That is why he doesn't know how to be a good husband. I blame myself for the way my son turned out."

Seymour drew a breath and then addressed his son.

"I never spoke to you as a boy," he said, "but now, finally, I speak to you as a man. You need to be a good husband. You need to listen to your wife. You need to be kind to your wife. You need to take care of your wife. You must never raise your hand to your wife."

Alyssa recalls this stunning confession as a piece of truth telling that would be rehashed over and over in future circles with Betty and Harry. Suddenly it became evident to everyone that Harry's aggressive and violent behavior was a direct result of his own childhood history of abuse. Harry had never learned *how* to be a kind and considerate man, let alone a good husband. And although Betty had known that Harry had had a rough childhood, he'd never let on just how bad it was. For the first time, Betty understood how ashamed Harry must have felt about his past.

As Betty began to better understand Harry's history, she also became more empathetic toward him and made a conscious effort not to always be "pummeling" him. In the circle, they began to talk about difficult issues in more depth. They also actively listened to each other. Even Hadassah's controlling behavior, always a trigger for a fight, was calmly discussed. The safety and frankness of the Healing Circles gradually drew them closer. Soon, Harry, much less nervous, cut back on his smoking, which Betty appreciated because this was a point of conflict for them. Then he enrolled in a real-estate class to obtain his license, so that he could get a higher-paying job. Finally, the couple resumed sexual intimacy as well.

"We've discovered foreplay," Betty cheerily reported.

At this point, the couple decided they felt comfortable ending the sessions with an understanding that they would contact Alyssa should they need further assistance. Alyssa didn't hear from Betty and Harry for several years. When she received a call from their rabbi alerting her that there might be a new problem in their relationship, Alyssa learned that the Steins now had six kids instead of three: a one-year-old, a two-year-old, a three-year-old, a five-year-old, a seven-year-old, and an eleven-year-old. Alyssa called Betty to see how the couple was doing. Betty told her that there had been no additional physical violence with Harry since the knife incident, but sometimes, Betty admitted, "there was a lot of screaming." Betty added that a couple of weeks before, there had been a crisis between Harry and their eldest son, David. David had written a letter to his father explaining "what he felt about their relationship." When David handed Harry the letter, Harry just ripped it up without reading it. When the son didn't show up for Sabbath prayers with his father that week, the rabbi got worried and called Alyssa.

When Alyssa then met with Betty and Harry, she asked Harry about his reaction to David. "I always feel like Betty and David are ganging up on me," he said quietly, looking down, "so I think I felt the letter was part of that." Because the letter was ripped up, no one ever saw exactly what it said. When Alyssa asked Betty if Harry's concerns about her relationship with David were legitimate, Betty readily admitted that she sometimes does align herself with David, and when she did, Harry probably felt displaced.

Alyssa then turned to Harry to ask him what he should have done when his son gave him a letter he'd written. "I know I did the wrong thing. I shouldn't have done that." After they talked further about the letter incident, and Alyssa felt satisfied that no physical violence was occurring in the household, it became clear that it would be useful to hold a Healing Circle. They decided to plan one for the following week, inviting all of the kids to attend.

The Circle was held in the Steins' living room. By now, Alyssa knew the couple and even their extended family well, so holding the circle in their home made sense. Healing Circles can have this kind of flexibility and familiarity and are often held where the participants feel most comfortable.

When Alyssa opened the Circle, she explained to the family members new to the program what the talking piece was and why it was important. She asked the kids what they should use as the talking piece. The five-year-old, Lisa, said she wanted to use her mother's gold watch. All the kids agreed that that was a good idea. Betty removed the watch and handed it to Alyssa.

Where everyone sits in a Circle can be telling: the kids sat on the couch, with Harry on one side of the room in a large chair and David on the other. The Circle keeper often begins by sending the talking piece in one direction of the circle or another, but this time Alyssa tried a different tactic. She placed the watch on an empty chair and told the Circle members that anyone could pick it up when they wanted to speak.

As she waited for someone to pick up the watch, she was struck by how much the Stein family had changed. When she had first met the children, years before, the family had seemed very chaotic, but things felt different now. Even though they were gathering in response to a family crisis, the room wasn't tense the way it used to be when she'd come over to meet with Harry and Betty. There was also a good deal of emotional warmth in the room, and both parents were contributing to that loving atmosphere. To help encourage the conversation, Alyssa asked an opening question, looking around at the group: "How do you feel important in this family?"

Finally, Lisa, the five-year-old, went over and picked up the watch. "I feel important because I take care of the baby a lot. I hold the baby a lot when the baby needs to be held." She returned the watch to the empty chair.

Then David picked up the watch and said, "I feel important because I do a lot of shopping for Mommy." Alyssa took up the talking piece when David finished. "What kind of shopping do you do?" Alyssa returned the watch to David. The boy explained that he went to the store five blocks from the house, picked up the dinner his mother ordered, and brought it back home. He was especially proud that he could count the change and check the dinner order, making sure that everything was right.

Then the seven-year-old, Ezekiel, explained how he felt important because he keeps the kids quiet when his parents take a nap on Shabbos afternoon. Then Harry noticed that the three-year-old, Charna, wanted to talk—he pointed this out to Alyssa. Her father helped Charna in her effort to speak: "Charna, you're very important, right?" Harry asked. Charna answered, "Yes." "How?" he pressed her. "Because," she answered, "I have lots of friends."

Then Betty took the watch and said, "I feel important when I know my children are listening to me. When they come home from school and take their shoes off and place them neatly by the door, and when they clear their dishes after eating."

Then it was Harry's turn. He said, "I feel important when my kids say thank you." Alyssa wanted to stress the value of each of these statements, and so she then asked the kids to repeat what one other person in the group had said. Interestingly, David chose to repeat what his father had said.

Alyssa decided that this was a good place to end the children's first Circle; she wanted to build a sense of trust—especially between David and his father—without immediately getting into the letter. After that first session, Harry confessed to Alyssa that he knew he had done something hurtful; he had already apologized to his son, and David had written Harry another letter, which Harry had read. Alyssa was pleased, but she still wanted to hold one more family Circle in order to reinforce the importance of open communication.

When the family came back to the Healing Circle the next week, Betty's parents joined them. Alyssa posed a different question to the group: "Who are you most like in the family?" When Hadassah answered, she said, "Betty, I'm most like Betty." Both Betty and Harry said, almost in unison, "Yeah, I knew you would say that." Betty, on the other hand, said, "I'm most like my father." When her father didn't say the same back (her father said he felt he was a bit like everyone in the room), Alyssa could see Betty's disappointment.

She understood that Betty strongly identified with her father but that it was her mother who showed her the most attention. She could also point out, the next time Betty and Harry met alone with her, that Betty should make sure that her alignment with David wasn't playing out Betty's unrealized attachment to her dad. Betty knew how uncomfortable it was to compete for her parents' attention, and Alyssa could help her see that she wouldn't want to repeat that pattern with her own kids.

The Circle ended that night with Harry saying, "I'm so proud of my kids. This is better than watching TV together, or even going to a baseball game together. This is the best time I've ever had." Alyssa, in keeping with the previous Circle, asked the kids to repeat what their father said.

A Circle with children, like this one—especially one with kids of different ages—can accomplish a great deal when the focus is on the strengths of the family and reaffirming everyone's important place in it. A few weeks after their last Circle, Betty reported to Alyssa that Harry and David were getting along much better. Alyssa reminded Betty that she and Harry could hold a circle whenever they needed to—and that they should do so—well before the tensions exploded. Betty agreed. This is part of the Circle tradition. Once families get comfortable with it, it becomes a tool they can use for solving family conflicts on their own.

Since Betty and Harry started working on their relationship and their family bonds in Healing Circles, many changes have occurred. There is no physical violence, and Harry never has contact with other women. He also found a higher-paying position and urged Betty to quit her job to become a stay-at-home mom—something she always wanted to do.

Last year, I interviewed each of the Steins in turn, to get a clearer picture on how they were feeling about their marriage. Betty reported that their lives had changed dramatically: "In the past, when we'd been to a rabbi or a marriage counselor, I found no structure existed. The result was chaotic with constant squabbling. But Healing Circles were different. They provided an orderly, peaceful, step-by-step process in which *everybody* had time to speak." Betty also assured me that Harry was "much calmer," "not violent *at all*," and "very romantic."

For his part, Harry had this to say: "Before I did all this with Alyssa, I didn't know what marriage was all about. The circles helped me come to love and respect my wife. Rather than just getting upset, I understand that it's important to communicate with my wife, to try and understand what she needs and wants." Harry also reflected on the most important lesson he learned in the circle: "We can't bring our parents into every argument—that is what really messed things up. When we stopped doing that, things really got better. I learned you have to appreciate each other, do nice things for each other, kiss each other."

Before participating in Circles, Harry had little hope for his marriage. He learned that, with commitment and hard work, an intimate relationship can radically improve: "Give it time, and it can get better, especially when you focus with your wife on each and every problem. Now I help her on the Sabbath, and I know this is important to her. I don't care that I'm a man—it is good to help your wife! This totally changed my life."

When I asked him about his relationship with his parents, especially his father, Harry said, "It's fine; it's good. They're my parents. But Betty and I have learned that we need to keep our relationship with our parents separate from our relationship. And that's what saved us."

When I wanted to expand the Healing Circle work, I contacted several Jewish agencies, hoping that one might want to adopt the program. Eventually, the

Jewish Family Services Program in Passaic, New Jersey, agreed. The executive director there, Esther East, was very excited about the possibility of piloting Healing Circles in their counseling unit. Until now, Jewish Family Services, which primarily serves the mental health needs of the Orthodox Jewish community in New Jersey, has only offered batterer treatment to the men who abuse their wives. But East believes the Healing Circles program has real potential: "It speaks to the lived experiences of the clients we have seen, in which the strong relationships that exist between spouses and their families can be brought into the treatment arena. In the process, we hope to increase understanding in the community of the complex dynamics that operate within these high conflict families."

Healing Circles can bring hope to millions of families who are hiding their violence from others because they are afraid of the criminal justice system and too ashamed to share their secret. Bringing folks out in the open with the support of those who care for them—and doing so in a way that is accepting of the person but intolerant of the violence—may be the perfect recipe for preventing abuse.

The beauty of the Healing Circle, as we saw with the Steins, is that the recovery work can go at the couple's own pace, in stages. The Circle keeper can hold an initial meeting with the couple and clarify the issues between them and then invite other participants who might have something to contribute (like Harry's father) to join in. Participants in the Circle can also sometimes help the couple break destructive patterns (such as when Hadassah agreed to stop calling her daughter every morning). Doing this work in a context in which the family feels comfortable (in this case, at home, using the Book of Psalms as the talking piece) and with people they trust (like the rabbi) allows for the greatest possibility of recovering from the violence, rather than denying it or hiding it.

One of the reasons Circles may appeal to people leery of couples counseling is that they move beyond the two members of the couple to include children, grandparents, friends, and community members. The Circle format simultaneously diffuses the hostility between the partners and supplies a supportive network. This gives participants a chance to air their feelings in front of not only the people to whom they are directly accountable but also the community at large. Owning one's behavior publicly suggests the hope of seeing beyond the conflict to another way of being. In addition, other participants will have a chance to witness the way in which the couple's dynamic evolves *outside* the Circle, in their daily lives and homes. Taken together, these unusual characteristics of Circle work suggest its enormous potential.

14

PEACEMAKING CIRCLES

A VISION BECOMES A REALITY

A few months after the roundtable of experts came together to develop the Healing and Peacemaking Circle models, I received an email from Mary Helen Maley, a criminal court judge in Arizona. Judge Maley had read *Insult to Injury* and wondered if I could help her establish Peacemaking Circles for people in her county who had been arrested for family violence crimes. I warned her that the process would involve enormous local support, but Judge Maley was committed to pursuing the idea. I agreed to come out to Nogales to introduce the concept of Peacemaking Circles to an assembled group of interested professionals and community leaders.

When we met at the airport, I was immediately struck by Judge Maley's energy and focus. On the drive to Nogales, she told me a little bit about her town. "There are twenty thousand people in Nogales," Judge Maley said, "mostly Hispanic and Spanish-speaking. Nearly everyone has relatives in Mexico, just five minutes from where I live." She and her husband, John Maynard (an elected member of the Santa Cruz County Board of Supervisors), have lived in Nogales for twenty years. "We love Mexican culture and appreciate the beauty of the land," she said. "It is a very special place." At the same time, she conceded, many families in Nogales are burdened by poverty, drug and alcohol addiction, and the uncertainty of their immigration status. Her job made her acutely aware of the problems plaguing her town.

She told me that she was expecting fifty people at the two-day conference, and that she'd invited them from all over Santa Cruz County. Why, I asked her, had she become so interested in this idea, and why did she think it would work for the people of Nogales?

"Last summer, I vowed to my husband that I was done being a judge unless I could find a treatment for the countless families who cycle through my court-room on family violence charges. If it isn't violence between the wife and hus-band, it's the son and mother. It's out of control." Maley went looking for possible treatment approaches in books about domestic violence at the local bookstore, but she was disappointed in what she found: an emphasis on solu-tions that weren't true to her experience. "The problem with batterer's treat-ment is that it doesn't work—it only treats half the problem. I was looking for a holistic solution, one that treated the whole family. The families in Nogales, they almost always stay together—they are Latino, Catholic, and held together by their links to Mexico. The idea that they will divorce, or even separate for longer than a day or two, is ridiculous." Then she learned about Circles, and wondered if they might be the approach she was looking for.

There was already a crowd of people at the hotel—judges, legal aid attor-neys, probation officers, treatment providers, and clergy—waiting for the con-ference to begin. Maley was clearly a force in her community—a bridge builder—who appeared to command the respect of Mexican, Anglo, and Latino people alike.

After introducing the general principles of the Healing and Peacemaking Circles, I asked the audience to think about how such a program might work in Nogales: "You could offer the program to a defendant either after he or she pleads guilty, or before—it's up to you and Arizona law. Once the defendant is in the program, he or she is called an —applicant.' The victim is called a 'partic-ipant.'" I reminded them that the process was strictly voluntary, however: "The participant can choose to participate in the Circle or not—it is up to them to decide."

Safety, I stressed, must be paramount: "An intake assessment determines whether it is safe for the victim to participate—you want to hear from both parties, in separate interviews, about how dangerous the relationship feels, and what the history has been." I explained how there are certain standard ques-tions to ask to determine the level of violence in the relationship and whether it's life-threatening for the victim. I described the importance of the Initial So-cial Compact—the document the applicant signs promising not to be violent and agreeing to simultaneously participate in any other treatments that might be necessary (treatment for alcoholism, for example). It was during these first discussions that the Circle keeper would identify a safety monitor with the help of the participants.

I also talked about who might participate in addition to the applicant and participant—extended family, support people, community members. "Some participants will want their extended family to come to all of the Circles; oth-ers will want them to participate in more limited ways. But it is good to include extended family to ensure that everyone is engaged in the healing process—

that someone isn't inadvertently undermining all the effort taking place in the Circle because he or she feels left out." I emphasized the importance of preparing each person who participates in the Circle for the fact that *all* participants must be supported so that they feel comfortable saying what's on their minds. Without such preparation, one person can end up dominating the circle and diverting attention away from the problem at hand. Members of the larger community should be engaged in the Peacemaking Circle process as well; the inclusion of religious leaders, engaged friends, and neighbors both reinforces the idea of a nonviolent standard of behavior and communicates that the community cares about the struggling couple—that they are not alone.

The rules and shared values of circles needed to be explicit from the beginning: no further violence; no blame; and instead a focus on acknowledgment, understanding, responsibility, and healing. It was also important to identify the underlying issues that might be contributing to the violence, and for everyone in the circle to participate in addressing those issues.

Circles could continue indefinitely; what span of time would be right for Nogales? Given that Peacemaking Circles were being considered as an alternative to the Batterer Intervention Programs offered through the courts, it was decided that the Circles would be held for the standard legal treatment period in Arizona: twenty-six weeks for first-time offenders. We envisioned that the program would therefore be one of two options for mandated treatment, along with BIPs, when someone was arrested for a family violence crime.

At that point, the large group broke into smaller groups to work on designing the specifics of a program to fit the needs of the Nogales community. They addressed questions such as the following: Where would they send clients who needed help with their drinking as well as their violence? (To a nearby alcohol-treatment program.) What if someone refused to sign the Initial Social Compact? (He or she would be excluded.) How would those assembled generate community support for the program? (Through events and publicity.) They formed a Restorative Justice Advisory Team that very afternoon—a community group willing to take responsibility for the development of the Circle program.

By the end of two days, the group had created their own Circles program and named it "Construyendo Circulos de Paz" or "Constructing Circles of Peace." It was the first restorative justice treatment program of its kind for intimate violence in the nation. With grants from the Andrus Family Fund—a small family foundation in New York City—it was up and running within months of my initial visit. The National Science Foundation (NSF) also approved funding to compare the CCP program to a batterer treatment program. This meant that offenders would be randomly sent to either CCPs or BIPs to judge which program was more effective at reducing violence.

To date, over fifty applicants have completed their six-month period of treatment. More than one hundred fifty community members now participate in the Circle process in Nogales by volunteering their time. Some contribute to the Restorative Justice Advisory Team, which meets monthly to discuss the program and its progress. Dozens of others sit in on Circles, week after week, supporting families through the healing process. The results of the NSF-funded study are still being analyzed, but anecdotally the program is considered a great success.

One applicant said of his experience:

> I am very happy that I participated. I was confused, worried, frustrated, nervous, and didn't know what to expect. I had participated in other groups, and I thought this would be the same—that I would attend just to get a signature and to get a release from the court—but I was wrong. As I continued with the circle, I started to see changes in my life. I learned that it takes hard work to change a bad habit and form a good one.
>
> I learned how to be more organized and practiced time management, which made my stress level come down. I also learned that the world didn't have to come to an end because of the incident and how good things can come from the bad.
>
> I hope to continue to apply what I learned by continued determination and perseverance and with the help of my family, which has been my support. My family also plans to continue the Circle once a month so we can continue to support each other. My family is also grateful because they made good changes and also learned new things that are helping them live better.

A victim participant who has three children with one of the applicants who participated was stunned by the Circle's success: "My husband . . . has changed dramatically. One of the reasons why he changed is because of the circle that we participated in. . . . Now he has a lot of communication with me. He's not violent at all. He talks a lot to the kids. He didn't used to do that much before, but now he's like a completely different person."

Judge Maley is also very pleased with the results of the Circles work in Nogales: "CCP has completely changed how our community thinks about how to address domestic violence. We finally have a way of healing the violence and dealing with the underlying issues. It really is a fantastic solution for all those involved. We are now using Circles for community problems—it is a process that works for so many social issues."

SETBACK OR TRANSITION?

Nevertheless, the Circles occasionally have setbacks. In a few cases, subsequent arrests for violent behavior have been reported; in other instances, people have been arrested for drug- or alcohol-related crimes after the Circle had begun. At first, any violations of the Social Compact were viewed as failures. If someone was arrested, even if it was for a crime that was unrelated to domestic violence, the case was immediately to be sent back to the judge for a jail sentence, and the offender would often be denied additional circles or treatment. (This is how BIPs customarily handle similar violations.) Then something important happened in one of the early Circles involving a twenty-year-old named José.

José had been assigned to a circle after hitting his mother during a fight and getting arrested. At first, José seemed to be responding very well to the treatment, but then his Circle participants were notified that he had been arrested again—this time for possession of cocaine. They were furious and bitter because they'd spent several weeks discussing José's drug problems; his relapse made them feel as though they'd been duped. Together, a number of the Circle participants marched over to the jail to confront José and tell him they were disbanding the Circle; his domestic violence case would therefore be sent back to the judge.

When they arrived, however, they discovered that José was embarrassed and apologetic, and their anger dissipated; instead of admonishing him, they held a Circle at the jail and encouraged him to speak his mind. He talked about how hard it was to give up his addiction. In response, the others reminded him of his hopes—to live with his girlfriend and baby—and he became more resolved than ever to change. José told them that he wanted so badly to be a good boyfriend and father, but he just didn't know how.

Insight into ways to handle these kinds of setbacks was further bolstered by the pioneering work of the Andrus Family Fund. Steve Kelban and the entire board of directors at Andrus believe that social change organizations that focus on the difficulties of transition are more likely to be successful in effecting lasting change than other groups. Kelban introduced the Nogales program to the Transition Framework model, developed by Bill Bridges in the 1970s, and we started to incorporate it into our thinking about Circles.

Bridges believes that people are constantly changing, but few of us pay close enough attention to the *process* of transition that underlies that change. Bridges and the Andrus Fund distinguish between "change," which is "external and situational" (moving to a new country, having a baby, ending the cycle of violence), and "transition," which is the "internal process of how one responds to the change," in other words, how it feels to go through these changes and how we manage those feelings.

Bridges believes that there are three stages of transition. First, an individual relinquishes an allegiance to something that has been part of his life for a long time: his bachelorhood, say, or his violent behavior. Bridges calls this the process of "Ending." This is perhaps the most difficult stage for many people; even when the anticipated change is theoretically a positive one, an individual may not be ready for all that the change might bring with it. ("I still may slap my wife if she deserves it.") In other words, old ways die hard.

The second stage is the "Neutral Zone," in which the person has agreed to the changes in principle but still feels the pull of old ways of being. This "limbo" period anticipates the future and therefore can be exciting, but it can also generate tremendous anxiety and insecurity. ("I want to stop hitting my wife, but maybe I can't. And will she still respect me if I *don't* hit her?") These feelings, in turn, encourage people to revert to old coping mechanisms, making it very difficult to stay on the path they've set for themselves. How one works through these ambivalent feelings is crucial.

A Circle can seize these moments of ambivalence as opportunities for reflection rather than condemnation, as it did in José's case, and this can make all the difference in the long-term results of the treatment. Rejecting or punishing the applicant during this critical period of transition may make him feel that his earlier efforts have been for nothing or that he'll never succeed in changing.

The final stage in the Bridges transition process is called "New Beginning." This is when the individual has embraced the change, and his feelings and his behavior are in accord. ("I no longer hit my wife, and now I find that we fight less. I *want* to hit her less, and it is also easier to control myself even when I'm angry. I feel better about myself than I have in years.")

The Transition Framework philosophy has been incorporated into the Constructing Circles of Peace (CCP) program in Nogales and has also become one of its hallmarks. This does not mean that a recurrent act of violence would be "excused" or "forgiven." Whether or not the Circle proceeds would depend on the feelings of all those involved, especially the victim participant, and the nature of the offense. But at the same time, one misstep would not necessarily capsize all the work and effort that had gone before. In José's case the court and CCP worked in concert—with interesting results. The judge allowed the Circle to continue meeting after the first drug arrest. After the second one, a few months later, he was sent to jail. After a few weeks of incarceration, however, he started to use what he learned in the Circle to fortify his commitment to drug treatment. He wrote a letter to Judge Maley thanking her for his Circle and vowing to "start fresh." JosÈ hasn't been arrested again since his release two years ago.

THE MENENDEZ FAMILY

Elena and Roberto Menendez appeared in Judge Maley's courtroom in the summer of 2005. Roberto, forty-two, and his wife, Elena, thirty-eight, had been married twelve years. They have lived in Nogales with their four children, Mario, fourteen, Juanita, ten, Micaela, six, and Jolie, three, for most of their lives. By Nogales standards, the family lives quite comfortably. They own a modest three-bedroom home and two cars. Roberto is on the road six days a week, selling, repairing, and delivering computers to various businesses. This leaves just one day a week for family time. Elena stays home with the children. From an outsider's perspective, the Menendez home is a model of order, and Elena takes enormous pride in it—especially in her collection of exotic plants. Before July 2005, neither husband nor wife had been arrested.

That summer, at nine o'clock one Saturday evening after a week on the road, Roberto became unexpectedly and alarmingly violent. According to the police report, he went out to the garage, returned with a sledgehammer, and smashed the Menendez's beautiful dining room table to bits. Then he destroyed each of the chairs. When his wife saw what he had done, she picked up one of the table legs and attacked her plants. After smashing the pots, she pulled each plant out by the roots. The children were terrified; nothing like this had ever happened before. Finally, Juanita couldn't stand it any more and called 911.

Within minutes, the Nogales police arrived, arrested Roberto, and charged him with disorderly conduct, a class one misdemeanor. The police chose not to arrest Elena—although they also charged her with disorderly conduct—because it would have left the children alone in the house without either parent. Although Elena did less damage than Roberto, she, too, the police believed, had contributed to the destruction. The police cuffed Roberto and took him away. Juanita, who felt responsible for her father's arrest, became hysterical, and soon all the children were crying.

When the Menendez couple arrived a few weeks later in Judge Maley's courtroom for disposition of their cases, the charges had been dropped against Elena; the prosecutor didn't feel that her behavior warranted a prosecution. Roberto, on the other hand, pled guilty; because his case came up prior to the NSF study—which randomly assigns the defendant to BIP or CCP—he was given two options. "You can attend batterer treatment or go to the Construyendo Circulos de Paz program," Judge Maley told him. Roberto asked what CCP was. "It's a new program here in Nogales," Judge Maley said, "in which the whole family can participate. You, your wife, the kids, support people for each of you—all can attend, if they choose to." Elena, sitting behind Roberto, nodded her head yes. The couple agreed to attend twenty-six weeks of Circles.

Each of the Menendezes' Circles ran about two hours, sometimes longer. Jessica and Steve served as Circle co-keepers. Jessica was a registered nurse with a history of working on domestic violence causes; she had displayed a passion for the CCP process ever since she'd been introduced to it at the first meeting in 2004. Steve was a social worker at a local hospital and also a stalwart supporter of Circles. Tom, an outspoken thirty-nine-year-old with a thriving computer business, was Roberto's employer and support person, which was unusual—few people choose their boss for this role—but the two men were close. Elena's support person was her mother, Lupe Machado.

On the evening of the seventh Circle meeting, Lupe looked weary. Still, she forced a smile, saying she was there out of devotion to her daughter and grandchildren. The Circle also included Janet as its community member, one of Nogales' civic-minded Circles volunteers.

Circle Seven was held in a spare room at the local firehouse. Jessica opened the meeting. She reminded the group that the talking piece is a vital tool and that as it moves from person to person, it becomes the catalyst for understanding, connecting, change, and healing. Indeed, the sharing in the circle was gradually providing a more nuanced backstory to the original incident; already, both Roberto's "crazy" explosion and his wife's furious response were beginning to make a little more sense to the others—and to themselves.

That Saturday night, Roberto first arrived at the house with his friend Juan, an independent trucker. Elena considers Juan to be a bad influence on Roberto. Among Juan's faults, says Elena, is that he often entices Roberto, when they are on the road, into patronizing Hooters after work to have a few drinks and unwind. Roberto explained to Elena that Juan had helped him deliver computers to a customer and that he'd given him $40 in exchange for his help. This further fueled Elena's unhappiness. It was bad enough that Juan was Roberto's drinking buddy; she didn't want Roberto also doing business with him. Later that evening, after Juan left, Roberto and Elena visited her unemployed brother, Jorge, who begged for some gas money; Roberto generously handed him $50. But on the way home, Elena—still angry about Juan—began complaining again to Roberto about his friendship with such a "low-life."

"Look, I just gave $50 to your brother," Roberto snapped back, "stop bitching at me."

After this remark, Elena simply stopped talking to her husband. When they got home, the couple had a few beers, and Roberto repeatedly tried to get Elena to speak to him. She continued to ignore him—even after he slammed a door and punched a hole in the living room wall as he became more and more frustrated. On his way to the kitchen for another beer, Roberto tripped and crashed into the dining room table; one of the legs buckled under his weight. At this moment, after several beers and hours of anger and tension, Roberto lost it entirely.

On the evening of Circle Seven, however, that night seemed very remote. Elena seemed shy, even timid; she barely made eye contact. Roberto, on the other hand, was expansive and direct, his handshake firm and friendly. He was far bigger than his wife, broad-shouldered and muscular, but his demeanor was in no way threatening. He and Tom were bemoaning the fact that they were missing an important football game on TV.

Jessica lit a candle and placed it in the middle of the Circle to begin. A feather was designated as the official talking piece. Although the group had already touched on the events that brought Roberto and Elena there, Jessica explained that she felt the underlying causes of the violence still remained mysterious, and that she wanted to initiate a deeper conversation by opening with a challenging statement.

"I think the dining room table is a symbol of the family," Jessica continued. "It is the heart and soul of the family. It is where the family gathers, where all the meals are eaten, and where all the holidays are celebrated." Jessica paused for a second and then finished her thought. "I believe that when the dining room table is attacked, the family is attacked."

Jessica paused as the others considered this notion. To accuse Roberto of destroying a table and chairs was one thing. But to connect that act to an act against his family was quite another. She then passed the feather to Elena's mother.

Yes," Mrs. Machado agreed, "the table is the center, the heart of the family." Then she quickly passed the talking piece to her son-in-law. He spoke slowly and seriously.

"I am ashamed of what I did to the dining room table and chairs," he admitted. "Very ashamed! Why did I do it? I've been thinking about that, and I think I know the reason. I went after the table and chairs because I knew that my wife cared so much about them. Afterwards, I tried to fix the table, but it couldn't be fixed. Then, I called the manufacturer to try to buy another one just like it. But they didn't have the exact table. I also made many calls to try and find a used table and chairs just like the one we had. But I had no luck. I bought a new table, but I know it's not the same. I know Elena loved that table. I know that she looks at the new table and what she really sees is a scar."

His eyes dropped to the floor. "What happened that night will never happen again," he promised.

Roberto passed the feather to Tom, who shook his head as if to say he understood his friend's feelings. "Sometimes," he joked, "you get into a fight with your wife and breaking a few cheap lamps just doesn't seem sufficient to make your point. Maybe sometimes you have to go for the dining room table," he said. "But if you do, consequences exist."

As Tom's humor lightened the mood, Steve, the Circle co-keeper interceded and asked for the talking piece. "Understand," Steve said, "Circles are not about placing blame. This is a very important point."

Roberto nodded. "I understand," he said, "and I appreciate that you are all not pointing fingers at me and telling me what a bad person I am. Still, I know I did a bad thing, something that I must be responsible for. What I want to try and do is understand why I was suddenly so violent. You know, I am away from home six days each week, and when I am home I want Elena to give me some attention. I guess I was feeling frustrated, not just that night but for many nights that stretch into many months. I just couldn't get her attention. So, I thought, and I know it's crazy, destroying our dining room table and chairs— now that will get her attention."

Roberto handed the feather to Janet, the community volunteer.

"I am divorced," she said. "And I know from being unhappily married that there are many ways to damage the heart. And one of the most damaging is to withhold communication. That is very dangerous to a marriage. I would like to hear what Elena has to say."

Janet gave the feather to Elena.

"I think I am just tired," Elena said. "I am worn out. I have so much to do with our children. And taking care of the house. Sometimes I just can't speak. Sometimes I just want to be left alone. I had nothing to say. I had nothing to give. Roberto should have understood how tired I was. I just needed some time. But he didn't give me time. Instead, he went crazy. When he began breaking these things that I love, that I worked so hard to keep beautiful, I became so . . . so . . . angry."

She paused and took a breath. Her face was flushed. Roberto stared at her, but she didn't return his look.

"When Roberto broke the table and chairs," Elena continued, "I thought, I will show him. I will break something. I, too, can be violent. I, too, can be crazy. But afterwards when I saw the state of our home, when I saw the look on our children's faces, when I couldn't stop them from crying, when I thought I was going to jail, I was so scared. What will happen to our beautiful home? What will happen to our children? What will happen to my husband? What will happen to me? What will become of us?"

She put her head in her hands and wept. Janet put an arm around her, and Roberto took the feather from Elena's lap.

"I think we need to fight *nicer*," he said softly to his wife.

For the first time during the evening Elena looked squarely at her husband. The feather was then handed to Jessica.

"Well," Jessica said, "we all like the notion of fighting *nicer*."

Janet asked for the feather and said that the conversation about the dining room table made her think about her own dining room table and how sad an object it is. Since her divorce, she had not invited anyone to her house to eat at her table. Perhaps it was time for her, too, to make some changes and bring joy back to her table.

Jessica retrieved the feather from Janet. "How lovely that we have come to this place in less than two hours," she said. "We have done a great deal, but more, of course, is still to be done. My hope is that eventually Jolie, Miguel, Juanita, and Mario will join our Circle, too. I think they would greatly benefit by telling us their stories."

Several weeks later, during Circle Fifteen, another significant breakthrough occurred. After sitting quietly through many of the Circles, Elena began talking about her life with the children during the workweek when Roberto was away. She talked about how much she and the children missed him. She talked about how difficult it was if one of the children was sick and needed special care.

"Sometimes I feel very alone," Elena said.

Roberto reached for the talking piece: "But I always call you throughout the day." "Yes," Elena answered. "I know. . . . I know. . . . During the day, you call me three or four times, even when you're busy working and driving all over—from here to California and back. That's good. And I appreciate these calls very much. But I think the problem is . . . is . . . deeper."

"So, what's the problem?" Roberto asked, as he handed the feather back to his wife.

"At night, that's the real problem," she responded. "It's different at night when you call. I often hear music in the background and people laughing and talking. Then I know you're in a bar. And if you're in a bar, I know that you're drinking. And that scares me because I know that you'll be getting back into your truck late at night to go to a motel, and that you'll be driving. And I don't know how much beer you've had, or how tired you are, or if maybe your head is heavy, and maybe . . . maybe you're even a little . . . a little . . . "

Roberto reached for the feather again. "Drunk!" he finished, uttering the word his wife refused to say.

The group stared at Roberto. He shook his head. They looked at Elena, who stared at the floor. Finally, Roberto spoke—softly, but firmly, "I am not a drunk. I am not an alcoholic."

Roberto passed the feather to Tom, his support person and employer.

"I've never met a person with a drinking problem who would admit he had a drinking problem," said Tom. "I also know that when alcohol is involved, stupid fights increase. When alcohol is not involved, stupid fights decrease."

The feather passed to Steve next, and he said, "I'd like to hear more from both Elena and Roberto."

At that particular moment, both Elena and Roberto were silent, perhaps stymied by their fears. Elena would not say the word "drunk." Roberto would not talk about why he drinks or why his drinking might be a problem for his wife. Nevertheless, the Circle participants now knew that Roberto's drinking was a larger part of the dynamic than they originally understood.

Steve expressed his satisfaction that the issue of drinking had come up, reminding the others that alcohol is a frequent trigger of violence, and that both Roberto and Elena had been drinking the night of the violence. "Roberto, was it Elena's silence that made you so angry?" he asked. "If so, why does her silence make you so angry? Is it possible that you destroyed the table just to break

Elena's silence? And Elena, was it your anger with Roberto, his drinking and carousing with his friend Juan, that made you go silent? It would be helpful to talk about how we communicate with one another, and how refusing to communicate can sometimes escalate situations. It would also be helpful to talk about when it's important to back off. If one partner needs space—or silence—maybe it's better to wait and talk later, when matters cool down."

For Circle Twenty, the group decided to meet at the Menendez home. A larger room than the one at the fire house was needed because all four of the Menendez children were going to attend. Because the Nogales Circle Program is anchored in the criminal justice program, the meetings are usually held in a community setting. The feeling in this case was strong, however, that the Menendez family had made so much progress that a Circle in their home would not be a problem. Indeed, the Circle keepers believed that there might be a healing benefit to meeting there, given that it had been so central to the violent incident. Before the next Circle, Jessica met with each child ahead of time, to prepare them for the evening.

Jessica addressed the children first, once everyone was assembled: "I know that you've been wondering what Circles are really about. I've thought about this question a lot. In a way, the answer is simple. And in another way, it's complicated. The reason we have Circles—and this is very important—is because it is a way for us all to come together to talk about things that have hurt us. Every week, we come together to listen to each other. We share our stories, and afterwards we find that we almost always feel better. We find that we always learn something about each other and from each other. And in Circles we also learn important things about ourselves. One other point: We feel very safe in Circles because we never judge each other. We never punish each other."

"Nobody *ever* gets grounded in Circles?" Mario asked. Jessica quickly passed the feather to Mario, who immediately returned it.

"No," Jessica said. "Nobody *ever* gets grounded in Circles. We just talk and listen. And we find that just talking and listening help us a great deal. And after awhile what happens is that we not only feel better, but we also see ourselves going through changes—good changes. Circles are a process—one that helps us grow and mature. You know, adults mature just like children."

The children listened carefully.

"What we are going to talk about—at least to start—is that night when the table was broken and Juanita called the police. We're not going to blame anybody for what happened. We just want to talk about it. And move forward from it."

Roberto asked for the feather, and Jessica passed it to him.

"Jessica," Roberto began, "I am so glad that you started with that night when the table was . . . was . . . destroyed. I have something to say to my children—something that I have wanted to say for months. But I think that this is the right moment because tonight we are all here together in a Circle in my home—my wife, my children, and my friends."

He paused and collected himself. He looked directly at his children, who were wide-eyed. Even Jolie, who was beginning to doze in her mother's lap, straightened up and listened. As Roberto continued, his voice quivered.

"I am very sorry for what happened that night when I destroyed the table," he said. "I know now that the dining room table is the symbol of the family. I want you to know that I would never want to hurt my family. I want to apologize to you—my children—from my heart for this terrible act. I want you to know that it will never, ever happen again."

The children stared at their father. Roberto paused again. He turned and glanced at the dining table.

"It's taken some time," he continued. "But the house is now as nice as it ever was. We have our beautiful new dining room table. The big hole that I made in the wall is fixed. Everything is plastered and painted. And now we have replaced all of the plants. They are beautiful—I hope as beautiful as the old plants. I feel good about the house being together . . . the way it used to be. Now we are *here* putting ourselves back together."

Again, he paused. "I have one more thing to say. Then I will pass the feather to whoever wants it. I want to say something about my drinking. I have been thinking a lot about my drinking. Particularly *why* I drink. I just wanted to say that."

"Mario," Steve asked, turning to the eldest Menendez child, "what do you think?"

Mario squirmed in his seat as Steve passed him the feather. "I think," he began tentatively, "I think I am happier." He squirmed some more. "I think," he began again, "my parents are happier together. That makes me happy."

He passed the feather, which suddenly seemed like a hot potato, to Juanita, who sat composedly in her chair.

"That night when I called the police," Juanita said, "I was very scared. I just wanted to stop the fighting and the yelling and everything from being smashed. So I told Papa—I am going to call the police.' And he said—Okay, call the police.' So I took the phone into the bathroom, and I dialed 911. I thought they would just come and stop the trouble. But they came and took Papa away. After that, I was even more scared than when they were fighting. I felt very bad about what I did. I felt what I did was wrong—worse than what Papa did."

Tom asked for the feather and addressed Juanita.

"All I can say, kiddo, is that you did the right thing," he said. "Yes, the police came and took your dad away. But they also brought order back to your house. I know it was a scary night. But let me tell you something: I came from a family where nobody talked—forget about yelled. In my house, it was so quiet you could hear the grass grow. The result was that all of our feelings got squashed.

And believe me, that was plenty scary, too. What I have found—especially in Circles—is that the more you talk, the more the trouble and hurt goes away."

Then Janet asked for the feather.

"When I was a little girl," Janet said, "my parents fought bitterly. I can remember my brothers and sisters huddling together, not knowing how my parents' battles were going to end. I actually thought sometimes that my parents might kill each other. In my day, there was no 911," she continued. "There was no one to call for help. Juanita—you are so lucky that there is a 911 to call for help. I only wish I'd had a 911 when I was your age."

Jessica retrieved the feather from Janet. "What I have found," Jessica said, "is that when life goes smoothly, we rarely have an opportunity to learn and grow. But when trouble happens, when we feel pain, that's when we learn and grow. I think the challenge is to use the pain as a kind of stepping stone to change."

Jessica asked Juanita what she was thinking. The child looked pensive. The feather was again passed. "I want to thank you for talking to me about that night," Juanita said. "You know, my brother and sisters were angry at me for what I did. They blamed me for the trouble when all I was trying to do was to stop the trouble."

Micaela plucked the feather from her big sister. "Yes, yes," Micaela said, "at first we were angry. Really, truly angry! But now we know that you did the right thing. Nobody's angry anymore." Micaela reached over and hugged her sister as Mario, grasping the feather, said that he, too, was no longer angry. Then Elena asked for the feather.

"I am very proud of my children," Elena said. "Especially tonight! I also want to say that I, too, am very sorry for what happened. I had a part in the violence of that night. It wasn't all Roberto's fault. I wish I could erase that night from my children's memory, but I know that I never can."

She handed the feather to Jessica.

"Juanita," Jessica asked, "is there anything else you want to add to what you've said? Is there anything you want to say specifically to your parents or your brother and sisters?"

Juanita thought for a moment and then asked for the feather. "I have one more thing to say," she began. "In my family, it feels to me as though I am a *bridge*. I don't think I want to be a *bridge* anymore."

At first, no one seemed sure what Juanita meant.

"When things in our house are bad," she continued, "when Mama and Papa aren't getting along, what happens is that Mama stops talking to Papa. When this happens, Papa comes to me and talks to me about his problems with Mama. And then he wants me to go and talk to Mama for him. Maybe, Papa thinks, Mama will talk to him through me. I . . . I . . . don't feel good doing this. This is hard for me. I love them both. I want them to work out their problems together. I don't think it's a good idea for me to be a bridge anymore."

The feather was passed to Roberto. "Yes," he admitted, "this is true. This is a problem. I see that. Yes, I see that. How did we come to such a place? All I really want to do is keep my children safe from pain and fear, and, here, again, I am only making things worse." He paused for a moment, collecting his thoughts. "I think Juanita has touched on a big part of the problem," he continued, "and I think it's all tied up with my drinking, too. Sometimes when Elena and I are not getting along, she just shuts off."

Again, Roberto nervously ran his hands through his hair as everyone waited to hear what he would say next. "My fear and hatred of the silences is one of the things that Circles has made me think about." Roberto continued. "I want to understand why Elena's shutting me out makes me so . . . so. . . . When Elena is silent and I am home, I know that's when I will take a drink. The night that I destroyed our dining room table, Elena wouldn't speak to me. I tried 101 ways to get her to talk to me. But she was mad at me. I can't even remember why. No matter what I did, she wouldn't say a word. Sometimes I think, maybe—and it sounds crazy—I attacked the table because I thought if I did something so . . . so . . . crazy . . . she'd *have* to speak to me. But then I attacked the table, and she never told me to stop. And she didn't say one word. That made me even crazier. And then our world went completely crazy, when Elena started attacking her plants."

Jessica retrieved the feather. "Roberto," she answered, "there's nothing — crazy' about what you've just said. In fact, it makes a lot of sense. Tonight we talked with your children about the core values of our Circle. These are values we also share beyond Circles. We want to have the love and trust of our family. We want them to be inclusive, to not shut us out. We want them to be empathetic and feel our heartache. And we want to have the courage to explore our deepest hurts with them. And to share these hurts honestly and openly."

Roberto shook his head and, with his sleeve, wiped some dampness from his eyes. The feather was returned to him as he struggled to compose himself.

"I just want to say to Juanita that I see how you've been a bridge," he said. "I also see why you've been a bridge. It's very good that you've told me of your discomfort. That takes courage. But until you talked tonight about how you felt like a bridge, I didn't understand the position that I was putting you in. For this, I am sorry. It won't happen again. I promise."

Juanita asked for the feather. "Thank you, Papa," she said softly.

Elena then asked for the feather and spoke directly to her eldest daughter: "Parents make mistakes," she said. "I've made mistakes with your papa. Your papa has made mistakes with me. And we've made mistakes with you. But we also learn from our mistakes."

Juanita smiled as Jessica retrieved the feather from Elena.

"Well," Jessica said, "we are coming to the end of Circle Twenty. I think this has been a wonderfully enlightening evening. I believe that tonight's conversation has led us deeper into places that we've only touched upon before. We are now delving into the subject of violence. After all, what do we really know about violence? One thing we know is that it rarely happens randomly. Violence almost always has a history. And violence isn't only about attacking something or someone. Violence has other ways of showing itself. In Janet's home, her parents fought with their fists. That's the violence we all recognize. But in Tom's home, the violence was different. The violence was in the silences. And perhaps in Elena and Roberto's home, the violence—or a part of the violence—is also in the silences. We also can see how violence moves from one generation to the next—how it touches lives, even changes lives, never for the better.

"We've also seen how by talking about our experiences, we face our pain—and sometimes even our mistakes. By doing this, we have a grand opportunity to change, ultimately, how we behave. Juanita won't carry the burden of her parents' silences. Roberto has connected the pain of Elena's silences with his drinking and his fear, anger, despair, even his violence. And Elena understands how profoundly her silences have affected her family. That's real progress."

By the time Elena and Roberto Menendez completed their Peacemaking Circles, they had made many important changes—as individuals and as a couple. Tom, who eventually told the Circle that he was a recovering alcoholic, continued to help Roberto think through his relationship to alcohol. Roberto started seeing less of his friend Juan; he also cut back on his drinking, although he has yet to join AA. He still works for Tom and maintains his difficult schedule, but he has made more of an effort to compensate for it: "I am making it a practice to call home from the road all the time," he reported. "And when I'm home, I am *truly* home." He and Elena even started going out on dates together to strengthen their relationship, and he plays games and talks at length with the kids on the weekends.

The Circle process allowed Elena to safely articulate her fears and express her anger, and she realized that her silences, while punishing Roberto, were also making her life and marriage more difficult. In fact, she saw how refusing to communicate had contributed to escalating the violence between them. She stopped giving Roberto the "cold shoulder" and said that her experience in Circles had made her calmer and more confident. "I want to improve my English. I also want to get my American citizenship. I see now with Jolie in school that my children are growing up. And I have to think about *my* future, too."

Mrs. Machado, Janet, and Tom also felt very good about the Circle, and they had personally learned a lot from participating in it. Janet resolved to communicate better in her relationships; she also held a reunion Circle—six months after their weekly sessions had ended—around her dining table, and everyone in the Menendez family attended. Tom decided to use the lessons he'd learned with the Menendez family to try to save his own marriage: "I realized from participating in all those Circles that anytime I engage in a conversation that deals with feelings, a potential for progress exists." At the beginning, Tom admitted, he'd seen the Menendezes' Circle "as a punishment for a crime that they'd committed against themselves and their children," but then it became something very different. "The truth is," he said, "the Circle has taken on a life of its own. It is a kind of sacred place that has helped us find the sacred places within ourselves."

HUMANIZING THE CRIMINAL JUSTICE SYSTEM

The authors of *Peacemaking Circles* envisioned a transformative process like the one we have just explored:

> As healing unfolds, the negative energies around wounds—the energies of anger, fear, shame, resentment, and self-protection—can be released and replaced by the positive energies flowing from connection, hope, compassion for ourselves and others, and a shared vision. Circles change the way our energies flow in relationships. We slow down and listen to each other, and this opens the door to deep change. . . . People often emerge from Circles feeling differently about themselves. They discover capacities for interacting with others—both in how they're treated and in how they respond—that they may never have experienced before.

What would it mean for all of us, as a country, if we could harness this sort of power to work in conjunction with our criminal justice system? For Roberto and Elena Menendez, as for Kate and James and so many other violent couples, the call to the police was not a call for legal action but a cry for help—a desperate attempt to break the destructive dynamic in play. Certainly, the authority of the court was a significant reason why both Roberto and Elena took their fight so seriously, and therefore its weight cannot be underestimated: sometimes it takes the arrival of the outside world to make the problem really hit home. But what is so striking about Peacemaking Circles is that they can build on that intervention in a truly productive way, by giving violent couples a chance to seriously confront their behavior, recognize its patterns and origins, and stop the abuse. They can do it among family and friends who care deeply about them but haven't had an avenue for helping them in the past.

Peacemaking Circles go one step further—they allow the couple to understand what is happening between them, and how they can each move forward in new ways that prevent violence. Circles offer us a lifelong tool—something people can continue to use on their own—at the dinner table or sitting around

the living room. The talking piece equalizes everyone and encourages participation. But perhaps the most exciting and sustaining part of Peacemaking and
Healing Circles is that they give people a safe forum in which they can share
their weaknesses and their strengths *beyond the couple*. The strength of
Roberto and Tom's relationship is fully revealed when Tom confesses to his
own alcoholism and recovery to help his friend. Employers like Tom and community members like Janet build the kinds of bridges we seek—bridges that
minimize our differences and maximize our similarities. Everyone is invested
in change.

ENDING THE CYCLE OF ABUSE

BRENDA AND LUCRETIA ARIS: BREAKING THE CHAIN

In late 2001, Lucretia was serving her sentence for car theft at Frontera—the same prison where Brenda had been incarcerated until 1999 for killing Rick. The ironies didn't stop there. Frontera was also, in a very real sense, Lucretia's emotional home: for ten years of her childhood, this had been the only place where she and her sisters had been able to spend time with their mother. Brenda had been popular at Frontera, and many of her fellow inmates remembered the Aris children's visits; when Lucretia herself was incarcerated, some of these women took her under their wings. Not long afterward, the prison's Convicted Women Against Abuse group asked if Brenda could be allowed to return to Frontera to tell her story, and the warden gave her consent.

This was a rare privilege, but Brenda had been a model prisoner, and her life after her release proved to be equally inspirational. At age thirty-six, Brenda finally had a full-time job: a lumber company in Southern California had agreed to hire her as a condition of her release. She found the work and the independence it brought her exhilarating, and her job quickly became the center of her life.

Many of Brenda's other dreams, however, were not so different from what they had been when she was sixteen. She wanted her own home, and her children close by. At the same time, she knew that she had to rebuild her family with extreme care: all three of her daughters were taking drugs and had criminal connections. Brenda was committed to her girls but equally determined not to let their troubles drag her down—as she had once let Rick drag her down. She repeatedly declared that she would commit suicide rather than re-

240

turn to Frontera as an inmate. On the other hand, she felt that lecturing her daughters, given her own recent history, was useless; she knew that she could only lead them through loving example.

Lucretia was ecstatic when she heard that her mother was coming; Brenda hadn't yet been able to visit her in prison because it was forbidden under the terms of her parole. Now, with Brenda returning to Frontera as a guest speaker, mother and daughter could be reunited at that triumphant occasion. Lucretia was therefore devastated to learn that she would not, in fact, be allowed to attend the event; precisely *because* the women had such an intimate bond, contact between them was deemed a security risk by the prison authorities. Once again, she was cut off from her mother, but now their situations were reversed: she was the one who was locked up, while her mother was a free woman, building a new life and moving into the future without her.

The shock of this disappointment proved to be a turning point for Lucretia. Although she had been attending group therapy and participating in 12-step programs since she'd arrived at Frontera, this was the moment when she realized that she was not willing to be left behind; instead of mimicking Rick's downward spiral, she wanted to follow in her mother's footsteps. She began to put new energy and focus into her recovery work.

When Lucretia was released from prison, she severed her ties with her old friends and went directly to Phoenix House, an inpatient drug-treatment program. Step by step, she tackled every difficult issue: how she used alcohol and drugs to cope with her own childhood; how her relationship with Bobby had been extremely destructive; and how her drug addiction prevented her from caring for her own daughter, who was still living with Bobby's parents. As Lucretia began writing and talking about her family history as part of her treatment, the complexity of her dependency became clearer. It wasn't simply that she'd grown up in a culture of drugs and alcohol; it was also that her father and grandparents and aunts were using drugs to cope with enormous reservoirs of grief and shame and rage—overwhelming feelings that their poor caretaking passed along to her, in turn.

At the same time, as Lucretia struggled to come to terms with the past, her mother's new existence provided an illustration of what a future free of drugs and violence might look like. Could her own recovery, she wondered, perhaps inspire Candice and Sheena to believe they, too, could change? As the eldest child, Lucretia carried a lot of guilt for having abandoned her sisters at Grandma Iona's—just as Brenda had, when she went to prison. Perhaps she and her mother could now work together to help heal their family.

Today, seven years later, Brenda and her daughters have transformed their lives. Brenda is happily married; she and her husband, Mike, own a condominium together. In 2001, while they were still dating, Mike suffered from a stroke. Brenda held his hand and prayed by his side for days, despite the fact that his doctors had given her little hope that he would recover. When it finally seemed that he'd get better, they both felt that a miracle had taken place. They came to believe that God had given Brenda a chance to help save a life in exchange for the one she had taken. Soon afterward, they dedicated themselves to becoming Jehovah's Witnesses—a path they'd started down earlier in their relationship—and got married. Brenda feels that Mike has proved to be a tender and loving husband. There has never been any physical or psychological violence between them. "I'm just at a really happy stage of my life right now," Brenda told me. "I own my own home. I have a great job. I enjoy the people that I work with. I'm involved in our congregation. I just love life at this time."

Brenda's three daughters are less settled and financially secure, but they, too, have made enormous strides. Candice began straightening out almost as soon as her mother came home from prison. Then, several years after Lucretia got clean, Sheena, too, went through rehab, and whenever visitors were allowed, Lucretia would be there. "Wow," Sheena recalls thinking. "I'm finally getting to know my sister." Before long, all three sisters were employed at the lumber company. (When Candice became pregnant, and she and her boyfriend, Nestor, decided to get married, Brenda got Nestor a job there as well.) What's more, none of Brenda's daughters are in an intimate relationship plagued by violence.

Nevertheless, they still find themselves wrestling with the legacies of the past. When I held a Circle with them, in the summer of 2007, Lucretia confessed, "Life is really, really hard, and I'm struggling financially; I'm struggling spiritually. I'm on a continuous learning journey, and it's not easy—it's not easy at all for me." Although she sees her twelve-year-old daughter regularly, she worries about the girl's grades in school and fears that her grandparents are no longer able to control her. Candice, who lives with her in-laws, longs for the time when she and Nestor can afford their own home. Sheena, who is studying in the evenings to be a dental assistant, feels guilty for spending too much time going out with her friends and not enough time with her family or in church.

Still, as I sit in Brenda's living room during the Circle, listening to these women talk and tease and support one another, it is difficult to keep in mind that all four of them have some sort of criminal record and drug history. Brenda's tremendous warmth and optimism are a life raft that the whole family can cling to: "I have a wonderful husband," she says during the Circle. "I have three wonderful kids who are all doing great, and two grandkids that I get to spend time with. I don't think life could be any better." At moments like this, that night in Riverside seems as if it belongs to another lifetime—but only because these women have fought so hard to give themselves and one another something better.

WHAT MAKES CHANGE POSSIBLE?

Often, we tell ourselves, criminals don't really want to change—and perhaps many of them don't. But one could also argue that most criminals are not given the support or tools necessary to change. In 2001, the sociologist Shadd Maruna published a study entitled *Making Good: How Ex-Convicts Reform and Rebuild Their Lives*. In it he compared people who had stopped their criminal behavior with those who had not. Maruna found that nearly every single person he studied from both groups *wanted* to stop offending. Those who succeeded, however, had found what he called a "redemption script"—a way of linking their past behavior to external circumstances, which they could conceivably alter, rather than connecting it to some essential sense of self. A treatment program, a new religion, or an inspiring family or community member all contributed to their commitment to a new life and a newfound identity. The women in Brenda Aris's family used all three of these tools during their recoveries.

Maruna argued that any new understanding of recovery must include a "love the sinner, hate the sin" approach that counteracts the rejection this person has probably felt for most of his or her life. As we have seen again and again in the preceding chapters, violent people often feel guilty and ashamed of their behavior, but they also feel aggrieved and misunderstood, or victimized by past injustices. Only when they can tell their whole story—how and why they learned to be violent—can they truly have the opportunity to "unlearn" that violence. Certainly, they are unlikely to embark upon that highly risky journey if they are not in an environment of trust and support.

A NEW UNDERSTANDING

What do we want the struggle against intimate violence to look like thirty years from now? In 2038, what forms might that struggle take? Before answering these questions, we need to expand and refine our ideas about violence and its consequences—rage, shame, grief, self-hatred—and recognize that they are all around us. Violence is present when we slap a toddler who misbehaves or taunt an adolescent for being gay. When we train our dogs to bite strangers or hang up the phone on our husbands. When we cut off a car on the highway or email a friend a racist joke. When we waterboard a suspected terrorist, sentence a murderer to death, or drop a bomb on a foreign country. Even when we believe that taking violent action is unavoidable, we must name it consciously, accept responsibility for it, and anticipate the consequences that may follow, because, as we have seen again and again, violence begets violence.

The pervasiveness of violence in our society means that our notions of victim and perpetrator must be fluid rather than fixed. Sometimes an abusive dynamic is alive and clearly discernible within the couple itself, as it was in the McPhersons' marriage and in James and Kate's relationship. But it also moves from the public sphere to the private and back again; a girl who's being molested in day care may come home and kick the dog; a disabled vet returns from Iraq and starts punching his wife; a mother who was sexually brutalized by her father tells her daughters that all men are pigs. Even those of us who don't live with physical violence in our lives see these currents moving through our families and our offices and our schools every day, as small acts of cruelty spread from work to home or from parent to child.

The fact that the forces of violence are always moving through time and space suggests that—even as we become less tolerant of violent behavior in ourselves and others—we need to increase our compassion for those whose lives are ruled by it. After all, today's abusers are often—like Rick and Ruth and Lucretia—the victims of ten or twenty or thirty years ago. And others who have been brutalized as children find themselves repeating that pattern over and over, unerringly seeking out the familiar even as they desperately hope for something better. If we view them simply as monsters or deluded masochists, we deny them their more complicated humanity.

NEW APPROACHES

Ideally, thirty years from now, the messages about battering won't all suggest that only one person is at fault and that all violent relationships should necessarily end. Some public service announcements will continue to educate the public about the realities of intimate terrorism. ("Are you a prisoner in your own home? Marriage should not feel like a life sentence. Seek help now.") But others might focus on the importance of family and community in the struggle to fight abuse with slogans like "Peaceful relationships, peaceful families, peaceful world," or "The face of violence is as diverse as our community—and violence is a problem that belongs to all of us." Some posters would be directed explicitly at the person who has been abusive instead of only at the person who has been victimized. A photograph of children could be accompanied with the slogan, "You didn't deserve to get hit when you were a kid. Neither do they. Together we can end the cycle of abuse." Or, "Are you teaching your kid to be a batterer when he grows up? Many children who are exposed to abuse become violent adults." Other public service announcements will specifically address women's capacity for violence: "Do you think that female aggression somehow doesn't count? Tell that to the 125,000 men who were treated last year for domestic violence injuries."

Primary and secondary schools must continue to become new frontiers in anti-violence work and conflict resolution; they must also become, in every sense, safe environments, so that they offer students who live in violent families or violent neighborhoods both a refuge and a model of other ways of being. We must teach children how to protect themselves from bullies; we must also reach out to the Rick Arises of the world before they end up dead or in jail. Most elementary school teachers can tell you who their violent and victimized kids are as early as third or fourth grade. Teen couples should be taught how to recognize and alter destructive patterns in their romantic relationships; as we have seen, group work with couples can be especially effective. What if we spent more money on trying to help children or young people before we ended up paying their room and board in the prison system or in shelters?

In 2038, of course, both adult partners trapped in a violent relationship will be encouraged to seek help *before* the law intervenes—by calling hotlines like SAFE and Violence Anonymous or seeking couples counseling. Some groups will follow the model of Family Wellness by offering to help victims whether or not they are ready to leave their abusive relationships; others, like the Northwest Network, may put less emphasis on labels than on identifying and changing destructive behaviors and patterns; some may find it helpful to confront their violence in groups with other couples who are struggling with the same issues, such as those offered by the Marriage and Family Therapy Program. And by 2038 Healing Circles will be offered in communities across the United States to address not only violence between partners but also how that violence has been handed down by their parents and how they may be in danger of passing it along to the next generation.

The criminal justice system will undoubtedly continue to play an important role in arresting abusive adults, but by 2038 it must also recognize that referring these adults to appropriate treatment programs—whether in prison or on the outside—is a crucial part of its role. There will always be those who will not confront their violence unless they are forced to do so by the criminal justice system. And yet any treatment that follows can still be meaningful: James and the Menendezes did extremely valuable therapeutic work with the threat of re-arrest hanging over their heads. Peacemaking Circles, working in tandem with the courts, hold the abuser accountable for his or her actions while simultaneously suggesting that growth and reconciliation are possible.

This is why Peacemaking Circles illustrate Maruna's "love the sinner" principle so well. In one sense, they provide the criminal justice system with a human face: they are an embodiment of the larger society whose values the courts are attempting to uphold and protect. At the same time, these Circles humanize the victims and abusers, too. They acknowledge that a violent drug addict like JosÈ isn't *only* a violent drug addict—that he may, in fact, yearn to be someone entirely different. JosÈ couldn't kick his habit without going to jail (where he received drug treatment), but he also couldn't imagine the life he now has—his job as a trucker, his home with his girlfriend and child—without his Circle: he needed them both to change.

What about the Rick Arises of the world? Are Circles too insubstantial a structure to contain such enormous violence? Perhaps. Certainly there will always be violent offenders who lie beyond any possibility of reform. But it is important to remember that Rick's violence was never successfully stopped by the current, far more rigid system; perhaps, if it had been interrupted earlier, his marriage wouldn't have become so lethal. Women like Brenda might call the police sooner in their marriages if a more responsive option like the Circles Program is available to them; Peacemaking Circles, backed by the threat of jail, should reach out to abusers while also bolstering the power of victims.

Only when we have put Circles into widespread use and studied them will we know their limitations. And only then will we know their full potential, as well. The truth telling encouraged by this sort of forum can have enormous power, as those who were involved with South Africa's Truth and Reconciliation Commission discovered.

LESSONS FROM SOUTH AFRICA

In 1995, South Africa's Truth and Reconciliation Commission (TRC), chaired by Archbishop Desmond Tutu, made the following offer: amnesty would be granted to those who had committed crimes under apartheid, but only if those participants provided "full disclosure relating to the crime for which amnesty was being sought." Those who did not come forward would risk prosecution for their crimes. Over a period of several years, scores of South Africans testified about their role in the murder, imprisonment, and torture of their fellow citizens, and thousands of survivors told their stories.

Pumla Gobodo-Madikizela, a psychologist who joined the TRC in 1996, was acutely aware of the potential pitfalls of this approach. What did it mean, for example, to offer amnesty to those who might still express contempt for those they had damaged in the past? (Remorse was not a precondition for amnesty.) Could her efforts to understand the psychology of her former oppressors be seen as minimizing or excusing their wrongdoings? And what about her own bias? Most of those who testified were black women, like her, and their traumas inevitably evoked her own. "I was not a neutral listener on the commission," she admits, although she struggled to keep her emotions in check. All of these complexities made her resistant to glib notions of good and evil and where they resided in the larger community.

She was particularly haunted by an incident that had taken place when she was lecturing at the University of Transkei in 1990. The black-run township was vocal in its opposition to the apartheid system, and eventually the apartheid government sent in forces under a black lieutenant colonel, Craig Duli, to overthrow the local leadership. When the attempted coup was thwarted and Duli was captured, Gobodo-Madikizela joined the others to celebrate in the streets. Only later, when she heard about his mutilated body, did she feel ashamed. Yes, he had been a traitor to his people, a pawn of the white South African government. But he was still a black man, with a family, who had been seized, tortured, and assassinated. What did it mean to glorify this act, as the Afrikaners had glorified such acts against her people?

Gobodo-Madikizela was further humbled when, as fate would have it, she was assigned by the TRC to hear his widow's wrenching testimony six years later. She knew that she couldn't have stopped Duli's murder, but her participation in the festivities had made her complicit in the dynamic that led to his death. She felt that the work of the commission, on the other hand, represented an attempt to "break the cycles of politically inspired violence that so often repeat themselves historically."

As the dramatic testimonies of the TRC unfolded, she was fascinated to discover just how redemptive its work could be for those who had been wronged under the former regime. It exposed the crimes of the past to public scrutiny and judgment while simultaneously putting the victims at the very center of the proceedings. "For the first time," she observed, "victims enjoyed the affirmation that they were denied in the years of apartheid. Because their experiences were validated, many victims who took the stand and spoke in public about their suffering felt justice was restored."

These observations have exciting implications for those willing to use Circle programs to combat intimate violence in the United States. Many people hurt by friends and family are less interested in locking up the perpetrators than they are in having the injustices they've suffered acknowledged and condemned. Circles offer just such a forum, whereas adversarial courtroom proceedings will always risk further injuring the victim, because the defense must strenuously attempt to discredit his or her testimony. The legal system is inherently about competing versions of the truth and will therefore never be an ideal arena for personal healing.

During her work for the TRC, Gobodo-Madikizela was also startled to discover that the victims' harrowing testimonies frequently elicited expressions of genuine remorse on the part of the accused. Evidence of remorse, in turn, was often very meaningful to the victims. She described a policeman's widow who was deeply moved by the apology of Eugene de Kock, the counterinsurgency commander who'd engineered her husband's assassination: "I hope that when he sees our tears, he knows that they are not only tears for our husbands, but tears for him as well," the widow later told Gobodo-Madikizela. "I would like to hold him by the hand, and tell him that there is a future, and that he can still change."

Gobodo-Madikizela goes on to say that these moments of forgiveness can be extraordinarily transforming for the perpetrator: "For all the horrific singularity of his acts, [de Kock] is seeking to affirm to himself that he is still part of the human universe." For these damaged and corrupted people, such moments are "an impossible demonstration of grace."

For such a moment to be possible, however, several principles must be in operation. There must be a sense that this wrong is being corrected not only between two people but in front of the larger community, and that the moral authority of that community has committed itself to righting past abuses rather than allowing them to continue to be perpetuated.

THE QUESTION OF FORGIVENESS

Many of us may find the idea of rehabilitating extremely violent offenders sickening to contemplate—as excusing and forgiving behavior that will forever remain inexcusable and unforgivable. In cases of intimate terrorism, where one person exults in his or her control over another, it is especially difficult to imagine. How does one forgive Rick's extreme and ongoing brutality toward his wife? Or, say, a trusted priest's brutalization of a child in his care? When crimes are committed collectively rather than individually, as they are in times of war, the horrors multiply: What does it mean to forgive the Serbian army for the sexual enslavement of young women during the Bosnian conflict or the Hutus for the slaughter of Tutsi children? After these conflicts, the damage is vast and irreparable: not dozens, but hundreds, thousands, even millions of lives have been destroyed. In the face of such injustices, one could argue, any belief in the power of forgiveness is meaningless, and many may feel the same way about individuals whose violence has destroyed the lives of their partners and children.

At the same time, as the example of South Africa has shown us, the difficulty of confronting such overwhelming questions also points to their urgency. It is one thing to jail or ostracize a rapist here or a murderer there, but what does it mean for a society to isolate and condemn a vast sector of its population? Does such a stance diminish future acts of violence? After all, in the United States today, over two million men and women are physically assaulted or raped each year by intimate partners, and more than 850,000 children are victims of maltreatment at the hands of their parents or caretakers. This means that there are, literally, millions of people committing crimes against those closest to them that we consider reprehensible. If we refuse to rehabilitate them, who benefits?

The question of whom we can forgive is, of course, one that each of us must answer for ourselves, on a case-by-case basis, but we must remain alert to the fact that our own fury at the horrors of abuse—our own desire to go to war with the Rick Arises of this world—may be of little use to them or to those who suffer from their violence. After all, the battered women's movement was meant to help women like Brenda, and yet she remained beyond its reach. As long as we deny the humanity of those who are violent, the burden of recognizing that humanity lies only with their victims—and that's a very heavy burden to carry alone. Many women like Brenda will stay with their partners until they see a way out for both of them.

Reintegrating violent couples into the community does not mean excusing the violence or increasing the likelihood that the abuse will go on unchecked. Indeed, bringing intimate violence out of the closet and making services more available to abusive individuals gives their family members an objective way to gage the abusers' desire to change. Are they keeping their pledges? Are they telling the truth in therapy? Are they attending meetings? Are they modifying their behavior? If help is available for the abuser and yet consistently resisted and refused, it is clearer to the victim that change will not be forthcoming. It is also possible that, once the violent person is in a therapeutic setting, the victim will feel safer and less disloyal about ending the intimate relationship. Perhaps if society had reached out to Rick, Brenda might have found it easier to leave him.

True forgiveness tends to come when a person who is violent takes responsibility for what he or she has done and follows it up with steps to change—to leave the behavior behind. As we all know, such transformations are exceedingly difficult; effecting them without the support of others, however, is almost impossible. Hatred and anger and shame may be the inevitable legacies of all the violence that has been done to us—whether collectively or personally. But they should not be weapons for fighting back.

Finally, it is important to remember that the act of forgiveness can be tremendously empowering for the victim. Because victims' granting of forgiveness is optional, as Gobodo-Madikizela observed, "they hold the key to what the perpetrator so desires—to rejoin the realm of moral humanity." But such generosity *can free the victim as well,* relieving him or her of the burden of anger and shame that has been carried for so long. It also separates the victim from the perpetrator by acknowledging a moral universe that the perpetrator ignored when committing the original act of violence. The act of forgiveness reinforces a common humanity between the victim and the perpetrator while simultaneously severing their bond of hatred and shame.

THE POLITICAL IS PERSONAL

I've come a long way in my thinking about intimate violence. As a wild and rebellious teenaged girl, I put myself in danger with no awareness that I was doing so. When my relationships with Chris and Dudley went drastically awry, I coped as best as I could by rejecting them and denying what had happened to me. I had no conceptual framework for these experiences, and their implications were almost too terrifying to think about.

As I grew older and learned more about feminism, these traumas made more sense to me: I could see where I fit into the patriarchy. By the time my relationship with David became violent, I felt more comfortable excusing myself and blaming him; after all, I was the victim, and he was the batterer.

But while embracing the role of victim may have been politically acceptable—even encouraged—it didn't feel entirely right for me. Although my unhappy romantic life could be explained by the fact that men were inherently domineering, hating Chris, Dudley, and David didn't make it any easier to forgive myself for having cared for them. My insufficiently examined intimate history also fed my deeper anxiety that I would remain incapable of finding a partner with whom I could be happy.

Only through therapy was I able to tease out the strands of power and powerlessness that were woven throughout my relationships with men. With Chris, I failed to recognize my vulnerability—which certainly felt very real to me when he punched me in the chest in broad daylight—but I also failed to acknowledge the significance of my social and financial privilege. With Dudley, I had not yet learned to take responsibility for my sexual power; with David, I fell into his manipulative games without realizing that he was far more threatened by the possibility of losing me than I had understood.

As I developed a new way of looking at my relationships that allowed me to take more responsibility for their failures, I felt *more* empowered than ever before, relieved rather than guilty. I also felt more confident that I could avoid such destructive patterns in the future. Outside of my therapist's office, however, I had nowhere to tell this story. It was subtle. It was messy. There was more than one bad guy. It wasn't a legitimate feminist narrative.

As my academic interest in domestic violence grew, I found myself longing for a different kind of feminism—one that acknowledged my desire for a more radical and transformative recovery for men and women alike. Like Brenda, I still held on to many of my old dreams—a woman's right to control her own body, equal pay for equal work. But I also wanted to be part of a movement with a more expansive, embracing vision, a movement in which migrant workers' rights, higher education for African American men, and women's desire to seek treatment with their violent spouses could all be seen as feminist issues.

Of course, my thinking has evolved alongside the movement itself. Thirty years ago, even the notion of considering women's struggles and desires apart from their husbands and children was a relatively novel one, and exploring that radical notion had profoundly valuable consequences. But now the time has come to reaffirm the fact that women and men live together and struggle together: our intimate lives are deeply intertwined. No matter what their sexual orientation, women are bound to men through our love for our fathers, brothers, sons, and friends. The political will always be personal.

When I started doing Circles work, I could immediately sense that this was part of a new feminist vision. I knew that I, too, would have benefited from a public yet nonconfrontational forum in which to explore my abusive encounters with the men in my life—a place where I could have felt both safe and heard. I also saw that Circles could include competing narratives, as well: Chris's feelings of inadequacy; Dudley's loneliness and rage, David's need for mastery and his terror of abandonment. The Circle can hold as many stories as we need to tell. Here everyone is supported equally, and the manipulations customarily hidden from view do not survive exposure. As the trust builds among the participants, the shameful secrets and burdens of the past can finally be released: a new family, in a sense, has addressed the wounds of the old one. At the same time, the Circle looks to the future, embodying a model of the world as we want it one day to be.

I believe that the struggle to eradicate intimate violence in this country has finally come of age. We have amassed a staggering amount of political support, financial backing, and intellectual understanding of the problem. Now the enormous gains we've made must give us the courage to confront our weaknesses and expand our horizons. In every political movement, as in every individual political awakening, there is a galvanizing period of righteous anger—an anger that, if properly channeled, can change laws and topple governments. Once this anger ossifies into a reflexive political stance, however, idealistic questioning becomes dogmatic certainty and past injustices the excuse for new tyrannies. If we allow for a freer exchange of ideas and begin fighting for what we love instead of against what we fear, the potential for what we can accomplish is immeasurable.

My thinking on intimate violence has provoked many hostile responses from academics and advocates alike, which has been discouraging. But I now try to take the spirit of Circles work into all aspects of my life—professional as well as personal—and this new approach both challenges and sustains me. I've gradually come to realize that my calling is to reach out to those who are moved by the same urgencies that I am, not to shout down those who have closed their minds against this new way of thinking. No one can be forced to join this Circle; my dream is that it will one day prove irresistible.

Acknowledgments

First and foremost, I want to thank Joan Marans Dim. Joan was central to the development of this project, and her skillful reporting contributed significantly to the book's case studies. I am deeply grateful to her.

I would like to thank Alice Truax, who was with me every step of the way. Alice is truly one of the most extraordinary women I have ever known. This book, which was an effort to share my thinking with a larger audience, was much more of a challenge than I had imagined. Alice would sit with me, and when I lost faith, she would fix it. We got there. Her caring and critical nature, as well as her good humor, carried me through. She brought new insights every day. Thank you, Alice—you are nothing short of amazing.

My office tolerated a great deal as we made our way through the process. Julia MacEwan was always there when I needed her—developing ideas, reading drafts, and entering changes. Julia is an incredible force—her contributions invaluable and profoundly influential; none of us could have functioned without her. Laura Beerits came to the project later, but she transcribed nearly every interview and was completely engaged with the material. She read chapters with a meticulousness that even Alice admired, and she found citations that no one else could locate. Laura is truly remarkable. Yael Shy is a gentle and wonderful spirit who understands the importance of restoration. She gave her soul to the citation work and to reading the manuscript—twice. Danielle Emery, who joined the effort in the final hour, also left her mark. Thank you, Danielle, for picking up the pieces. Nancy Morrison, who is my colleague and good friend, has been a godsend. Thanks for your intelligence and grace.

Peggy Grauwiler, who has run the Center on Violence and Recovery for several years now, has always been an inspiration to me. Peggy's important study of the Family Wellness Program was so imaginative that I had to feature it in the book. Together with Peggy, Briana Barocas, who is the research director at the center, has done truly outstanding work in designing our studies and seeing them through. Thanks to both of you for your efforts in pushing the boundaries.

Judge Maley has been a great partner in our effort to design a new paradigm for treating intimate abuse. Meeting Mary Helen and becoming a part of the

Nogales community have completely transformed my life. Thanks to Teresa Morales and everyone I have met through CCP who has patiently built this groundbreaking program. The board at Andrus Family Fund has provided unrelenting support and infinite wisdom; the Santa Cruz Community Foundation was invaluable to the launch of this program. More recently, the Arizona Foundation for Women has helped us move the effort beyond county boundaries. Bellows Foundation was also incredibly generous when we needed it.

Colleagues Kay Pranis, Gwen Chandler-Rhivers, Murray Straus, Gale Burford, Larry Sherman, Zvi Eisikovits, Zeev Winstok, Duncan Lindsey, Stuart Kirk, Zeke Hasenfeld, and Colleen Friend have all contributed to my rethinking of intimate abuse; their insights have been my inspiration throughout the years.

It is very special to work with David McLaughlin, who has been a stalwart supporter of my work. Bob Berne is there when I need him; I count on his astute advice and his unending humor. John Sexton is always a mentor and a guide—especially as I navigate telling my story publicly. Thanks to all three of you for believing in me and for nurturing my passion.

Ellen Schall, from whom I draw incredible strength, and Steve Kalban, who gives so much to the world and to me, have been intrinsic to my work and to my being. I literally could not have undertaken this effort without their unwavering support.

To everyone at Admissions, Public Safety, Student Affairs, the Wellness Exchange, the Registrar's Office, the Deans, Senior Team, and Child Study—my thanks for your zazz.

Other friends were core to my thinking and to the development of this project. Susan Greenwald, my oldest friend, read drafts and helped me sort through my feelings—she is nothing short of the best! Edwin Cohen, always the tipping point, introduced me to Alice; I am so very grateful he is in my life. David Lewis and the fellas at San Quentin are an enduring spirit at the center of my work. Caty Shannon and her whole family, including Jacqueline, are magnificent additions to our routines. Liz Swados has taught me that anything is possible—and she does it all. Susan Thaler and Michel Rosenfeld have tolerated long discussions of the book—I am grateful to them for listening. Thanks, too, for sharing some of my favorite Saturday evenings together.

My sincere thanks go to Amanda Moon, my editor at Basic Books, who helped me through to the home stretch. Amanda has been incredibly generous—as well as attentive and committed to the project. I am greatly in her debt. Thanks also to Sydelle Kramer, my agent, who added so much to the initial proposal; I greatly appreciate her guidance at key moments.

As for the people featured in the book who spent hours talking to me, I am humbled by not only what you contributed to me personally but how you've put your vulnerabilities and your work into the world. You have been my guiding light.

Ultimately, it is family who is so often taken for granted and who supports us through the difficult times. This is certainly true of my parents, Anne and Harold, my sister, Adele, my brother-in-law, Paul, and Craig and Marissa. Thank you for everything tangible and intangible you do for me. Peter's family has always encouraged me to work on issues I care about—your support means the world to me. Holly Shawhan has a limitless ability to surprise us and adds immeasurably to our home.

And then there is Ronnie: you consistently inspire me with your chat and soul—and with your incomparable insight into the human psyche. Peter, you hold me and our life together. I will never repay you for the dinners you cooked, the hours you listened, the drafts you read (and improved), and your humor. You have tolerated everything, which was too much, I know. I count on the dynamic of our love and all that it brings.

Resources

PROGRAMS

Center for Family Services
Marriage and Family Therapy
Program
Virginia Tech–Northern Virginia
Center
Eric McCollum, Ph.D.
703.538.8470
7054 Haycock Road
Falls Church, VA 22043

Children's Aid Society
http://www.childrensaidsociety.org
Family Wellness Program
Kerry Moles, C.S.W.
kerrym@childrensaidsociety.org
212.503.6842
150 East 45th Street
New York, New York 10017
Information on *The Relationship
Workbook* can be found at
http://www.sunburst-media.com, or
email Kerry Moles at
kerrym@childrensaidsociety.org.

**Construyendo Circulos de
Paz/Constructing Circles of Peace**
520.377.0563
1859 N. Grand Avenue, Suite 4
Nogales, AZ 85621

Jewish Family Service
Esther East, L.C.S.W.
http://www.jfsclifton.com
jfs.eeast@verizon.net
973.777.7638
199 Scoles Avenue
Clifton, NJ 07012

**The Northwest Network of
Bisexual, Trans, Lesbian and Gay
Survivors of Abuse**
http://www.nwnetwork.org
info@nwnetwork.org
206.568.7777
P.O. Box 20398
Seattle, WA 98102

**Stop Abuse For Everyone (SAFE
International)**
http://www.safe4all.org
Business phone: 503.853.8686 (not
a crisis line)
16869 Southwest 65th Avenue,
P.M.B. 212
Lake Oswego, OR 97035–7865

**SAFE International Executive
Director (direct line)**
319.522.4817

PROGRAMS, *continued*

SAFE-NH (NH Chapter Stop Abuse For Everyone)
http://www.SAFE-NH.org
603.859.0859 (business and twenty-four-hour crisis line)
P.O. Box 523
Rochester, NH 03867

SAFE Illinois (PEACE4 ALL/SAFE)
http://www.peace4allonline.org/
815.455.SAFE (7233) (business and twenty-four-hour crisis line)
44 North Virginia Street, Suite 1A2
Crystal Lake, IL 60014

University Marital Clinic
http://www.psychology.sunysb.edu/marital-/index.htm
631.632.7850
Psychology Department
Stony Brook University
Stony Brook, NY 11794

Violence Anonymous
http://www.violenceanonymous.com

THERAPISTS AND RELATED PROFESSIONALS

Bill Burmester, M.A., M.F.T.
Marriage and Family Therapy
http://www.psychreview.com

Janet A. Geller, L.C.S.W., Ed.D.
docgeller@aol.com
212.866.1003

Sandra Stith, M.S., Ph.D.
Professor and Program Coordinator
sstith@ksu.edu
Marriage and Family Therapy Program
Kansas State University
101 Campus Creek Complex
Manhattan, KS 66506

RESOURCES FOR PRACTITIONERS

Samuel Aymer, Ph.D.
Assistant Professor
Hunter College School of Social
Work
saymer@hunter.cuny.edu
212.452.7115

Virginia Goldner, Ph.D.
Faculty Emeritus
Ackerman Institute for the Family
vgoldner@aol.com
212.982.9359
102 East 22 Street
New York, NY 10010

The Honorable Mary Helen Maley
MMaley@courts.az.gov
520.375.7762
2150 North Congress Drive
Nogales, AZ 85621

Notes

INTRODUCTION

00   **The popular conception:** Johnson, "Conflict and Control," 1010–11.

00   **Yesterday's victims often become:** See for example, Dutton, *The Domestic Assault,* 119; Straus et al., *Behind Closed Doors,* 111; Athens, *The Creation of Dangerous,* 47; Gilligan, *Violence,* 45–55, 110–15; and Mills, *Insult to Injury.*

00   **and yet most batterer intervention programs:** Jackson et al., *Batterer Intervention Programs,* 7; see also "Recent Research."

00   **Violence is dehumanizing:** See generally, Mills, "Shame and Intimate Abuse"; Gilligan, *Violence,* 45–55, 110–15; Athens, *The Creation of Dangerous,* 27–62.

00   **Women frequently strike out at their:** Hamel, "Domestic Violence," 8–9; Straus et al., *Behind Closed Doors,* 37; Straus, *The Controversy Over,* 17–18.

00   **Brenda Aris:** All the stories featured here are contained within the book and are drawn from interviews with either one or both partners. Some names have been changed to protect their identities. Source notes on individuals and couples are contained in the chapters in which their stories are told.

CHAPTER 1: MY PERSONAL ENCOUNTERS WITH INTIMATE VIOLENCE

00   **I cited as an example:** I interviewed two jurors several years after Brenda Aris's trial about their perspectives on her guilt and innocence. For further information about the Aris trial, see chapter 3.

00   **Chris was my first serious boyfriend:** The descriptions of my abuse experiences are recollections from my past in some cases more than thirty-five years ago. The dialogue presented here and in the rest of the chapter is as I remember it. I have changed the names of the people involved and some of the distinguishing facts in order to protect their identities.

CHAPTER 2: A BRIEF HISTORY OF THE BATTERED WOMEN'S MOVEMENT: ENORMOUS STRIDES AND UNEXPECTED CONSEQUENCES

00   **This grassroots response:** Schneider, *Battered Women and Feminist Lawmaking.*

00   **The first known shelter:** Schechter, *Women and Male Violence,* 11.

00   **by 1977, there were:** Roberts, "Myths, Facts, and Realities," 17–18.

00   **The tenets of the:** Schneider, *Battered Women and Feminist Lawmaking,* 13–27.

00   **Police officers have traditionally:** Robinson, "The Effect of a Domestic Violence Policy Change," 607–9; See also, Toon et al., *Layers of Meaning,* 2.

00   **The inadequacy of this perspective:** The facts of this case are drawn from *Thurman v. City of Torrington,* 595 F. Su1521, 1984; Statement of Tracey Motuzick, *Women and Violence before the Senate Comm. on the Judiciary* (1990); Anderson, "Chronicle"; Gombossy, "Torrington Suit Held Valid."

00   **Buck worked at a local:** Gombossy, "Torrington Suit Held Valid."

00   **The officers' astonishing passivity:** Buzawa and Buzawa, *Domestic Violence,* 102–3.

00   **But significant numbers:** Hirschel and Dawson, *Violence Against Women,* 2.

00   **When the woman wasn't serious:** Ibid.

00   **Advocates also pointed:** Baker, "And I Went Back," 67–68.

00   **To address the concerns:** See, for example, New York State Office for the Prevention of Domestic Violence, "Bulletin: Primary Aggressor Law."

00   **By 1989, just six years:** Sherman, "The Influence of Criminology," 2.

00   **And prosecutors were unenthusiastic:** Fagan, *The Criminalization of Domestic Violence,* 3.

00   **In the late 1980s, prosecutors:** Hanna, "No Right to Choose," 11–12.

00   **A primary focus:** National Coalition Against Domestic Violence, *Violence Against Women Act Appropriations.*

00   **It became much easier:** Kane, "Police Responses to Restraining Orders," 562.

00   **As a result of such serious concerns:** Bernstein, "Living Under Siege," 532–546.

00   **By 1999, a woman's visit:** McFarlane, "Mandatory Reporting of Domestic Violence," 13; see also, American Prosecutors Research Institute, "Summary of Laws," 2.

00   **Public education campaigns:** Klein et al., *Ending Domestic Violence,* 93–96.

00   **Ellen Pence and Michael Paymar:** "Recent Research Countering Confusion."

00   **For one thing, it was:** Mills, *Insult to Injury,* 60–63.

00   **The victims were held:** *Los Angeles Times,* "Never Set a Finger On Us," and *Chicago Tribune,* "Bank Hostage Says Gunman."

00   **The Stockholm Syndrome came:** "The Stockholm Syndrome."

00   **In a series of experiments in the late 1960s:** Seligman, "Learned Helplessness," 407.

00   **Walker tested this hypothesis:** Walker, *Battered Woman Syndrome,* 116; Walker, *The Battered Woman,* 50–53.

00   **Her theory gained significant:** Stevenson, "Self-Defense or Murder?"; Walker, "A National Emergency," 33–35.

00   **In 2005, Congress:** National Coalition Against Domestic Violence, *Violence Against Women Act Appropriations.*

00   **The campaign to institute:** Miller, *Domestic Violence: A Review of State,* 27–30.

00   **Visible injuries:** Ibid., 28.

00   **At this point, Alaska:** Ibid., 36.

00   **But several states:** Ibid.

00   **Nearly every jurisdiction:** "Victims' Bill of Rights."

00   **A number of states mandate:** Miller, *Domestic Violence: A Review of State,* 33.

00   **A national registry:** Ibid., 34; See also, Cecala and Walsh, *New York State's Response,* 31–32.

00   **New York has been especially:** Cecala and Walsh., *New York State's Response,* 33–35, 4.

00   **As of 2007:** Labriola et al., *Court Responses to Batterer Program Noncompliance,* 1. For fee requirements see Arizona Revised Statutes, 13–3601.01 (2007); California Penal Code 1203.097 (2007); Florida Family Law 12.05(2007); Louisiana Revised Statutes, 14:35.3 (2007); New Mexico Code, 31–12–12 (2007); Oklahoma Statutes, 21, 644 (2007); South Carolina Code, 16–25–20 (2006); Virgin Islands Code, 6, 99a (2007).

00   **For example, couples counseling:** See, for example, NY CLS Exec 576 (2007); Cal Pen Code 1203.097 (2007); N.M. Stat. Ann 31–12–12 (2007); 16 V.I.C. 99a (2007).

00   **Consider these statistics:** Fernandez-Lanier et al., *Comparison of Domestic Violence Reporting,* 1; see also, Cecala and Walsh, *New York State's Response,* 32.

00   **California has seen:** "Attorney General's Domestic Violence Prevention Program."

00   **Domestic violence homicides:** U.S. Department of Justice, Bureau of Justice Statistics, *Homicide Trends in the U.S.*

00   **In an interview with Oprah:** *The Oprah Winfrey Show.*

00   **In a 2007 research report:** Sampson, *Domestic Violence,* 3.

00   **Richard L. Davis:** Davis, "Domestic Violence Awareness Month."

00   **Davis also observes:** Ibid.

00   **Davis cites study after study:** Ibid.

00   **A Ms. Foundation study:** Dasgupta and Eng, *Safety and Justice for All,* 3.

00   **Indeed they went so far:** Ibid., 13.

00   **The first scientifically rigorous study:** Sherman, "The Influence of Criminology," 2.

00   **Eight years later, when:** Sherman et al., "The Variable Effects," 160–61.

00   **Sherman underscored:** Ibid., 10.

00   **In addition, many more African:** Sherman makes the important point that abusers who come to the attention of the police (in a city like Milwaukee) are likely to be "ghetto poor unemployed" because "most of these cities . . . have substantive minority populations, in which victims disproportionately call on the police for assistance." Sherman, "The Influence of Criminology," 37–38.

00   **Sherman estimated that if three:** Sherman et al., "The Variable Effects," 10.

00   **"It is clear that our zeitgeist . . . ":** Ibid., 45.

00   **The report concluded that:** Dugan, Nagin, and Rosenfeld, *Exposure Reduction,* 34; see also Mead, "When an Order."

00   **A 2002 study also funded:** Wells and De Leon-Granados,, *Analysis of Unexamined Issues,* 21.

00   **Overall, the researchers concluded:** Ibid.

00   **Given that the largest:** Catalano, *Intimate Partner Violence in the United States,* 10; Hsu, "Domestic-Partner Violence in U.S. Fell Sharply."

00   **On the evening of:** Associated Press, "Man Kills Wife"; Tressler, "Man Charged."

00   **In one study of California:** Wells and De Leon-Granados, *Analysis of Unexamined Issues,* 21; see also Johnson, "A New Side to Domestic Violence."

00   **In 2000, Patricia Tjaden:** Tjaden and Thoennes, *Extent, Nature.*
00   **Tjaden and Thoennes discovered:** Ibid., v; 50. See also Felson, "The Legal Consequences," for another perspective on this study.
00   **Such findings led:** Ibid., v.
00   **Several states have instituted Fatality:** See Arizona Coalition Against Domestic Violence, *Arizona Domestic Violence Fatality Review*; for a study of Florida's fatality review team, see, Johnson, Lutz, and Websdale, "Playing the Psychiatric Odds," 271.
00   **When the partner also killed:** Johnson, Lutz, and Websdale, "Playing the Psychiatric Odds," 269.
00   **Some of the results:** Tjaden and Thoennes, *Extent, Nature ,* iii.
00   **Only 13.5 percent of these men:** Ibid., 49.
00   **Stanley Green, a licensed:** I interviewed Stanley Green on November 1, 2007; I have heard Stanley speak on numerous occasions.
00   **"Looking at only one side . . . ":** Cook, introduction to *Abused Men,* xvi.
00   **Indeed, when same-sex couples:** "Domestic Violence in Same Sex Relationships."
00   **Researchers found that batterers:** Jackson et al., *Batterer Intervention Programs,* 10, 12, 7, 13, 9.
00   **The Brooklyn study:** Ibid., 19.
00   **But as researchers at the Center:** Labriola et al., *Court Responses,* 1.
00   **In 1999, the football:** *St. Petersburg Times,* "Brown Acquitted of Threat"; CNN.com, "Wife of Former NFL Star"; Hall, "New OJ Faces Jail."
00   **"The greatest frustration . . . ":** Adcock, "Professor Targets Roots."
00   **When I talk with legal professionals:** I did extensive interviews with a defense lawyer and prosecutor in spring 2007; they both handled domestic violence cases in criminal courts. For a recent study on Arizona's criminal justice response to domestic violence and the perspectives of legal professionals, see Toon and Hart, *System Alert.*
00   **Two years ago:** This material is taken from extensive interviews with Jeff and Sarah McPherson between April 2007 and May 2007. Their names have been changed to protect their identities.
00   **After an incident:** Fedders, "Lobbying for Mandatory-Arrest," 292.
00   **Ironically, Hare comments:** Hare, "What Do Battered Women Want?" 613.

CHAPTER 3: ENLARGING THE FRAME: COMPLICATING OUR PERSPECTIVES ON SEVERE ABUSE

00   **The Brenda and Rick Aris murder case:** I have known Brenda Aris and her children for over ten years. I have formally interviewed all of them and spent time with each of the Aris children at family gatherings. I have also interviewed two of Brenda's three siblings, Kathy and Jack Lane. I have had access to all of Brenda's memorabilia from her relationship with Rick, including love letters. I have performed a detailed review of the trial transcript and related documents, including police and parole board records, probation reports drawn from Rick's childhood, Lenore Walker's evaluation of Brenda before her murder trial, and the Court of Appeals decision in Brenda's case, *The People of the State of California v. Aris.* I have interviewed Brenda's defense attorney, Joyce Bubello, as well as two jurors from the trial. Several additional anonymous sources have contributed to this story. The dialogue

presented here is taken from these documented sources, together with Brenda's recollection of these interactions and events.

CHAPTER 4: THE ANATOMY OF INTIMATE ABUSE

00   **In 2005, there were over sixteen thousand:** U.S. Department of Justice, Federal Bureau of Investigation, *Crime in the United States 2005,* Table 1 and Table 1A; and Harrison and Beck, *Prisoners in 2005,* 1.

00   **In fact, the U.S. Centers:** "Intimate Partner Violence: Fact Sheet."

00   **The truth is:** Propp, "Words Can Hurt," 2; see also Geffner and Rossman, "Emotional Abuse," 2–3; O'Leary, "Psychological Abuse," 19.

00   **Stalking should always:** McFarlane et al., "Stalking and Intimate Partner Femicide," 311–12.

00   **Israeli social work professors:** Eisikovits and Buchbinder, *Locked in a Violent Embrace,* 104.

00   **It is also important to remember:** Murphy and O'Leary, "Psychological Aggression," 582.

00   **On the other hand, one sort of abuse:** Woffordt, Elliott, and Menard, "Continuities in Marital," 216–21.

00   **For example, studies show significant:** Propp, "Words Can Hurt"; and Rubin, "Shalom Bayit," 108. For Chicago statistics, see Block and Christakos, "Intimate Partner Homicide," 501; Tjaden and Thoennes, *Extent, Nature,* v.

00   **Of the 8.5 million total:** Tjaden and Thoennes, *Extent, Nature,* iii.

00   **Intimate partner violence results in nearly:** Tjaden and Thoennes, *Extent, Nature,* v.

00   **For the year 2005:** U.S. Department of Justice, Bureau of Justice Statistics, *Homicide Trends in the U.S.*

00   **In a study on family violence:** Straus and Stewart, "Corporal Punishment," 55.

00   **Similarly, sociologist David Finkelhor:** Finkelhor, Ormrod, Turner, and Hamby, "The Victimization of Children," 9.

00   **In a study of over seventeen thousand:** Felitti and Anda, *Adverse Childhood Experiences Study.*

00   **After thirty years:** Gelles, "An Exchange/Social Control Theory," 157–59.

00   **In 1980, sociologists:** Straus, Gelles, and Steinmetz, *Behind Closed Doors,* 37.

00   **The results of this research:** Straus, "The Controversy over Domestic Violence," 17.

00   **Emblematic of this fact:** Felitti and Anda, *Adverse Childhood Experiences Study.*

00   **Studies show that many men:** Clarke, Burns, Kenealy, and Darling, *Horseplay and Hitting.*

00   **This explains the fact that:** Tjaden and Thoennes, "Prevalence and Consequences of Male-to-Female," 155.

00   **Members of the Task Force:** Knollenberg, Douville, and Hammond, "Community Organizing," 99.

00   **One study found that 90 percent:** Lockhart, White, Causby, and Isaac, "Letting Out the Secret," 480.

00   **In another study of over a thousand:** Lie and Gentlewarrier, "Intimate Violence in Lesbian," 41–59.

00   **The Department of Justice reports:** U.S. Department of Justice, Federal
      Bureau of Investigation, *Crime in the United States 2000.*

00   **A study by Murray Straus published in 2008:** Straus, "Dominance and
      Symmetry," 25.

00   **When Straus and his colleagues:** These comments are drawn from
      interviews with Murray Straus and his lectures I have attended over the years.
      His writings have also been incorporated into this section. See, for example,
      Straus, "The Controversy over Domestic Violence" and "Processes Explaining
      the Concealment."

00   **Gelles and Steinmetz were also:** Straus, "The Controversy over Domestic
      Violence"; Gelles, "The Hidden Side," 4.

00   **A large national study of child abuse:** U.S. Department of Health and
      Human Services, *Child Maltreatment 2005,* 58, 67.

00   **A study of teen violence:** Ellickson, Saner, and McGuigan, "Profiles of Violent
      Youth," 987.

00   **The psychologist Miriam Ehrensaft:** Ehrensaft et al., "Intergenerational
      Transmission," 741.

00   **It should therefore be no surprise:** Straus, Gelles, and Steinmetz, *Behind
      Closed Doors,* 100.

00   **Boys like Rick Aris:** Ibid., 114 .

00   **Psychologist Donald Dutton:** Dutton, *The Domestic Assault of Women,* 119;
      see also Ehrensaft et al., "Intergenerational Transmission," 748.

00   **For example, psychologists:** Murphy and O'Leary, "Psychological
      Aggression," 582.

CHAPTER 5: WHERE DOES INTIMATE ABUSE COME FROM?

00   **Doctors, psychologists, and sociologists:** Mednick, Pollock, Volavka, and
      Gabrielli, "Biology and Violence"; Meyer-Lindenberg et al., "Neural
      Mechanisms," 6269; Lewis, *Guilty by Reason of Insanity,* 117–20.

00   **Drugs and alcohol:** Greenfield, *Alcohol and Crime,* v.

00   **Anthropologist David Levinson's:** Levinson, *Family Violence in Cross-
      Cultural Perspective.*

00   **For example, Cagoba, Columbia:** Ibid., 12.

00   **In the societies Levinson studied:** Ibid., 81–82.

00   **In light of these findings:** Ibid., 82.

00   **Bang Chan was a:** Ibid., 104–7.

00   **The study of this bond between child:** Henderson, Bartholomew, Trinke, and
      Kwong, "When Loving Means Hurting," 219.

00   **John Bowlby:** Bowlby, *A Secure Base,* 166–67.

00   **In 1998, psychologists Jamila Bookwala:** Bookwala and Zdaniuk, "Adult
      Attachment Styles," 186.

00   **That same year:** Roberts and Noller, "The Associations between Adult
      Attachment," 340.

00   **Canadian psychologist Antonia Henderson:** Henderson, Bartholomew,
      Trinke, and Kwong, "When Loving Means Hurting," 226–27.

00   **in fact, it is estimated:** Gormley, "An Adult Attachment," 793.

00   **"Men who had seen parents . . . ":** Straus, Gelles, and Steinmetz, *Behind
      Closed Doors,* 100.

00   **Women with violent parents:** Ibid.

00   **Bonnie Carlson, a professor:** Carlson, "Children's Observations," 160.

00   **Psychologists and social workers:** Jaffe, Wolfe, and Wilson, "Children of Battered Women," 26–31, 34.

00   **In 1989, psychology researchers:** Ibid., 79.

00   **In a particularly sobering:** Jaffe, Wolfe, Wilson, and Zack, "Similarities in Behavioral and Social Maladjustment," 144–45; see also Kitzmann, Gaylord, Holt, and Kenny, "Child Witnesses to Domestic Violence," 347. Psychology professor Katherine Kitzmann and her colleagues examined a total of 118 studies on the effects of exposure to abuse that had been published between 1978 and 2000. This overview concluded that exposure to violence between parents had significant effects on the children's psychosocial functioning. They found no substantial evidence that these outcomes varied depending on the child's gender, but they did tentatively find that the very youngest children were at the greatest risk for emotional and behavioral problems.

00   **Indeed, Straus, Gelles, and Steinmetz:** Straus, Gelles, and Steinmetz, *Behind Closed Doors,* 111.

00   **In 2003, psychology researcher:** Ehrensaft et al., "Intergenerational Transmission," 741.

00   **Straus and his colleagues discovered:** Straus, Gelles, and Steinmetz, *Behind Closed Doors,* 109–10.

00   **Not surprisingly, domestic violence:** Appel and Holden, "The Co-Occurrence of Spouse," 586.

00   **Lonnie Athens, a criminologist:** Rhodes, *Why They Kill,* 1–37.

00   **He interviewed over:** Ibid., 64. I also communicate often with Lonnie Athens, who told me on February 28, 2007, that he has interviewed 110 subjects over the course of his career.

00   **"Novices are always taught . . . ":** Athens, *The Creation of Dangerous Violent Criminals,* 47.

00   **"My mother and grandmother . . . ":** Ibid., 54.

00   **Shame has been defined:** Feiring and Taska, "The Persistence of Shame," 337; see also Morrison, *Shame,* 1.

00   **This unresolved shame:** Miller, *Women Who Hurt Themselves,* 1–26.

00   **James Gilligan, a psychiatrist:** Gilligan, *Violence,* 45–55; 110–15.

00   **If a child feels implicated:** Ibid.

00   **Lonnie Athens:** Athens, *The Creation of Dangerous Violent Criminals,* 27–62.

00   **"The beatings I took . . . ":** Ibid., 62.

00   **A twenty-eight-year old actress:** Dillon, Ross, and Gendar, "Girl, 14, Nabbed in Nicole Slay."

00   **In the immediate aftermath:** Bulliet and Geller, "Blazing Tribute," 7.

00   **Gilligan explains that:** Gilligan, *Violence,* 110–13.

00   **"I still get upset . . . ":** Athens, *The Creation of Dangerous Violent Criminals,* 60.

00   **"The beatings my stepfather . . . ":** Ibid., 60–61.

00   **"After I got my ass . . . ":** Ibid., 69.

00   **But many of us have:** Gillespie, *Pissed Off.*

00   **"Exposure to violence . . . ":** Ehrensaft et al., "Intergenerational Transmission," 749.

00   **Bernice Andrews:** Andrews and Brewin, "Attributions of Blame," 764–66.

00   **In an enlightening study:** Buchbinder and Eisikovits, "Battered Women's Entrapment."

00   **Usually it is because:** Thomlison, "Risk and Protective Factors," 58, 65.

00   **Samuel Aymer:** Aymer, *Exposure.*

00   **"I like my coach . . . ":** Ibid., 121.

00   **Andrea Ashworth's book:** Ashworth, *Once in a House on Fire,* 265.

00   **"It was easier not . . . ":** Ibid.

00   **"Why does it have to be Them . . . ":** Ibid., 229.

00   **"For years, I had lived . . . ":** Ibid., 263.

00   **Lucretia's memories of life in Riverside:** I have interviewed Lucretia on numerous occasions over the ten years I have known her. This material is drawn from those interviews; this section is written from Lucretia's point of view. I met Bobby a few times and have corresponded with him while he has been in prison, but he has not reviewed this material.

CHAPTER 6: THE DYNAMICS OF INTIMATE ABUSE

00   **"Dynamics" is a word:** *Webster's New World Dictionary.*

00   **A particularly striking example:** Lansky, "Shame and Domestic Violence."

00   **" . . . either he is not experienced enough . . . ":** Ibid., 345.

00   **"Mario doesn't drink . . . ":** Ibid., 341–42.

00   **"He made me feel . . . ":** Ibid., 344.

00   **"She has no idea . . . ":** Ibid., 348.

00   **Lansky points out:** Ibid., 356.

00   **"Anna seems to have a talent . . . ":** Ibid., 343.

00   **Although Mario proudly:** Ibid., 359.

00   **despite assurances:** Ibid., 351.

00   **"He wants to start at the top . . . ":** Ibid., 347.

00   **"I can sit there for three hours . . . ":** Ibid., 343.

00   **"It's almost like I have to . . . ":** Ibid., 344.

00   **All forms of violence:** See for example, Babcock, Waltz, Jacobson, and Gottman, "Power and Violence"; Scott and Wolfe, "Change among Batterers."

00   **Michael Johnson:** Johnson, "Conflict and Control," 1009–10. For a broad overview of Johnson's work, see Johnson, "Two Types of Violence"; "Patriarchal Terrorism and Common Couple Violence"; "Research on Domestic Violence in the 1990s"; and Johnson and Leone, "The Differential Effects."

00   **In 97 percent of these relationships:** Ibid., 1010; see generally, Johnson, "Two Types of Violence."

00   **In 96 percent of these cases:** Ibid.

00   **"Just as intimate terrorism . . . ":** Johnson and Leone, "The Differential Effects," 346.

CHAPTER 7: SITUATIONAL COUPLE VIOLENCE

00   **When psychologist Antonia Henderson:** Henderson, "It Takes Two," 48.

00   **The violence that erupted:** This material is taken from extensive interviews with Jeff and Sarah McPherson between April 2007 and May 2007. Their names have been changed to protect their identities.

00   **The "violence presents . . . ":** Eisikovits and Buchbinder, *Locked in a Violent Embrace,* 13.

00   **Eisikovits and Buchbinder, who have:** Ibid., 13–28.

00   **The vicious circle:** Ibid., 27.

CHAPTER 8: THINKING BEYOND LABELS: THE ODIERNOS AND THE WOODSES

00   **In April 2005, Ben Odierno:** The facts of this case are drawn from the
following newspaper articles: Feldman, "Jurors Find More Sympathy"; Feuer
and Wilson, "Amid Luxury, Domestic Strife"; Greene, "Slain Wife"; Hartocollis,
"The Decline of a Family"; Hartocollis, "Murder Trial Hears Account";
Hartocollis, "Woman Killed by Husband"; Hartocollis and Feldman, "Man Who
Stabbed Wife"; Hartocollis and Moynahan, "Murder Trial Paints"; Italiano, "Jury
Hears Wife's Dying"; Italiano, "Killer's New Slice of Life"; Italiano, "Killer's
Story"; Jacobs, "Woman Killed by Husband." I also interviewed jurors Joanne
McGrath on November 6, 2007, and Mike Stoller on November 7, 2007.

00   **For years, no one took Ruth:** This account is derived from interviews with
both Ruth and David Woods between May and June 2007, and email
conversations with both of them. I also reviewed the *John Walsh Show* on
which the Woodses appeared in January 2004.

00   **"Their joint reality . . . ":** Eisikovits and Buchbinder, *Locked in a Violent
Embrace,* 28.

CHAPTER 9: COUPLES COUNSELING

00   **One of the earliest:** Schechter, *1987 Guidelines for Mental Health
Practitioners,* 16.

00   **"People who are being either hit . . . ":** New York State Office for the
Prevention of Domestic Violence, "The Legal Corner."

00   **"According to battered women . . . ":** New York State Office for the
Prevention of Domestic Violence, "Finding Safety and Support."

00   **I spoke with five prominent therapists:** Mat Williams was interviewed on
March 29, 2007; Janet Geller on April 13, 2007; Samuel Aymer on April 18,
2007; and August 23, 2007; and Virginia Goldner and Bill Burmester on April
26, 2007. I have also consulted Geller's publications, specifically, "Conjoint
Therapy for the Treatment of Partner Abuse," as well as Goldner's, including
"Morality and Multiplicity," "The Treatment of Violence," and "When Love
Hurts."

00   **Pamela Brown and her colleague:** Brown and O'Leary, "Therapeutic
Alliance," 343.

00   **In a study of more:** Pan, Neidig, and O'Leary, "Predicting Mild and Severe
Husband to Wife Physical Aggression," 980.

00   **He relies on a method:** Brown and Reinhold, *Imago Relationship Therapy;* see
especially chapter 5.

00   **According to University:** Babcock, Canady, Graham, and Schart, "The
Evolution of Battering Interventions," 228.

CHAPTER 10: THE NEW GRASSROOTS MOVEMENT: SAFE AND VIOLENCE ANONYMOUS

00   **This informal assistance eventually:** Fulcher, "Domestic Violence and the
Rights," 16.

00   **Jade Rubick is the founder:** I interviewed Jade Rubick on April 24, 2007, and
also drew from Wright, "Male Abuse," 1.

00   **The NAC on VAW:** U.S. Department of Justice, *Charge to the National
Advisory Committee on Violence Against Women.*

00   **In fact, the following appears:** U.S. Department of Justice, Office on Violence
      Against Women, *National Advisory Committee Recommendations,* 11.

00   **Lee Newman was one:** I interviewed Lee Newman on several occasions
      between May and November 2007.

00   **I first met James:** I have known James M. and Kate M. since early 2006. I
      interviewed them in spring 2007 for several hours. This material comes from
      those interviews. I also listened in on a Violence Anonymous phone meeting;
      in addition, I corresponded with a Violence Anonymous participant in
      November 2007.

00   **Each of the 12-step programs:** Alcoholics Anonymous, "This Is A.A.," "A.A.
      at a Glance," and "The Twelve Steps of Alcoholics Anonymous,"
      http://www.aa.org.

00   **Members of AA:** Alcoholics Anonymous, "A.A. Fact File" and "An
      Introduction to the A.A. Recovery Program," http://www.aa.org.

00   **The enormous gains that:** See, for example, Connors et al., "A Longitudinal
      Model"; Moos and Moos, "Paths of Entry"; Gossop et al., "Is Attendance at
      Alcoholics Anonymous Meetings."

00   **In fact, AA's policy:** For a broad discussion of this issue, see White, *Slaying
      the Dragon.*

CHAPTER 11: THE POWER OF THE GROUP

00   **Kerry Moles, a social worker:** I interviewed Kerry Moles on May 2, 2007,
      regarding the Family Wellness Program, and this material, including quotes,
      comes from that interview, together with other published work cited here,
      including Moles, *The Relationship Workbook.*

00   **Grauwiler was particularly:** Grauwiler, "The Voices of Women," 87–88; 103;
      116–17. I work closely with Peggy Grauwiler, who verified the stories of Emily
      and Helen as they appear here.

00   **Each week the group focuses on:** Moles, *The Relationship Workbook,* 39–40.

00   **Another important exercise:** Ibid., 83–86.

00   **In 2000, Professor Einat Peled:** Peled, Eisikovits, Enosh, and Winstok,
      "Choice and Empowerment," 14, 17.

00   **Sandra Stith, who was:** I interviewed Sandra Stith and Eric McCollum about
      their professional backgrounds and the Marriage and Family Therapy
      Program on April 14, 2007. This material, including the quotes, comes from
      the interview, together with other written and published work cited here.

00   **First, they believe that:** Stith, McCollum, and Rosen, *Domestic Violence
      Focused,* 10.

00   **To ensure that the couple:** Ibid., 10–14.

00   **One female participant:** Ibid., 5–6.

00   **Commenting on this duality:** Ibid., 5.

00   **In 2004, seven years:** Stith, Rosen, McCollum, and Thomsen, "Treating
      Intimate Partner," 305.

00   **To her amazement, Stith has:** This material and these quotes come from my
      interview with Stith and McCollum on April 14, 2007.

00   **"Whether we're at a drag king . . . ":** Northwest Network,
      http://www.nwnetwork.org/index.html.

00   **"The Network never assumes . . . ":** I interviewed Connie Burk on April 18,
      2007, about the Northwest Network. This material, including the quotes,

comes from this interview, together with other written materials cited here, including the "Assessment Tool Worksheet."

00   **The class is offered:** Northwest Network, "Assessment Tool Worksheet."

00   **Erin K. told me that:** I interviewed Erin K. on April 26, 2007, about her experiences at the Northwest Network.

CHAPTER 12: MY POLITICAL ENCOUNTERS

00   **Prosecutors, however, were:** See, for example, Rebovich, "Prosecution Response to Domestic Violence," 176, 185–86.

00   **But Cheryl Hanna, a former prosecutor:** Hanna, "No Right to Choose."

00   **Donna Wills argued:** For a review of her presentation, see Wills, "Domestic Violence," 173.

00   **She drew on a homicide case:** Ibid., 177–78.

00   **Wills argued that prosecutors:** Ibid., 179.

00   **Advocates like Wills believe:** Ibid., 180.

00   **My arguments focused on:** For a review of my presentation, see Mills, "Intuition and Insight," 183–99.

00   **The study showed that:** Ford and Regoli, "The Criminal Prosecution of Wife Assaulters," 156.

00   **In 1999, I published an article:** Mills, "Killing Her Softly," 551.

00   **In an article published in 1991:** Crenshaw, "Mapping the Margins," 1258–59, 1265.

00   **Crenshaw believed that:** Ibid., 1265.

00   **"Women of color . . . ":** Ibid., 1250.

00   **Deborah Sontag, a reporter:** Sontag, "Fierce Entanglements,"55.

00   **Over the next few years, I wrote:** Mills, *Insult to Injury.*

00   **Many men didn't continue with the treatment:** Jackson et al., *Batterer Intervention Programs,* 7, 9, 13.

00   **Whereas the men kept asserting:** Henning and Holdford, "Minimization, Denial," 122; see also chapter 9 for a discussion of the importance of childhood histories to men who batter.

00   **Nor were advocates fully confronting:** Peled, Eisikovits, Enosh, and Winstok, "Choice and Empowerment," 9.

00   **Restorative justice:** For an overview of the following arguments on restorative versus retributive justice, see Mills, "The Justice of Recovery," 466–77.

00   **Victims who are actively involved:** Ibid., 481–98; and Strang and Sherman, "Repairing the Harm," 17–25.

00   **The Amish community's reaction:** Dueck, "There's a Lot We Can Learn," A25; and Hewitt, "Forgiveness," 58.

00   **Indeed, many family members:** see King, *Don't Kill in Our Names,* and King, "The Impact of Capital Punishment," 296.

00   **Retributive justice also often fails:** An excellent example of this repetition is found in the Tracey Thurman case. Her son, who was two and a half at the time that his mother was brutally beaten by his father, was later arrested for violating his probation and assaulting a woman. See Davis, "Domestic Violence and the Problem"; see also Mills, "The Justice of Recovery," 481–84.

00   **When apartheid was abolished:** Goodman, "Why Killers Should Go Free," 169; see also, Tutu, *No Future without Forgiveness;* Tutu, *God Has a Dream,* 52–58.

00   **Although some victims' families:** Ibid.; see also Minow, *Between Vengeance and Forgiveness.*

00   **In exchange for sparing:** Goodman, "Why Killers Should Go Free."

00   **Hawaii is using Circles:** For a description of Hawaii's program, see Porter, "Restorative Programs"; Minnesota's programs are described in "Restorative Justice." For a review of England's juvenile restorative justice programs, see Crawford and Newburn, "Recent Developments"; see also Crawford and Newburn, 'Youth Offending and Restorative Justice." Australia has not yet implemented a program but intends to; a description of their legislation can be found in Australian Capital Territory Consolidated Acts, *Crimes (Restorative Justice) Act 2004óSect 12.* See also Stubbs, "Restorative Justice."

00   **Circles are actually:** Pranis, Stuart, and Wedge, *Peacemaking Circles,* xiii.

00   **According to William Isaacs:** Isaacs, *Dialogue and the Art of Thinking Together,* xvi.

00   **Social workers Joan Pennell and Gale Burford:** Pennell and Burford, "Feminist Praxis," 109.

00   **Pranis reports:** Pranis, Stuart, and Wedge, *Peacemaking Circles,* 77–79.

00   **According to Pranis:** Ibid., 6–7.

00   **and many of my critics:** Coker, "Race, Poverty, and the Crime-Centered"; Raphael, "Rethinking Criminal Justice"; Stark, "Insults, Injury and Injustice"; see also, Mills, "Intimacy and Terror."

00   **My consultations with other experts:** Pennell and Francis, "Safety Conferencing."

CHAPTER 13: HEALING CIRCLES

00   **Alyssa Nice is a clinical social worker:** I interviewed Alyssa Nice, whose name has been changed, on May 10, 2007, and June 19, 2007, for this chapter and also consulted with her on how to help the Steins through the Healing Circle process. I have interviewed the Steins to get their feedback about the usefulness of the program. Their names have been changed to protect their identities.

00   **Two-thirds of Orthodox:** Wertheimer, "Jews and Jewish Birthrate," 3–4.

CHAPTER 14: PEACEMAKING CIRCLES

00   **After introducing the general principles:** This information is drawn from presentation notes and my recollection of this conference held at the Rio Rico Hotel, Nogales, Arizona, May 10–11, 2004.

00   **With grants from the Andrus Family Fund:** For information on the Andrus Family Fund, see http://www.affund.org.

00   **The National Science Foundation:** For further information on the study, see Grant SES–0452933 and http://www.nyu.edu/cvr/. The study results will be available late Spring 2008.

00   **One applicant said:** These comments, gathered over a three-year period, come from applicants and participants in the CCP program.

00   **Steve Kelban and the entire:** For more information about the Transition Framework, see http://www.transitionandsocialchange.org.

00   **Elena and Roberto Menendez:** I was intimately involved in the treatment of the Menendez family as they went through the Circle process. I served as a clinical consultant to the case throughout their participation in the program

and attended one circle with the permission of the circle participants. This description is drawn from the reports given by the participants of progress in the circle (including an interview with the circle co-keeper and community member participant on November 12, 2007). The names of all the circle participants have been changed to protect their identities.

00 **The authors of** *Peacemaking Circles*: Pranis, Stuart, and Wedge, *Peacemaking Circles*, 223.

CONCLUSION: ENDING THE CYCLE OF ABUSE

00 **In late 2001, Lucretia:** I have interviewed Lucretia on numerous occasions over the ten years that I have known her. This material is drawn from those interviews. I have also spoken at length with Brenda, Candice, Sheena, and Lucretia during a recent circle we held at Brenda's condominium on June 11, 2007.

00 **Not long afterward:** This is the group of convicted women I visited in Frontera Prison in 1996.

00 **In 2001, the sociologist Shadd:** Maruna, *Making Good.*

00 **Maruna found that:** Ibid., 85–108; 3–14.

00 **A treatment program:** Ibid., 117–30.

00 **Maruna argued that:** Ibid., 131–45.

00 **Tell that to the:** Tjaden and Thoennes, *Extent, Nature,* v.

00 **In 1995, South Africa's:** Office of the President (South Africa), *Promotion of National Unity.*

00 **"full disclosure relating . . . ":** Ibid., 30.

00 **Over a period:** Goodman, "Why Killers Should Go Free."

00 **Pumla Gobodo-Madikizela:** See, Gobodo-Madikizela, *A Human Being;* see also Mabuza, "The Truth and Reconciliation"; Steinman, "The Truth Shall Set You Free."

00 **"I was not a neutral . . . ":** Mabuza, "The Truth and Reconciliation."

00 **She was particularly:** Gobodo-Madikizela, *A Human Being,* 10–12.

00 **Gobodo-Madikizela was further:** Ibid., 11–12.

00 **"break the cycles of . . . ":** Mabuza, "The Truth and Reconciliation."

00 **As the dramatic testimonies:** Gobodo-Madikizela, *A Human Being.*

00 **"For the first time,":** Mabuza, "The Truth and Reconciliation."

00 **"I hope that when . . . ":** Gobodo-Madikizela, *A Human Being,* 14–15; see also 32.

00 **"For all the horrific singularity . . . ":** Ibid., 47.

00 **"an impossible demonstration of grace":** Steinman, "The Truth Shall Set You Free."

00 **After all, in the United States:** "Intimate Partner Violence: Fact Sheet"; U.S. Department of Health, *Child Maltreatment,* xiv–xv.

00 **"they hold the key . . . ":** Ibid. See also Gobodo-Madikizela, *A Human Being.*

Bibliography

ARTICLES, BOOKS, REPORTS

Adcock, Thomas. "Professor Targets Roots of Violence; Says Criminal Justice System Can Worsen Victims' Plight." *New York Law Journal* (March 2006), News sec.

American Prosecutors Research Institute. "Summary of Laws Relevant to the Mandatory Reporting of Domestic Violence When the Victim Is a Competent Adult." National Center for Prosecution of Violence Against Women at APRI (2006). http://ndaa-apri.org/pdf/dv_summary.pdf.

Anderson, Susan Heller. "Chronicle." *New York Times,* April 13, 1991.

Andrews, Bernice, and Chris R. Brewin. "Attributions of Blame for Marital Violence: A Study of Antecedents and Consequences." *Journal of Marriage and the Family* 52, no. 3 (August 1990): 757–67.

Appel, Anne E., and George W. Holden. "The Co-Occurrence of Spouse and Physical Child Abuse: A Review and Appraisal." *Journal of Family Psychology* 12, no. 4 (1998): 578–99.

Arizona Coalition Against Domestic Violence. *Arizona Domestic Violence Fatality Review: A Review of 2000 and 2001 Murder Suicides.* Arizona Coalition Against Domestic Violence, 2002.

Ashworth, Andrea. *Once in a House on Fire.* New York: Metropolitan Books, 1998.

Associated Press. "Man Kills Wife Hours After Domestic Violence Complaint." ABC News Charleston. http://www.abcnews4.com/news/stories/1007/464628.html.

Athens, Lonnie H. *The Creation of Dangerous Violent Criminals.* New York: Routledge, 1989.

Aymer, Samuel. "Exposure: An Explanatory Study of Adolescent Males' Coping to Domestic Violence." Ph.D. diss., New York University, 2005.

Babcock, Julia C., Jennifer Waltz, Neil S. Jacobson, and John M. Gottman. "Power and Violence: The Relation between Communication Patterns, Power Discrepancies, and Domestic Violence." *Journal of Consulting and Clinical Psychology* 61, no. 1 (1993): 40–50.

Babcock, Julia C., Brittany E. Canady, Katherine Graham, and Leslie Schart. "The Evolution of Battering Interventions: From the Dark Ages Into the Scientific Age." In John Hamel and Tonia L. Nicholls, eds., *Family Therapy for Domestic Violence: A Practitioner's Guide to Gender-Inclusive Research and Treatment,* 215–44. New York: Springer, 2007.

Baker, Phyllis L. "And I Went Back: Battered Women's Negotiation of Choice." *Journal of Contemporary Ethnography* 26, no. 1 (April 1997): 55–74.

Bernstein, Susan E. "Living Under Siege: Do Stalking Laws Protect Domestic Violence Victims?" *Cardozo Law Review* 15 (1993): 535–67.

Block, Carolyn Rebecca, and Antigone Christakos. "Intimate Partner Homicide in Chicago Over 29 Years." *Crime & Delinquency* 41, no. 4 (October 1995): 496–526.

Bookwala, Jamila, and Bozena Zdaniuk. "Adult Attachment Styles and Aggressive Behavior within Dating Relationships." *Journal of Social and Personal Relationships* 15, no. 2 (1998): 175–90.

Bowlby, John. *A Secure Base.* New York: Basic Books, 1988.

Brown, Pamela D., and K. Daniel O'Leary. "Therapeutic Alliance: Predicting Continuance and Success in Group Treatment for Spouse Abuse." *Journal of Consulting and Clinical Psychology* 68, no. 2 (2000): 340–45.

Brown, Rick, and Toni Reinhold. *Imago Relationship Therapy: An Introduction to Theory and Practice.* New York: Wiley & Sons, 1999.

Buchbinder, Eli, and Zvi Eisikovits. "Battered Women's Entrapment in Shame: A Phenomenological Study." *American Journal of Orthopsychiatry* 73, no. 4 (2003): 355–66.

Bulliet, Mark, and Andy Geller. "Blazing Tribute." *New York Post,* February 4, 2005.

Buzawa, Eve S., and Carl G. Buzawa. *Domestic Violence: The Criminal Justice Response,* 2nd edition. Thousand Oaks, Calif.: Sage, 1996.

Carlson, Bonnie E. "Children's Observations of Interparental Violence." In Albert R. Roberts, ed., *Battered Women and Their Families,* 147–67. New York: Springer, 1984.

Catalano, Shannan. *Intimate Partner Violence in the United States.* Washington, D.C.: U.S. Department of Justice, Office of Justice Programs, Bureau of Justice Statistics, 2006.

Cecala, Suzanne, and Mary M. Walsh. *New York State's Response to Domestic Violence: Systems and Services Making a Difference.* Office for the Prevention of Domestic Violence, 2006.

Chicago Tribune. "Bank Hostage Says Gunman Wasn't Brutal," August 30, 1973.

Clarke, Sara A., Andrew R. Burns, Deborah Kenealy, and Nancy Darling. *Horseplay and Hitting: An Experimental Study of the Perception of Male and Female Aggression.* Bard College and Oberlin College, 2006. http://www.oberlin.edu/faculty/ndarling/lab/SRA%20ECG%20poster%20presentation.pdf.

CNN.com. "Wife of Former NFL Star Jim Brown Denies Death Threat," September 2, 1999. http://www.cnn.com/US/9909/02/jim.brown.trial/index.html.

Coker, Donna. "Race, Poverty and the Crime-Centered Response to Domestic Violence: A Comment on Linda Mills' *Insult to Injury: Rethinking Our Responses to Intimate Abuse.*" *Violence Against Women* 10, no. 11 (2004): 1331–53.

Connors, Gerard J., J. Scott Tonigan, and William R. Miller. "A Longitudinal Model of Intake Symptomatology, AA Participation and Outcome: Retrospective Study of the Project MATCH Outpatient and Aftercare Samples." *Journal of Studies on Alcohol* 62 (November 2001): 817–25.

Cook, Philip W. *Abused Men: The Hidden Side of Domestic Violence.* London: Praeger, 1997.

Crawford, Adam, and Tim Newburn. "Recent Developments in Restorative Justice for Young People in England and Wales." *British Journal of Criminology* 42, (2002): 476–95.

Crawford, Adam, and Tim Newburn. *Youth Offending and Restorative Justice: Implementing Reform in Youth Justice.* London: Wilan, 2003.

Crenshaw, Kimberlé. "Mapping the Margins: Intersectionality, Identity Politics and Violence Against Women of Color." *Stanford Law Review* 43 (1991): 1241–99.

Dasgupta, Shamita D., and Patricia Eng. *Safety and Justice for All: Safety Program: Examining the Relationship between the Women's Anti-Violence Movement and the Criminal Legal System.* Washington, D.C.: Ms. Foundation for Women, 2003.

Davis, Richard L. "Domestic Violence Awareness Month." The Price of Liberty, http://www.thepriceofliberty.org/06/09/18/davis.htm.

Davis, Richard L. "Domestic Violence and the Problem of Indifference." Men's News Daily, http://mensnewsdaily.com/archive/c-e/davis/2005/davis013005.htm.

Dillon, Nancy, Barbara Ross, and Alison Gendar. "Girl, 14, Nabbed in Nicole Slay: Accused Killer's Gal Pal Knew of Gun and Helped Start Attack, Police Say." *Daily News,* February 2 , 2005, city final edition, News sec.

Dueck, Lorna. "There's a Lot We Can Learn from the Amish." *Globe and Mail* [Toronto], November 3, 2006, Comment sec.

Dugan, Laura, Daniel Nagin, and Richard Rosenfeld. *Exposure Reduction or Backlash? The Effect of Domestic Violence Resources on Intimate Partner Homicide, Final Report.* Washington, D.C.: U.S. Department of Justice, 2001.

Dutton, Donald G. *The Domestic Assault of Women: Psychological and Criminal Justice Perspectives.* Vancouver, B.C.: University of British Columbia Press, 1995.

Ehrensaft, Miriam K., et al. "Intergenerational Transmission of Partner Violence: A Twenty-Year Prospective Study." *Journal of Consulting and Clinical Psychology* 71, no. 4 (2003): 741–53.

Eisikovits, Zvi, and Eli Buchbinder. *Locked in a Violent Embrace: Understanding and Intervening in Domestic Violence.* Sage Series on Violence Against Women. Thousand Oaks, Calif.: Sage, 2000.

Ellickson, Phyllis, Hilary Saner, and Kimberly A. McGuigan. "Profiles of Violent Youth: Substance Abuse and Other Concurrent Problems." *American Journal of Public Health* 87, no. 6 (1997): 985–91.

Fagan, Jeffrey. *The Criminalization of Domestic Violence: Promises and Limits.* Washington, D.C.: U.S. Department of Justice, National Institute of Justice, 1996.

Fedders, Barbara. "Lobbying for Mandatory-Arrest Policies: Race, Class, and the Politics of the Battered Women's Movement." *New York University Review of Law and Social Change* 23 (1997): 281–300.

Feiring, Candice, and Lynn S. Taska. "The Persistence of Shame Following Sexual Abuse: A Longitudinal Look at Risk and Recovery." *Child Maltreatment* 10, no. 4 (2005): 337–49.

Feldman, Cassi. "Jurors Find More Sympathy for Defendant." *New York Times,* February 14, 2007.

Felitti, V. J., and R. F. Anda. *Adverse Childhood Experiences Study: Prevalence of Individual Childhood Experiences.* Centers for Disease Control and Prevention, http://www.cdc.gov/nccdphp/ace/prevalence.htm.

Felson, Richard B. "The Legal Consequences of Intimate Partner Violence for Men and Women." *Children and Youth Services Review* (forthcoming).

Fernandez-Lanier, Adriana, Deborah J. Chard-Wierschem, Phyllis L. Baker, and Donna Hall. *Comparison of Domestic Violence Reporting and Arrest Rates in New York State: Analysis of the 1997 and 2000 Domestic Incident Statistical Databases.* New York: New York State Division of Criminal Justice Services, 2003.

Feuer, Alan, and Michael Wilson. "Amid Luxury, Domestic Strife Apparently Took Deadly Turn." *New York Times,* April 26, 2005.

Finkelhor, David, Richard Ormrod, Heather Turner, and Sherry L. Hamby. "The Victimization of Children and Youth: A Comprehensive, National Survey." *Child Maltreatment* 10, no. 1 (February 2005): 5–25.

Ford, David A., and Mary J. Regoli. "The Criminal Prosecution of Wife Assaulters: Process, Problems and Effects." In N. Zoe Hilton, ed., *Legal Responses to Wife Assault: Current Trends and Evaluation,* 127–64. London: Sage, 1983.

Fulcher, Juley. "Domestic Violence and the Rights of Women in Japan and the United States." *Human Rights Magazine* 39, no. 3 (Summer 2002): 16–17.

Geffner, Robert, and Robbie Rossman. "Emotional Abuse: An Emerging Field of Research and Intervention." *Journal of Emotional Abuse* 1, no. 1 (1998): 1–5.

Geller, Janet A. "Conjoint Therapy for the Treatment of Partner Abuse: Indications and Contraindications." In Albert R. Roberts, ed., *Battered Women and Their Families,* 76–96. New York: Springer, 1998.

Gelles, Richard. "An Exchange/Social Control Theory." In David Finkelhor, Richard J. Gelles, Gerald T. Hotaling, and Murray A. Straus, eds., *The Dark Side of Families: Current Family Violence Research,* 149–65. Beverly Hills, Calif.: Sage, 1983.

Gelles, Richard. "The Hidden Side of Domestic Violence: Male Victims." *The Women's Quarterly* (1999).

Gillespie, Spike. *Pissed Off: On Women and Anger.* Emeryville, Calif.: Seal, 2006.

Gilligan, James. *Violence: Reflections on a National Epidemic.* New York: Vintage Books, 1996.

Gobodo-Madikizela, Pumla. *A Human Being Died That Night: A South African Story of Forgiveness.* New York: Houghton Mifflin, 2003.

Gobodo-Madikizela, Pumla. "Remorse, Forgiveness, and Rehumanization: Stories from South Africa." *Journal of Humanistic Psychology* 42, no. 1 (Winter 2002): 7–32.

Goldner, Virginia. "Morality and Multiplicity: Perspectives on the Treatment of Violence in Intimate Life." *Journal of Marital and Family Therapy* 25, no. 3 (July 1999): 325–36.

Goldner, Virginia. "The Treatment of Violence and Victimization in Intimate Relationships." *Family Process* 37 (1998): 263–86.

Goldner, Virginia. "When Love Hurts: Treating Abusive Relationships." *Psychoanalytic Inquiry* 24 (2004): 346–72.

Gombossy, George. "Torrington Suit Held Valid: Wives May Sue Police for Protection." *The Hartford Courant,* October 24, 1984.

Goodman, David. "Why Killers Should Go Free: Lessons from South Africa." *Washington Quarterly* 22, no. 2 (March 1999): 169.

Gormley, Barbara. "An Adult Attachment: Theoretical Perspective of Gender Symmetry in Intimate Partner Violence." *Sex Roles: A Journal of Research* 52, nos. 11/12 (June 2005): 785–95.

Gossop, Michael, et al. "Is Attendance at Alcoholics Anonymous Meetings After Inpatient Treatment Related to Improved Outcomes? A 6-Month Follow-Up Study." *Alcohol and Alcoholism* 38, no. 5 (April 2003): 421–26.

Grauwiler, Peggy A. "The Voices of Women: Perspectives on Domestic Violence Policy and Practice." Ph.D. diss., New York University School of Social Work, 2007.

Greene, Leonard. "Slain Wife: 'I Want Him Dead, Dead.'" *New York Post,* January 30, 2007.

Greenfield, Lawrence A. *Alcohol and Crime: An Analysis of National Data on the Prevalence of Alcohol Involvement in Crime.* Washington, D.C.: U.S. Department of Justice, Bureau of Justice Statistics, 1998.

Hall, Maggie. "New OJ Faces Jail for Horror Attack." *Sunday Mail,* September 26, 1999, News sec., 21.

Hamel, John. "Domestic Violence: A Gender-Inclusive Conception." In John Hamel and Tonia L. Nicholls, eds., *Family Interventions in Domestic Violence,* 3–26. New York: Springer, 2007.

Hanna, Cheryl. "No Right to Choose: Mandated Victim Participation in Domestic Violence Prosecutions." *Harvard Law Review* 109 (1996): 1849.

Hare, Sara C. "What Do Battered Women Want? Victims' Opinions on Prosecution." *Violence and Victims* 21, no. 5 (October 2006): 611–28.

Harrison, Paige M., and Allen J. Beck. *Prisoners in 2005.* Washington, D.C.: U.S. Department of Justice, National Institute of Justice, Office of Justice Programs, Bureau of Justice Statistics, 2006.

Hartocollis, Anemona. "The Decline of a Family, Played Out on the Stand." *New York Times,* February 6, 2007.

Hartocollis, Anemona. "Murder Trial Hears Account of Marital War's Last Fight." *New York Times,* January 31, 2007.

Hartocollis, Anemona. "Woman Killed by Husband Provoked Family, Son Says." *New York Times,* January 27, 2007.

Hartocollis, Anemona, and Cassi Feldman. "Man Who Stabbed Wife Is Acquitted." *New York Times,* February 14, 2007.

Hartocollis, Anemona, and Colin Moynahan. "Murder Trial Paints Portrait of a Family Torn by Strife." *New York Times,* January 12, 2007.

Henderson, Antonia J. Z. "It Takes Two to Tango: An Attachment Perspective Exploring Women's and Men's Relationship Aggression." Ph.D. diss., Simon Fraser University, 1998.

Henderson, Antonia J. Z., Kim Bartholomew, Shanna J. Trinke, and Marilyn J. Kwong. "When Loving Means Hurting: An Exploration of Attachment and Intimate Abuse in a Community Sample." *Journal of Family Violence* 20, no. 4 (August 2005): 219–30.

Henning, Kris, and Robert Holdford. "Minimization, Denial, and Victim Blaming by Batterers." *Criminal Justice and Behavior* 33, no. 1 (February 2006): 110–30.

Hewitt, Bill. "Forgiveness." *People Magazine,* October 23, 2006: 58–61.

Hirschel, David J., and D. J. Dawson. *Violence Against Women: Synthesis of Research for Law Enforcement Officials.* Washington, D.C.: U.S. Department of Justice, 2003.

Hsu, Spencer S. "Domestic-Partner Violence in U.S. Fell Sharply." *Washington Post,* December 29, 2006, sec. A.

Isaacs, William. *Dialogue and the Art of Thinking Together: A Pioneering Approach to Communicating in Business and in Life.* New York: Doubleday, 1999.

Italiano, Laura. "Jury Hears Wife's Dying Gasp." *New York Post,* January 12, 2007.

Italiano, Laura. "Killer's New Slice of Life." *New York Post,* February 14, 2007.

Italiano, Laura. "Killer's Story." *New York Post,* January 30, 2007.

Jackson, Shelly, et al. *Batterer Intervention Programs: Where Do We Go From Here?* Washington, D.C.: U.S. Department of Justice, National Institute of Justice, Office of Justice Programs, 2003.

Jacobs, Andrew. "Woman Killed by Husband Was Abusive, His Lawyer Says." *New York Times,* May 4, 2005.

Jaffe, Peter, David Wolfe, Susan Wilson, and Lydia Zak. "Similarities in Behavioral and Social Maladjustment Among Child Victims and Witnesses to Family Violence." *American Journal of Orthopsychiatry* 56, no. 1 (January 1986): 142–46.

Jaffe, Peter J., David A. Wolfe, and Susan Kaye Wilson. *Children of Battered Women.* Developmental Clinical Psychology and Psychiatry Series 21. Newbury Park, Calif.: Sage, 1990.

Johnson, Janet A., Victoria L. Lutz, and Neil Websdale. "Playing the Psychiatric Odds: Can We Protect the Public by Predicting Dangerousness? Symposium Speeches: Death by

Intimacy: Risk Factors for Domestic Violence." *Pace Law Review* 20 (Spring 2000): 263–96.

Johnson, John. "A New Side to Domestic Violence; Arrests of Women have Risen Sharply since Passage of Tougher Laws; Critics Say Some Men Manipulate the System; Others Say Female Abusers Have Long Been Overlooked." *Los Angeles Times,* April 27, 1996.

Johnson, Michael P. "Conflict and Control: Gender Symmetry and Asymmetry in Domestic Violence." *Violence Against Women* 12, no. 11 (November 2006): 1003–18.

Johnson, Michael P. "Patriarchal Terrorism and Common Couple Violence: Two Forms of Violence Against Women." *Journal of Marriage and the Family* 57 (May 1995): 283–94.

Johnson, Michael P. "Research on Domestic Violence in the 1990s: Making Distinctions." *Journal of Marriage and the Family* 62 (November 2000): 948–63.

Johnson, Michael P. "Two Types of Violence Against Women in the American Family: Identifying Patriarchal Terrorism and Common Couple Violence." Paper presented at the Annual Meeting of the National Council on Family Relations, Irvine, Calif., November 1999.

Johnson, Michael P., and Janel Leone. "The Differential Effects of Intimate Terrorism and Situational Couple Violence: Findings from the National Violence Against Women Survey." *Journal of Family Issues* 26, no. 3 (2005): 322–49.

Kane, Robert J. "Police Responses to Restraining Orders in Domestic Violence Incidents: Identifying the Custody-Threshold Thesis." *Criminal Justice and Behavior* 27, no. 5 (October 2000): 561–80.

King, Rachel. *Don't Kill in Our Names: Families of Murder Victims Speak Out Against the Death Penalty.* New Brunswick, N.J.: Rutgers University Press, 2003.

King, Rachel. "The Impact of Capital Punishment on Families of Defendants and Murder Victims' Family Members." *Judicature* 89, no. 5 (2006): 292–96.

Kitzmann, Katherine M., Noni K. Gaylord, Aimee R. Holt, and Erin D. Kenny. "Child Witnesses to Domestic Violence: A Meta-Analytic Review." *Journal of Consulting and Clinical Psychology* 71, no. 2 (2003): 339–52.

Klein, Ethel, Jacquelyn Campbell, Esta Soler, and Marissa Ghez. *Ending Domestic Violence: Changing Public Perceptions/Halting The Epidemic.* Thousands Oaks, Calif.: Sage, 1997.

Knollenberg, Sue, Nancy Douville, and Nancy Hammond. "Community Organizing: One Community's Approach." In Kerry Lobel, ed., *Naming the Violence: Speaking Out about Lesbian Battering,* 98–99. Seattle: Seal, 1986.

Labriola, Melissa, Michael Rempel, Chris S. O'Sullivan, Phyllis B. Frank, Jim McDowell, and Richard Rosenfeld. *Court Responses to Batterer Program Noncompliance: A National Perspective.* New York: Center for Court Innovation, 2007.

Lansky, Melvin R. "Shame and Domestic Violence." In Donald L. Nathanson, ed., *The Many Faces of Shame,* 335–62. New York: Guilford, 1987.

Levinson, David. *Family Violence in Cross-Cultural Perspective.* Frontiers of Anthropology vol. 1. Newbury Park, Calif.: Sage, 1989.

Lewis, Dorothy Otnow. *Guilty by Reason of Insanity.* New York: Ivy Books, 1998.

Lie, Gwat-yong, and Sabrina Gentlewarrier. "Intimate Violence in Lesbian Relationships: Discussion of Survey Findings and Practice Implications." *Journal of Social Service Research* 15 (1991): 41–59.

Lockhart, Lettie L., Barbara W. White, Vicki Causby, and Alicia Isaac. "Letting Out the Secret: Violence in Lesbian Relationships." *Journal of Interpersonal Violence* 9, (December 1994): 469–92.

Los Angeles Times. "'Never Set a Finger on Us': She Feared Police More than Captors, Bank Hostage Says," August 27, 1973.

Mabuza, Nthabiseng. "The Truth and Reconciliation Commission: An Interview with Pumla Gobodo-Madikizela." South Africa Partners, Inc., Fall 2000.

Maruna, Shadd. *Making Good: How Ex-Convicts Reform and Rebuild Their Lives.* Washington, D.C.: American Psychological Association, 2000.

McFarlane, Judith M., et al. "Stalking and Intimate Partner Femicide." *Homicide Studies* 3, no. 4 (November 1999): 300–316.

McFarlane, Mia M. "Mandatory Reporting of Domestic Violence: An Inappropriate Response for New York Health Care Professionals." *Buffalo Public Interest Law Journal* 17 (March 5, 1999): 1–41.

Mead, Julia C. "When an Order of Protection Does Not Work." *New York Times,* July 3, 2005.

Mednick, Sarnoff A., Vicki Pollock, Jan Volavka, and William F. Gabrielli Jr. "Biology and Violence." In Marvin E. Wolfgang, Neil Alan Weiner, and Philip J. Cook, eds., *Criminal Violence,* 21–79. Beverly Hills, Calif.: Sage, 1982.

Meyer-Lindenberg, Andreas, et al. "Neural Mechanisms of Genetic Risk for Impulsivity and Violence in Humans." *Proceedings of the National Academy of Sciences* 103, no. 16 (April 2006): 6269–74.

Miller, Dusty. *Women Who Hurt Themselves.* New York: Basic Books, 1994.

Miller, Neal. *Domestic Violence: A Review of State Legislation Defining Police and Prosecution Duties and Powers.* Alexandria, Va.: Institute for Law and Justice, 2004.

Mills, Linda G. *Insult to Injury: Rethinking our Responses to Intimate Abuse.* Princeton, N.J.: Princeton University Press, 2003.

Mills, Linda G. "Intimacy and Terror: Making Peace with My Critics." *Violence Against Women* 11, no. 12 (December 2005): 1536–42.

Mills, Linda G. "Intuition and Insight: A New Job Description for the Battered Woman's Prosecutor and Other More Modest Proposals." *UCLA Women's Law Journal* 7, no. 2 (1997): 183–99.

Mills, Linda G. "The Justice of Recovery: How the State Can Heal the Violence of Crime." *Hastings Law Journal* 57, no. 3 (2006): 457–508.

Mills, Linda G. "Killing Her Softly: Intimate Abuse and the Violence of State Intervention." *Harvard Law Review* 113, no. 2 (1999): 550–613.

Mills, Linda G. "Shame and Intimate Abuse: The Critical Missing Link between Cause and Cure." *Children and Youth Services Review* (forthcoming).

Minow, Martha. *Between Vengeance and Forgiveness: Facing History After Genocide and Mass Violence.* Boston: Beacon, 1998.

Moles, Kerry. *The Relationship Workbook: Activities for Developing Healthy Relationships and Preventing Domestic Violence.* New York: Wellness Reproductions and Publishing, 2001.

Moos, Rudolf H., and Bernice S. Moos. "Paths of Entry into Alcoholics Anonymous: Consequences for Participation and Remission." *Alcoholism: Clinical and Experimental Research* 29, no. 10 (October 2005): 1858–68.

Morrison, Andrew P. *Shame: The Underside of Narcissism.* Hillsdale, N.J.: Analytical, 1989.

Murphy, Christopher M., and K. Daniel O'Leary. "Psychological Aggression Predicts Physical Aggression in Early Marriage." *Journal of Consulting and Clinical Psychology* 57, no. 5 (1989): 579–82.

National Advisory Committee (NAC) on Violence Against Women. *National Advisory Committee on Violence Against Women Response to the Charge.* 2005.

National Coalition Against Domestic Violence. *Violence Against Women Act (VAWA) Appropriations.* Washington, D.C., 2007. http://www.ncadv.org/aboutus.php.

Northwest Network of Bisexual, Transgender and Lesbian Survivors of Abuse. "Assessment Tool Worksheet." http:///www.nwnetwork.org.

O'Leary, K. Daniel. "Psychological Abuse: A Variable Deserving Critical Attention in Domestic Violence." *Violence and Victims* 14, no. 1 (1999): 3–23.

Pan, Helen S., Peter H. Neidig, and K. Daniel O'Leary. "Predicting Mild and Severe Husband-to-Wife Physical Aggression." *Journal of Consulting and Clinical Psychology* 62, no. 5 (October 1994): 975–81.

Peled, Einat, Zvi Eisikovits, Guy Enosh, and Zeev Winstok. "Choice and Empowerment for Battered Women Who Stay: Toward a Constructivist Model." *Social Work* 45, no. 1 (January 1, 2000): 9–25.

Pennell, Joan, and Gale Burford. "Feminist Praxis: Making Family Group Conferencing Work." In Heather Strang and John Braithwaite, eds., *Restorative Justice and Family Violence*, 42–61. Cambridge: Cambridge University Press, 2002.

Pennell, Joan, and Stephanie Francis. "Safety Conferencing: Toward a Coordinated and Inclusive Response to Safeguard Women and Children." *Violence Against Women* 11, no. 5 (2005): 666–92.

Pittman, Bill. *AA: The Way It Began.* Seattle: Glen Abbey Books, 1988.

Porter, Abbey J. "Restorative Programs Help Hawaii Inmates Reconnect with Community." *International Institute for Restorative Practices: Restorative Practices E-Forum* (September 25, 2007). www.iirp.org.

Pranis, Kay, Barry Stuart, and Mark Wedge. *Peacemaking Circles: From Crime to Community.* St. Paul: Living Justice, 2003.

Propp, Karen. "Words Can Hurt." *Lilith,* December 31, 2005.

Raphael, Jody. "Rethinking Criminal Justice Responses to Intimate Partner Violence." *Violence Against Women* 10, no. 11 (2004): 1354–66.

Rebovich, Donald J. "Prosecution Response to Domestic Violence" in Eve S. Buzawa and Carl G. Buzawa, eds., Do Arrests and Restraining Orders Work? Thousand Oaks, Calif.: Sage, 1996.

Rhodes, Richard. *Why They Kill: The Discoveries of a Maverick Criminologist.* New York: Vintage Books, 2000.

Roberts, Albert R. "Myths, Facts, and Realities Regarding Battered Women and Their Children: An Overview." In Albert R. Roberts, ed., *Handbook of Domestic Violence Intervention Strategies: Policies, Programs, and Legal Remedies*, 3–22. New York: Oxford University Press, 2002.

Roberts, Nigel, and Patricia Noller. "The Associations between Adult Attachment and Couple Violence: The Role of Communication Patterns and Relationship Satisfaction." In Jeffry A. Simpson and W. Steven Rholes, eds., *Attachment Theory and Close Relationships*, 317–50. New York: Guilford, 1998.

Robinson, Amanda L. "The Effect of a Domestic Violence Policy Change on Police Officers' Schemata." *Criminal Justice and Behavior* 27, no. 5 (October 2000): 600–624.

Rubin, Carrie J. "Shalom Bayit (Peace in the Home): An Explanation of Orthodox Jewish Women and Domestic Violence." Ph.D. diss., New York University.

Sampson, Rana. *Domestic Violence.* Washington, D.C.: US Department of Justice, Office of Community Oriented Policing Services, 2007.

Schechter, Susan. *1987 Guidelines for Mental Health Practitioners in Domestic Violence Cases.* Washington, D.C.: National Coalition Against Domestic Violence, 1987.

Schechter, Susan. *Women and Male Violence.* Boston: South End, 1982.

Schneider, Elizabeth M. *Battered Women and Feminist Lawmaking.* New Haven, Conn.: Yale University Press, 2000.

Scott, Katreena L., and David A. Wolfe. "Change among Batterers: Examining Men's Success Stories." *Journal of Interpersonal Violence* 15, no. 8 (August 2000): 827–42.

Seligman, Martin E. P. "Learned Helplessness." *Annual Review of Medicine* 23, (February 1972): 407–12.

Sherman, Lawrence W. "Introduction: The Influence of Criminology on Criminal Law: Evaluating Arrests for Misdemeanor Domestic Violence." *Northwestern University School of Law Journal of Criminal Law & Criminology* 83, no. 1 (spring 1992): 1–46.

Sherman, Lawrence W., et al. "The Variable Effects of Arrest on Criminal Careers: The Milwaukee Domestic Violence Experiment." *Northwestern University School of Law Journal of Criminal Law & Criminology* 83, no. 1 (spring 1992): 137–69.

Sontag, Deborah. "Fierce Entanglements: Why Battered Women Return Again and Again to Their Assaulters and What That Means for the Law." *New York Times Magazine,* November 17, 2002.

Stark, Evan. "Insults, Injury and Injustice: Rethinking State Intervention in Domestic Violence Cases." *Violence Against Women* 10, no. 11 (2004): 1302–30.

Steinman, Louise. "The Truth Shall Set You Free." *LA Weekly,* February 27, 2003, Books sec.

Stevenson, Jennifer L. "Self-Defense or Murder? Battered-Spouse Theory Goes on Trial with Tampa." *St. Petersburg Times,* March 13, 1989, Tampa sec., 1.

Stith, Sandra, Karen Rosen, Eric McCollum, and Cynthia Thomsen. "Treating Intimate Partner Violence within Intact Couple Relationships: Outcomes of Multi-Couple Versus Individual Couple Therapy." *Journal of Marital and Family Therapy* 30, no. 3 (2004): 305–18.

Stith, Sandra M., Eric E. McCollum, and Karen H. Rosen. *Domestic Violence Focused Couples Treatment: Multi-Couple Treatment Manual.* Virginia Polytechnic Institute and State University Department of Human Development, 2007.

St. Petersburg Times. "Brown Acquitted of Threat." September 11, 1999, Sports sec.

Strang, Heather, and Lawrence W. Sherman. "Repairing the Harm: Victims and Restorative Justice." *Utah Law Review* 15, no. 1 (2003): 15–42.

Straus, Murray A. "The Controversy over Domestic Violence by Women: A Methodological, Theoretical and Sociology of Science Analysis." In Ximena B. Arriaga and Stuart Oskamp, eds., *Violence in Intimate Relationships,* 17–44. Thousand Oaks, Calif.: Sage, 1999.

Straus, Murray A. "Dominance and Symmetry in Partner Violence by Male and Female University Students in 32 Nations." *Children and Youth Services Review* (forthcoming).

Straus, Murray A. "Processes Explaining the Concealment and Distortion of Evidence on Gender Symmetry in Partner Violence." http://pubpages.unh.edu/~mas2.

Straus, Murray A., Richard Gelles, and Suzanne K. Steinmetz. *Behind Closed Doors: Violence in the American Family.* New York: Anchor, 1980.

Straus, Murray A., and Julie H. Stewart. "Corporal Punishment by American Parents: National Data on Prevalence, Chronicity, Severity, and Duration, in Relation to Child and Family Characteristics." *Clinical Child and Family Psychology Review* 2, no. 2 (1999): 55–70.

Stubbs, Julie. "Restorative Justice, Domestic Violence and Family Violence." *Australian Domestic & Family Violence Clearinghouse,* issues paper 9 (2004): 1–23.

Thomlison, Barbara. "Risk and Protective Factors in Child Maltreatment." In Mark W. Fraser, ed., *Risk and Resilience in Childhood: An Ecological Perspective,* 50–72. Washington, D.C.: National Association of Social Workers, 1997.

Tjaden, Patricia, and Nancy Thoennes. *Extent, Nature, and Consequences of Intimate Partner Violence.* Washington, D.C.: U.S. Department of Justice, National Institute of Justice, Centers for Disease Control and Prevention, 2000.

Tjaden, Patricia, and Nancy Thoennes. "Prevalence and Consequences of Male-to-Female and Female-to-Male Intimate Partner Violence as Measured by the National Violence Against Women Survey." *Violence Against Women* 6, no. 2 (February 2000): 142–61.

Toon, Richard, and Bill Hart. *System Alert: Arizona's Criminal Justice Response to Domestic Violence.* Phoenix: Morrison Institute for Public Policy, Arizona Sate University, 2007.

Toon, Richard, Bill Hart, Nancy Welch, Nora Coronado, and Dan Hunting. *Layers of Meaning: Domestic Violence and Law Enforcement Attitudes in Arizona.* Phoenix: Morrison Institute for Public Policy, Arizona State University, 2005.

Tressler, Jonathan. "Man Charged in Wife's Murder Has Violent Past." *Sun News,* October 22, 2007.

Tutu, Desmond. *God Has a Dream.* New York: Doubleday, 2004.

Tutu, Desmond. *No Future without Forgiveness.* New York: Doubleday, 1999.

U.S. Department of Health and Human Services, Administration on Children, Youth and Families, Children's Bureau. *Child Maltreatment 2005.* Washington, D.C.: U.S. Department of Health and Human Services, 2007.

U.S. Department of Justice, Bureau of Justice Statistics. *Homicide Trends in the US: Intimate Homicide.* http://www.ojp.usdoj.gov/bjs/homicide/tables/intimatestab.htm.

U.S. Department of Justice. *Charge to the National Advisory Committee on Violence Against Women.* Washington, D.C.: U.S. Department of Justice, 2006.

U.S. Department of Justice, Federal Bureau of Investigation. *Crime in the United States 2000: Table 33: Ten-Year Arrest Trends.* Washington, D.C.: U.S. Department of Justice, 2000.

U.S. Department of Justice, Federal Bureau of Investigation. *Crime in the United States 2005: Table 1: Crime in the United States by Volume and Rate Per 100,000 Inhabitants, 1986–2005.* http://www.fbi.gov/ucr/05cius/data/table_01.html.

U.S. Department of Justice, Federal Bureau of Investigation. *Crime in the United States 2005: Table 1A: Crime in the United States Percent Change in Volume and Rate Per 100,000 Inhabitants for 2 Years, 5 Years, and 10 Years.* http://www.fbi.gov/ucr/05cius/data/table_01a.html.

U.S. Department of Justice, Office on Violence Against Women. *National Advisory Committee Recommendations: Responding to Domestic Violence, Sexual Assault and Stalking.* Washington, D.C.: U.S. Department of Justice, 2005.

Walker, Lenore. *The Battered Woman.* New York: Harper & Row, 1980.

Walker, Lenore. *Battered Woman Syndrome.* 2nd ed. New York: Springer, 2000.

Walker, Lenore. "A National Emergency: Child Abuse and Neglect." *Colorado Woman News,* 5, no. 8 (August 31, 1990): 33–35.

Wells, William, and William De Leon-Granados. *Analysis of Unexamined Issues in the Intimate Partner Homicide Decline: Race, Quality of Victim Services, Offender Accountability, and System Accountability, Final Report.* Washington, D.C.: U.S. Department of Justice, National Institute of Justice, 2002.

Wertheimer, Jack. "Jews and Jewish Birthrate." *Commentary,* October 2005.

White, William L. *Slaying the Dragon: The History of Addiction Treatment and Recovery in America.* Bloomington, Ill.: Chestnut Health Systems, 1998.

Wills, Donna. "Domestic Violence: The Case for Aggressive Prosecution." *UCLA Women's Law Journal* 7, no. 2 (1997): 173–82.

Woffordt, Sharon, Delbert M. Elliott, and Scott Menard. "Continuities in Marital Violence."
     Journal of Family Violence 9, no. 3 (1994): 195–225.
Wright, Jeff. "Male Abuse: Survivor Stands Up for the Stigmatized." *PI Register-Guard*
     (Eugene Oregon), January 25, 2005.

CASES AND CONGRESSIONAL TESTIMONY

The People of the State of California v. Brenda Denise Aris. 215 Cal. App 3d 1178; 1989.
Tracey Thurman et al. v. City of Torrington et al. 595 F. Supp. 1521; 1984 U.S. Dist. LEXIS
     22524.
Women and Violence Hearings before the Senate Committee on the Judiciary. 101st Congress,
     Part 2, 99 (1990) (statement of Tracey Motuzick).

STATUTES

Arizona Revised Statutes. Domestic Violence; Treatment; Definition. Sec. 13–3601.01, Title
     13, Chapter 36.
Australian Capital Territory Consolidated Acts. *Crimes (Restorative Justice) Act 2004.* Sec.
     12.
California Penal Code. *Conditions of Probation for Crime of Domestic Violence.* Vol. Sec.
     1203.097.
Florida Family Law. *Final Judgment of Injunction for Protection Against Domestic Violence;*
     Marriage; Domestic Violence. S. 17, Ch. 95–195; s. 3, Ch. 2001–183. Vol. 12.05, 741.325.
New Mexico Code. *Domestic Violence Offender Treatment Fund Created; Appropriation;*
     Program Requirements. Ch. 387, Sec. 2. Vol. 31–12–12.
New York Executive Law. *Article 21; New York State Office for the Prevention of Domestic*
     Violence. Sec. 576.
Office of the President (South Africa). *Promotion of National Unity and Reconciliation Act*
     1995. Act 95–34, 26 July 1995.
Oklahoma Statutes. *Assault—Assault and Battery—Domestic Abuse.* 644, Title 21, Part III,
     Ch. 20.
South Carolina Code. *Crimes and Offenses: Criminal Domestic Violence: General Provisions.*
     Sec. 1. Vol. 16–25–20.
Virgin Islands Code. *Domestic Relations: Domestic Violence, Deferred Sentence and*
     Counseling. Vol. Act 6905, Title 16, Chapter 2.

TELEVISION

The Oprah Winfrey Show: Casey Gwinn Interview. January 23, 2003.

WEBSITES

Alcoholics Anonymous. "AA at a Glance," "This Is AA," "AA Fact File," "An Introduction to
     the AA Recovery Program," "The 12 Steps of Alcoholics Anonymous."
     http://www.alcoholics-anonymous.org/en_information_aa.cfm?PageID=10.
Andrus Family Fund. http://www.affund.org.
"Attorney General's Domestic Violence Prevention Program: Domestic Violence–Related
     Calls." Table 57. Safe State: Preventing Crime and Violence in California.
     http://safestate.org/index.cfm?navId=9.
"Center for Violence and Recovery." New York University Center for Violence and
     Recovery. http://www.nyu.edu/cvr/.

"Domestic Violence in Same Sex Relationships." An Abuse, Rape and Domestic Violence
    Aid and Resource Coalition. www.aardvarc.org.
"Intimate Partner Violence: Fact Sheet." Centers for Disease Control and Prevention,
    National Center for Injury Prevention and Control.
    http://www.cdc.gov/ncipc/factsheets/ipv_factsheet.pdf.
New York State Office for the Prevention of Domestic Violence. "The Legal Corner. Stop
    F.E.A.R Rockland Court Policy."
    http://www.opdv.state.ny.us/public_awareness/bulletins/fall2003.
New York State Office for the Prevention of Domestic Violence. "Bulletin: The Primary
    Aggressor Law" (1999).
    http://www.opdv.state.ny.us/public_awareness/bulletins/spring1999.
New York State Office for the Prevention of Domestic Violence. "Finding Safety and
    Support: Help for My Partner."
    http://www.opdv.state.ny.us/about_dv/fss/batterer.html.
"Recent Research: Countering Confusion about the Duluth Model." Minnesota Program
    Development, Inc. http://www.duluth-model.org/recentresearch.htm.
"Restorative Justice." Minnesota Department of Corrections.
    http://www.doc.state.mn.us/rj/Default.htm.
"The Stockholm Syndrome." International Survivors Action Committee.
    http://www.isaccorp.org/stockholm.asp.
"Transition Framework." Transitions. http://www.transitionandsocialchange.org.
"Victims' Bill of Rights." The National Center for Victims of Crime.
    http://www.ncvc.org/ncvc/Print.aspx?PrintableXoneID=Cell_3&Print.
"Violence Against Women Act Appropriations." National Coalition Against Domestic
    Violence. http://www.ncadv.org/aboutus.php.